D0081621

HQ
1064
U5
A633

THE AGE OF AGING

A Reader in Social Gerontology

Edited by
Abraham Monk

Ⓟ Prometheus Books
Buffalo, New York 14215

Published 1979 by Prometheus Books
1203 Kensington Avenue, Buffalo, NY 14215

Copyright © 1979 by Abraham Monk
All Rights Reserved

Library of Congress Catalog Number: 79-2727
Cloth: ISBN 0-87975-111-8
Paper: ISBN 0-87975-114-2

Printed in the United States of America

Contents

Introduction

Gerontology is an emerging field of knowledge. Notwithstanding the plethora of textbooks and readers produced over the past two decades, workers with the aged often complain that the current knowledge base does not satisfy their practice needs. Yet policy provisions contained in Title IV of the Older Americans Act specifically mandate filling the manpower gaps in the field of aging through a persistent training effort at all levels: regular career programs, as well as continuing and inservice education.

Both trainers and trainees are confronted with the imperative of service and must, therefore, condition their interventions to the best information they find available. They cannot afford the luxury of postponing the performance of those service duties until gerontology reaches a more authoritative or richly endowed "state of the art." This reality is experienced even more acutely by agencies hiring staff without any training in gerontology. The fact is that, even in times of service retrenchment, manpower development programs in aging cannot keep up with the demand for adequately trained personnel. This reader was conceived as a contribution to the educational requirements in gerontology. It is addressed to undergraduate and beginning graduate students seeking a better understanding about the issues and concerns of old age. The book was organized with two types of students in mind: those in human service related careers and those in the academic social sciences wishing to bridge the gap between science and practice, between theory and empirical applications. This book does not exclude, however, the general reader among its potential publics. At a time when the demographic impact of the aging cohorts on society is reaching unprecedented dimensions, aging already appears sufficiently universalized to transcend a selective professional audience.

Editors of readers usually begin with defensive disclaimers of comprehensiveness. We are no exception, as this book makes no pretense of exhausting all there is to know about aging. It is at best a sample of issues, problems, policies, and services. More has been left out, in fact, than has been included. Our essential criterion has been to facilitate an understanding of aging by integrating life development processes, social conditions, and service supports. The six chapters thus constitute a continuum ranging from how aging is perceived to how it is interpreted: what are some of its significant changes, how is it being experienced, what is being done and, finally, what ought to be done. In more detail:

Chapter 1 focuses on "Images, Myths, and Reflections." It calls attention to the fact that the aged are not perceived or accepted for what they really are. It explores the way the younger generations value the aged, how the reality of aging differs from prevailing attitudes, and finally, how older persons feel about themselves.

Chapter 2, "The Social Condition of the Aged: Theories and Interpretations," goes beyond images and perceptions in search of their underlying meanings. The earlier theoretical frameworks of the disengagement and activity theories are reexamined in light of more recent conceptual propositions.

Chapter 3 deals with "Transitions." It aims to dispel the notion that aging is a static or uneventful stage of life and dwells instead on its significant social and developmental changes.

Chapter 4, "The Aging Experience: Life Styles and Life Events," reviews a number of experiences such as widowhood, ethnicity, loneliness, and victimization. Again, it does not pretend to cover the whole experience of aging, but makes the case that a composite presentation of selected facets provides a more revealing portrait of what it means to reach old age in the American society.

Chapter 5 on "Interventions" reviews a few of the service resources available to the aging, including preretirement preparation programs and legal and protective services for the frail and disabled. The express intention has been to deal with community-based services. The whole constellation of health care, and more specifically, long-term care services, has been excluded. It is complex and vast enough to warrant separate treatment in a more specialized text.

Chapter 6, "Policy Debates and the Future of Aging," recognizes that services for the aging are also in their pristine stages of development. Their effectiveness is jeopardized by inexperience, duplication, inconsistent eligibility requirements, and vast, unjustified gaps. Authors in this chapter discuss ways and means of providing better attention to the aged. Precisely because sound policy decisions depend on a reliable understanding of what old age is all about, this book seems to complete a full circle: it starts examining images and perceptions and it concludes with policy directions that are in turn contingent on adequate perceptions and assessments.

Each of the six chapters is preceded by a brief introduction highlighting its major themes. All papers have been transcribed as in their original versions, with no abridgements. References and bibliographic citations have been standardized, however, in order to provide editorial consistency. I am particularly grateful to my colleague Rosa P. Resnik for completing this yeoman job, as well as for many other thoughtful editorial suggestions. Ms. Barbara Bergstrom of Prometheus Books deserves a special expression of thanks for her skillful aid in the preparation of the final manuscript.

Abraham Monk
Brookdale Professor of Gerontology
Columbia University School of Social Work

CHAPTER I

IMAGES, MYTHS, AND REFLECTIONS

Aging has become a high priority issue on the agenda of policy makers, public forums, and human service agencies. Social scientists are acknowledging in turn that the age profile of the American society is tilting in the direction of its elderly cohorts.

There is an overwhelming realization that the very texture and dynamics of the American society may be changing on account of these demographic transformations. As new age related role sets and new patterns of intergenerational transactions are coming into being, it is argued that we are entering into an "age of aging," a new era characterized by prolongevity and dominated by age stratified relations.

The emerging "age of aging" is fraught, however, with scores of misconceptions and stereotypes. Older people do live longer and their numbers increase both in actual numbers and relative to the rest of the population, but they are not necessarily accepted for what they really are. Are the aged valued positively by younger age groups or are they considered as excess baggage, an unproductive burden? How different is the reality of aging from prevailing attitudes? Furthermore, how do older people feel about themselves: do they share the pejorative stereotypes about old age and accept them as their own subjective reality?

The three questions in reference constitute the very gist of this first chapter. Following a prudent epistemological point of view, we begin examining how the aged are perceived and how they see themselves, their "images and reflections," before we go on exploring how they really are.

Monk's paper, "The Age of Aging," underscores some of the tensions and fears that have surfaced in the policy and social services arena. They range from the alleged imminent collapse of the social security system to the runaway costs of institutional care. He finds some of the solutions being advocated as purely evasive and inconsistent with the very nature of the needs of older persons. The author also touches on the other side of the coin: the illusions of prolongevity that are invading the scientific realm and caution against a relentless extension of the life span without concomitant improvements in the quality of life. The paper finally concludes with five hermeneutic rules aimed at safeguarding the policy-making process on behalf of the aged.

Robert M. Butler inventories the myths about aging that have permeated into the helping professions, most specially psychiatry. Published in 1970, this paper retains its validity because of the resilience of the myths in question. Human service workers often exhibit a therapeutic pessimism and even a destructive nihilism when dealing with psychiatric disorders in old age. Butler tears apart the myths about the tranquility, unproductivity, resistance to change, brain damage, and unresponsiveness to therapy of older patients. It is a yeoman task but the author undertakes it with a sense of moderate optimism. Some attitudes, he contends, are changing, even if slowly.

Bernice L. Neugarten shares initially the same optimistic assessments. In her paper on "Patterns of Aging: Past, Present, and Future," she points out that negative stereotypes of old age, while deeply entrenched in our society, are now giving gradually way to a more realistic appreciation of the heterogeneity of the aging cohort. Longevity has been prized almost as a utopian aspiration through the ages, but now that a "dramatic" extension of the life span does occur, society does not seem prepared to handle either its immediate or long range effects. Neugarten inventories some of the crucial questions that have recently arisen: Will increased longevity be attained without marginalizing the aged from society? Will the higher use of social and health services by older persons inevitably lead to clogging these services to the point of rendering them ineffectual? Will the quality of life then substantially drop? Will the economies of even the more affluent industrial nations be able to sustain larger numbers of retirees? Neugarten does not venture into lighthearted forecasting exercises, but she alerts the reader that there are, in effect, several strategies aimed at the lengthening of the life span. Once they succeed, the possibility of intergenerational confrontations, similar to political and economic class struggles, may very well occur.

Are the aged the object of negative attitudes or are they put aside and ignored altogether? Peterson and Karnes undertook a content analysis of some of the contemporary adolescent literature. They sought to determine the types, images, and roles of their older characters. They did not find negative stereotyping or a sense of pervasive discrimination, a fact that appears to contradict the basic assumptions of some of the other contributions contained in this chapter. Yet more important than the pejorative or negative stereotyping was the fact that in the majority of cases older persons were cast in marginal, "shadow" roles. Their presence was not essential to the real action. A sort of neutral aura of indifference seems to envelop them as if they were superfluous people, neither loved nor hated, but simply ignored or removed from the mainstream of life.

The two following papers explore the attitudes about
aging and the correlative acceptance of age among older
persons. Borges and Dutton embarked in an empirical
investigation of the negative attitudes toward aging. They
differentiated ratings by age of respondent and inquired
whether such attitudes were congruent with the way in
which older persons assess their own lives. The authors
report that as a person grows old, he perceives the years
ahead more optimistically. Older persons rated their lives
better than the younger respondents projected their lives to
be. In their analysis of this patent disparity, Borges and
Dutton state that society puts distance among generations,
and young people have no opportunity to become better
acquainted with the old. Young people thus grow with a
lack of awareness of the satisfaction potential in later years
and even with a lack of belief in the possibility of continuous growth and fulfillment in the later stages of life.

The study by Russell A. Ward investigated the impact
of shifts in age identification by older respondents, from
"middle aged" to "elderly." Acceptance or attachment of
the label elderly did not affect age identification nor did it
negatively impinge upon their self-esteem. Attachment of
negative stereotypes to growing old was, however,
strongly associated to self-derogation. In essence, both
papers empirically arrive at similar conclusions: that aged
persons are not distressed by old age. It fosters neither
pessimism nor denial.

After examining the images, attitudes, and stereotypes about aging, it is only befitting to close the first
chapter with a corrected reflection of the reality of aging.
Donald O. Cowgill focuses on the fundamental changes in
family life brought about by the "demographic revolution,"
namely, by the unprecedented and presumably permanent decline of both mortality and fertility rates. Its ultimate
effect is the increasing preponderance of older persons in
society, a novel historical fact that is bound to cause deep
effects in family relations, life styles, and living arrangements. Cowgill finds a remarkable sense of resilience,

adaptability, and continuity among the aged. Most older persons, he claims, are not isolated or cut off from kin but maintain affectionate, close ties with their families. True, they wish to remain independent and keep their separate residences at all costs but patterns of mutual assistance and reciprocal care are strong and pervasive. Cowgill finds that "the safest generalization to be made is that it is not safe to generalize": older persons are too diverse and more heterogeneous than any younger group. They are too busy experimenting with life in its infinite potentialities.

Aging remains a puzzle and a challenge to social scientists and human services practitioners. It is too complex an issue to apprehend it in naïve or simple-minded stereotypes. There is need instead for more fundamental, theoretical interpretations. This is the topic of our second chapter.

1.1

The Age of Aging

Abraham Monk

Public interest in the problems of aging in our society has been growing relentlessly in recent years. Far from being a temporary fad, this
awareness is rooted in new demographic realities. The number of
older persons is increasing as a result of both a static birthrate and a
higher life expectancy. In other words, there are more older people in
absolute numbers, their proportion relative to the total population is
higher, and they simply live longer.

Although the aged do not act as a monolithic block, the fact that
they constitute nearly 25 percent of the American voters has strategical
significance carefully noticed by politicians at all levels of government.
No wonder then that we are in the midst of a legislative rediscovery of
the aged. This can be traced back to the Social Security Act of 1935, but
it has been only in the past eighteen years, after the creation of the
Senate Special Committee on Aging of 1959, that an intense flurry of
public policy-making began to steamroll. It included the 1961 White
House Conference on Aging; the Medicare and Medicaid amendments to the Social Security Act; the Older Americans Act of 1965,
signed into law with the intent of fostering planning and services for
the aged at the local level; the Age Discrimination in Employment Act
of 1967; the 1975 Comprehensive Service Amendments to the Older
Americans Act; the 1971 White House Conference on Aging; the 1974
Supplemental Security Income Amendments to the Social Security

Reprinted from *The Humanist*, September/October 1977.

Act, a major pensions-reform bill; and, in 1975, the pegging of the social-security benefits to the Consumer Price Index. True, some of this legislation exerted little impact because of inadequate funding or because they were too cumbersome or nearly impossible to actually enforce.

On the whole, however, and notwithstanding gaps and deficits, the United States has already shaped a social policy for the aging. It may lack comprehensiveness and it still falls short of meeting basic needs of the elderly, but there is no doubt that the "age of aging" has arrived. It is being received with mixed emotions, ranging from exacerbated fears about the cost of an ever-expanding package of geriatric services and income supports, to the euphoria of prolongevity, and even the illusion of eternal youth and indefinite survival. Let us examine succinctly some of those hopes and fears.

Fears of Aging

Much has been speculated lately about "gerontophobia," the fear of aging and the incomplete assimilation of the aged in what has been labeled a "youth oriented" society. Aging has recently also conjured visions of ever-mounting payroll taxes, and conversely, of shrinking disposable incomes for the working, nonaged adults. It is claimed that this will be the unavoidable corollary of both letting social security assume its obligations to provide adequate benefits and footing the bills of institutional health-care through Medicaid or any other national health scheme. True, the ratio of workers to retired persons is dropping from three-to-one to a two-to-one level, but the dependency ratio for the aged may be offset by the smaller dependency ratio for children, given the lower birthrate. If the expectation of a rising gross national product is also taken into account, the alarm about social security's demise may be exaggerated. The issues must nevertheless be reviewed in closer detail.

To begin with, because older people live longer, their morbidity also increases. They are a higher-risk population, twice as likely to have chronic illnesses, and when hospitalized, their average stay is twice as long as those of the population under sixty-five. The dread of prolonged hospitalization or institutionalization is pervasive. For older persons, the prospect of spending the rest of their lives in seemingly impersonal, exploitative, and poorly run nursing homes is tantamount to abandonment and confinement. For the taxpayer it again evokes nightmares of never-ending fiscal scandals and skyrocketing costs. Nobody denies that nursing-home costs are prohibitive and resources are being strained. However, it has become fashionable, because of isolated cases of patient abuse, outright larceny, and fraudulent billings by unscrupulous administrators, to bring wholesale indictment against this service.

Nursing homes and homes for the aged are often labeled Medicaid mills and accused of preying on human misery. However, the question of whether institutional services are intrinsically needed has seldom been addressed. Since the Senate Special Committee on Aging exposés of 1974 and 1975, the flaws of Medicaid became obvious: It is a lax system with poor controls that invited abuse. It was consequently learned that when federal subsidies and grants are allocated without rigorous accountability standards fraud becomes inevitable. But the lesson concerning the extent of societal need for sheltered institutional services like those provided in nursing homes was never learned. Much to the contrary, the alleged failures of Medicaid were subsequently used as the main reason for proposing to do away with institutions altogether.

It was assumed, in the same vein, that relatives or kin can—or should—invariably take care of the older members of their family. Such assumptions overlook the fact that the institutionalized population has a mean age of eighty-two, with more than 70 percent over seventy. Most of them are widows, including a large portion of single, never-married women. Nearly half of them do not have close relatives, and many widows have outlived their own children. The accusation that those who seek to place an older relative in an institution are guilty of filial or kin neglect is also unfounded and unfair. As Elaine Brody has pointed out repeatedly, there is no such thing as the "dumping" of older relatives into nursing homes. Relatives apply only after they have already exhausted all other avenues of assistance, including their own physical and psychological stamina. Even when families and relatives are available as active primary support systems, they are often not equipped to provide the round-the-clock complex services required by their ailing elderly relatives.

It is true that many nursing home patients do not belong there and could be transferred to lower and less expensive levels of care, but this would require revamping all our health-care systems in a way that provides for a real continuum of services, ranging from independent living to hospitalization, and including a wide spectrum of sheltered, semi-independent, and congregate forms of care. Unfortunately, the appeal for "alternatives to institutionalization" often conceals the outright abandonment of the aged at their own mercy. Viable alternatives, such as in-home services, are desirable because they enable the older person to remain in his familiar environment and at a meaningful level of self-sufficiency. Yet, mounting and sustaining such services is a costly enterprise. Furthermore, they are a valuable part of the continuum of services, not a substitute for institutional care. Nursing homes will always be necessary for the 5 percent of high-risk, chronically disabled older persons who lack viable home supports. We better learn to accept them and turn them into more humane settings.

Concerning our retirement system, there is the fear that the social-security fund will go broke as the ratio of wage earners to retirees declines. The situation seems to be aggravated by the upsurge in early-retirement decisions, thanks to the social-security option that makes it possible for men to retire at sixty-two, and women at sixty, at actually reduced pension levels. Health considerations, but most particularly the endemic unemployment among middle-aged workers, are behind this trend. No wonder then that nearly 20 percent of the aged are legally poor, a proportion twice as high as the overall national estimates.

Humanistic arguments that mandatory retirement is a form of discrimination, that it infringes upon the human and constitutional rights of older workers, and that it causes profound psychological injuries, have failed to sufficiently impress Congress. Legislators began paying some heed only after they realized that the present system is on the way to becoming a luxury that our younger wage earners will soon be unable to afford. On July 14, 1977, the House Education and Labor Committee approved legislation that would end age limits of mandatory retirement in government and prohibit mandatory retirement in the private sector before age seventy. Four days later, Secretary of Labor Ray Marshall supported the proposal. Doing away with mandatory retirement will bring about a higher measure of justice for older Americans, but it will not bring, in itself, the assurance of more jobs. If anything, it would keep the labor force larger, thus creating the risk of a new form of intergenerational strife around the competition for jobs.

The replacement of mandatory retirement by a more flexible system will give workers the opportunity to decide when they will exit from the labor force. To be effective, however, it needs to go hand in hand with comprehensive programs of jobs development, not only for the elderly, but also for the young and the unemployed of all ages.

The Illusion of Prolongevity

The marked upsurge in life expectancy is turning us into an "aged society." It has also rekindled the mythical illusions of prolongevity. The search for Ponce de León's fountain of youth and the visions of supercentenarians roaming around in seven- or eight-generation households did not rest with the caustic minds of Aldous Huxley or Kurt Vonnegut. Scientists are still searching for a serum or medium, some unusual substance or environmental equation, that has the property of extending the life of the normal cell, or at least slowing the rate of aging. Life expectancy may climb to eighty or ninety years if aging is decelerated through some specific serum (antioxidants, enzymes, antitoxins, and so on) and if the major chronic diseases are effectively cured or prevented. This, however, does not guarantee a better or less-traumatic aging. Older people may still remain subject to social conditions over which they have little control. In addition to a severe drop in income, they find health services inadequate and suffer a loss of emotional supports due to the death of relatives and friends. Each of these injuries contributes to the erosion of their self-esteem and to increasing feelings of anxiety and insecurity. No wonder that older persons experience greater psychological stress and more reactive depressions. The latter result from attacks on the individual's self-sufficiency, from limitations on the ability to attend to basic needs, and from the anticipation of impending new losses, that is, from the fear that things will not be getting better—if anything they will be worsening. Life, in essence, could be extended only to result in the same wasted potential. Prolongevity, without concomitant improvement in the quality of life for the aged, is prolongation of suffering. Prescriptions for a better quality of life are manifold and still controversial. Fortunately, prescriptions and policy proposals have multiplied as a result of the new societal awareness about aging. We do not intend to spell out additional proposals here, but only a few safeguards or rules for the game of policy development.

First: Care should be taken to recognize the heterogeneity of the older population. Policies that treat them in a uniform fashion end in regimentation that serves no one.

Second: No programs should be instituted without the older persons' involvement in the planning process. They do not have to be dictated solutions; they should enable older persons to negotiate and speak for themselves.

Third: New outlets and environments should be created for the expression of their interests and for the application of their experience and knowledge.

Fourth: Aging should be accepted as a normal stage of life. It should not be intrinsically defined as a problem. Neither should it be idealized in mythical terms.

Fifth: Life, however, is ever-changing, and what is desirable or may work today may be inadequate and unsuitable for tomorrow. Each new cohort of older persons has the right to redefine and act upon new interests and aspirations.

Some of these "rules" may appear as truisms or simplistic self-evident propositions. They may save our society a lot of difficulties. We need to approach the impending "age of aging" without the concerns, exaggerated fears, or unrealistic optimism alluded to earlier.

1.2

Myths and Realities of Clinical Geriatrics

Robert N. Butler

Despite the therapeutic pessimism, and at times, nihilism concerning the psychiatric disorders of old age, physicians who actually work with elderly patients report impressive therapeutic results. Unfortunately, many general physicians refer the aged to a psychiatrist only late in the course of their illnesses or never refer them at all. These practitioners feel that they cannot treat geriatric patients because their "mental" conditions are "irreversible." Some psychiatrists, on the other hand, regard the mental disorders of old age as primarily physical—and thus beyond the scope of psychiatric treatment. Fortunately, these attitudes are changing—even if slowly—as is the social and economic situation of the elderly.

But even under the most favorable socioeconomic and cultural circumstances, the latter years of man are a time of psychologic crises, characterized by loss, grief, and efforts at restitution. First of all, there are the profound human losses of marital partner, children, loved friends and associates—losses for which it is now difficult to find a substitute. The result is often an abiding sense of isolation and loneliness.

Reprinted from *Roche Medical Image and Commentary*, International Medical Press, Inc., June 1970, p. 116-118.

Social losses similarly influence the inner life and the behavior of the aged. These include a reduction of income and a loss of status and prestige—all the result of retirement, which is often involuntary and apt to occur earlier in the U.S. than in Western Europe. A sense of uselessness, a feeling of nonparticipation in society, heightens the desolation of the elderly. For a significant proportion of our aging population, these conditions are aggravated by economic distress. It is estimated that some 7,000,000 out of the 20,000,000 Americans aged 65 or over fall below the poverty line.

What's more, the numbers of the aged are increasing. By the year 2000 it is estimated that there will be 33,000,000 retired persons in the country. In this connection it is well to remember that older people—70 per cent of whom have one or more chronic ailments—suffer more severe illnesses than do younger persons and remain ill twice as long. One in four has some degree of hearing loss, and perceptual impairment is common. The prevalence of mental illness increases decade by decade; the incidence of depression specifically rises with age; and the suicide rate attains its peak in white males in their 80s.

The Tranquility Myth

This brings us to the first of the many prevalent myths about geriatric care—namely, that old age is a time of relative peace and tranquility, when people can relax and enjoy the fruit of their labor after the storms of active life are over. Actually, older persons experience more stresses—and their stresses are more devastating and less susceptible to treatment—than any other age group. Seen from that perspective, the strength of the aged to endure vicissitudes is remarkable. In many instances, it is these stresses, often external (such as solitude or poverty)—and not the process of aging itself—that produce, at least in large part, such mental states as depression, anxiety, and paranoia, and the many psychosomatic illnesses that are commonly associated with the geriatric patient.

Depressive reactions are particularly widespread in old age. To the psychotic depressions and the depressions associated with cerebroarteriosclerosis must be added the everyday depressions that stem from prolonged physical illness, from grief and despair, and from diminished social and personal status, with inevitable lowered self-esteem. Remember that some 10 to 20 per cent of all aged persons live alone and are essentially isolated.

Anxiety reactions are similarly common in old age, manifested in various forms—in rigid thinking, for instance, and in behavior that is often mistakenly attributed to "aging." Actually, some mellowing of symptoms may be observed as people grow older, particularly in the obsessional-compulsive person. A man who has been a fussbudget in earlier life, who has always been meticulous, insisting on managing everything, may find these qualities useful in retirement. Taking care of the house and watching over everything may keep him occupied and busy.

Paranoid states occur more commonly in older women than in men. They are frequently associated with hearing loss, probably because this deficiency increases the sense of isolation and a tendency to misinterpret conversations. A woman in her 70s, for instance, though apparently free of major psychiatric problems, insisted that at night her overhead neighbors deliberately pounded on the floor with a cane and sent noxious fumes through the radiator. Discussions indicated that this discreetly circumscribed delusion was related to her fears of being alone at night—a characteristic isolation symptom.

The Myth of Unproductivity

A common chronologic myth holds that at the age of 65 or 70—or at some similarly arbitrary figure—old people become significantly different from their younger neighbors. They are then presumed to become unproductive and to decline, disengaging themselves from life and preferring to live alone in a state of segregation.

In reality, granted the absence of disease and social adversity, old people tend to remain actively concerned about their personal and community relationships. Many persons of achievement continue to be productive late in life (Picasso, for instance, who was 88, and Artur Rubinstein, who plays dazzling piano concerts at 81). Some, in fact, become unusually creative for the first time in their old age. Many notable examples of this phenomenon have been cited, from the painter Grandma Moses to the novelist William de Morgan, but it is by no means limited to exceptional personalities of this type; the discovery and expression of inborn talents late in life may occur at any social level, often appearing long after the individual has been freed from the routine responsibilities of the so-called "productive years."

When the elderly patient suffers from a sense of insignificance ("being over the hill" or "being put out to pasture"), the physician can often help him find a role, a place, or an activity of authentic interest. The older person's natural interest in teaching and sponsoring the activities of younger people should be encouraged. Certainly, social participation, when it is desired, should be encouraged.

Since old age is a period of numerous rapid and profound losses—including the loss of choice—medical and psychiatric efforts must be directed toward making restitution when possible and promoting realistic acceptance when fundamental change is impossible. With the more serious depressions—and it is dismaying how refractory the depressions of later life can be—psychiatric referral is indicated. Psychotherapy, drugs, and/or electroconvulsive therapy may be used. But it does not always follow that supportive psychotherapy is needed. The help of another person—sometimes a friend—in open discussion may be very liberating.

The resources of the community must also be exploited. Home care is probably the therapeutic trend of the future. Certainly the physician can play a crucial role as coordinator of services that are fragmented. Comprehensiveness and continuity of evaluation and care are essential.

Myth of Resistance to Change

Although the stability of the adult character structure is remarkable, old people are more open to change than is generally recognized. Indeed, their alleged conservatism is exaggerated: some of it derives, again, not from "aging" but from socioeconomic pressures. A good example would be the decision of older persons to vote against school loans or tax increases. Not enough consideration is given to the fact that property—the home—may be the only equity of an aged person and that his income may be both fixed and low.

This kind of presumed reduction in social commitment gives rise to many theories about withdrawal and loss of vitality. But when one considers the effects of physical disease in old age and the pressure of adverse social and economic factors, the extent to which "disengagement" and "interiority" are crucial in the citizen over 65 remains controversial.

The Brain Damage Myth

There is a tendency to think all old people have damage to the brain. Two major disorders create brain damage: cerebral atherosclerosis and senile brain disease. On the other hand, old people—like young people—are subject to such emotional states as anxiety, grief, depression, and paranoia. Age and brain damage cannot be held accountable for all this psychopathology. In fact, fundamental aging processes per se probably play a very small role, if any, in the production of psychopathology.

Older persons frequently display such symptoms as disorientation, confusion and other mental states that may be temporary, reversible, and caused by external factors. Careful diagnosis is therefore necessary to differentiate these states from chronic organic brain syndromes, which might better be called irreversible brain damage. Both reversible and irreversible brain disorders may occur in the same person, making the problem of diagnosis and treatment even more difficult. If a reversible brain syndrome is assumed by the physician to be a chronic brain disorder, the elderly patient is apt to be transferred to a mental hospital or nursing home without active treatment and without hope of discharge.

The fact that aged patients seem very preoccupied and that their capacity to respond in terms of learning and memory may be greatly compromised sometimes results from deep concern over money problems or family worries. A depressive state arising from such concerns may be overlooked and a misdiagnosis of organic brain disorder made. The physician should also be alert to vitamin deficiencies, since many older persons who live alone often eat poorly or may even, because of poverty, go hungry.

The Unresponsive-to-Therapy Myth

Under reasonably good circumstances, more older psychiatric patients improve or recover because of psychotherapy than fail to react to it, but the physician needs to work realistically within the constrictions imposed by the patient's age and waning years. Depending on his personal training, interest, skill, and experience, the general physician may well be able to undertake such psychotherapy with his elderly patients. Since he may want to do so under the supervision of a psychiatrist, it is important to develop his judgment as to when referral is indicated. Alone or in collaboration with the psychiatrist the physician may thus work with the elderly patient up to and through the process of dying itself.

Physicians often resist referring their older patients for psychiatric care for a variety of reasons: therapeutic pessimism, the retired person's restricted finances (although here the advent of Medicare has helped somewhat), and the sense of stigma felt by the family. Consequently, the aged are often seen by the psychiatrist only when mental disease is well advanced and hence more resistant to treatment. Also, many mentally ill persons over 65 unfortunately bypass outpatient care and are admitted to mental hospitals and nursing homes. The latter rarely offer psychiatric skills, a fact that leaves the patient committed to long term custodial care, with a progressively poorer prognosis.

In contrast to this prospect, it is well to remember that psychotherapy of varying depths has been successfully used with patients in their 60s, 70s, and 80s. With these older-age groups, it is important to listen attentively and to indicate that the aged person has something to teach. Just as one must avoid false reassurances, so one must also deal honestly with motivation, anxiety, grief, defenses, and restitution to the extent that it is possible. The physician must never, however, be destructive to the processes of illusion and denial needed by his patients. He must discuss the fact of death, the fact of loss, and the problems of grief, but always within the context of possibilities, restitution, and resolution.

The same principle applies as in work with patients of other ages: one must work compassionately and carefully to discover the roots of the patient's defenses rather than to attack them overtly. Both age and illness are sometimes used as a defense, which, if permitted to get out of hand, can promote invalidism. When the physician collaborates, albeit unwittingly, in this form of defense, a state of helplessness is induced. On the other hand, excessive pride may sometimes deter an elderly person from seeking the help he sorely needs.

The aged have also been found to be responsive to group therapy. Group sessions for hospitalized patients as well as for outpatients have spurred improvements in social behavior, mood, and mental status. Even groups set up in an informal social setting—such as afternoon teas—can be effective. Community and senior citizen centers offer good backgrounds for such self-help groups. Short-term therapy, consisting of perhaps six 15-minute sessions with a physician, are useful in resolving grief, in effecting reconciliation with siblings whom the patient may have refused to see for years, and in aiding the aged person to adjust himself to a more restricted life, with reduced physical activity, as might be mandated by a cardiac regimen.

Advice from the physician on living arrangements and social commitments may be necessary. But the physician must be careful not to encourage excessive "collaboration" with the aging process by offhand "take-it-easy" warnings against exercise, social engagements, and work. The doctor-patient relationship is crucial to the older person, who is often more fearful of losing people close to him than of his own death.

The physician must also be prepared for this patient's greater need to be physically touched, for a garrulity that is often only the expression of a profound loneliness and for the allowance of adequate time to avoid any sense of pressure.

For old people who remain alone at home the physician should advise—and help them procure—telephone reassurance programs, which are now becoming increasingly available in many cities through public and private agencies. It is shocking to learn that no less than 5,000,000 of America's 20,000,000 aged persons lack even the rudimentary aid of a telephone with which to make an emergency call or to maintain contact with a relative or friend. Yet the telephone can often allay anxiety more effectively than a tranquilizer.

The Myth of Institutionalization

In general, older people do best at home. But overemphasis on age, brain damage, and hypochondriasis leads many physicians, including psychiatrists, to favor institutionalization. They also have a tendency to apply to the phenomena of old age concepts that were conceived to explain the behavior of childhood. Thus, facile references are made to "regression" and "second childhood," and the fear of death (which should be understandable in an aged person) may be designated as "castration anxiety." To all of this I would suggest that the answer to the sense of futility felt by so many physicians concerning treatment of the aged lies in greater exposure to the elderly patient and a more serious effort to discover the extent to which his mental disorders are reversible.

The family is sometimes blamed for rejecting its older relatives and thus condemning them to institutionalization. Although this does happen on occasion, the extent of such rejection is exaggerated. Many families, in fact, endure enormous hardships to maintain their older relatives in the community. Even so, the physician must carefully assess the family's attitude toward his patient and its objective capacity to help sustain him. He must determine: What is the role of the patient in the family? How objectively does the family see the organic decline of the patient? Can the family be helped in its response to the patient? Can the family members become components in the treatment plan? Are they fostering childishness in the patient?

The psychiatrist will learn a great deal about his older patient from consultation with the family. Although he must bear in mind who is his primary patient and preserve confidentiality, he should be flexible enough to move away from the traditional psychiatrist-to-patient model when indicated. Home visits, family counseling, and consultation with the patient's physician may be mandatory.

Caution is necessary in using the blanket designation of senility as a cause for hospitalization. Senility is a wastebasket term, not acceptable in medicine. We have no measurable indicators for it. So-called senile symptomatology may indicate (1) the beginning of a depression, manifested as a state of confusion, (2) the development of a reversible brain disorder, or (3) a chronic brain disorder that may either remain stable or progress at various rates of speed. Old persons without families are much more susceptible to psychiatric disorders and are likely to need hospitalization.

The early symptoms to look for in organic brain disorder are a change in the capacity for attention, in memory, in intellectual grasp or comprehension, in orientation, in judgment, and in response to the physician. Neurotic and psychotic behavior may occur. Disorientation in time precedes that of place. Impairment in the capacity to recognize others precedes the inability to recognize oneself.

There is no specific treatment for the major organic brain disorders of old age—cerebral arteriosclerosis and senile brain disease. Structuring of a medically and socially prosthetic milieu is important. Simplification, order, a balance of care and self-care, moderation of stimuli, and the use of objects and personnel to preserve orientation are among the procedures that are valuable in helping the patient with an organic brain syndrome either at home or in an institution. Again, home-care systems are probably the trend of the future. Supportive psychotherapy for the patient and his family is often advisable.

Acute brain disorders are less distinguished by the rapidity of their onset than by the fact that they may be reversible. It is very important to make a careful differential diagnosis to avoid hospitalization, if possible, especially so because acute brain disorders are often misdiagnosed. To identify an acute brain syndrome, look for a fluctuating level of awareness—from stupor to active delirium, with hallucinations (visual, rather than auditory), and evidence of misidentification. The physician at the bedside, for instance, may be identified as the patient's son or his dead brother. Great restlessness may be present.

Acute reversible brain disorders are often associated with febrile, debilitating, or exhausting types of physical illness; in fact, they sometimes represent the first clues to such physical disorders as dehydration, electrolyte disturbances, or even appendicitis (in instances without manifestation of pain, fever, and leukocytosis).

Advances in internal medicine and surgery have abetted the prevention and treatment of acute brain syndromes. Careful preoperative preparation, for example, should include orientation; the recovery period calls for the presence of familiar persons and objects. Such measures have significantly reduced the incidence of delirium after cataract surgery in the aged.

When institutionalization is unavoidable, I have found the psychiatric units of general hospitals or the private mental hospitals preferable to nursing homes or state mental hospitals. The present controversy concerning the mental hospital versus the nursing home as the place for the elderly psychiatric patient might be eliminated by improved admission studies and standards of care. A socially and medically supportive environment requires personnel not ordinarily available in nursing homes; rarely do these homes have any psychiatric coverage. Restorative services directed toward discharge of the patient are more likely to be provided by the mental hospitals. But the diagnosis, care, and treatment of the elderly patient in the average state mental hospital is also discouraging. Results from private hospitals and general hospital psychiatric units are much better, probably reflecting the fact that the elderly patient is treated on a par with the younger patient in this setting and that more money is available.

Some key points must be remembered in institutionalizing the aged:

1. They should not be segregated but rather maintained on active adult treatment wards until such time as their needs in the way of physical nursing justify care that is essentially custodial. But custodial care need not have a pejorative meaning; it can include the application of psychiatric principles and use of adjunctive services.
2. In whatever institution, the older patient (like the younger) should participate in establishing ground rules for his living. Experiments in resident and patient government have been encouraging. Choice is important.
3. The physical structuring of space should provide freedom and safety for the wandering, confused geriatric patient. Privacy in easily accessible bathrooms favorably influences incontinence.
4. Color coding, name plates on doors, and the use of personal furnishings and belongings (pictures, slippers, purses, footstools) help maintain orientation.
5. By eliminating restrictive visiting hours, institutions should encourage visitors. To allay anxieties, social services should look after the aged patient's home possessions, such as furniture, plants, pets, and mail, including pension and social security checks.

Finally, whether the patient remains at home or is hospitalized, contact with persons close to him can be the single most important factor in his environment. This crucial contact may be provided by a relative, a friend or neighbor, a visitor to whom the patient becomes attached, or a nurse or aide in the institution itself. To the elderly person this contact signifies that he is not totally isolated, that he still participates in the world of living people, and that he has not been completely discarded into the limbo of those not yet dead but no longer truly alive. Fortunately, more churches and synagogues now train Friendly Visitors.

1.3

Patterns of Aging: Past, Present, and Future

Bernice L. Neugarten

The topic of aging and longevity has become an "in" thing in the mind of the American public. The mass media have discovered it, as witnessed by the recent cover story in *Newsweek*, the article "Is Senility Inevitable?" in *Saturday Review*, the article in *National Geographic* about remote villages in Ecuador and the Soviet Union where persons are said to live to the advanced ages of 125 and 130, and by a rash of newspaper headlines such as "Scientists Seek the Key to Longevity."

This "discovery" by the mass media stems from the fact that a few biologists are predicting that we stand on the brink of a scientific breakthrough that will add from twenty-five to thirty years to the average life-span. Understandably enough, these claims have caught the attention of the science editors and reporters.

Aging is neither an "in" nor an "out" topic, but one that has always been here and is here to stay. Interest in aging constitutes the wave of the future as far as social scientists, social workers, and medical practitioners are concerned. The reason is obvious. Since the turn of the century, the total United States population has increased nearly threefold; but the number of persons aged 65 and over has increased almost sevenfold. In 1970, there were about 20 million older people in the United States; by the year 2000, there will be over 28 million. The latter figure is based on persons already alive and on projection of present death rates. Because it takes no account of possible medical advances or breakthroughs in biology, it is a conservative estimate.

Published in *Social Service Review*, 47 (4) 1973, pp. 571-580. This paper is based on the Sidney A. and Julia P. Teller Lecture presented at the School of Social Service Administration of the University of Chicago on May 2, 1973.

The growing number of aged persons is not in itself a social problem if a social problem is defined as a state of affairs which needs correction. Few persons would seriously maintain that it is wrong to have many older people in the population or that remedial steps should be taken to pare down their numbers. On the contrary, nations prize longevity and count it an accomplishment, not a failure, that increasing numbers of men and women live to old age. The problem is the lack of preparation for the "sudden" appearance of large numbers of older people and the lag in adapting social institutions to their needs.

To be more exact, the social problems are of two types. First, a certain proportion of older people suffer from poverty, illness, and social isolation. These people, whom we call the needy aged, create acute problems in the field of social welfare. Second, broader problems arise from the need of all individuals in the society to adjust to the new rhythms of life that result from increased longevity. All members of society must adapt to new social phenomena such as multigenerational families, retirement communities, and leisure as a way of life. The second set of social problems, as much as the first, leads to the innumerable questions of social policy that arise as the whole society accommodates itself to the new age distribution.

How should society meet the needs of older people? How does their increasing presence affect other groups in the society? What new relationships are being generated between young and old? More and more people are asking these questions in their professional as well as their private lives. For example, biological and social scientists have evolved a new science, gerontology; the Gerontological Society, created in 1940, now has a membership of some twenty-two hundred scientists and professional workers; and there are now some fifty-five gerontological societies and organizations in different countries belonging to the International Gerontological Association. The medical profession is arguing over the creation of a new specialty, geriatrics. While the move toward developing new specialties is regarded by many physicians as a step backward rather than forward, nevertheless the first professor of geriatrics in an American university was appointed in 1973. Social workers are experimenting with new types of services for older clients; adult educators are seeking ways of serving the older as well as the younger adult; recreational workers are trying new programs for older people; a few law schools are turning attention to the special legal problems that arise. Business corporations are concerned with the nagging questions of arbitrary or flexible retirement, the vesting of pension funds, and ways of preparing middle-aged workers for the adjustments they will make after retirement. Commissions, committees, and public agencies are proliferating at local, state, and national levels to cope with problems of older people.

All this is leading to a different climate of awareness and to changing images of old age as one looks to the recent past, the present, and the future.

The Past

Negative stereotypes of old age were strongly entrenched in a society that prided itself on being youth oriented, future oriented, and oriented toward doing rather than being. Old people were usually regarded either as poor, isolated, sick, unhappy, desolate, and destitute—the "old age, it's a pity" perspective—or, on the contrary, as powerful, rigid, and reactionary. The first of these inaccurate images, usually inadvertently repeated through the mass media, probably originated from social workers, physicians, and psychiatrists who served the disadvantaged, the poor, and the physically and mentally ill—the needy aged.

In that climate—and, of course, it has not entirely disappeared—most people saw aging as alien to the self, and they tended to deny or repress the associated feelings of distaste and anxiety. In a society in which the frequency of death among the young had been drastically reduced by the conquest of infectious disease, and in which death had become increasingly associated only with old age, these pervasive attitudes, irrational and unconscious though they may have been, served also to maintain a psychological distance between young and old.

There was also the fact—and it is still true, although rapidly changing—that, in comparison with other age groups, the aged were economically and socially disadvantaged. They included a disproportionate number of foreign-born, unskilled men, who had come to the United States without much formal education, who had worked most of their lives at low-paying jobs, who had accumulated no savings through their lifetimes, and who were living in relative poverty after a life of hard work.

To reiterate, the image of old age was, from many different perspectives, a negative one.

The Present

Images are now changing in the direction of reality; and reality means diversity. Older people are coming to be recognized for what they are:

namely, a very heterogeneous group. With 10 percent of our population now over sixty-five years old, and with nearly half that group now great-grandparents, a very large number of young people are interacting with older members of their own families. With people now becoming grandparents between the ages of forty and fifty, and with more than one-half of all women in that age group are in the labor market, young children see their grandmothers going to work every day and their mothers staying at home with them. We are beginning to delineate a "young-old" population and to see it as different from the "old-old."

The image of the old man in the rocking chair is now matched by the white-haired man on the golf course. Even television images are beginning to change. "Maude" is a forceful, liberal, middle-aged woman; "A Touch of Grace" portrays an elderly widow being courted by an elderly man, with both persons portrayed sympathetically; "Sanford and Son" are a black father and his adult son who have a close and mutually supportive relationship in which the old father emerges as the wiser and more astute.

A different example of the changing images of aging appeared in a newspaper picture a few months ago. Captioned "Happy Pappy," it showed Strom Thurmond, the sixty-nine-year-old senator from South Carolina, with his young wife, their eighteen-month-old daughter, and their newborn son. Only six years earlier, in contrast, a newspaper report of the marriage of Supreme Court Justice Douglas to a twenty-three-year-old coed had included some very venomous comments. Five members of the House of Representatives had introduced resolutions calling on the House Judiciary Committee to investigate the moral character of Douglas: one said he should be impeached. If the newspaper account of Justice Douglas's marriage appeared today, it would probably take a much less hostile form, judging at least from the story about Senator Thurmond.

There are other social forces at work which change the images and status of the aged. The so-called youth culture seems to be recognizing new affinities with older people. That culture forgoes instrumentality—work, achievement, production, competition—for expressivity. "Being" rather than "doing," it values reflection, relatedness, and freedom to express one's authentic self. Some young people regard these qualities as characteristic of older people, and they find allies in the old. Some young people perceive the old as alienated from the dominant culture and from the "establishment," although, of course, there is no evidence that a higher proportion of the old than of the young or middle-aged are in truth alienated.

It is possible, also, that sizable segments of the young are seeking to strengthen their ethnic identifications and turn to their grandparents for reaffirmation of ethnic cultural values.

Findings of Social Scientists

The findings of social researchers are contributing to the changing images of aging. For example, studies of large and representative samples of older people have shown that they are not isolated from other family members. While most older people prefer to live in their own households, they live near children or relatives and see other family members regularly. Overall, a higher proportion of old people who are sick live with their families than do those who are well. Old persons, contrary to the stereotype, are not dumped into mental hospitals or nursing homes or homes for the aged by cruel and indifferent children. Furthermore, older persons are not necessarily lonely or desolate if they live alone.

Few older persons ever show overt signs of mental deterioration or senility. Only a small proportion ever become mentally ill; for those who do, psychological and psychiatric treatment is by no means futile.

Retirement is neither good nor bad; some men and women want to keep on working, but more and more choose to retire early, as soon as they have enough income to live without working. The newest studies show that there is an increasing alienation from work and that increasing proportions of the population seem to value leisure more than work. Retired persons do not grow sick from idleness or from feelings of worthlessness. Three-fourths of the persons questioned in a recent national sample reported they were satisfied or very satisfied with their lives since retirement, a finding that is in line with earlier surveys. Most persons over sixty-five years old think of themselves as being in good health and act accordingly. On the average, after a short period of readjustment after retirement, men do not fail to establish meaningful patterns of activity.

Although there are some signs of increased age segregation, as in the retirement communities that have multiplied in the United States, this trend involves only a small proportion of older persons, and they constitute a self-selected group who appear to be exercising a larger rather than a smaller degree of freedom in choosing where to live. Furthermore, what studies are available indicate that in such communities, where the density of older people is relatively high, social interaction has increased. On the whole, it cannot be said that urban industrial societies preclude the social integration of the old.

In a series of studies of individuals between the ages of fifty and eighty carried out over a period of years at the University of Chicago, great diversity was found in the social and psychological patterns associated with successful aging. (Neugarten, 1968.) Various kinds of data were gathered on several hundred persons, all living "normal" lives in the community, including information on types of social interaction, role performance, investment in various roles and life-styles, degree of satisfaction with life—past and present—and personality type. It was found that as they grew older some persons sloughed off various role responsibilities with relative comfort and remained highly content with life. Others showed a drop in social role performance (e.g., as worker, friend, neighbor, or community participant), accompanied by a drop in life satisfaction. Still others, who had long shown low levels of activity accompanied by high satisfaction, changed relatively little as they aged.

For instance, in one group of seventy- to eighty-year-olds, eight different patterns of aging were empirically derived. They included the Reorganizers, Focused, Disengaged, Holding-on, Constricted, Succorance-seeking, Apathetic, and Disorganized. It appeared, furthermore, that the patterns reflected long-standing life-styles; within broad limits—given no major biological accidents or major social upheavals—an individual's pattern of aging was predictable from his way of life in middle age. In other words, aging is not a leveler of individual differences—until, perhaps, at the very end of life.

If there is no single social role pattern for the aged in 1970, the diversity is likely to become even greater in the future. With better health, more education, and more financial resources, older men and women will exercise—or at least will wish to exercise—greater freedom to choose the life-styles that suit them.

All this is not to deny the fact that, at the very end of life, there will continue to be a shorter or longer period of dependency, and that increased numbers of the very old will need care, either in their own homes or in special institutional settings. For persons who are terminally ill or incapacitated, it will be idle, in the future as in the present, to speak of meaningful social roles or of increased options in life-styles. For the advanced aged, the problems for the society will continue to be those of providing maximum social supports, the highest possible levels of care and comfort, the assurance of dignified death, and an increasing element of choice for the individual himself or for members of his family regarding how and when his life shall end.

Questions for the Future

In looking to the future, rather than focus upon the diversities among individual older people, one might well look at the society as an age-differentiated system and at relationships among age groups. In this context, questions about the prolongation of life can be reconsidered.

Generational conflict and relationships among age groups fluctuate according to historical, political, and economic factors. Under fortunate circumstances, an equilibrium is created whereby all age groups receive an appropriate share of the goods of the society and an appropriate place for their different values and world views. Under other circumstances, conflict may increase, as when the old, through some presumed historical failure, become "de-authorized" in the eyes of the young or when the young become overly advantaged in the eyes of the old. Whatever the forces of social change, the quality of life for all members of society and the social cohesion among age groups are influenced by the relative numbers of young, middle-aged, and old present at any given time.

If, indeed, the life-span is to be further extended, resulting in a dramatic increase in the numbers of the old, will industrialized societies be more ready for them than before and better prepared to meet their needs? Will the status of the aged become better or worse?

The answers are by no means clear. For one thing, generational conflicts may be increasing. If so, will they involve, on the one hand, the young and society at large and, on the other hand, the old and society at large? Is a new age divisiveness appearing and are there new antagonisms that can be called "ageism"? Is the world entering a period of social change in which, like earlier struggles for political and economic rights, there is now also a struggle for age rights? If so, will the struggle be joined not only by the young but also by the old who might otherwise become its victims?

Such questions have no easy answers, for the underlying social dynamics are complex. In the United States, for example, resentments against delinquency, student activism, the drug culture, and the counterculture often become uncritically fused into hostility toward the young as an age group. At the same time, there have been new attempts to integrate the young, as witnessed by the recent lowering of the voting age from twenty-one to eighteen. And there are the dramatic instances, such as the election of a youthful mayor or youth-controlled city councils of Berkeley or Madison, in which traditional age values were swept aside by other political considerations.

Anger toward the old may also be on the rise. In some instances, because a growing proportion of power positions in judiciary, legislative, business, and professional arenas are occupied by older people, and because of seniority privileges among workers, the young and middle-aged become resentful. In other instances, as the number of the retired increases, the economic burden is perceived as falling more and more upon the middle-aged taxpayer.

These issues are not merely academic, as illustrated in recent journalistic accounts.

An editorial, syndicated in many metropolitan newspapers and occasioned by the 20 percent rise in social security benefits, was headlined, "Budget Story: Bonanza for Elderly." It said, "America's public resources are increasingly being mortgaged for the use of a single group within our country, the elderly." It went on to distort the situation by saying, "One-fourth of total federal spending is earmarked for only one-tenth of the population . . . clearly this trend cannot continue for long without causing a bitter political struggle between the generations."

Another example is an article that appeared two years ago in the *New Republic*. The author advocated that all persons lose the vote at retirement or age seventy, whichever was earlier. Reviewing changes that had occurred in his native California, he said: "We face a serious constitutional crisis—California faces civil war—if we continue to allow the old an unlimited franchise. There are simply too many senile voters and their number is growing" (Steward, 1970).

However, older people are becoming more vocal and more active in the political process. As they become accustomed to the politics of confrontation they see around them, they are beginning to voice their demands. For instance, appeals to "senior power" came into prominence in 1971 at the White House Conference on Aging. There are more frequent accounts of groups of older people picketing and protesting over such local issues as reduced bus fares or better housing projects. Whether such incidents remain isolated and insignificant or whether an activist politics of old age is developing in the United States is still a debatable question, but it would be a mistake to assume that what characterized the political position of older people in the past decades will be equally characteristic in the future.

Another factor to be considered is the creation of advocacy groups. The American Association for Retired Persons, which makes it appeal primarily to middle-class older persons, claims a membership of 3.5 million. The National Council of Senior Citizens, oriented primarily toward blue-collar groups, claims a membership of some 3 million. The Grey Panthers, smaller but more militant, is now organizing nationwide.

Given the complexity of such trends, we presently lack good indexes for assessing the degree of social cohesion among age groups. As we develop so-called intangible social indicators (e.g., of levels of life satisfaction or levels of alienation), social scientists might well build indexes relating to expectations and attitudes of various age groups toward each other and monitor those attitudes in assessing the social health of the nation.

Some observers take an optimistic and others a pessimistic view of the progress thus far achieved in equalizing the needs of various age groups. All in all, it is probably fair to say that, in at least the affluent societies of the world, the status of the aged has begun to show marked improvement during the past few decades. The question is whether such gains as have been achieved can be continued in the face of a dramatic extension of the life-span.

Two general strategies for lengthening the life-span are being pursued: the first is the continuing effort to conquer major diseases. It has been variously estimated that, if the problems of cancer and cardiovascular diseases are solved, life expectancy at age 65 will be increased five to ten years, thus redistributing deaths so that they will come more often at the end of the natural life-span, at about age eighty to ninety.

The second strategy involves altering intrinsic biological processes, which are presumed to underlie aging and which seem to proceed independent of disease processes. That is, the genetic and biochemical secrets of aging should be discovered, and then the biological clock that is presumably programmed into the human species could be altered. This second approach is directed at control of the rate of aging rather than control of disease. A few biologists claim that such a breakthrough will occur within the next twenty years and that it will result in an extension of the natural life-span itself, so that men will have not an additional ten, but an additional twenty-five years of life.

If the natural life-span were to be increased in the relatively short period of a few decades, the effects upon society might well be revolutionary. It is an unhappy fact that few social scientists, and even fewer biological scientists, have given serious thought to the social implications, although speculative essays and fictional accounts by journalists have begun to appear alongside more familiar forms of science fiction.

One writer has published a social satire describing a society in which people when they reach the age of fifty are automatically segregated from others, even from their own children, then painlessly put to death when they reach sixty-five. Another has described the solution in opposite terms in a society in which the old are in control, and the few young who are allowed to be born seek ways to accelerate their own aging in order to take their places in the society of elders. These parodies are examples of ageism carried to the extreme: in the first instance ageism is directed against the old; in the second, against the young.

There have been few serious attempts to extrapolate from available data in pondering such questions as these: Can an increased life-span be achieved without keeping marginally functioning individuals alive for extended periods? Would a major increase in the proportion of the aged so aggravate the problems of health, medical care, income, and housing that the old would be worse off than now? What would be the major deleterious and the major beneficial effects of a prolonged life-span upon the rest of society? Given present economic and governmental institutions, can even the affluent societies support greatly enlarged numbers of retired persons? Can income be divorced from work rapidly enough to balance off inequities among age groups? Will free time be truly free—that is, will it be desired by most individuals? Can it be supported by adequate income and by a reasonable level of good health? Will it be socially honored—that is, will the work ethic change rapidly enough into a leisure ethic? Or, if the employable age were to be extended, would the effects be deleterious upon both young and old? Could spectacular unemployment be avoided in either or both groups? Could technological obsolescence be overcome in the old? Could our educational systems be transformed rapidly enough into opportunity systems for self-fulfillment for the middle-aged and old as well as for the young? Will our social and humanistic and ethical values accommodate to a drastically altered age distribution? What will be the effects upon successive groups of young, and what will be the eventual effects upon their old age?

Lest we be overwhelmed by unanswerable questions, it should be said that, in contrast with those biologists whose statements make newspaper headlines, most biologists take a more conservative view of the future and believe that dramatically lengthened life-spans are still far off.

But whether or not a breakthrough is imminent, we are nevertheless already witnessing transformations in the age distribution of the society, in which the number of older people is rapidly increasing. And we can be quite sure that medical advances will continue to prolong life, even if we are far from solving the biochemical or genetic secrets of aging. Many gerontologists believe that if average life expectancy is increased by only five more years—to say nothing of twenty-five years—the effects upon our present economic and welfare institutions will be profound.

Man's desire for longevity can now be whetted by the findings of social scientists, such as those already mentioned. If—as now appears true—the institutional arrangements of industrialized societies do not inevitably lead to the social isolation of the old, if—as also appears true—man does not lose his ability to learn as he grows old, and if there is no universal set of personality changes that lead inevitably to disengagement from society, then the old person stands to benefit as much from social advances as does the young person.

What, then, will be the new social and ethical pressures for prolonging life? What will be the risks of a prolonged life-span, not only to older people themselves, but to the society as a whole? How can these risks be weighed against the benefits? How can social values be weighed against economic values, and how can a new priority of social values be effected?

These are questions that will inevitably preoccupy us more and more over the next decades. In pursuing our research programs and our action programs and in working out broad-scale social solutions, the social scientist will join with the biological scientist, the policy maker, the jurist, the ethicist, and the social worker. We will need, as never before, the insights and the experience and the social philosophy of the profession of social work.

References

Neugarten, Bernice L., ed. *Middle Age and Aging*. Chicago: University of Chicago Press, 1968.
Steward, Douglas J. "The Lesson of California: Disfranchise the Old." *New Republic* (August 29, 1970).

1.4

Older People in Adolescent Literature

David A. Peterson and Elizabeth L. Karnes

The measurement of attitudes toward older people has generated extensive research in the gerontological field during the past 30 years. This activity was stimulated by concern over the prevalence of negative stereotypes and opinions about the elderly and a desire to measure accurately the extent and distribution of these views. Findings have rarely been completely consistent (Arth, 1968; Bell & Stanfield, 1973; Bengtson & Smith, 1968; Duncan, 1963; Harlan, 1968; McTavish, 1971).

In an excellent review of these studies, McTavish (1971) distinguished those which concentrate primarily on the stereotypes held by individuals from those which focus on the cultural or societal status of the older person across various time periods. In reviewing these studies, he identified two approaches used by researchers—participant observation and analysis of ethnographic records. The latter approach has often utilized content analysis of published literary works to assess the roles which older people play and to determine the attitude toward old age which is evidenced.

Literature may be expected to have some effect on the attitudes and stereotypes which readers hold. The process of attitude acquisition, including those concerning old people, begins early in life. The persistence of these attitudes and stereotypes is related in some extent

Copyright 1976 by The Gerontological Society. Reprinted by permission. *The Gerontologist*, Vol. 16, No. 3, 1976, pp. 225-231.

to subsequent experiences of the individual with older persons. Rosencranz and McNevin (1969) observed that college students who had close positive contacts with grandparents or other older persons exhibited more favorable attitudes toward older people than did subjects who did not have such experiences. Students who had acquaintanceships with institutionalized older people, however, were less likely to hold favorable attitudes. It may be postulated that vicarious experiences with older people would have similar effects. In this regard, some research interest has been evidenced in the stereotypes and attitudes regarding older people that are conveyed by the electronic and print media.

The view of aging that is presented by the mass media is widely distributed, consequently, it is often assumed that it influences the stereotypes and attitudes of the consumer. This assumption is difficult to test, since the initial opinion or attitudes and the unlimited number of intervening variables all affect the final disposition of the consumer. Consequently, researchers must be content to quantify the input from the print or electronic media and then assume that over the long run this stimulus will have some reinforcing or modifying effect. In this process, content analysis is typically utilized. Such an approach provides an organized process of reviewing the material presented and separating it into categories. In most content analyses dealing with aging, the number of older people, the positive or negative characteristics of their activities, the importance of their roles, or the changes that have occurred over time are presented.

Northcott (1975), in an examination of older people in prime-time television, reported that senior citizens comprised only 1.5 percent of the role portrayals. He concluded that older persons tended to be seen in contrast to a competent adult male and/or an attractive young adult female rather than as individuals able to rely upon themselves. In a brief review of television programming between 1969 and 1971, Aronoff (1974) found that only 4.9 percent of the characters were old. He concluded that aging in prime-time drama was associated with evil, failure, and unhappiness. Petersen's (1973) data do not support this negative conclusion. She reported that nearly 13 percent of the persons appearing on prime-time television were over age 65. The image of older persons was examined, and 59 percent of the roles were judged to be favorable portrayals, while only 18 percent were unfavorable. She concluded that visibility of older people on television was proportionate to their numbers in the USA population and that existing programming projected a favorable image.

Martel (1968) examined magazine fiction to assess sociological changes that have occurred in American society from 1890 to 1955. He found little emphasis on older people but did conclude that over the sixty-five-year period in question, the aged suffered a "symbolic abandonment," became relegated to less prominent roles, and were excluded from membership in the mainstream of life.

Studies of newspaper coverage of aging have been undertaken by Evans and Evans (1975) and MacDonald (1973). MacDonald's study categorized news articles relating to older people in a major Midwestern daily newspaper and compared them with those that appeared ten years earlier. His findings suggested that significant progress had not been achieved in attaining a sympathetic and balanced reporting of aging news. Evans and Evans, reporting on a content analysis of five major metropolitan daily newspapers, confirmed MacDonald's conclusion that no increase in coverage or balance in aging-related articles occurred over the period. They observed that some cities received much superior coverage to others and suggested strategies to increase and improve aging coverage in the press.

In a study similar to the one reported here, Seltzer and Atchley (1971) examined a number of children's books which had been published over the last 100 years and reported that negative attitudes and stereotypes about older people were not as common as had been expected. The present study was undertaken in the hopes of clarifying some of the questions raised by Seltzer and Atchley and others. This research was designed to supplement these efforts by analyzing a heretofore unexamined ethnographic source—adolescent literature. In the process, care was exercised to select a sample which could be justified as representing the highest quality of writing in the adolescent field.

The Study of Newbery Medal Books

This study determined the types, extent, and importance of older characters in adolescent literature, the attitudes toward oldness that were conveyed by the authors of adolescent literature, and the differences among older characters who appear in books of various time periods. The sample of adolescent literature selected for review comprised fifty-three books which had been awarded the John Newbery Medal. Each year, since 1922, the members of the children's section of the American Library Association have selected one book as the outstanding piece of adolescent literature for the year. The fifty-three books thus honored are the most distinguished collection of literature for adolescents of the past half century (Kingman, 1965).

Since these books are so highly recommended by librarians, they are vigorously promoted in schools and public libraries. Consequently, Newbery Medal Books are likely to be more widely read than others and may be expected to have wider influence. The Newbery Medal winners include fiction and nonfiction, contemporary and historical settings, American and foreign authors. They are extremely diverse and cannot easily be categorized except to say that they represent the best of literature written for adolescents.

Because these books and others of similar quality have been and continue to be read by young people, the material they include and the attitudes their authors' evidence may be supposed to have a lasting effect on the youthful readers. Whether this is a primary source of attitude is doubtful, but the books are likely to reinforce or modify existing stereotypes and attitudes held by young people.

Content Analysis Methodology

The Newbery Prize books were read to identify each of the characters of whatever age. In another report, Karnes will analyze the roles which women play in these books. For this analysis, however, as each older character was identified, every piece of information about the person was recorded verbatim. These data were later assigned to one of several demographic, behavioral, or descriptive categories which were used in the testing of hypotheses and are described in this report.

Six hypotheses were generated from the literature and perusal of a preliminary sample of adolescent books. Three of these hypotheses dealt with the entire group of fifty-three books. In research format, it was hypothesized that: (1) older characters would be portrayed as peripheral to the major focus of the book, i.e., they would be underrepresented, underdeveloped, and supporting rather than major characters; (2) the authors' attitude toward older characters would be generally positive, i.e., words chosen to describe older people would have positive connotations, pictures would be positive, and descriptions of older characters would be positive; and (3) older people would be portrayed as members of a family rather than as members of other social groupings, i.e., they would be referred to as family members, would live with or near relatives, and would be relatives of major characters.

A second set of hypotheses was adapted from the Seltzer and Atchley study. These hypotheses concern changes in the presentations of older people that appear in adolescent literature in different time periods. In general, it was hypothesized that: (4) attitudes toward older people would have become decreasingly positive over the past half-century; (5) there would have been a decrease in the number of references to older people in the more recent books; and (6) more recent adolescent literature would reveal an increased variability in the descriptions of older people.

General Findings of the Study

Of the 53 Newbery Medal books which were reviewed, 51 included at least one character considered by the author to be "old." There were a total of 159 such older persons in the 51 books, a mean of 3 older people per book. Nearly 12 percent of all characters of whatever age in the books were old. Male older characters were more numerous than females, with 94 of the older characters being male and only 65 being female. Thus the older population of the Newbery books included only 41 percent females, a significant difference from the 58 percent in the USA today (Brotman, 1971). It was interesting, however, that when characters of all ages were considered, females only accounted for 32 percent. Thus, older females were underrepresented but not nearly as much as younger and middle-aged females.

The typical demographic information was not able to be determined for many of the characters since they were not well developed in the books. From the data which could be extracted, it was found that ethnic or racial minorities made up 13.2 percent of all older characters, with blacks, Chinese, and native Americans being the largest groups. Occupations were indicated for sixty of the older characters, predominantly men. These were distributed over a wide range of employment with farmers, peddlers, and workmen being the most common. Women are generally not given an occupation, but, of those so designated, maids and owners of rooming houses were most common. Older characters were well distributed across the economic spectrum, with twenty-seven being identified as poor, thirty-four as middle class, and thirteen as well-to-do. Older characters tended to live in their own home (66 percent) while others lived with families, in a hut, or in an apartment. In general, then, the demographic data on older characters were similar to those of the contemporary USA population with the exception of the disproportionate number of males in the adolescent literature.

Limited confidence should be placed on the representativeness of the older characters, since complete data were not available on most. The authors tended to describe the appearance of the older character rather than to provide specific demographic information. For instance, a feeling for the older character would be provided through a description of the individual's eyes. Descriptions such as "bright," "friendly," "mellow," "sharp," "twinkling," and "wrinkles at the corners which made him look like he were smiling," were used to give positive feelings. On the other hand, "fat, paunched, tired eyes," "eyes hidden by heavy folds of eyelids," "worried eyes," and "hard of eye" were used to describe less positive characters.

In numerous ways the authors indicated their recognition of the process of aging as a slow accumulation of environmental injuries and insults which reach a point of awareness late in life. Descriptions of older characters included passages such as the following from *Up A Road Slowly:*

> Signs of age, so long held in abeyance, suddenly appeared in many little ways. Lines of fatigue, or possibly pain showed up around his mouth. His eyes looked tired, and what was unusual, he was given to long periods of silence (Hunt, 1966).

In other books, younger people gained an awareness of older persons and evidenced a desire to help them in their frailty or at least to understand what was happening to them. " 'I wish I had a great grandmother,' said Garnett enviously. 'Great grandmother's nice. She tells me a lot of stories. Only she sleeps all the time. Old people always do. I wonder why?' " (Enright, 1938). Some authors demonstrated their understanding of behavioral continuity into the later stages of life and described older characters as doing what they had always done. "She had spent a lifetime interfering—days, weeks, years. There was not a thing she could do better or enjoy more" (Sawyer, 1936). Other authors recognized the sense of fulfillment and integrity that may occur at the end of life for those who have reconciled aging and death as a natural part of the continuum of life. In the case of *The Cat Who Went to Heaven:*

> I'm poor and I'm old,
> My hair has gone gray,
> My robe is all patches
> My sash is not gay.
> The fat God of luck,
> Never enters our door,
> And no visitors come,
> To drink tea any more.
> Yet I hold my head high,
> As I walk through the town,
> While I serve such a master,
> My heart's not bowed down.
>
> (Coatsworth, 1931.)

The authors of the literature reviewed did not provide as extensive a demographic profile of the older characters as desired, but collectively they did include a more detailed and insightful view of the aging process than expected. This view illustrates an awareness of the diversity of age and sympathy for the pain and growth that can accompany the last of life.

The Hypotheses Are Rejected

Six hypotheses were tested; none could be accepted since the submeasures for the hypotheses were not consistent in any instance. The first hypothesis stated that older characters would be portrayed as peripheral to the major focus of the book. The expectation was that older people would be underrepresented, underdeveloped, and found in supporting roles rather than as major figures. As pointed out above the proportion of older people in the 53 books was approximately equal to their distribution in contemporary America. However, only 25 of the 159 older characters could be considered as major in any sense. The designation of major was applied to those roles which were necessary to the development of the book's plot. Although this included some subjective judgment on the part of the researchers, the importance of the character and the degree to which he or she was emphasized was usually obvious. Older persons were generally excluded from the central action of the books.

The older individuals in the adolescent literature reviewed were not well developed. The mean number of items of information available on each older character was found to equal 4.6. This is a minute number when one considers the dozens and even hundreds of information references available on major characters. It was concluded that the aged were greatly underdeveloped. Thus, the tendency was in the direction suggested by the first hypothesis; older people were usually in supporting roles and they were underdeveloped. However, they were not underrepresented, so the hypothesis could not be accepted.

The second hypothesis, that the authors' attitudes toward older characters would be generally positive, was also rejected. Three separate content analyses were used to make this determination—one for words used to describe the behavior or disposition of the older person, one for words used to describe the appearance of the older person, and one for the pictures which included older persons. To avoid researcher bias, judgments on whether the words and descriptions used by the authors were positive, neutral, or negative, were made by a panel of gerontological professionals. Words and descriptions which were rated by a majority as being positive or negative were used in the analysis. Words on which there was no consensus by the judges or which were rated as neutral were dropped from consideration. The inter-rater reliability was calculated and was found to be significant beyond the .01 level ($\chi^2 = 41.05$, $df = 8$).

Positive words were used more often than negative words to describe the behavior or disposition of an older character. There were a total of 32 words or phrases used which were judged to be positive while only 21 were viewed as negative. Although this indicated a positive tendency on the part of the authors, the chi-square probability ($p < .15$) did not reach the level of statistical significance (.05). Pictures which included older people were clearly positive. Of 16 pictures of older characters, only three were considered to convey a negative image. This difference is statistically significant ($p < .02$) and indicates a positive attitude on the part of illustrators and authors.

The appearance of older characters was also judged to be positive. Seventeen of the descriptions were positive while only 11 were seen as negative. A majority (29) were viewed as neutral with statements such as "sharp, black eyes," "long nose," "thin lipped," and "blue veined hands" falling into this category. There was no statistically significant difference in the descriptions ($p < .25$) but the tendency was positive. The second hypothesis, then, could not be accepted, since two of the three measures (behavior and appearance) did not reach the level of statistical significance. The tendency on all three measures was in the expected direction, however.

The third hypothesis, that older individuals would be portrayed as members of families rather than as members of social groups, was rejected. Sixty of the characters were provided an occupational identity. This number was greater than the 41 who were given a family identification.

The fourth, fifth, and sixth hypotheses predicted that differences would be found among older characters who appeared in books of various time periods. To test these hypotheses, the books were divided into five time intervals. Those books which received the Newbery Medal betwen 1922 and 1931 were included in the first period. Those from 1944 to 1953 were placed in the third; and those from 1966 to 1975 were in the fifth. This provided three groups of books to be examined, each encompassing 10-year periods and separated by 13 years.

The fourth hypothesis stated that attitudes toward older people would become decreasingly positive over the past half century. The hypothesis was not confirmed because the data were inconsistent. Two criteria were used—the appearance of the older characters and the behavior and disposition of the older people. When the descriptive words were examined, it was found that in 1922-1931 seven descriptions were positive and only one was negative. In 1944-1953, seven were positive and five were negative; in 1966-1975 none was positive and one was negative. Although this analysis involves a small amount of data, the comparison clearly indicates a trend toward less positive views of older people in the more recent books.

When the appearance of the older persons was considered, however, the trend was just the opposite. In 1922-1931 zero descriptions were positive and one was negative; in 1944-1953, ten were positive and five were negative; and in 1966-1975, six were positive and one was negative. The hypothesis that attitudes would become decreasingly positive could not be accepted since descriptive words and characters' appearance were inconsistent.

The fifth hypothesis concerned a decrease in the number of references to older people in the more recent books. Seltzer and Atchley found this trend to be generally true but curvilinear in character with the largest number of references being observed in 1870 and 1960. Data from the present review also demonstrated a curvilinear pattern. In 1922-1931 there were 30 older characters; in 1944-1953, 43 older persons, and 1966-1975, 17 older characters. This indicates a clear decline in the number of older characters from the first period to the third, but is confused by the second period which included a higher number than either of the other two. In general, then, the hypothesis cannot be accepted.

The final hypothesis, that the more recent adolescent literature would reveal an increased variability in the descriptions of older people, was also rejected since no significant difference could be determined among the three time frames. In employment, for instance, the first period included such occupations as a sailor, a plantation owner, a peddler, a scholar at a university, and a cook. The second period had an older person as a teacher, a public crier, a gardener, a wise man of the tribe, and a llama herder. The most recent time frame had a literary critic, a sailor, a toy tinker, a sharecropper, and a teacher. In other categories the characters from the three periods seemed consistently diverse. Financial conditions were rather equally distributed and minority individuals were evident in all time frames. There did not appear to be any trend toward the increased variability hypothesized.

Conclusion: Older People in Adolescent Literature

This review of older people in adolescent literature assumed that books written for teenagers reflect the reality of the world as perceived by the authors. The findings of this study have borne this out to a larger degree than previously anticipated. Older characters in these books were not consciously discriminated against; were not portrayed as overwhelmingly senile, crippled, or ill; tended not to be excluded from the stories entirely; and were generally not all grandparents in a three-generation household. Rather, the men were employed and the women were at home; some were rich and some were poor; a few were wise and a few were ignorant; many bore the outward appearance of age; and wrinkles, white hair, and burdens of time were described with sympathy or scorn depending upon character of the individual.

The roles assigned to women by the authors incorporate a traditional bias. Women were portrayed as wives, mothers, and grandmothers rather than being shown in relation to a community or employment role. Men were portrayed just the opposite with most being shown in the vocational area. It is this sort of stereotyping that is more common in the adolescent literature than the explicit negative images that gerontologists often seek to find. So long as the older woman is described only in relation to the family, it will be difficult for young people to break away from the concept of the older woman living in a life-space bounded by neighborhood and kinship roles.

The reasons for this bias as well as that directed toward all older characters is possibly related to the age of the author. In order to determine if the author's age at the time the book was written could be an intervening variable, a comparison was made of this age with the number of older characters in the book. The results did not show any consistent trend. Authors between the ages of 21 and 30 averaged 3.6 older characters per book; those between 31 and 40, 3.0 characters; those 41-50, 5.2 characters; 51-60, 1.6 characters; and 61-70, 2.7 characters.

The explicit stereotyping of the aged which was expected did not materialize. As Seltzer and Atchley (1971) concluded, "It is possible that we will find attitudes and stereotypes toward the old are not so negative as social gerontologists expected them to be." Perhaps we are looking for overt stereotyping and feel a bit nonplussed when our expectations are not confirmed. What may be more important than the direct negative stereotyping, is the indirect picture of the older population that is shown. In an overwhelming number of cases, older people were portrayed as only shadows who moved into and out of the major flow of the story at expeditious times. They were not within the mainstream of the plot; they were the bit players who inhabited the fringes of the stage and who received neither the love nor the hate of the heros or the villains.

Only 5 of the 159 older characters died during the course of the 53 books. Few other older persons were ill, disabled, or senile. Problems which face real older people each day were not recognized nor struggled with in the books. Older adults led a quiet, self-sufficient life, affecting few people and being seldom affected by others. In fact, the older persons seldom really existed in the eyes of others but quietly wandered through the pages, without trouble, gratification, or suffering.

Older people in adolescent literature, then, have a distinct similarity to older people in contemporary America. They are only partial people; they are not developed; they are not necessary to the real action that transpires about them. They are useful only for their relationship with the important people. In short, they are there, but no one seems to notice.

References

Aronoff, C. Old age in prime time. *Journal of Communication*, 1974, *24*, 86-87.

Arth, M. J. Ideals and behavior: A comment on Ibo. *Gerontologist*, 1968, *8*, 242-4.

Bell, B. D., & Stanfield, G. G. Chronological age in relation to attitudinal judgments: An experimental analysis. *Journal of Gerontology*, 1973, *28*, 391-6.

Bengtson, V. L., & Smith, D. H. Social modernity and attitudes toward aging: A cross-cultural survey. *Gerontologist*, 1968, *8*, 26. (abstract)

Brotman, H. *Facts and figures on older Americans: An overview*, AoA, USDHEW, Washington, 1971.

Coatsworth, E. *The cat who went to heaven*. Macmillan, New York, 1931.

Duncan, K. J. Modern society's attitude toward aging. *Geriatrics*, 1963, *18*, 629-35.

Enright, E. *Thimble summer*. Rinehart, New York, 1938.

Evans, K., & Evans, D. Media coverage of aging, 1965-1975: An exploratory study, 1975. (mimeo)

Harlan, W. H. Social status of the aged in three Indian villages. In B. L. Neugarten (Ed.), *Middle aged and aging*. Univ. Chicago Press, Chicago, 1968.

Hunt, I. *Up a road slowly*. Follett, New York, 1966.

Kingman, L. *Newbery and Caldecott Medal Books: 1956-1965*. Horn Book, Boston, 1965.

Macdonald, R. Content analysis of perceptions of aging as represented by the news media. *Gerontologist*, 1973, *13*, 103. (abstract)

Martel, M. U. Age-sex roles in American magazine fiction (1890-1955). In B. Neugarten (Ed.), *Middle age and aging*. Univ. Chicago Press, Chicago, 1968.

McTavish, D. G. Perceptions of old people: A review of research methodologies and findings. *Gerontologist*, 1971, *11*, 90-101.

Northcott, H. Too young, too old—Age in the world of television. *Gerontologist*, 1975, *15*, 184-6.

Petersen, M. The visibility and image of old people on television. *Journalism Quarterly*, 1973, *50*, 569-73.

Rosencranz, H. A., & McNevin, T. E. Factor analysis of attitudes toward the aged. *Gerontologist*, 1969, *9*, 55-59.

Sawyer, R. *Roller skates*. Viking Press, New York, 1936.

Seltzer, M. M., & Atchley, R. C. The concept of old: Changing attitudes and stereotypes. *Gerontologist*, 1971, *11*, 226-230.

1.5

Attitudes Toward Aging: Increasing Optimism Found with Age

Marilyn A. Borges and Linda J. Dutton

In our apparently youth-oriented society, with negative stereotypes regarding old age (Bringmann & Rieder, 1968; Golde & Kogan, 1959; Kogan & Shelton, 1962a, b), it is plausible that the older one gets, the more dissatisfied one is. But is this the case? The present study was undertaken to investigate the prevalence of negative attitudes toward old age among various age groups, and whether such attitudes are consistent with the way in which older people evaluate their own lives.

Prior Findings Inconclusive

Mason (1954) found that older subjects did not enjoy living as much as they did when younger, and Gurin, Veroff, and Feld (1960) found that self-report responses of "very happy" decreased while "not too happy" increased with age. Bradburn and Caplovitz (1965) also found a negative correlation between happiness and age, but these results were confounded with a corresponding negative correlation between age and income and age and education. Bortner and Hultsch (1972)

Copyright 1976 by The Gerontological Society. Reprinted by permission. *The Gerontologist*, Vol. 16, No. 3, 1976, pp. 220-224.

showed that optimism decreased with age—that is, as the respondent's age increased, the past looked increasingly better, the future increasingly worse, when compared to the respondent's present. Nearly two-thirds of Lieberman's (1970) young adult subjects agreed that their "best years" were "now," whereas only one-fifth of his elderly subjects felt that their best years were "now."

On the other hand, Morgan (1937) reported that subjects 65 and over responded that the "happiest time" of their lives was the middle-adult years, and Landis (1942) and Lehr (cited in Buhler & Massarik, 1968) found similar evidence that life satisfaction does not plummet after youth gives way to adulthood. Gardner's (1949) elderly subjects reported being "just as happy now" as when they were middle-aged; Chiriboga and Lowenthal (1971) failed to find the expected proportional increase in "deficits" (Bradburn, 1969) with age; Cameron (1967) reported no difference in happiness between his aged and young subjects; and Bortner and Hultsch, in spite of the findings mentioned above, reported that the ratings of the *present* showed little difference as a function of age. Meltzer (1963) even suggested that happiness increases with age, as did Cumming and Henry (1961), provided that disengagement occurs. (Other studies have indicated that social involvement, rather than disengagement, is a source of happiness in old age, but these studies did not focus on *changes* in happiness over the years.)

Taken together, these studies fail to prove a reliable connection, either positive or negative, between aging and happiness, which suggests that some other variables—correlates of age, perhaps, such as health, income, activity level, or even self-knowledge—are responsible for happiness, and not age (or youth) *per se* (Kaplan, 1971; Neugarten, 1964).

Present Study Compares Attitudes

Perhaps what should be dealt with are the cultural *projections* regarding the aging process. If, as seems plausible, happiness in old age is dependent upon the kinds of factors and adjustments that happiness at any age is dependent upon, then the cultural projections are dysfunctional. Is there a discrepancy between what people think "getting old" will be like and what it "really" is like? The results of this study suggest that there is.

Undergraduates enrolled in a developmental psychology class at a state university selected the subjects (N = 532). Each student presented a questionnaire to the person he knew best in each of seven age groups: 6-12, 13-18, 19-24, 25-36, 37-48, 49-65, and 65+. This covers

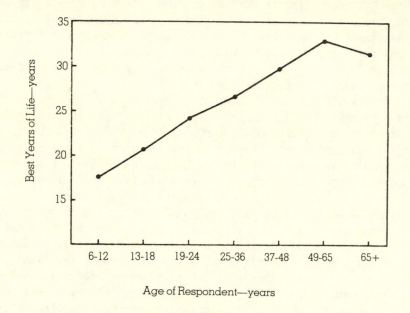

Figure 1. Mean ratings of "best year" of a person's life as a function of respondent's age (N = 76 at each age interval)

a more complete age range than the groupings established in any other known investigation of this type, due to the inclusion of very young subjects. Each grouping is sufficiently narrow to eliminate much of the ambiguity found in studies using only two or three ("generational") groups, and the groupings have a fair correspondence with the empirically established groupings of Cameron (1969) and Gould (1972).

Respondents were asked to use a seven-point scale, ranging from "Very Good" to "Very Bad," in evaluating their own lives (assessing their past, present, and futures) at each of eight age intervals (the original seven age intervals plus the age interval from 0-5). Respondents also evaluated the "average person's life" at each of the age intervals and the "best year" of their lives (either to date or projected). This combination of parameters (age of respondent, age of referent

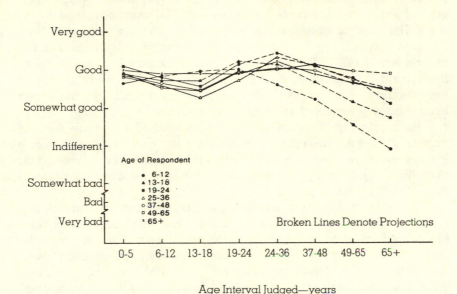

Age Interval Judged—years

Figure 2. Mean ratings of respondent's own life as a function of respondent's age (N = 76 at each age interval; broken lines denote projections)

group, and context of discrimination) is in keeping with Bengtson's (1971) suggestions for research in inter-age perception. Results were as follows.

Increasing Optimism

Fig. 1 shows that the "best year" selected increased with the respondent's age until age 65, at which point there was a slight decline from "34" (cited by the 49- to 65-year-olds) to "32" (cited by the 65+ group). Subjects younger than 24 chose best years which were above their own age, while most subjects over 25 chose best years below their own age, but above the "24" year point.

A three-way analysis of variance (age of respondent × age interval judged × own life vs. average person's life) was performed on the data. The most notable findings were in the "own life" ratings at various age levels (Fig. 2). These vary significantly with the age of the respondent, $F (42, 3675) = 6.95$, $p < .01$ (see contrast in Fig. 2 between heavy and broken lines). Younger subjects projected that their future lives would not be as good as older subjects actually reported their lives to be or projected their future lives would be.

Ratings of the average person's life followed the same general pattern. When the two rating curves ("own life" and "average person's life") were compared, it was noted that the respondents rated their own lives significantly higher than they rated the average person's life, $F (1, 525) = 43.73$, $p < .01$.

When "own life" and "average person's life" ratings were plotted for the subjects' own age levels—that is, "own life" projections were eliminated and the age interval judged was the same as the age of the respondent—"own life" was again rated higher in general than "average person's life." Moreover, respondents actually at each age interval above the peak-rated interval of 25 to 36 consistently rated their lives higher than any other younger subjects projected life would be like at that age. The only exception was the 49- to 65-year-old group, who optimistically projected a higher rating for their own 65+ age interval than members of that age group actually rated their lives.

In all measures, the responses grew increasingly differentiated as a function of both the age level being evaluated and the respondents' age. The implication from these data is that, as a person grows older, he perceives the years ahead more optimistically.

Adults Adapt to New Age Status

Why do younger people think that "getting old" is worse than it apparently is? Cameron (1972) theorized that members of any permanently socially disadvantaged group will tend to rate themselves within the limits of what they can reasonably expect to achieve in their lives in our society. Since the aged have a social status equivalent to that of ethnic minorities and suffer similar prejudices (Kogan & Shelton, 1962a), and since Cameron and others have found that older persons report being as happy as any other generalized group, such adaptation to limits may indeed occur.

Bengtson and Lovejoy (1973), in establishing a "social age status" scale, explained that involvement in various social behaviors add up to give one a social age, and "older" people are more accepting of society and the limits it imposes on individual lives. This somewhat circular argument may point to an essential element of aging in our society, namely that individuals accommodate their values and behaviors to fit the values and expectations of society.

Lieberman (1970), instead of postulating continual adjustment to increasingly fewer meaningful components for decision-making (Loeb, 1973), hypothesized that early in life a "set" is established, an orientation toward satisfaction that stabilizes and is maintained throughout life within a very broad range of circumstances. Goldstein (1966) suggested that values of the young and old remain roughly continuous, but finances frequently prevent older persons from keeping up a youthful style of life. Money or health has frequently been cited as the biggest problem of old age (Birren, Butler, Greenhouse, Sokoloff, & Yarrow, 1963; Bradburn, 1969; Gurin et al., 1960).

Perhaps younger people underrate later maturity because culturally we expect "adults" to emerge full-blown from "youth" and remain static from then on. Such an unnatural concept allows for only one kind of change: deterioration. It is far more likely that adults continue to grow and develop (Gould, 1972), and that, as they do, the various factors which are associated with self-satisfaction or self-derogation combine in different ways (Kaplan, 1971). Thus, what is perceived by a 25-year-old as essential to happiness is not so perceived by a 50-year-old, but the younger person, knowing only that this "essential" ingredient is likely or certain to be missing at age 50, perceives age 50 as a definite comedown from glorious 25.

Youth Unaware of Happiness Potential

Our mobile society has made familiarity with old persons unavailable to many younger people. Gordon (1970) found that older role models do influence the attitudes of younger people toward those who are 65 and over as well as toward their own eventual 65-and-over period. Furthermore, younger respondents who had lived in the same household with someone 65 or older held a more positive view of old people. Bengtson (1971) found a large "cohort gap" between generations in the broader society but a much smaller "lineage gap" between generations within the family. Closer contact between the generations might reduce the discrepancy between the life age judgments of younger and older subjects.

Some of the findings reported here should be interpreted in light of certain phenomena observed by Goldings (1954), who substantiated his hypothesis that, on direct inquiry, happiness tends to be avowed and unhappiness disavowed and that most people will rate their own happiness as greater than average. He also found that people who rate themselves as moderately happy (or unhappy) will tend to project their sentiments onto others like themselves. In the present study, no mean ratings fell below the midpoint on the scale, and most clustered around "Good" for all age intervals judged, regardless of the respondent's age. Thus, although significant differences were found, these differences reflected consistent directional trends in the ratings rather than changes of a large magnitude.

It should also be noted that the subjects were asked, "Which of the following judgments best describes your own life / an average person's life . . . ?" and not "How happy are you?" or "How are things these days?" No controlled study has yet been done to evaluate the possible response differences these variously worded questions might elicit.

Above all, this study should not be taken as an argument in favor of the status quo of aging persons in this country, and Kogan and Shelton's (1962) conclusion that the aged have a status equivalent to that of ethnic minorities should be borne in mind. The point of the inquiry was to reveal the lack of awareness, on the part of younger people, of the satisfaction potential in middle-age and later maturity. Further research into the processes behind the attitudes found in the present study may increase understanding of how identity and self-acceptance change with growth.

The implications of this study extend into many social and political areas. This society is apparently operating under a set of beliefs that are not in line with reality. The grim specter of a lonely dejected unproductive old age haunts Americans and is reinforced by the youth bias of the mass media. Such attitudes are difficult to change. Certainly, education is a first step—formally in the schools, and informally in the community and in the home.

But belief in the possibility of continuous development will be difficult to foster in a society which imposes age segregation upon the young and the old. Of course, social fragmentation is currently a major device to coerce the majority to attend to the problems of all sorts of minorities. But the results thus obtained are at the risk of increasing the isolation and alienation of those minorities from the mainstream. The young have already embraced their imposed isolation, by policy and by custom, from adult society. The elderly may soon do likewise as they organize to demand fair treatment in social security, medical care, retirement laws and benefits, housing, recreational facilities, and nursing home care.

Integration, not segregation, should be the goal, first recognizing that development proceeds through all stages of life. Happy productive adulthood is not a state of existence on limited hold; rather it is a dynamic process in which problems are attacked and pleasures sought, with personal equipment whose powers and limitations, though changing with age, do not necessarily favor one age as opposed to another. Lust for life is available to all ages.

References

Bengtson, V. L. Inter-age perceptions and the generation gap. *Gerontologist*, 1971, *11*, (4:2), 85-89.

Bengtson, V. L., & Lovejoy, M. C. Values, personality, and social structure: An intergenerational analysis. *American Behavioral Scientist*, 1973, *16*, 880-912.

Birren, J. E., Butler, R. N., Greenhouse, S. W., Sokoloff, L., & Yarrow, M. R. (Eds.) Human aging: A biological and behavioral study. USPHS Pub. No. 986. NIMH, Bethesda, 1963.

Bortner, R. W., & Hultsch, D. F. Personal time perspective in adulthood. *Developmental Psychology*, 1972, 7, 98-103.

Bradburn, N. M. *The structure of psychological well-being*. Aldine, Chicago, 1969.

Bradburn, N., & Caplovitz, D. *Reports on happiness*. Aldine, Chicago, 1965.

Bringmann, W., & Rieder, G. Stereotyped attitudes toward the aged in West Germany and the United States. *Journal of Social Psychology*, 1968, 76, 267-268.

Buhler, C., & Massarik, F. (Eds.) *The course of human life*. Springer, New York, 1968.

Cameron, P. Ego strength and happiness of the aged. *Journal of Gerontology*, 1967,22, 199-202.

Cameron, P. Age parameters of young adults, middle aged, and aged. *Journal of Gerontology*, 1969, *24*, 201-202.

Cameron, P. Stereotypes about generational fun and happiness vs. self-appraised fun and happiness. *Gerontologist*, 1972, *12*, (2:1), 120-123.

Chiriboga, D., & Lowenthal, M. F. Psychological correlates of perceived well-being. *Proceedings of the 79th Annual Convention of American Psychological Assn.*, 1971, *6* (pt. 2), 603-604.

Cumming, E., & Henry, W. E. *Growing old: The process of disengagement*. Basic Books, New York, 1961.

Gardner, L. P. Attitudes and activities of the middle aged and aged. *Geriatrics*, 1949, *4*, 33-50.

Golde, P., & Kogan, N. A sentence completion procedure for assessing attitudes toward old people. *Journal of Gerontology*, 1959,*14*, 355-363.

Goldings, H. J. On the avowal and projection of happiness. *Journal of Personality*, 1954, *23*, 30-47.

Goldstein, S. The effect of income level on the consumer behavior of the aged. *Proceedings of the 7th International Congress of Gerontology*, vol. 7. Viennese Academy of Medicine, Vienna, 1966.

Gordon, E. W. Role models for later maturity (Doctoral dissertation, American Univ., 1969). *Dissertation Abstracts International*, 1970, *30*, 4017A. (University Microfilms No. 70-3168).

Gould, R. L. Phases of adult life. *American Journal of Psychiatry*, 1972, *129*, 521-531.

Gurin, G., Veroff, J., & Feld, S. *Americans view their mental health*. Basic Books, New York, 1960.

Kaplan, H. B. Age-related correlates of self-derogation: Contemporary life space characteristics. *Aging & Human Development*, 1971, *2*, 305-313.

Kogan, N., & Shelton, F. Beliefs about "old people": A comparative study of older and younger samples. *Journal of Genetic Psychology*, 1967, *100*, 93-111. (a)

Kogan, N., & Shelton, F. Images of "old people" and "people in general" in an older sample. *Journal of Genetic Psychology*, 1962, *100*, 3-21. (b)

Landis, J. T. What is the happiest period in life? *School & Society*, 1942, *55*, 643-645.

Lieberman, L. R. Life satisfaction in the young and the old. *Psychological Reports*, 1970, *27*, 75-79.

Loeb, R. Disengagement activity, or maturity? *Sociology & Social Research*, 1973, *57*, 367-382.

Mason, E. P. Some factors in self-judgments. *Journal of Clinical Psychology*, 1954, *10*, 336-340.

Meltzer, H. Age differences in happiness and life adjustments of workers. *Journal of Gerontology*, 1963, *18*, 66-70.

Morgan, C. M. The attitudes and adjustments of recipients of old age assistance in upstate and metropolitan New York. *Archives of Psychology*, 1937, *214*, 131-138.

Neugarten, B. L. *Personality in middle and late life*. Atherton Press, New York, 1964.

Tissue, T. Old age and the perception of poverty. *Sociology & Social Research*, 1972, *56*, 331-344.

1.6

The Impact of Subjective Age and Stigma on Older Persons

Russell A. Ward

Social gerontologists have paid considerable attention to the determinants of "subjective age"—whether older persons view themselves as "middle-aged," "elderly," etc. Comparatively less attention has been paid to whether such labels are of consequence to the aging individual. Such issues have been of interest, however, to sociologists in the field of "deviant behavior."

The recent labeling theory of deviant behavior has somewhat shifted the emphasis of study from the causes of norm-violating behavior to processes by which certain behaviors are defined as "problems" or "deviant" (Becker, 1963; Schur, 1971). The field has also been broadened to include deviant individual *attributes*, or "stigma," as well as deviant *behavior* (Goffman, 1963).

The labeling perspective has also been accompanied by increased commitment to an "appreciative" view of deviant phenomena—a consideration of the deviant's viewpoint and an understanding of the world in which he lives (Matza, 1969). Partly this involves concern for the effect of stigmatization on deviants themselves, in terms of their reactions to labels and stereotyped views of others.

Copyright 1977 by The Gerontological Society. Reprinted by permission. *Journal of Gerontology*, Vol. 32, No. 2, 1977, pp. 227-232.

This paper will assess the usefulness of including old age within such a framework, particularly the applicability of the labeling perspective to understanding the impact of aging. It will also hopefully add to the continuing debate over the theoretical and substantive usefulness of labeling theory (e.g., Scheff, 1974).

Old age as stigma

Following Goffman (1963), old age can be viewed as a combination of abominations of the body (loss of physical attractiveness, crippling chronic diseases, etc.) and blemishes of individual character (dependency, diminishing intelligence, etc.). Negative attitudes toward the aged have been attributed to the presumed problems of older people (Bennett & Eckman, 1973), their inability to fulfill the "achievement syndrome" of modern societies (Clark, 1967; Cowgill & Holmes, 1972), and their isolation from younger generations because of age stratification (Riley, Johnson, & Foner, 1972).

Research in numerous contexts, utilizing a variety of methods, indicates that largely negative stereotypes are attached to old age and that older persons themselves may subscribe to these negative stereotypes to an even greater degree than younger persons (McTavish, 1971). Such stereotypes will shape the expectations and reactions of others, and often the perceptions of the individual himself.

Identity and old age

Given indications that old age is a stigmatized status, what will be the reaction of older persons themselves? Though not always important to an actor, the self becomes a significant issue during so-called "identity crises" when the bases of self are changing or questioned. As with adolescence, aging is characterized by personal change and status ambiguity, and "an intensification of the intimate and self-reflexive" (Clark & Anderson, 1967). Changes in roles (e.g., retirement and widowhood), health, and activities remove bases of identity and constrain personal continuity, initiating "turning points" in identity transformation (Strauss, 1962).

Stigmata may become a "pivotal category" (Lofland, 1969), which is seen as the "essential" nature of that individual by those with whom he interacts, affecting the nature of that interaction and their willingness to validate certain identities. Thus, a person may be viewed as "really" an "old person," rather than as a person who, along with other identities, is "old."

The changes in the symbolic environment which accompany entrance into a pivotal category, as others adjust their reactions and expectations, make the aging person more aware of changes in his own characteristics and in the interaction of others with him. The consequent fluidity of identity makes possible the effects of a label such as "old person." The *personal* impact of labeling, however, requires awareness of the label and the stigma attached to it, perception that the label is potentially applicable to oneself, and self-labeling as that kind of person.

The implications of aging awareness

Individuals may deny the personal appropriateness of a label, either by reforming or denying possession of the characteristic. Stigmatized attributes, such as obesity, physical disability, and old age, cannot easily be denied once the label is applied, so denial typically occurs before the fact. Substantial proportions of those over 65 consider themselves "young" or "middle-aged," rejecting the labels "old" and "elderly" (Riley & Foner, 1968). Felt need to avoid such labels should depend on personal acceptance of stigma attached to them. Thus, it was hypothesized that older persons who subscribe to negative stereotypes about aging should be more likely to avoid attaching the label "old person" to themselves.

Individuals may also accept the label for a variety of reasons, including recognition of reality. The psychological impact of that label depends upon its meanings for the individual. Those who accept both the applicability of the label and stigma attached to it are vulnerable to feelings of personal unworthiness and insecurity. On the other hand, the deviant may accept the label, but substitute positive meanings for the negative ones held by society.

Labeling by others may have consequences because of alterations in interaction. The impact of labeling on self and identity, however, must be sought at the personal level, as an outcome of self-labeling processes. Meanings for the label may come from the society (as the "generalized other") or from the counter-attitudes of a subculture, but their effect arises from internalization by the deviant. Thus, the *personal* impact of labeling depends upon the personally-held meanings for the label, whatever their original source. It was, therefore, hypothesized that the impact of age identification, as a potentially stigmatizing label, on self-esteem would depend on the personal meanings attached to age identification labels.

Method

Sample

Interviews were conducted with 323 noninstitutionalized residents of Madison, Wisconsin, who were at least 60 years of age. The sample was purposive, using systematic sampling from group membership lists (Senior Citizen Clubs, American Association of Retired Persons), clients of social service agencies (e.g., telephone reassurance programs), and recipients of Old Age Assistance. This resulted in 497 names, of which 28 were younger than 60 or deceased. Interviews were completed for 80.1% of all persons both eligible and actually contacted during the study.

Given the nature of this sample, it was not expected to be truly representative of the aging in Madison. Although the intent was to investigate theoretical issues rather than to delineate population parameters, an attempt was made to insure inclusion of a wide spectrum of aged subgroups. This goal was attained. Compared with the aged population in the USA and in Madison (Riley & Foner, 1968; U.S. Bureau of the Census, 1973 a&b), the sample was representative with regard to sex distribution (56% female) and marital status (43% currently married). However, respondents in the sample were more highly educated (35% with some college), had higher income (only 10% below $2,000), were in better health (25% had no chronic illness conditions), and were more likely to be retired (90% were fully retired) than the aged population. In all such areas, however, the sample included all portions of the target population. Respondents ranged in age from 60 to 92, with a mean age of 74.1.

Variables

Age identification.   Respondents were asked if they thought of themselves as "young, middle-aged, elderly, or old," a commonly studied series of labels (Riley & Foner, 1968). In tabular presentations, responses will be collapsed into the two most frequently selected choices: "middle-aged" (44.8%) and "elderly" (55.2%).

Attitudes toward old people.   Respondents were asked to indicate extent of agreement with 19 statements, such as "old people are cranky," "old people grow wiser with age," and "old people cannot manage their own affairs," most of which were adapted from Tuckman and Lorge (1953). Using categories from "strongly agree" to "strongly disagree," the possible range was 19-76 (a high score indicating more negative attitudes), with a mean of 44.0 and standard deviation of 5.71. Inter-item reliability was .80 (Cronbach's alpha).

Self-esteem. The study used a global measure of self-esteem (Rosenberg, 1965). Again using four response categories, the possible range was 10-40 (a high score indicating more positive self-esteem), with a mean of 29.4 and standard deviation of 3.07. Inter-item reliability was .74 (Cronbach's alpha).

Age-related deprivation. This variable constitutes a measure of over-all change, both perceived and experienced, since age 55, combining eight possible changes since age 55: retirement, widowhood, worsened financial status, worsened health, decreased ability to do housework, decreased inter-personal activity, residential move, and lessened ability to continue favored activities. The possible range was 3-24 (increasing score representing greater deprivation), with a mean of 14.3 and standard deviation of 4.48. Age-related deprivation was strongly related to the respondent's open-ended comparison of his life now with his life at age 55.

Activity. This is a composite score based on 12 activities and hobbies which respondents might engage in (e.g., housework, yardwork, watching TV, crafts, writing, sports, etc.). Scoring 1 for a "yes" on each activity yielded a possible range of 0-12, with a mean of 6.73 and standard deviation of 1.79. This is a relatively weak measure of activity, particularly since it focuses upon more solitary pursuits, but it does provide some rough indication of the ability of the respondent to engage in a variety of activities.

Health. An overall health assessment was made by the author based on the presence of chronic illness conditions and limitations imposed by those conditions, as indicated by responses to specific interview questions. The distribution of categories was: (1) no chronic illness conditions and no activity limitation due to health (24.8%), (2) chronic illness conditions but no activity limitation (27.6%), (3) minor activity limitation due to health (22.3%), (4) major activity limitation due to health (18.6%), and (5) bedridden due to health (6.8%). Independent coding by another rater yielded 94% agreement with health ratings made by the author.

Findings

Correlates of age identification

A number of studies have examined shifts in age identification, indicating the importance of role change (e.g., widowhood, retirement), failing health, institutionalization, and other factors (see Riley & Foner, 1968). While not a major consideration of this paper, the current study found shifts in age identification to be related primarily to age-related deprivation, age, health, activity, and employment status. Females had a younger age identity than males. While this sex difference was not large, it was statistically significant and persisted despite controls on such variables as health and age-related deprivation. Streib and Schneider (1971) found a similar sex difference, perhaps reflecting a double standard whereby aging is viewed more negatively for women than for men (Sontag, 1975).

It was expected that willingness to assume the status "elderly" would also depend on meanings held for that status—those holding more negative attitudes toward old people would more often identify themselves as middle-aged. This hypothesis was not confirmed. Actually, the opposite was true: those who identified themselves as elderly or old had more negative attitudes toward old people. This was apparently spurious, since the relationship disappeared when health, age, and age-related deprivation were controlled. Thus, there was no relationship between age identification and attitudes toward old people.

The impact of age identification

Age identification had a correlation of −.28 with self-esteem, indicating that those who identified themselves as elderly or old had significantly lower self-esteem. This relationship disappeared, however, when variables which caused age identification (notably health, age-related deprivation, and age) were controlled. Thus, the age identification label itself appears to make no unique contribution to self-esteem.

It was expected that personally held meanings for being old would affect self-esteem only if there was self-labeling as "elderly." Table 1, however, indicates that attitudes toward old people were related to self-esteem regardless of age identification. Those with negative attitudes toward old people also had lower self-esteem.

Since respondents experiencing more negative change with age

Table 1. Self-Esteem by Attitudes Toward Old People, by Age Identification

Self-esteem	Middle-aged[a] Attitudes Toward Old People (%)			Elderly[b] Attitudes Toward Old People (%)		
	Positive (0–42)	Neutral (43–46)	Negative (47+)	Positive (0–42)	Neutral (43–46)	Negative (47+)
High (30+)	70.8	52.5	34.2	62.3	30.5	26.6
Low (0–29)	29.2	47.5	65.8	37.7	69.5	73.4
	$N = 65$	$N = 40$	$N = 38$	$N = 53$	$N = 59$	$N\ 64$

[a] $\chi^2 = 13.27$ (2 d.f.), $p = .002$.
[b] $\chi^2 = 18.06$ (2 d.f.), $p = .0001$.

also expressed more negative attitudes toward old people, Table 1 might be indicative of a more general "negativism." Multiple regression (Table 2), however, indicates retention of a strong relationship between personal attitudes toward old people and self-esteem when personal change and current situation variables are controlled. Looking at the standardized regression coefficients for the entire sample in Table 2, attitudes toward old people are in fact the best predictors of self-esteem when all of the variables are considered simultaneously. This result was consistent for both males and females, again indicating a strong relationship between self-derogation and negative attitudes toward old people.

While the basic findings relevant to this paper show no sex differences, there are some intriguing differences in determinants of self-esteem for males and females, as indicated by a comparison of the standardized regression coefficients for both groups. Education and income were considerably more important in determining male self-esteem, while age-related deprivation and current activity were more important for female self-esteem. Thus, males are affected by socio-economic status (and, in a sense, by their *past* status), while females are affected by current activities and the extent to which aging has been accompanied by loss. A longitudinal study by Maas and Kuypers (1974) found something similar—that males are affected more by early situations in their lives, while females are more subject to the effects of current circumstances.

Meanings attached to growing old appear to qualify the impact of *age* on self-esteem, rather than the impact of age identification. Although increased age was significantly related to self-derogation (zero-order correlation with self-esteem was −.14), this relationship was not significant when attitudes toward old people were controlled.

Respondents were also asked if they felt "older people are looked down on by others." This taps more directly the respondent's perception of societal reaction, and this perception about others was related to personal attitudes toward old people (χ^2 = 12.87, p = .002). Feeling that older people are looked down on by others interacted with age identification to apparently affect self-esteem—identification as elderly was significantly related to lower self-esteem only for those indicating that older people are looked down on (Table 3). Thus, the label in this case made a difference, whereas it did not with personal attitudes toward old people.

Implications and Conclusions

The implications of these findings may be drawn out in terms of both the experience of aging and the applicability of the labeling perspec-

Table 2.   Multiple Regression Analysis of Self-Esteem

Dependent variable = Self-esteem

Independent variables	Entire sample (294)		Females (166)		Males (128)	
	O-order[a]	Beta[b]	O-order[a]	Beta[b]	O-order[a]	Beta[b]
Negative attitudes toward old people	−.41	−.31	−.40	−.27	−.43	−.36*
Age-related deprivation	−.38	−.15	−.47	−.25	−,24	.07
Activity	.31	.11	.39	.17	.19	−.02*
Health	.37	.16	.43	.16	,27	.19
Age	−.13	−.01*	−.13	.04*	−.13	−.03*
Education	.20	.06*	.10	−.04*	.34	.16
Income	.26	.04*	.21	.02*	.38	.21
		R^2 = .30		R^2 = .35		R^2 = .32

[a]Zero-order correlation coefficient.
[b]Standardized regression coefficient.
*Not significant at p = .05.

Table 3. Self-Esteem by Age Identification by Perception That Others Look Down on Older People

| | Older People Looked Down On (%) | | | |
| | No[a] | | Yes[b] | |
Self-esteem	Middle-aged	Elderly	Middle-aged	Elderly
High (30+)	55.9	42.7	57.1	32.9
Low (0-29)	44.1	57.3	42.9	67.1
	N = 93	N = 103	N = 49	N = 73

[a]χ^2 not significant at $p = .05$.
[b]$\chi^2 = 6.10$ (1 d.f.), $p. = .02$.

tive to aging. Old age may be viewed as a stigmatized attribute—one to which negative meanings may be attached by people in general and by specific persons who "enter" the status. Labeling theory concentrates on (1) the emergence and attachment of labels and (2) the impact of those labels on the labeled individual. Inherent is the argument that the *labels* we attach to others and to ourselves make a difference beyond the consequences of being in a certain category of people. Thus, being labeled an "old person" creates problems which are additional to those inherent in the status and which would not be present if the label was not attached to the person or group of persons.

Within this context, it was felt that "elderly" would be a meaningful and consequential label for older people and that, given the presence of negative meanings for the label, would be resisted and have a self-derogating effect if successfully attached. The labels used here do make sense for older people—respondents were able to give specific reasons for labeling themselves as "middle-aged" or "elderly"—and have been studied extensively by social gerontologists. These labels did not have the expected psychological impact, however.

First, acceptance of the label was not related to attitudes toward old people. It is likely that persons come to identify themselves as middle-aged and continue to do so through continuity and habit. Change in that continuity, due to retirement, health problems, etc., leads to age identification shifts regardless of attitudes toward growing old. Thus, resistance lies in perceived personal consistency, rather than in the perceived traits of old people.

The label could still be important in the sense of fulfilling a "gatekeeping" function—those who reject or avoid the *label* do not feel the force of the stigma. This brings labeling down to the personal level of self-labeling and the meanings held by the individual regarding possibly stigmatizing identities. Again, the age identification label studied here was not important in this regard—it did not affect the relationship between negative stereotypes and self-derogation. These findings indicate that the particular form of age labeling studied here, and widely used in other studies, may have little impact on the well-being of older people. "Age identification" may, of course, represent more than one attitudinal dimension. It may refer to feelings about oneself, as was the intention here, or it may refer to feelings of identification with age peers. The extent to which these dimensions intermix will obscure the effects of either one. Thus, the labels we study must be conceptually clear.

One interpretation of the results reported here is that labels make no difference in the realm of aging and that labeling theory is at least a partially inappropriate framework for this area. It has been suggested that the self-concept of older people may become less dependent on external factors (Atchley, 1972). Others, however, suggest that older people may be *more* susceptible to social labeling due to social reorganization (Bengtson, 1973). Perhaps the appropriate labels are more subtle, and implicit, rather than explicit. Recognition of a certain chronological age may itself be a label, so that, for example, all persons over 60 view themselves as "eligible" for stigma. Thus, researchers must remain sensitive to the subtleties of labeling at the individual level and the possibility that apparently meaningful labels may be ignored by the individual. People are often aware of their own characteristics, even if only implicitly, without the necessity of "prodding" by formal or informal labeling.

This study did, however, find a strong and consistent relationship between acceptance of negative attitudes toward old people and self-derogation. Linking such personal attitudes to societal stigmatization (an assumption partly confirmed here, but requiring more specific investigation), these results indicate that stigmatization does have an important impact on the well-being of older people. Thus, general labeling of this group as stigmatized appears to have an effect, and further discussion of old age within the context of stigma appears fruitful. It must be recognized that the results could have occurred because self-esteem affects attitudes toward aging and old people, rather than *vice versa*. Until the direction of the relationship can be adequately tested with longitudinal data, the interpretation of the impact of stigma must remain tentative.

There was some indication that personal meanings were related to the perceived attitudes of others. While personal attitudes toward old people were directly related to self-esteem, belief about others' attitudes was related more indirectly through interaction with age identification. Thus, personal and perceived societal attitudes were related to self-esteem, but personal attitudes were related more strongly and in more direct fashion.

The results of this study seem indicative that a "stigma" approach would be fruitful in studying personal reactions to aging, but that the labels which are generally studied may have little importance. Application of labeling theory requires sensitivity to the meaningfulness and interpretations of specific labels for the individuals involved. The impact of being labeled must be sought at the personal level and viewed in terms of personal experience and meanings.

References

Atchley, R. *The social forces in later life*. Wadsworth, Belmont, CA, 1972.

Becker, H. *Outsiders: Studies in the sociology of deviance*. Free Press, New York, 1963.

Bengtson, V. *The social psychology of aging*. Bobbs-Merrill, Indianapolis, 1973.

Bennett, R., & Eckman, J. Attitudes toward aging: A critical examination of recent literature and implications for future research. In C. Eisdorfer & M. P. Lawton (Eds.), *The psychology of adult development and aging*. American Psychological Assn., Washington, 1973.

Clark, M. The anthropology of aging: A new area for studies of culture and personality. *Gerontologist*, 1967, 7, 55-63.

Clark, M., & Anderson, B. *Culture and aging: An anthropological study of older Americans*. Charles C Thomas, Springfield, IL, 1967.

Cowgill, D., & Holmes, L. C. *Aging and modernization*. Appleton-Century-Crofts, New York, 1972.

Goffman, E. *Stigma: Notes on the management of spoiled identity*. Prentice-Hall, Englewood Cliffs, NJ, 1963.

Lofland, J. *Deviance and identity*. Prentice-Hall, Englewood Cliffs, NJ, 1969.

Maas, H., & Kuypers, J. *From 30 to 70*. Jossey-Bass, San Francisco, 1974.

Matza, D. *Becoming deviant*. Prentice-Hall, Englewood Cliffs, NJ, 1969.

McTavish, D. Perceptions of old people: A review of research methodologies and findings. *Gerontologist*, 1971, *11*, 90-101.

Riley, M., & Foner, A. (Eds.) *Aging and Society. Vol. I: An inventory of research findings*. Russell Sage Foundation, New York, 1968.

Riley, M., Johnson, M., & Foner, A. (Eds.) *Aging and society, Vol. III: A sociology of age stratification.* Russell Sage Foundation, New York, 1972.

Rosenberg, M. *Society and the adolescent self-image.* Princeton Univ. Press, Princeton, NJ, 1965.

Scheff, T. The labelling theory of mental illness. *American Sociological Review,* 1974, *39,* 444-452.

Schur, E. *Labeling deviant behavior: Its sociological implications.* Harper & Row, New York, 1971.

Sontag, S. The double standard of aging. In *No longer young: The older woman in America.* Occasional papers in Gerontology No. 11, Inst. of Gerontology, Univ. Michigan-Wayne State Univ., Ann Arbor, 1975.

Strauss, A. Transformations of identity. In A. Rose (Ed.), *Human behavior and social processes.* Houghton Mifflin, Boston, 1962.

Streib, G., & Schneider, C. *Retirement in American society.* Cornell Univ. Press, Ithaca, 1971.

Tuckman, J., & Lorge, I. Attitudes toward old people. *Journal of Social Psychology,* 1953, *37,* 249-260.

U.S. Bureau of the Census. Some demographic aspects of aging in the United States. *Current population reports,* Series P-23 No. 43. USGPO, Washington, 1973. (a)

U.S. Bureau of the Census. *Census of population: 1970. Detailed characteristics.* Final Report PC(1)-D51 Wisconsin. USGPO, Washington, 1973. (b)

1.7

The Revolution of Age

Donald O. Cowgill

With the celebration of our Bicentennial last year, Americans acknowledged that we are becoming one of the older nations of the world; but there was no celebration and little acknowledgement of the fact that we are also becoming older in a second sense—as a population. While it included many pleasant and prideful ceremonies, the marking of our national birthday brought no basic changes in our way of life, but the demographic revolution we are experiencing is producing some very fundamental changes in family life and how people relate to each other.

No one knows how many old people were in this country at the time of its founding. The first census, which did not take place until 1790, did not bother to determine the age of the people; and we were already approaching our centennial before we were even able to count the number of people sixty-five and over. In 1870, we had only a little more than a million persons of that age, less than 3 percent of a total of almost forty million. No doubt we had already aged a bit by this time, but by any standard we were still a young population. At that time, England, Holland, and Sweden had about 5 percent, and France had already passed 7 percent. A hundred years later we have an elderly population of more than twenty-two million, and they constitute more than 10 percent of the total. Thus, in a century, we have changed from a "young" population to an "old" one. We made the change so quickly that we are still not fully aware of it, and we certainly have not

Reprinted, with permission, from *The Humanist*, September/October, 1977.

fully adjusted to it. Indeed, our values are still very "youth-oriented"; so much so that the very act of pointing out that we are aging seems to have an ominous ring.

Actually it is an achievement worthy of celebration; surely the doubling of the average length of life is one of the greatest achievements of our two-hundred-year history. Americans have always believed in progress; what better measure of progress than the prolongation of life; what better basis for pride than that, whereas the children of our founding fathers only lived about thirty-five years, our children being born today may expect to live at least seventy-two years.

This is indeed a demographic revolution. While many European countries are a bit further along in it than we, the change is a novel development in human history; it has never happened before. It is not only new; it is unprecedented in scope; and the speed with which it happens appears to be accelerating in each new society as it begins the process. In Europe it began earlier and has been more gradual than in the United States; it began later but is taking place more rapidly in Japan; and the newly developing countries are likely to experience it with still greater speed, if and when it begins.

At the present time there is no assurance that it will happen at all, since two conditions are necessary to produce demographic aging, and thus far only one of those conditions has been met in most developing countries. Not only must mortality decline, permitting people to live longer and thus allowing more people to live to old age; but until fertility declines, thus reducing the proportional number of children, the population will not age very much. Indeed, most of the developing countries are probably younger now than before their death rates began to fall, since the initial effect of a declining death rate is likely to be the "younging" of its population rather than its aging. This is mainly because the earliest and easiest improvements in public health are the prevention or control of epidemic and contagious diseases, those that mainly affect infants and children. Reducing the death rate from these causes has the immediate effect of increasing the number of children in a population, thus making it younger; only much later will this increase the *number* of elderly persons and even this will not necessarily increase the *proportion* of older people; that will happen only when the birthrate goes down, completing what demographers call the "demographic transition"—a presumably permanent decline of both mortality and fertility. This is the basic demographic process, of which the Revolution of Age is the unintended and sometimes unrecognized by-product.

At the same time that a population ages, some other very significant socio-demographic changes are also taking place that affect the makeup of the surviving older population and its way of life. In the first place, for reasons not fully identified, women outlive men—by a margin of about seven years in the United States—and the differential has been increasing steadily during the past century. One of the effects of this is that, among the elderly population of our country, for each four surviving females there are only three males of comparable age. This badly unbalanced sex ratio partially accounts for the fact that more than half of those surviving females are widows, whereas only one-fourth of the males are widowers; other variables accounting for this difference are age differences of husbands and wives—husbands not only are at greater risk of death even if they are the same age as their wives, they are in fact usually several years older—and widowers more frequently remarry and thus appear to the census-taker as married persons rather than as widowers, and they are likely to marry women somewhat younger than themselves. In consequence, it is not surprising that three-fourths of the older males are living with wives in independent households, whereas only one-third of the older women are married and living independently with their husbands. However, the American insistence upon independence is evident even among the widows, and we find about one-third of the older women living alone. This belies the common illusion that most old people are decrepit, dependent, and, if not presently institutionalized, imminent likely prospects. As a matter of fact, less than one out of four older women and one out of fourteen older men lives with one of their children, only 5 percent are in institutions at any given time, and only one out of four will ever spend time in a nursing home.

In the midst of all of these demographic changes, the family life-cycle has undergone radical alteration. People get married a few years earlier than they did a century ago; they have fewer children, and the children in turn marry earlier. Thus, generations have been shortened; the average difference in age between parents and children has decreased. At the same time, there is a sharper delineation of generations: since the two or three children in a family are born during their mother's twenties, the age spread between youngest and oldest children is only two to five years; and rarely anymore do children have the experience of growing up with aunts and uncles their own age, a frequent occurrence in earlier generations. This means that the period of parenting has considerably contracted, and since both of the parents increasingly survive the parenting phase, they are now left in an "empty nest" by the late forties or early fifties. For the most part, this is a new phase of life and a new social phenomenon, since a century ago the father was usually dead before all of the children had left home. It is probable that that accounts for the fact that more people remained single in those times; younger children, out of a feeling of obligation, stayed home to look after their widowed mothers. For many couples, the "empty nest" is an opportunity for unfettered enjoyment of companionship; but for those for whom children are the only glue binding the marriage together, the departure of children often signals middle-aged divorce.

At the same time, the earlier cessation of childbearing, along with the availability of modern domestic gadgetry, has relieved women of household drudgery. Many return to the labor force as soon as the youngest child is in school, and others do so with the onset of the empty-nest phase. Certainly the contraction of the parenting role has contributed to the expansion of the work role for women and to greater leisure for both sexes. But there are other concomitants as well; the breakup of more marriages in middle age and subsequent remarriage of one or more of the partners is new only in the sense that earlier the break occurred because of the death of one partner, whereas now the usual means of a break at that stage is divorce. At the same time, it appears that remarriage, whatever the reason for the break of the prior marriage, is becoming more frequent and acceptable.

In theory, the increasing mobility of American society and the increasing tendency for people, including older people, to live independently should lead to increasing geographic separation of generations and increasing isolation of older family units from younger. The evidence on this point is at present inconclusive and contradictory. Certainly America is a mobile society, and young people upon marriage strongly prefer to establish their own separate households (and their parents agree with this objective). However, neither the establishment of separate households nor geographic separation should be interpreted as social isolation or disaffection. Indeed, high mobility does not necessarily lead to geographic separation; about one-sixth of the older people of America live in the same household as one of their children, and fully four-fifths are within one hour's commuting distance of at least one child. Furthermore, with modern postal services and telephonic communications, even if generations have become widely separated geographically they are not sociologically separated or alienated. In fact, much research, both here and in Europe during the past twenty years, leads to a contrary set of conclusions, namely (1) that high mobility and neolocal marriage patterns have not led to as wide a geographic separation of older people and their children as was expected, (2) that even when the generations are geographically separated, they are not sociologically isolated, and (3) that both generations, although they agree that they should not live in the same household, prefer to be close. This has been called "intimacy at a distance" by Austrian sociologist Leopold Rosenmayr, and from another perspective, by American sociologists, "the modified extended family," meaning that many kinship relationships and obligations continue even if the members are separated by residence and by geography.

One measure of increasing residential separation, though not clearly of wide geographic separation, is the finding that over the past thirty years older people have increasingly concentrated in different sections of metropolitan areas. Some of this no doubt reflects the growth of retirement villages, high-rise retirement housing, and nursing homes; but the separation is a two-way process and has mostly rested with the initiative of the younger generation, who have pursued the American dream to the suburbs while their parents remained behind in the central city or retired from their farms into small towns in rural America. However, this increasing geographic segregation of the older generation does not yet clearly portend sociological isolation or political alienation.

Relations between parents and middle-aged children are in general, according to the bulk of the research done both here and in Europe, strong, affectionate, and mutually supportive. Contrary to general impression, the older generation still contributes more heavily financially to the younger generation than the reverse, but there is a mutual reciprocity of relationships that adapts to changing needs. Up to now there is no general evidence of the shirking of conventional responsibilities on the part of either generation; each generation appears to be contributing more in money and services to the other than is expected.

While the parenting role has been foreshortened, there is no evidence that it has lost any affective quality or effective consequence. On the other hand, the grandparenting role appears to have diminished both quantitatively and qualitatively. In the first place, the current generation of people who are in the grandparenting phase, that is, those whose grandchildren are still immature, have many fewer grandchildren than their forebears. This is the intrafamilial counterpart of the aging of the population resulting from the decline of the birthrate. Second, while the evidence is not very extensive or clear, it appears that grandparenting has lost some of its former warmth and intensity. But, after all, the modern grandmother in her fifties is very likely to be holding down a full-time job away from home, thus having contacts, interests, and responsibilities apart from the family. The same must be said of the grandfather, but in his case this is not so new. In other words, grandparenting today is an after-hours role that must be arranged and scheduled; and while this is by no means to say that there is not affection and interest, it does appear that there is less spontaneity and more formality in the relationship. Furthermore, as the grandchildren mature, the distance increases and may even amount to alienation.

By the time of retirement, many people have become great-grand-parents. With the lengthening of life and the telescoping of generations, increasing numbers and proportions of people ultimately experience this stage of life. About four out of ten people who are sixty-five and over report that they have great-grandchildren. But this role is still more attenuated than grandparenting. Mobility, distance, competing interests, and demands of intervening generations severely dilute the relationship, and contacts are frequently limited to family reunions and rites of passage. A modern child may experience a glut of grandparents—possibly four grandparents, several great-grand-parents, and even some great-great-grandparents. This is a bewildering array; it certainly does not favor much sharing of time or intimacy. One aspect of competing relationships is posed in terms of: With which set of grandparents shall we spend this holiday? There is often some strain in making the rounds and keeping things balanced, such as alternating Christmases with different grandparents. When generations become four or five deep, such alternation and sharing becomes too complicated. Adjacent generations maintain contact, concern, and sharing, but great-grandparents are forced to take a back seat in favor of their children, the current grandparent generation, and be content with occasional filial visits or being included in the gatherings centered around one of their children.

Even though there is an effort to maintain balance and reciprocity and not to play favorites in these relationships, this ideal is often impossible, and patterns of preference and intimacy do emerge, with females being the primary links within and between generations. Sisters are more likely to maintain meaningful lifelong relationships than brothers or cross-sexual siblings. The mother-daughter link is the most common intergenerational bond. Couples tend to live closer to the wife's parents than to the husband's, when elderly parents give up the homestead, they commonly move to be near a daughter; and when a widow moves into the household of a child, it is usually a daughter. Females are usually the "kinkeepers"—those who keep track of all of the kin—the focus of communication, and the organizers of reunions.

The most common critical events of later life are the departure of children, retirement, and widowhood. Each is now being subjected to scholarly scrutiny, which is gradually stripping away the mythology that has grown up around it. The emptying of the nest in most cases occurs without trauma, and the mother of the bride is more often happy than tearful. Likewise, retirement is not the lethal event it is often supposed to be. Oft-recited stories of the man who retired and died within a few months fails to establish a causal relationship. Frequently, failing health is a motivating factor in retirement; and if death occurs shortly thereafter, it is the culmination of the disease that was already in progress; retirement may have had nothing to do with it. Careful before-and-after studies have failed to discover any dire consequences of retirement. Of course widowhood is traumatic, but after the shock of bereavement, most widows find solace in companionship with other widows, while many widowers remarry.

Some prophets of doom are saying that the aging of the population imposes an intolerable economic burden upon the workers. This is mostly a specious and, in one respect, a hypocritical argument. The increasing proportion of aged in the population does *not* produce an increasing proportion of the economically dependent. In all populations, the aged are a minority of those who are dependent. If we define economic dependency as the condition of not working or not being in the labor market, there are about four major categories of people included: young children, students, housewives, and nonemployed elderly. In the United States in 1970, children (under fourteen) accounted for 43 percent of the total dependent population; students (over fourteen), 16 percent; and the nonworking aged (sixty-five and over), only 14 percent.

It is a common illusion that as the proportion of the aged increases in a population the dependency load increases. In fact, just the opposite is true. As noted above, the proportion of aged does not increase until the birthrate goes down, that is, when the proportion of children decreases. Because the child population is such a large segment of the total dependency load in any society, almost invariably when the child dependency load decreases, the total dependency load declines.

I have recently tested this proposition in two different ways. In a cross-sectional study of eighty-two countries for which comparable data was available, I found that in the less developed countries about 70 to 75 percent of the population was not working, and these were the same countries that had low proportions of aged; in the more advanced countries, in which there were more aged, only 55 to 60 percent of the population was not working. Thus the total dependency load was lower in the more advanced, more aged societies. The second test was a longitudinal study of the United States, in which I found that in 1879, when less than 3 percent of our population was sixty-five and over, more than two-thirds of the population (68 percent) was not in the labor force; while a hundred years later, with 10 percent of our population sixty-five and over, the proportion not in the labor force was below 60 percent. In other words, at the same time our population was aging, the dependency load was declining.

The reason for suspecting a bit of hypocrisy in the contention that we, the most affluent society in human history, cannot afford to support our moderate load of aged dependents is that this same society, through its compulsory-retirement rules, forces many of the elderly to become dependent. An obvious corrective for the current drain upon the Social Security Fund is to abolish compulsory retirement, permitting those who wish to work to do so and thereby to continue to pay into the fund rather than draw out of it. About a third of those now retired say they would prefer to work.

To argue that our affluent society cannot afford to support its elderly members in comfort is self-serving rationalization. Other, much less affluent societies are, with less grumbling, carrying much higher dependency loads than we are; and with less affluence, we have in the past borne heavier burdens ourselves. The mere facts that fewer of our dependents are children and more of them old, and that we have elected to support the latter through a public mechanism for the transfer payments (social security), cannot serve as an excuse for avoiding our manifest responsibility.

All of these changes of demography, familial relations, and economic arrangements have, of course, been accompanied by changes in the lifestyles of the older people themselves. Each new generation of elderly are better educated and healthier than the last, and they become more diverse and varied in their backgrounds, experiences, and capabilities. No single stereotype is adequate to describe them or their lifestyles.

But the rising levels of education and health imply a more active and involved lifestyle. More older people with wider horizons are traveling greater distances. Their more extensive intellectual interests are taking them back to school, and they in turn are beginning to change the schools. Some just want to try out new leisure interests; others are preparing for new careers. Second, and even third, careers are becoming commonplace. For more than one out of five, the drive for involvement leads to volunteering—a new career without pay. The variety of retirement activities of today's elderly defies cataloging, but certainly the rocking chair has lost its popularity.

The varied interests and capabilities of older people are also giving rise to new types of community settings. Many small towns have evolved into retirement communities as young people have left and old people have stayed or retired from a nearby farm. The same kind of process gives rise to the "gray ghettos" of our inner cities. Old transient hotels are evolving, or being converted, into residential hotels for the elderly, while new high-rises and condominiums are being constructed to serve similar purposes for different social strata. Meanwhile nursing homes have become a big business to meet the specialized needs of the "old-old" whose health or support systems have failed.

A few communes of elderly people have sprung up, distinguished from other living arrangements by the extent of the sharing of costs and responsibilities. Perhaps the most widely publicized of these is the Share-a-Home Association, in Winter Park, Florida, where twenty "aunts" and "uncles" live together as a family in a jointly owned twenty-seven room house.

More widely known, well advertised, and easily visible are the planned retirement communities that have been built in all parts of the country, but particularly in the sun belt. These include varying types of housing, such as mobile homes, with a wide range of services and facilities. Many of them purport to be self-contained, with shopping centers, churches, recreation facilities, and health services. There is strong stress on "leisure world" activities, but even these appear to be operating on the basis of stereotype and fail to appreciate the diversity of needs of their clientele; Jerry Jacobs reports that only about 15 percent of the residents account for most of the activity in "Fun City," the rest being largely invisible, including 25 percent who "never leave their homes."

So while the Revolution of Age is producing some marked changes in family relations, living arrangements, and lifestyles, it is also demonstrating much resilience, adaptability, and continuity. In the face of major structural changes in families and living arrangements, most older people are not isolated from kith and kin, but maintain strong ties of affection and mutual assistance with their families. Still they are fiercely independent, maintaining their own separate residences if at all possible, avoiding common residence with their children, and dreading the possibility of having to resort to a nursing home. They are increasingly healthy, active, and involved, and the current generation is busy experimenting with new activities and new lifestyles. Still, the safest generalization to be made is that it is not safe to generalize; older people are too different among themselves, more diversified than any younger age group; after all, they've had longer time to get that way.

CHAPTER II

THE SOCIAL CONDITION OF AGING: THEORIES AND INTERPRETATIONS

Theories are symbolic devices that make sense out of a body of facts and throw light onto a confusing reality. Because of their conjectural or hypothetical nature, theories have a temporary quality. They must undergo tests of empirical validation before they gain acceptability.

When Elaine Cumming and her co-workers stated their disengagement theory of aging in 1960, they were probably not aware of the controversy they were to originate. The clamor has not subsided yet, as repeated field studies are still designed to test its basic propositions. Cumming reappeared in 1975 after a long retirement from the field of gerontology, in order to restate the disengagement theory, examine the preceding discussions, and even dispel some of the semantic misunderstandings that had seemingly arisen. Above all, she found it necessary to set the limits of the theory and disclaim what it never intended to cover. This chapter includes Elaine Cumming's third and most recent formulation of the disengagement theory.

That the theory remains in its conjectural state is evidenced by the response her paper drew from Stanley H. Cath. In an essay entitled "The Orchestration of Disengagement," Cath claims that the disengagement theory does not take into account the rich complexities of human existence or the appreciation of coping behavior in later life. The author fears the idea that disengagement, as a mutually freeing and somewhat beneficial process for the normal aged, may even induce or encourage discriminatory attitudes and practices against the aging. Cath agrees that normal aging consists of a series of insults, losses, and impairments, but many aged have no alternative but to contend with their depletion anxieties in a social environment that is hostile and uncaring. The fact that the external world reinforces the internal losses turns the disengagement theory into a sort of circular, self-fulfilling prophecy.

James J. Dowd in "Aging as Exchange: A Preface to Theory" aims to overcome that circularity with a new paradigmatic alternative that he draws from the social psychological theory of exchange. If disengagement theory assumes that progressive decline in social involvement is mutually desired by both the individual and society, and if the activity theory postulates the opposite, that involvement throughout life is necessary, the exchange theory then rejects both contentions. It assumes instead that the degree of engagement or involvement in old age is an empirical outcome of the transactions between each individual and his social environment. Because power resources diminish with age, older people become increasingly unable to enter into balanced exchange relations with other groups. From this perspective, disengagement is the symptom or effect of the relative loss of power of the aged vis-à-vis their exchange partners. When such loss of power occurs, there is nothing left for the older person but to exchange compliance in return for continued sustenance.

Irving Rosow reiterates the theme of depletion and power imbalance from a role theory perspective. In "The Social Context of the Aging Self," he draws attention to the reality of systematic role loss for an entire population cohort. It is a reality that segregates and devalues people and ultimately undermines their social identity. Society freed the aged from role constraints and expectations but left them with no norms for restructuring their lives. Coping with stress is an almost impossible feat when appropriate role sets are not at hand. While response to role loss and stress is tied to many personality factors, it tends to improve with strong and viable group supports. The social world of the aged is, however, in a process of disintegration and shrinkage, and effective group supports are no longer available. Rosow does not believe that all is lost: he concludes with the positive observation that losses can be arrested and compensations generated through social policy designs, social services programs, and most specially, through the militant action of the aged on their own behalf.

Far from being a static or uneventful stage, aging is filled with changes and transitions. Some have a social-environmental origin and others are more psychogenic in nature. Theories add intelligibility to those changing realities. This was our rationale for having a hermeneutic foundation precede our next chapter, where we review a select number of transitions.

2.1

Engagement with an Old Theory

Elaine Cumming

Because the first tentative statement of disengagement theory (Cumming et al., 1960) was reprinted in a recent book of readings (Chown, 1972) just after the major statement, *Growing Old* (Cumming and Henry, 1961) went out of print, I am assuming that the specter of this theory has not yet been put to rest. It seems reasonable, therefore, to review the theory, and also to consider some of the controversy it has generated. Accordingly, I shall try to re-state the bare essentials of the theory, suggesting some new studies that might confirm its usefulness in making sense out of what we know about the aging process, and I shall also discuss briefly those aspects of both the theory itself and the context in which it was set forth that seem to have generated controversy, polemics, and even invective.

Copyright 1975 by Baywood Publishing Co. Reprinted by permission. *International Journal of Aging and Human Development*, Vol. 6 (3), 1975, pp 187-191.

Everything here is attributable to me alone. None of my previous co-authors are at all responsible. I am, however, grateful to participants in a discussion at the 1973 Gerontology Meetings in Miami Beach for some valuable ideas. I regret that I do not know their names. I would like to thank my colleague, Charles Lazer, for helpful suggestions and to absolve him too, from responsibility for what I am saying here.

The Core of the Theory

The first statement of the theory, which was based on the findings of the Kansas City Study of Adult Life, contained three propositions.

1. The life space of an individual decreases with age, in that he interacts with a narrower variety of role partners and spends a smaller proportion of his time in interaction. This proposition was later elaborated to highlight the importance of vacating the key life roles of work and family.
2. The individual anticipates this change and participates in the process.
3. The individual's preference for interpersonal rewards becomes more individualized and expressive, and less role-connected as he grows older, and thus his *style* of interaction changes.

These three elements were summarized by the word "disengagement." It appears to me now that without the second element, the statement would have been almost a truism.

The second statement of the theory added a fourth proposition, which was directly derived from propositions one and three, and which suggested that if the individual has relinquished obligatory roles, and if he has become more individuated and expressive, which is to say less normative and conforming, then he is unlikely either to seek out or to be sought out for new obligatory roles. This is the same as saying that once started, disengagement has a momentum of its own. The implicit trade-off for the aging individual is that in giving up obligatory roles he gains freedom as he loses centrality.

Subsequent statements of the theory were essentially elaborations of the original two statements although they sometimes included speculations relating to the connection between disengagement, death, retirement, the needs of the labor market and various kinds of temperamental and personality characteristics.

Where We Are Now

I have not kept up with this field, so I may have missed important work, but it is my impression that although light has been thrown on some aspects of disengagement theory, it remains on the whole poorly operationalized and largely untested. Were I to work in this field again, I would attack first propositions one and two. (The empirical base of the theory has never been strong, although with the exception of the late Margaret Blenkner, I don't recall anyone criticising it for that reason.) I would want to press forward with Marjorie Lowenthal's questions about "voluntary withdrawal," and I would want to know more about the variance among individuals of different generations in this matter as well as the variance among situations in which disengagement occurs. I would be particularly interested in finding evidence of any reversibility of the process. In short, I do not think this theory can be dismissed until all four propositions have been adequately tested. If I were to broaden the scope of my enquiry, I would turn first to the neurophysiological findings of the past few years. Most importantly, I would make every effort to improve the reliability of the measures used in order to facilitate comparative studies and replications. A simple measure of the variety in the life space, for example, might be:

$$\text{Variety of Life Space Score} = 1 - \frac{\sum\limits_{i=1}^{n} X_i^2}{(\Sigma X_i)^2}$$

where X is the number of people in any one role category. With such a measure, scores would approach unity as the number of kinds of role partners increased and would be zero if all role partners were in the same category. If, for example, a person had three role partners within a given time period but they were all his own children, his score for that period would be zero. If two role partners were children and the third a friend, his score would be .44, and if all three role partners were in different categories, the score would be .67. With four partners, all in different categories, the score would rise to .75, and so on. Such a measure would perhaps be most useful for comparing cohorts at different intervals. A longitudinal study using such operations together with enquiries into perceptions of the life space would go a long way toward testing propositions one and two.

The Controversies

There were a number of inappropriate[1] responses to disengagement theory; after all, it is only theory, not a policy statement or a political platform. Some of these responses arose from misunderstandings of the nature of the theory, some from misunderstandings of what we were trying to say, and some we brought on ourselves through our manner of setting the theory forward. Some controversies have surrounded misapplications of the theory, and these are the most serious.

Theory qua theory

A theory is a system of linked propositions that makes sense of a body of data. No theory can take up all the variance in the phenomena to which it addresses itself. This particular theory does not address itself to biological concomitants of aging nor to cultural variation in the treatment of the aged, but to the social and psychological aspects of the aging process.

I do not personally think that the theory can be faulted for not doing what it never set out to do, although it may be in the end that a theory based on either cultural or biological variables, or political or economic ones, or some combination of these may take up so much of the variance in normal aging as to make disengagement theory unimportant whether it is upheld or not.

Misunderstandings

The major misunderstandings appear to have arisen in semantic confusion surrounding the word disengagment. This word appears to carry connotations, not derived from the theory but from general knowledge and experience, that are similar to those around such concepts as isolation, loneliness, marginality, and passivity. Inasmuch as proposition four above included an assumption of lessened normative control of the individual, disengagement can logically be considered to be a form of marginality, but the others appear to me to be independent. A man who has negotiated a new contract with society such that he has fewer roles or less interaction or both may be travelling around the world, cultivating his garden, playing tennis, talking to his wife, sitting in a rocking chair, writing a book, climbing a mountain, or almost anything else. Some of these undertakings are rather more active than passive, others not. Whether activity *qua* activity increases or decreases with age is not clear, but nothing in disengagement theory is inimical to high levels of activity, and nothing in it implies loneliness and isolation.[2]

Controversies we brought on ourselves

Two problems we brought on ourselves: first, a stultifying polarization of discussion apparently resulted from the use of a straw man in the major statement of the theory, and second, there was confusion over the use of "morale" as a variable. Taking the first error first: it seemed to us at the time that the literature was full of statements related to an *ideal* of aging, which we read as a constantly expanding life space. By creating a straw man from this line of thinking, we created the mistaken impression that disengagement was an alternative ideal. We should have stuck to our question, "What *is* the normal aging process?" and ignored questions of what *should be*. If we had, I think we would have avoided the subsequent unenlightening controversy over "activity versus disengagement."

Allied to this misunderstanding has been the morass of argument over morale, life satisfaction, happiness, and so on. In disengagement theory, morale is obviously a dependent variable. It should not be addressed until the utility of the theory has been established. The confusion of purpose that allowed us to include data regarding morale in the general statement of the theory has led to profound misunderstandings. Disengagement theory *does not predict morale*, and findings of high or low morale among people with high or low patterns of engagement, though interesting, are essentially irrelevant. My own later speculations about the theory contributed to this confusion, and made the theory the target of invective.[3] I suspect that a number of intervening and contingent variables must be isolated before disengagement theory, supposing that it survives testing, can be linked with the concept of morale.

Misapplications of the theory

Disengagement theory was addressed to normal aging. The sick and the poor were excluded from the initial study, and consideration of the effect of illness and poverty, the two scourges of old age, were omitted and stated to be omitted. Nevertheless, numerous studies of the beneficent effect of increased stimuli on the sick old are described as "disproofs" of disengagement theory, and what is much worse, I am told that some administrators of facilities catering for the dependent old use this theory to support *laissez-faire* policies and negligent practices. Inasmuch as our straw-man tactic and our premature introduction of the morale question led to this tragic misuse of our theory, we must take the blame. I personally, regret deeply that this has happened, but I do not think that such fraudulent practices should deter us from making every effort to understand the process of growing old, or any other aspect of the human condition.

Notes

1. I have in mind both the epithets and the "that's telling them!" kind of fan letter that I have received from time to time.

2. It is interesting to note in passing that a statement by Henry and Cumming (1961) about the *intrinsic* character of the disengagement process did not create anything like the controversy that its radical implications deserved.

3. For the record, we did identify in the Kansas City Study, one small group of disengaged widows who showed high morale on our measures, and we did argue that this tended to show that disengagement is not automatically accompanied by low morale, but we never at any time said that there was a positive association between morale and disengagement, and we did state categorically, that disengagement is "neutral for morale."

References

Chown, S., Editor. *Ageing*, London: Penguin, 1972.

Cumming, E., Dean L. R., Newell, D. S., & McCaffrey, I. Disengagement, a Tentative Theory of Aging. *Sociometry*, Vol. 23: 23-35, 1960.

Cumming, E., & Henry, W. E., *Growing old*. New York: Basic Books, 1961.

2.2

The Orchestration of Disengagement

Stanley H. Cath

The history and science of man is a crazy concert indeed—sometimes 4, 5, or 20 orchestras or, if you prefer, institutions of care, all play different though simultaneous tunes, using different scores, librettos or languages and have different climaxes, stopping points, or codas in sight. All clamor simultaneously not only to be heard, but to be applauded for originality, depth and value. In the process they may well lose sight of their common object of concern—man, his welfare and his dignity.

It is a haphazard and ambivalent harmony at best whenever organized community institutions are asked to fill in vacant seats of family players who are absent because of "morale problems." To appreciate one tune over the rest without listening to or being sensitive to important themes from other sections of the orchestra may be necessary to protect from overload or discord or playing the other person's part. But it also isolates one's self from hearing many inspired performances and interesting or important harmonic contributions. Motifs, which at first may seem strange or insignificant, may add to the overall richness like harmonic overtones.

In language, "being engaged" has many meanings or overtones, including being prepared for or involved in various new adventures, intimacies, and confrontations. The word varies in extremes from in-

Copyright 1975 by Baywood Publishing Co. Reprinted by permission. *International Journal of Aging and Human Development*, Vol. 6 (3), 1975, pp. 199-213.

tense love in the state of "about to be married" to intense hate or destructiveness in a state of war or in a battle unto death.

As to be expected, "disengagement" may also be similarly defined in emotionally charged, polar terms. One extreme may represent a welcome separation from overwhelming circumstances and responsibility; the other may herald an inevitable confrontation with hopelessness and death. It seems to me that in human research, we should start with the premise of a *multidetermined phenomena with potential for many individually chosen, adaptive interpretations along a wide spectrum.*

Disengagement theory, if it is to be criticized, cannot be faulted on its essential core. The theory truly reflects an objective series of observations made by serious scientists. Yet it may be said it failed to appreciate the *spectrum* involved. First, as Cumming interpreted her data, with increasing age there develops in many people a progressively diminishing life space with reduced time spent in social interaction. Anticipating this change, the individual participates in a social process, which is characterized by his "changing preferences," moving on a scale of interpersonal rewards from "role-connected" to more individualized interactions (Cumming, Dean, Newell, & McCaffrey, 1960; & Cumming, 1975).

Secondly, it included a reference to "a withdrawal of normative control intrinsic to certain role obligations, especially connected to child-raising and work that would allow an increase of egocentricity which militates against the future resumption of new obligatory roles" (Cumming, 1975). The process, once started, then may be regarded as "circular." Excepting the intentional, volitional characteristics implied in her statements up to this point, one might still consider disengagement theory quite consistent and harmonious with medical, demographic, and psychodynamic observations by allied social scientists.

It is the next "hence" which may still lead to being misunderstood and misapplied, should we accept Cumming's current position without qualification: *"Hence, disengagement was conceived of as a circular, mutual, freeing process in which society and the individual arrived at an equilibrium different from that of middle age both in amount and kind of involvement."*

There is little to disagree with in the last half of that sentence—namely, the differences between qualitative and quantitative aspects of many phenomena of equilibrium of middle and later years. But the implications in the first half of "mutual, freeing," mirrored earlier writing "of mutual benefit" (Cumming et al.) is at the core of the controversy, and now one may indeed question the "harmonic values" of the "new equilibria."

In an effort to create some harmony out of the discord, I will speak to four points selected from Cumming's most recent outline in her present revisions of Disengagement Theory.

Theory and Technique

There have been misapplications attributable to the complexities of the relationship and priorities of theory and practice. According to subsequent statements by the author and her collaborators, the sparks—if not flames—generated by this theory seemed out of proportion to the heat consciously intended. Still, many people have been burned. I am inclined to believe Cumming still does not understand the reasons for the misapplications of her theory, especially when, after all these years, she writes: " . . . it is only a theory, not a policy statement or a political platform" (Cumming, 1975).

Criticism

In social science and psychologically enlightening health research, there has always been a mutually challenging interaction between established techniques and new theories. Whether correct or not, and without a conscious wish to determine policy, Cumming's theory did play into the hands of important policy makers—usually politicians, nursing home administrators, and the like. Social science demography unwittingly became an advisory ally to those who were most concerned with the care of the elderly. Unfortunately, some of these influential people still have unconscious gerontophobic, geronto-rejecting and geronto-sadistic attitudes. They interpreted such research results according to their personal motivation and limitation—often colored by financial considerations. Somehow the differentiation between regressive *reversible* disengagement and equilibrium stations, associated with ordinary loss and depression, and the more serious *irreversible* impairments was lost.

Some generalizations seem necessary in describing the relationship of theory to technique and political policy. Over the past 20 years progress in understanding the dynamics and interdigitation of organic and psychological life processes over the total life span has been extremely rapid. Enriching reports from a multitude of researchers are not always easily communicated across the borders of contiguous fields. Still, a generally held view is that normal aging proceeds through a series of epigenetic phases beginning at birth, each of which contains age-specific challenges with potential for growth, maintenance of status quo, or regression. Each challenge is experienced with greater or lesser degrees of crisis, depending on many personal and environmental circumstances which are being defined and studied. To discuss the crisis of disengagement without consideration for, and isolating it from, depression or paranoia is to place an *artificial barrier and naive handicap* on the phenomena of theory leading to technical advocacy. A developmental interdisciplinary approach was needed to tease out many extremely important independent and dependent variables, but including the potential for reversibility of disengagement at various way stations.

When we consider that the responsibility for the destiny of many of our elderly has moved from the family into the hands of various community caretakers, including legislators, politicians, nursing home administrators, medical personnel, social work agencies, businessmen, and various boards of directors (i.e., hospital and other residential units), the application or misapplication of our theoretical assumptions assumes tremendous heuristic importance. While not always easy, it rests heavily upon researchers to be as careful as possible in overseeing to what use tentative inquiries and early impressions are put, especially on a large or global scale, by human engineers with limited backgrounds and differing motivations. The step from incomplete and inconclusive research to complete advocacy by offering naive solutions is all too easily taken.

From another viewpoint, there is much compliance by the elderly with their own exclusion from society. Progressive or regressive potential is heavily influenced by awareness in the elderly themselves of judgments related to burdens or comforts they place upon their loved ones or from community responses to their progressive aging, depletion, disengagement, and anticipated demise. They often consciously wish so much not to be a burden that they are likely to fail to recognize or deny negative input from their bodies dealing not only with aging or loss of function, but with disease itself. Accordingly, one is often hard put to know how to weigh the validity of their responses to questionnaires in which only their conscious reactions are considered and which ignore human defensiveness and their own self-hatred—built in and reinforced by cultural adoration of youth. Old people may believe the last gift to those who remain on the face of this earth will be to lay down or sacrifice needs and preferences in the service of others. Accordingly, they may minimize illness or ignore the rage felt at their own decline in order not "to rock the boat." They also rarely "rage against the dying of the light" so as not to cause further censure or abandonment. It is reminiscent of the Eskimo mother who gave her life to a son by instructing him how to murder her, commanding him to eat her flesh afterwards so that he and their progeny might survive. Similarly, modern man demonstrates many mixed attitudes toward his elderly, who may drain his emotional, financial and physical resources while contributing little, while reminding him especially of his own vulnerabilities.

Years of painful experience should teach us that it is not possible for any scientific endeavor to separate theory from technique and practice. All technique is ultimately based upon theoretical frameworks or constructs—good, bad or incomplete. Theory, in turn, is an amalgam composed of experience, observations, and most importantly, the harmonic synthesis of data processed by human brains from different viewpoints—but always filtered through subjective and objective screens, always subject to considerable distortion. New theory is particularly difficult to encompass because it requires a break with tradition, with what was comfortable and believed in the past. Assuming a new position may require a destruction of the old or established pattern. Because of this destructive quality and attendant guilt, conflict is engendered and new resolutions, compromises, and harmonious interactions will be sought, but often influenced by political and socioeconomic considerations. Possibly Cumming failed to stress how mutual reinforcement of individual and society can be destructive, reflecting depressive gerontophobic self-hate as well as hate of the elderly by significant others. The "riddance" reaction has always been enhanced by political necessity. We cannot ignore these considerations any more than we can ignore the contributions of other fields.

Furthermore, it is all too easy for families, administrators, and planners to ignore the restituitive potential and the various steps taken by elders to cope with their increasing dependency, depression, psychosomatic concerns, and various levels of paranoia. Most institutional programs reflect a general attitude of blindness to these adaptive routes and actually enhance rejection and isolation. This can hardly be said to be basically sound and mutually beneficial. Recent research on isolation suggests tremendous biochemical sensitivities to the effect of this ecological and psychological state.

Rather than shifting the balance of care toward ego restitution, independence, and social enhancement; rather than being concerned with the maintenance of ego integrity on a level consonant with ability, disengagement has moved many social resources and programmers toward *diminishing* resonance and *reduced* interaction with the elderly. It leads toward more static and less active systems. The elderly, if not the middle-aged, are considered as mismatched, poorly accepted, neither a rehabilitable nor a marketable commodity. Disengagement theory reinforces outmoded, anachronistic and increasingly detrimental retirement policies as well as other more complicated program development.

Activity and Passivity

Cumming now asserts nothing in disengagement theory is inimical to high levels of activity. Similar misinterpretations have arisen related to the statement, "culture-free," although she adds, "the form it takes will always still be 'culture bound'." She admits semantic ambiguity may have cultivated polarities in concepts of isolation, loneliness, marginality, and passivity in contrast to group interaction, social programming, stimulation, and activity. Yet such theory has added to the shift of the caretaking community from high levels of activity to a more passive stance.

Criticism

There is a need for the interweaving of activity and passivity, of studying the roles of the culture-free and culture-bound vs. that of object ties in maintaining continuity of integrity and development. I doubt if we are ever completely culture-free or culture-bound. I am also uncertain about how we come to know, possess, and especially how we relinquish our real world. We attempt to understand the natural lives and deaths of animals around us. Should we not do the same with people? How do we relinquish attachments to people? Under what circumstances do we disengage from objects? Certainly the human animal remains the most puzzling of enigmas, especially when we consider how scant our knowledge is about his normal-to-pathological development. Some believe he is seduced into this world. At any rate, he remains reluctant to leave it. It is another basic tenet of dynamic psychology that people have various realities and capacities, often based upon residual memories and earliest experience of interacting with others. These in turn determine various subsequent stages of life. One's life style is colored, if not significantly influenced, by the emerging capacity to relate to or engage others; by the ability to be intimate or bound to significant people; and by the capacity to tolerate loss, grieve for loss, and repair it by restitution. As one's world "depletes," it is natural to attempt to replenish it. No one who lives long avoids the final common path of a series of complex grieving interdigitations with destiny. The outcomes determine the strength or relative degrees of influence of fact and fantasy, faith and despair. These mood or "morale" factors may strongly determine the tendency toward isolation or intimacy, trust or mistrust, active searching vs. passive compliance, confidence in one's integrity and physical intactness vs. a sense of ego fragmentation in a world that seems deserting and dangerous to the fading self. One's storehouse of narcissism required to fuel these years is based upon interactions between self and object love. The capacity to maintain identity differentiation as one ages is further influenced by the vicissitudes of aggressive drives of targets chosen—i.e., the self or others. In the aging process, much research lacks appreciation for these segments of research on "normal" longitudinal social variables—all of which result, hopefully, in the acquisition of ego strength or healthy narcissism needed to cope with chronic depletion, loss, and the ultimate confrontation with one's own partial annihilation or total death.

The aging crisis requires a preparatory process over years—in all probability from the mid-30's on—when one's father and mother, friends, sisters, brothers, all may threaten to leave, actually become seriously ill, or impaired, or die. When there is no one between the self and the grave, a tragic theme intrudes itself into the composition of life and must be coped with by an ego often itself less than intact. All of these interrelated themes may seem global rather than circumscribed by special "morale" or affective responses. Individual judgments are *reinforced by both cultural expectations and ego ideals.* What was once a minor theme may become major. It is not possible to separate cultural factors from ego responses to perceptions of the changes from within. Long years of preparatory adaptive adjustments lead to a protest against the relinquishment, not only of instrumental roles, but of all influence and meaningful purposes of life. One may be called upon to abandon cherished ideals and one's expectations of the young as extensions of one's self. Step by step, progression and regression can be observed to occur in most lives.

I will grant that the responses to one's own aging, reinforced by responses of those to whom the elderly are particularly sensitive, lead to a combined effect which is often a matter of conscious and unconscious communication between the participants. But judgments as to comfort or discomfort, assets or liabilities, and the degree of burden to be tolerated by the significant members of the family may accelerate disengagement and depletion. Such a "withdrawal" may lead to a "voluntary" decathexis of life. In such a developmental and multifactorial system, even as one traces some of the factors of the process, ongoing homeostasis and harmonious regulation of still functioning parts of the self and the self's other interactions do go on. Cumming's theory seemed without appreciation for the need to maintain psychic integrity, despite normal failures or abnormal pathology of component parts, which do insist on various degrees of disengagement, or release from previous role expectations. Sad reality informs us that Cumming is basically correct. There is, for most people, a regressive move down the ladder in a series of personal interactions and a move from independent individuation to more symbiotic living. In some cases, the regression may progress to almost autistic-like, self-preoccupied isolation.

Lewinsohn and MacPhillamy (1974) recently confirmed that there is a significant decrease in the frequency of the pleasant activities, in terms of occurrence and subjective enjoyability, in both depressed and older people. Yet the main finding of this study, while confirming Cumming's basic observations, called attention correctly to the need for finer discrimination in research. For example, especially in depressed people of *all* ages, there is a decrease in pleasant activity, particularly in the subjective enjoyability of pleasant events. This is not the same in elderly people. Thus, we may conclude the decrease in subjective enjoyability is uniquely part of depression, and this takes place in many old people too. In this counterpointing paper, it is hypothesized that a person feels depressed because he is not engaging in behaviors which elicit positive reinforcement. The elderly in this study were also supposedly selected because they were normal, well, and without overt psychiatric problems. The older individuals resembled the depressed ones in having lower pleasant activity scores and also showed a decrease in enjoyability rating. The hypothesis to explain this discrepancy was that the individual, as he ages, is less *able* to engage in activities which are potentially reinforcing (requiring physical endurance or special skills) so that he is less likely to emit behaviors which elicit social reinforcement. With the diminished social reinforcement, society tends to supply the elder's needs noncontingently, without expecting any behavior from him—even when capable of being self-sufficient (e.g., enforced retirement). This may deprive the elderly of many behaviors which are potential sources of enjoyment for them. This is an example of discriminating paradoxical research I think Cumming would find helpful in validating her hypotheses, but at the same time, invalidating the implications which have been drawn from it.

Appreciation for Coping Behavior

My own work with the aged has resulted in an increased appreciation of how all middle-aged and depressed people, sick or well, must cope with increasing quantities of depressive affect, diminished activity, a tendency toward psychosomatic concern, a turning toward the past, and decrements in all types of mental and physical resources and pleasures. Survival, daily care of the self, and retaining hold on people and/or objects become increasingly important motifs or demands placed upon psychic energy through the later years. Maturity under such circumstances may all too often yield to immaturity, and independence may be surrendered to the type of marginality which many people feel encompasses the elderly. I cannot consider such fluctuating states irreversible or to be advocated, for it is a matter of quality or the structure of defenses brought to bear upon the process of loss, depletion and restitution. Temporary equilibria, if you will, may give impressions of static systems.

In our culture we must keep our minds open to the possibility of progressive maturity and achievement in some elders, even to the century mark in rare cases. Disengagement Theory seems to exclude an expansion of the mind and/or socio-economic circumstances, well demonstrated by a particular elite group of long-lived people.

Furthermore, another section of the orchestra seems to have been initially ignored, especially in terms of the fine-tuning adjustments required related to activity and passivity in the last trimester of life. If there is any one physiological finding of significant research over the past 20 years in terms of primary or secondary prevention of aging, it is the prescriptive advice to keep active, exercise to the point of tolerance, and remain busily engaged. Every research project I know of has a rather pessimistic prognosis when people disengage, and atrophy from disuse is almost as certain as night following day. These reports on the disastrous effect of passivity ranges from brain cells to muscle size, to mental activity and capacity. Not only is it true of humans, but in our closest relatives, the primates, and in all other animal studies.

In the normal person, except for speed of processing information, virtually no changes in certain areas of intellectual capacity are identifiable until well beyond the age of 60. So it is that most clinicians believe keeping the long-lived as active as possible, in the mainstream, reinforced by environmental stimulation, by common respect, and a mutual need for their performance, may result in the most enriched of later years. On the West Coast researchers found exercise expands the brain. At the University of California, Mark R. Rosenzweig (1972) countered an old dictum—the brain was physiologically unchanged by experience—and uncovered the phenomenon that the cerebral cortex, the nerve cell rich outer layer of the brain, changes in weight as a result of enriched experiences. It is something to think about when we advocate disengagement. This has also been observed in apes, as well as in humans—children and adults. Whenever taxed, resources are called upon, and everyone perks up, performs sometimes "superhuman" feats and may even develop ingenuous ideas. The challenge should be to learn what is the proper level of activity, training, and enriching experience for various older minds. Until we know such patterns, we can only respect findings which bring us to the point of appreciating Cumming's research, especially for its suggestion society is playing a minimal, unwilling, but crucially significant role. Without realizing it, Cumming was swimming against a stream or an avalanche of research findings and did not seem to take it all into account. Still, her initial hypothesis is in essential harmony with my own on depletion and depletion anxiety.

Other relevant studies tell us the elder can adjust, but at a slower rate of speed. Subjectively, he even experiences the duration of time as 3/5 that of clock time. To an observer he seems to show less need for change, avoiding it as much as he can. For reasons that seem clear, he keeps himself in familiar channels or in a routine environment, so as not to be disoriented. He moves slowly, so as to be able to process slowed incoming stimuli. There seems to be a decreased rate of biological interaction within the body, suggesting slowed metabolic processes. Some cellular regeneration, or return to more usual physiological equilibrium after stress or disuse, is accepted. Thus, there may even be various pacemakers built in to predetermine some of these changes which, with age, ultimately lead to a type of shut-off or, as Freud suggested, an intrinsic death force or built-in pattern leading to an inorganic state. Many elders, when overstimulated, do respond as if external reality (e.g., children and their noise) intruded on privacy, but in truth they experienced these as demands they were incapable of meeting. Rather than pleasure and enthusiasm, increased stimuli may elicit fear and avoidance. While we think of some of these people as bored, apathetic, and living a life of tedium, many elders tell us that waking up in the morning, getting dressed, having breakfast, shopping, lunching, resting in the P.M., possibly playing a card game or visiting, supping, and going to bed is a full-time occupation which takes all their resources. They really want no more to do. Some, but not all, are indeed contented with this disengaged state of affairs. The concept of time as "filled" or "empty" relates to needs and satisfactions, which may vary as age-specific changes occur. This must be included in our appreciation of what Cumming has found.

Furthermore, I have found there may be elements of shame and embarrassment about progressive impairments in self or spouse. A wife may find her husband's short-term memory loss, his limited capacity to concentrate on a task, to understand instructions about how to do simple things or play bridge extremely humiliating. Leaving the TV on, the record player running, something burning on the stove, or forgetting to button one's buttons or zipper one's fly—all lead to such embarrassment, the intact elder tends to reduce the possibility of exposure and criticism, even if it's primarily her own superego that's involved. In some cases treatment may reduce these responses and limit disengagement. Similarly, if one becomes aware of the potential gross errors in one's judgment, the possibility of not knowing about current events or general information others possess when the observing ego is still partly intact, one may accelerate disengagement, increase isolation, and hasten the depletion process. Deterioration in physical habits, in care of the self, in cleanliness, may mount to a point where it is better not to be seen or exposed. Old people still look for scapegoats and are never satisfied with the reality reasons dredged up for their normal aging. These ironies of aging may lead to depression and sometimes to a form of relative paranoia. Fate may have been unkind, children may be unappreciative, society ignoring and uncaring. Despite all this, some elders flourish while others form the type of interaction in which a part of the self, finding such painful reality too hard to bear, reactivates the past and begins to repeat stories of one's earlier life.

Thus, there are some who seemingly "choose" increasing isolation and seclusion, disengagement, or ultimate depletion as a way of responding to the demands to live up to an ego ideal which can no longer be met by diminishing resources. One can describe this as "free will," respond as if it were conscious and volitional, and listen to responses of the aged individual without concern for deeper emotional motivation and biological factors; and, as society has done, respond by withdrawal even if inappropriate and premature. The general belief that some outside force was involved, to impel, constrict, or inflict this fate, may lead to an accentuation of normal variations—especially paranoid ones—which, surprisingly, leads to a form of re-engagement. For example, one old couple is convinced they are bugged "a la Watergate" by their neighbors and make protective forays into society to protest.

In that work is generally regarded as expressive and non-instrumental with retirement, the former may assume primacy over instrumentality. There is a close connection between aging and the expectations of increased leisure time. In one study (Gordon, Gaitz, & Scott, 1973) 17 leisure time activities were found to decline with age in terms of participation, time spent therein, and number of interactions. These included dancing, drinking, listening, attending movies, travelling, reading, hunting, participating in sports or physical exercise. With the exception of reading, all these activities are done outside the home; involve substantial degrees of excitement, escape, and physical exertion; and are associated with markedly high intensity involvement. However, across age grades, four leisure time activities showed stable patterns—entertaining friends, television viewing, cultural consumption (e.g., listening to music), and cultural production (e.g., playing music, painting, and the like). Situated primarily within the home or context of family and friends, they showed little change with age and seem more sedentary, with lower levels of intensity. This research supports the concept of disengagement—should one differentiate intensity, home-centeredness, media-based symbolic interaction, etc.

Some other peaks of participation are clubs and organizations around ages 40 to 54; discussions on important issues, by age 65; observing spectator sports in both sexes either in public arenas or on television, by the age of 40.

Confusion Over Predictability of "Morale" Related to the Polarities of Ideals of Expanding vs. Diminishing Life Space

Cumming would regard "morale" as a dependent but irrelevant variable best excluded from such a study.

Criticism

When one listens to the theme related to "diminishing life space," one is hardly surprised to recognize that the phenomena reflects, to some degree at least, diminished motility and overall reserve capacity. This may be, under more favorable circumstances, attributable to decreased biological energy and diminished range of muscular and joint movement, but in less favorable ones, related to arthritic, cardiac, or CNS changes. Everyone old enough has lessened biological reserves for long trips and feels a need to conserve and protect one's self from stress and/or exertion. Through the middle years one learns to tolerate diminished cardiac output and to adjust to new rather than anachronistic schedules and demands. When organic changes (still dimly understood) enter the picture, one recognizes a lessened ability to learn, increased difficulty in concentration and memory, altered sense of time, and many other decremental variables. Still, I have not seen these phenomena generally advocated as "beneficial" or "mutually freeing." They may be of some psychological help for the inadequate personality who is looking forward to a release from responsibility, but for most characterological types, such developmental decrements are traumatic when perceived and may be partially or completely denied, with many deleterious, if insidious, effects. One does not willingly and mutually make "Lebensraum" for the younger generation or give up one's ego ideals, sense of mastery, sphere of influence, or power to control. To think so is to ignore human grief and suffering over losses of parts of the self even if altruistically and gracefully accomplished.

Cumming's observations of reduced numbers of interpersonal activities may well be related to the reluctance of old people to reinvest emotionally, or to risk grieving over and over again, just when so many losses have been and are being worked through. It is this very inability to fuel the fires of object ties which demands that society reach out, move in and attempt to refuel whenever possible. The human equation now demands the advocacy of input—not of disengagement.

Thus it is that the question of morale is intimately linked with the adaptive and grieving capacity of the ego. For the relatively intact, aging also brings with it a reawakening of conflicts, memories, and experiences of earlier years in the form of reminiscences—a turning inward, with the tendency to be absorbed in an abstract and intellectual exercise; taking an inventory of one's life; and attempting once again to master and work through the past in the poignant awareness of the limitation of the future. The need to accomplish what there is to accomplish in whatever remaining time is sensed may lead to a desperate attempt to engage, cling to, and even remake the real world. This final thrust of activity may lead one to ask new questions about the meaning of man's past and future, as well as one's own, in a creative, philosophical, historical effort at resynthesis. One tries to see what has been in order to assess what is and what can or should be in an individual or in the collective future. The ongoing process of depletion, disengagement, and restitution may result in a freeing of energy, and one spends time attempting to revive memories and experiences leading to a newly acquired sense of dignity and worth.

Some have reported feeling relieved or "freed" from the physical "duties" of sex, the obligations of family, work, or marital responsibility. Some have proceeded to mental achievement of a new and finer order. This can be possible even in the face of disastrous physical disease, as it was with Freud, who had a long history of cancer with interminable surgical efforts to relieve his pain and restore his speech. Despite this and advanced years, he never disengaged. Others, in the face of much less a catastrophe, lost morale and manifested evidence of what we call the "giving up phenomena." Most studies of morale point to the crucial variable—namely, the absence or presence of serious physical disease or important decrements in mental health—as determinants of major regressive changes. Many cope until they lose an important faculty, capacity, or significant other. In those where the death of a symbiotically involved person triggers a rapid disengagement or giving up, a constriction of life space and extraction from the mainstream of living or interaction follows almost immediately—but still not necessarily irreversibly. While morale may seem to be a dependent variable on some levels, I am not sure how to exclude it from a most significant role in our studies or in theories derived from these studies, and especially in therapeutic attempts to aid restitution. Disengagement and regression, in many cases, are appropriate. After a moratorium the individual and his culture should retain the capacity to generate the vital buoyancy of hope. Re-engagement is possible and should balance disengagement as restitution balances depletion.

The Normal Aging Process

Cumming (1975) currently adds, "We should have stuck to our question. Disengagement was addressed to normal aging, as the original study excluded the sick and the poor."

Criticism

Today it is hardly possible for geriatric experts to distinguish normal aging ("maturescence") from pathological implications of senescence related to organicity. Others (including this writer) remain confused about when normality merges into pathology and accordingly have always considered normal aging to be intimately involved with, or shade into, pathological processes. Remember, in our segment of the orchestra, we are likely to hear tones of deep sorrow; tragic, repeated themes of loss— sometimes in crescendo—summating in unbelievable proportions. We hear of progressive decline in problem-solving ability and navigational capacity, often linked to a painful, gradual dissolution of memory systems. One doesn't have to carry the musical analogy too far to appreciate how discordant it is to realize one cannot process, store, or retrieve certain types of new information. All too often we have witnessed the progress of tiny strokes, one after another, hardly noticed in the busy thrust of life. Clinically, I have found these small strokes all too often result in silent tragedies. They are like little thieves who rob people of their strength, creative ability, spontaneity, gaiety and longevity. With lessened resistance to infection; decreased ability to perform and act; diminished capacity to think, master and remember; declining physical strength, and with fewer resources in coping with stress, one is all too aware of the depletion of approximately 1-1½ percent per year of the organic structure and matrix of every organ and system within the body. I submit that normal aging is a randomly scattered series of progressive insults, diminishing peaks, major losses and impairments on *(1) organic or biological, (2) family, (3) social, (4) economic, and (5) abstract sublimated levels of life.* These pathological events of senescence I have subsumed under the concept of "normal depletion," something which will occur if one but lives long enough. I consider the basic divisions listed above as *five basic an-*

chorages of security. It is unfortunate, but many aged are forced to cope with depletion anxieties related to the losses in these basic anchorages in an environment that is negativistic, hostile, rejecting, and, in itself, sometimes pathologically unsupporting. So it may be his shrinking external world mirrors or reinforces the events within.

Summary

The phenomena under discussion transcend the very real distinctions between normal and abnormal, rich and poor. While many start with a marginal position in society, others end that way. All men must undergo the same critical losses and attempted restitutions. Disengagement Theory seems to me to have ignored in its conceptualizations and applications the genetic, fetal, environmental (good enough mothering and fathering), family, social, and economic anchorages, as well as much ecological and anthropological research. All evidence from such fields suggest the rich complexities of human existence. While some of these variables are difficult to evaluate in terms of present knowledge, much research starts off with an assumption that some of these issues are conceptualized and clarified enough to form a knowledge base not to be ignored.

Cumming's contributions lacked conceptual clarity and to some extent, still do. This leads to misunderstanding despite the essential truths contained in its sincere, well-meaning, scientific inquiry. Accordingly, we have a responsibility to listen to it and then attempt to integrate it into other sections of the orchestra.

I believe Cumming was correctly attuned to the elders' social and economic anchorages of security. I would think the enigmas to which she addressed herself (as I and others have also done) can be phrased as: *"How does one extricate one's self gracefully and effectively from no-longer-appropriate obligatory demands on one's behavior and resources characteristic of the child-bearing-rearing and work-a-day world without extricating one's self from life-support and enhancing systems and/or exchanges?"*

Her error was not to clarify these distinctions and to ignore the contributions of the biological studies, the socio-physical basic family structure, and the sublimated levels of life, which include some of the most meaningful purposes that the human mind can devise. Furthermore, the concept that this was a mutually freeing and a somewhat beneficial process for the normal population obviously fails to take into account the complexities involved and may encourage greater geronto-rejecting attitudes.

Not only is man a unique conglomeration of atoms, molecules, cells, organs, and systems, but also a miracle of evolution, growth, and development. The odds against these parts integrating into a whole human, functioning perfectly according to a predetermined time schedule based upon average expectations, seems stupendous. That all humans on this earth could or would age in the same way, from any psychological, sociological, or demographic point of view, can only be extended so far. When we present any image of man to other people, we must take into account unique variations. Not only are the whorls of each fingertip of each individual different from others, but life styles have remarkable individual variations stamped into them. Acclimated as we try to be to the expectations of aging and death, we are denying them simultaneously. There is a strange paradoxical awareness and denial of all the processes under discussion. The human brain, while private in its utmost recesses, is remarkably open to modification by incoming stimuli. So, behavioral conditioning, learning, and multiple sources of motivation derived from experiences, conscience, instinctual needs, habitual gratification, and our social environment all become grist for the mill of restitution. As we attempt to understand the depression-depletion-disengagement phenomenon, the output of various sections of the scientific orchestra may yield a more harmonious whole.

References

Cumming, E., Dean, L. R., Newell, D.S., & McCaffrey, I. Disengagement, a Tentative Theory of Aging. *Sociometry*, 1960, 23:23-25.

Cumming, E. Engagement with an Old Theory. *Aging and Human Development*, 1975.

Gordon, C., Gaitz, C. M., & Scott, J. Value Priorities and Leisure Activities among Middle Aged and Older Anglos. *Diseases of the Nervous System*, 1973, 34: 1, 13-26.

Lewinsohn, P. M., & MacPhillamy, D. J. The Relationship between Age and Engagement in Pleasant Activities. *Journal of Gerontology*, 1974, 29: 3, 290-294.

Rosenzweig, M. R. Keep that Brain Busy. *Parade* (magazine), 5/7/72.

2.3

Aging as Exchange:
A Preface to Theory

James J. Dowd

Theoretical development within social gerontology has been limited to date to an almost exclusive preoccupation with the theories of *disengagement* and *activity*. The absence of alternative paradigmatic development in the study of aging is especially puzzling, since both of these approaches have been found wanting empirically. The tradition of life satisfaction researches within social gerontology—life satisfaction considered to be the correlational attribute *sine qua non* of both disengagement and activity theories—is illustrative of our lack of a reliable inventory of tested propositions.

The essence of Activity theory has been stated to be the "positive relationship between activity and life satisfaction." Consequently, the "greater the role loss, the lower the life satisfaction" (Lemon, Bengtson, & Peterson, 1972). These hypotheses have been tested on numerous occasions with very little, if any, of the findings achieving even the most modest consensus. (For an overview of this controversy see, for example, Adams, 1971; Alston & Dudley, 1973; Cumming & Henry, 1961; Cutler, 1973; Edwards & Klemmack, 1973; Lemon et al., 1972; Martin, 1973; Tallmer & Kutner, 1970; Tobin & Neugarten, 1961; Youmans, 1969.)

Copyright 1975 by The Gerontological Society. Reprinted by permission. *Journal of Gerontology*, 1975, Vol. 30, No. 5, pp. 584-594.

What seems so obviously necessary, then, in this stage of development of social gerontological theory is a new beginning. The disengagement/activity paradigm which has guided research for almost 15 years must be shelved—if at least only temporarily—in order to provide the opportunity for competing views of human behavior in the later stages of the life cycle to emerge. The developing sociology of age stratification represents an important and promising contribution in this regard; its focus, however, is less *old* age than it is *age per se*. What follows is an initial attempt at theory construction—a prolegomenon—which will hopefully anticipate a larger theoretical base within social gerontology. The intent is to draw upon the research tradition known as Exchange theory, particularly the later developments of this theory which detail the nexus between exchange and power, in order to reconceptualize the relationship between age and social structure as—above all else—a process of exchange.

Disengagement and Activity Theories of Aging

In order to briefly summarize the essential postulates of the disengagement and activity theories of aging, it may prove beneficial to follow the lead of Rose (1964) and first describe what the theories are not. Disengagement theory, although consistent with, is not identical to the oft-observed generalizations that, as people get older, they become increasingly removed from their associations and social functions; or, as their health deteriorates and income becomes depleted, older persons are often forced to abandon these same associations and functions. What the theory of disengagement does refer to, as detailed in Cumming and Henry's *Growing Old* (1961), is the hypothesis that

> society and the individual prepare *in advance* for the ultimate "disengagement" of incurable, incapacitating disease and death by an *inevitable, gradual, and mutually satisfying process of disengagement from society* (Rose, 1964).

The disengagement postulates stress the fact that the decreased rates of social interaction observed in the daily lives of older persons, in addition to being functionally advantageous to both the individual and the larger society, are often initiated by the older person himself. It is often, but not necessarily, a voluntary process satisfying to the individual because of the increased personal autonomy induced by decreased expectations of normative behavior and the opportunities for leisure time; it is functional for society as the disengagement of the older person releases his formerly held roles and statuses for the eventual occupancy by younger and presumably more efficient role incumbents (cf. Atchley, 1971; Cumming, 1964; Cumming, Dean, Newell, & McCaffrey, 1960; Havighurst, Neugarten, & Tobin, 1964; Tissue, 1968).

Activity theory, often proferred as an alternative explanation of social aging supposedly contradistinctive to the disengagement hypothesis, actually assumes much the same behavioral phenomena in old age as disengagement theory. Neither theory argues that old age is characterized by anything but a generalized decrease in social interaction.

Although some advocates of activity theory have designed studies relating life satisfaction with degree of social interaction as a "critical test" of the disengagement/activity debate (a finding of life satisfaction positively associated with greater degrees of social interaction taken as supportive of activity theory), most statements of activity theory do not deny the disengagement theory postulate that old age is characterized by decreased social interaction. They, too, take as "given" the assumption that, vis-à-vis younger statistical aggregates, the rate of social interaction for older persons is just not as great.

The specific difference between the two theories concerns whether the observed negative association between aging and social interaction is voluntary and preceded by psychological disengagement on the part of the individual or imposed unilaterally on the individual by the structural requirements of the society (Havighurst, 1968; Lowenthal & Boler, 1965). Supporters of an activity theory of aging posit the latter and offer as proof the positive correlation often reported between higher levels of social interaction and life satisfaction (Carp, 1968; Lipman & Smith, 1968; Maddox, 1963; Prasad, 1964).

The conclusion often drawn is that neither theory is sufficient by itself to explain all of the myriad patterns of aging, many of which require further information of a sociological and social psychological nature to elaborate meaningfully. Disengagement theory appears hopelessly antiquated in its functionalist insistence on the necessity of social withdrawal for "successful aging" (read morale and sense of well-being). Activity theory, on the other hand, is less an actual theory complete with defined concepts and empirically verifiable propositions than it is a well-intentioned, but thoroughly value-laden response to the less-than-ebullient characterization of aging attributed to the disengagement theorists. Neither theory, however, while focusing for the most part on descriptive accounts of the peculiar relationships between social interaction and life satisfaction, attempts to offer anything but the most perfunctory of explanations for the *decreased social interaction* itself. Rather, this phenomenon is given the status of a sociological "given"; that is, it is treated as something requiring no additional explanation. The fact of the decreased interaction in old age, considered in this fashion as a nonproblematic "given," may subsequently be included in a particular test of a theory—not as the problem itself—but merely as an empirical touchstone, a datum against which the conclusions from the major analysis are later measured. For some, the reasons appear all too obvious: decreased social interaction is "simply a matter of logic and has long been known to be a fact" (Rose, 1964).

The methodological difficulty which this assumption poses for both the disengagement and activity theories of aging (and, for that matter, theory construction in social gerontology generally) is that the answer to *why* social interaction decreases in old age can be so effortlessly produced as to effectively preclude further search for possible alternative responses. The reason is simple: older persons as a statistical aggregate suffer from lower income and poorer health than their more youthful counterparts (Palmore & Whittington, 1971). Consequently, they are physically and financially unable to be "engaged" to the same degree as when they were younger. Furthermore, the loss of role partners through the death of a spouse, friend or relation—a frequent occurrence in old age—places additional limits on the range of possible interaction available to the aged individual.

It is upon this mutually shared perspective, then, that the activity and disengagement theories are built. I contend that the commonsense logic of this assumption, while compelling in its face-validity, has functioned to divert more systematic analyses into its *why* component. No one can argue convincingly against the hypothesis that failing health or lowered income tends to stifle social interaction. But is it not possible that additional factors might also be operating to produce the same phenomenon and which, going unrecognized and, hence, not taken explicitly into account, precludes the construction of a complete theory? This, it would seem, has been the case with previous attempts at theory construction in social gerontology. They have failed to recognize that decreased social interaction in old age is a result, not only of the previously mentioned conditions of widowhood, poor health, and lowered income, but also of an intricate process of exchange between society and the aged resulting from their power-dependent relationship. This is the alternative perspective of aging developed through an exchange theory analysis of the problem.

The remaining pages will be an attempt to elaborate this exchange view of aging, beginning with the innovative notion of social behavior as offered by Homans (1961) and further developed by Blau (1964) and Emerson (1962, 1972) in their analyses of exchange and power in social life and power-dependence relations.

Exchange Theory—Introduction

While very few social gerontologists continue to seriously espouse a disengagement view of the aging process, the theoretical void left by its discreditation leaves one to wonder whether the cure has been any more tolerable than the original ailment. That the disengagement postulate was very limited in its generalizability is a well-supported criticism. In its functionalist statements concerning the *mutual* process of disengagement between society and the individual, the theory clearly failed to recognize the implicit power advantage—and the consequent threat of future reprisal—society may utilize to achieve its desired ends. The disengagement theorists tacitly accept the functionalist dictum that because a certain structure exists, it is functional. Because the aging individual is observed to give up social roles and statuses, this disengagement is posited to be mutually desired and mutually benefiting for both the individual and the society. One advantage of an exchange theory approach to social aging in our society would be a rejection of the functionalist-disengagement notion of reciprocity and an explicit analysis of both sides of each social transaction (or exchange) as problematic (cf., Wallace, 1969).

Exchange Theory: Concepts and Propositions

The basic assumption underlying much of the research collectively known as exchange theory is that interaction between individuals or collectivities can be characterized as "attempts to maximize rewards (both material and non-material) and reduce costs (both material and non-material)" (Knipe, 1971). Certain patterns of interaction among social actors (either groups or individuals) are sustained over time not, as the functionalists would have it, because there exist normative expectations specifying the maintenance of such an interaction or because such a pattern of interaction fulfills some socially required need; rather, interaction is maintained because men find such interaction rewarding—for whatever reasons. In the process of seeking rewards, however—whether the rewarding activity be intrinsic to the interaction itself such as love or extrinsic to the relationship such as an exchange of recipes among gourmet cooks—*costs* are inevitably incurred. Costs refer either to the negative value or unpleasantness actually experienced in the course of obtaining a reward or to the positive value associated with an alternative course of action which is forsaken to pursue the chosen rewarding activity. In effect, therefore, all behavior entails costs even if the cost involved is only the probability of rewards that are associated with activity other than the activity presently being pursued. As in economic exchanges, the profit one derives from social exchange is equivalent to the difference between rewards minus costs (Homans, 1961). A major proposition of exchange theory is that interaction between two or more social actors will most probably be continued and positively evaluated if the actors "profit" from the interaction. In other words, actors engaged in an exchange of behavior will continue their exchange only so long as the exchange is perceived as being more rewarding than it is costly (cf., Byrne, 1971; Shaw & Costanzo, 1970).

It is often the case that one of the participants in the exchange values the rewards gained in the relationship more than the other. It is in these situations that the variable of *power* enters the analysis. The exchange theorist's view of power is that it is derived from imbalances in the social exchange. From this perspective, power is synonymous with the dependence of Actor A upon Actor B. It is based in the inability of one of the partners in the social exchange to reciprocate a rewarding behavior. As we shall see in our analysis of the exchange relationship between the aged and society, whoever "commands services others need, and who is independent of any at their command, attains power over others by making the satisfaction of their need contingent on their compliance" (Blau, 1964). The compliance of the dependent partner in the exchange thus becomes an important source of rewarding, albeit costly, behavior which he can then exchange for continued rewards from the other partner in the interaction. Thus, for Blau, much of social life is

> an intricate exchange in which every participant in interaction approaches and withdraws in patterns that add to or subtract from his store of power and prestige. Everyone accumulates, by the judicious use of favors and services, a credit of power which he then invests in subsequent transaction (Bierstedt, 1965).

Aging as a Process of Social Exchange

Having elaborated the essential concepts and propositions of the exchange paradigm, we return now to the question raised earlier, namely, how do we account for the decreased social interaction frequently observed in the daily lives of older persons in our society? Acknowledging that the tremendous impact associated with impaired health, depleted income, and/or the loss of a spouse or associate is partially responsible for this phenomenon, it is our position that an exchange analysis of the problem would enable the researcher to discover addi-

Table 1.   Constructs of Exchange Theory

		Society	
Readiness to Disengage		Positive	Negative
	Positive	a. Power balance: Mutually satisfying exchange.	b. Power imbalance: The individual with critical expertise is forced to remain engaged.
Individual	Negative	c. Power imbalance: The individual with little critical expertise is forced to disengage.	d. Power balance: Continued role incumbency is institutionally sanctioned, e.g., religious and political leaders.

tional—and heretofore untapped—sources of variation. The perspective discussed above, and in the pages that follow, emphasizes the concept of human behavior as an exchange of more or less rewarding behaviors between two or more social actors. Intrinsic to the concept of exchange is the notion of power. As discussed above, the partner in a social exchange who is less dependent on that exchange for the gratifications he seeks enjoys a *power advantage*. Such an advantage can then be utilized to effect compliance from the exchange partner.

In the case of the aged, decreased social interaction is the eventual result of a series of exchange relationships in which the relative power of the aged vis-à-vis their social environment is gradually diminished until all that remains of their power resources is the humble capacity to comply. Where once the now-retired worker was able to exchange expertise for needed wages, the final exchange required of most older workers would be their compliance (in the form of acquiescence to mandatory retirement) as exchange for sustenance (Social Security, Medicare, etc.).

Disengagement theory's view of the problem, while objectionable in its functionalist view of disengagement as mutually satisfying, is nonetheless accurate in its identification of the problems of aging as those caused by the frequent lack of equilibrium between the individual's readiness to withdraw from his social world and the requirements of the social structure for continuous succession of role incumbents. We can formalize this general statement on personal versus societal readiness to disengage with the constructs of exchange theory.

From Table 1, one can see that the probability of continued engagement in social relationships is principally a function of the existing power relationships between the aging role incumbent and the society. In both instances of power imbalance included in this Table (cells b & c), the power advantage favors society. This is the case in modern postindustrial society with its constant demand for current knowledge and technological innovation. The skills of many aged individuals become quickly outmoded, presuming they were sufficiently adequate in the first place. As power generally accrues from the prestige associated with higher status occupations, the supply of power resources of the older worker frequently is meager from the start; hence, the bargaining position of the aged social actor upon retirement quickly deteriorates as his supply of power resources becomes depleted.

This table, then, is obviously time- and culture-bound, representing the structural realities of twentieth century industrial society. The aged of pre-industrial society, for example, were able to accumulate a much larger share of power resources than their twentieth century counterparts (cf., Adams, 1972; Cowgill & Holmes, 1972). They engaged in exchanges more often voluntarily than not, of expertise gained from a lifetime of living in a much more stable society for deference and prestige. With the onset of the Industrial Revolution, however, and the concomitant specialization of knowledge, the aged have had less to offer. The actual craft or trade or the more general expertise of leadership and experience which sufficed as barter in exchanges of long ago are no longer considered rewarding. Consequently, whatever power advantage they once enjoyed gradually shifted to others in the society. And, as the growth rate increased in exponential leaps and bounds, the relative power of the aged decreased further as the resultant surfeit of available labor decreased their range of available employment opportunities.

This interpretation is supported by recent cohort analyses that suggest the difference between older and younger age cohorts is not so much the debilitating aspects of aging *per se* that result in the differential patterns of attitude constellations, cognitive functioning, and task efficiency, etc., as it is the tremendous modal differences in the cohort-defining experiences of educational level, socioeconomic status of the family of origin, and occupational aspirations. From this view, the problem of the older worker is not only his diminished skills but also the fact that he was never trained initially in skills which are currently marketable (Cutler, 1974; Glenn & Zody, 1970; Riley, 1973; Ryder, 1965).

The institutionalization of *retirement*, where the older worker was mandatorily—and often involuntarily—released from the work force, was an inevitable outcome. In order to legitimate this forceful removal as an equitable exchange, the aged were allowed a much wider range for deviant behavior; the "role" of the retired older person in our society prescribes greater freedom to deviate from normative expectations based on the work ethic. In effect, society exchanges leisure time (and the financial burden thereof) for additional positions in the work force.

The difference between this view and that of disengagement theory is not that professional social scientists like Cumming and Henry fail to recognize that older members of society are regularly discarded to make room for the younger. Rather, it is a matter of ideological commitment. Like other structural-functionalists, Cumming and Henry are unable to accept the possibility that men are *forced* to act—not because that act is normatively governed—but simply because they have no other reasonable alternative. Disengagement theorists are well aware that the disproportionately large number of young adults who are competing for the jobs that are becoming more scarce as industry automates are forcing older workers from the job market. Their particular set of lenses through which they view the world allows them only to recognize what is functional for society. That certain institutions may not be "mutually satisfying" to the individual remains, for them, a source of wonderment (cf., Cumming, 1964).

The Nature of Exchange: Power-Dependence Relations

As Emerson (1962) has noted, power resides implicitly in the Other's dependence. Dependence of actor A on actor B (notable as D_{ab}) is both directly proportional to actor A's motivational investment in the rewards offered by actor B, and inversely proportional to the availability of those rewards to actor A from sources other than B. If both parties in the exchange relation are equally dependent upon each other (that is to say, they both are equally desirous of the rewards offered by the other and have similar outside resources from which to obtain the reward), the relation is said to be *balanced*. When the exchange relation is unbalanced, the exchange partner who is the more dependent—hence less powerful—will attempt to rebalance the relation and thereby reduce the costs he incurs from the exchange. Emerson notes that the relation can be balanced through one of four possible *balancing operations*:

(a.) *Withdrawal*, i.e., motivational investment in rewards offered by the Other is reduced. This is the balancing operation clearly descriptive of Cumming and Henry's disengaged individual.

(b.) *Extension of Power Network*, i.e., alternative sources of the rewarding behavior are cultivated. Unlike the disengagement implied in the first example, this balancing operation resembles more activity theory's protestations supporting the development of new roles for the aged.

(c.) *Emergence of Status*, i.e., motivational investment in rewards offered by the less powerful partner is increased by the more powerful partner. The exchange relation could be balanced by the emergence of status of the less powerful partner as when, for example, revivals of formerly valued skills (e.g., the knowledge of construction of pot-bellied stoves during an energy crisis) serve to increase his power resources.

(d.) *Coalition Formation*, i.e., the more powerful member is denied alternative sources for achieving his goals. The interesting possibility of a coalition forming between older and younger cohorts is often hypothesized as a means of equalizing the power of the wage-earning middle-aged cohorts.

Should none of these options be exercised—which has been the case with the majority of older persons in our society—the less dependent and therefore more powerful participants in the relation (i.e., the middle-aged and young adult cohorts) are able to establish a rate of exchange favorable to them. The danger for the less powerful partner—the aged—is that, once established, this unbalanced exchange rate becomes institutionalized and thereby provides a normative basis for future unbalanced exchanges (cf., Martin, 1971). As for the claims that the aged are not really powerless or that the relation between the larger society and the aged is one of balance, the evidence clearly indicates otherwise (Blau, 1973; Clark, 1972).

Positing, then, that the aged as a group are less powerful than younger age cohorts in our society, the next question to be answered concerns the actual use of power. In Emerson's (1972) scheme, power is not a discrete quantity of stuff which can be used or not used voluntarily or only at certain times. Rather, to have power is to use it. If A has a power advantage in his exchange relation with B, and if B has additional resources potentially rewarding to A, "A's use of power will increase, cutting further into B's resources, until its use is offset by incurred or anticipated costs to A." Only if the relation is balanced, where $P_{ab} = D_{ba}$ and $P_{ba} = D_{ab}$, will an increased use of power be unlikely.

The relationship between the aged and society, previously defined as an unbalanced exchange relation, is consequently one in which power is being exercised. Of course, the power being utilized in this case is not the power afforded by a superior military force or technological expertise; rather, it is the economic and social dependence of the elderly—legitimated by persistent social norms that specify many adult behaviors as inappropriate for those who have reached a certain age—which is the source of society's power. The younger worker who is promoted into a position left vacant by the retirement of its former occupant certainly does not perceive that power has been utilized in his behalf or that the retired role incumbent was in any way in competition with him. Yet we would only have to consider the probable sequence of events that would result should that older worker have refused to leave his particular machine or office to retire. Because most individuals have sufficiently internalized societal norms specifying institutions such as retirement as legitimate, the specter of society's sanctioning power is rarely realized. Yet in the individual relations between the aged and other groups in society, power *is* being used.

Many of these exchange relations between the aged and other age-groups within society can be seen as a special case of the balancing operation described above as Coalition Formation. Blau (1964) notes that, in any complex organization with given limited resources,

> it is only possible for management to balance one exchange relationship by unbalancing others. As one group gains a relative advantage, other groups are roused into opposition . . . .

It is important, then, in attempting to understand the exchange between management and the older worker, we include in the analysis a consideration of the relationship between management and the remainder of the work force. Younger workers exchange their labor for wages and the implicit promise of job security and promotions. However, as the older worker remains on the job, he is blocking this path of career mobility for younger work cohorts. Hence, the forced retirement of older workers or the decision of employers to divert more monies into increased wages than into employee pension plans reflect the changes within formal organizations that Blau (1964) argues

> tend to take a dialectical form as the intermittent refocusing of conflict and consensus is accompanied by realignment of internal exchange relationships.

Table 2.   Types of Rewards (or Power Resources)

| | Type of reward | | |
	Intrinsic	Extrinsic	Unilateral
Spontaneous evaluation	Personal attraction	Social approval	Respect–prestige
Calculated action	Social acceptance	Instrumental services	Compliance–power

Source: Blau, 1964.

Aging and the decline of power

Prerequisite to the exercise of power, however, is the possession of sufficient power resources. Resources are essentially anything which the exchange partner perceives as rewarding and which consequently renders him susceptible to social influence. Examples of power resources include money, knowledge, persuasiveness, and social position.

A frequent exchange entered into by most older people is the exchange of his position in the labor force for the promise of economic and medical sustenance in the form of Social Security and Medicare. Or, the widowed woman living with her married children may be required to exchange compliance or approval for her room and board. The possible exchange situations are of infinite variety but, in general, the types of rewards (or power resources) are shown in Table 2.

From an exchange theory perspective, then, the problems of aging are essentially problems of *decreasing power resources*. The aged have very little to exchange which is of any instrumental value. What skills they once had are often outmoded; the skills which remain can often be provided more efficiently and with less cost by others. Since the aged have no specific benefit—or power resource—to offer their exchange partner, they typically have no alternative but to offer some generally available response which is universally experienced as rewarding. In Blau's analysis of exchange and power, there appear to be four such generalized power resources: money, approval, esteem or respect, and compliance.

Money, even if the older retiree was able to afford parting with it, is "clearly inappropriate as a means of repaying diffuse social obligations" (Mulkay, 1971). A dinner invitation can hardly be repaid with a personal check. Approval would be an effective power resource were it not for the fact that approval is too plentiful and easy to obtain to be sufficiently rewarding. Consequently, esteem and compliance are the resources that generally tend to be utilized as social currency in exchange relations. Since esteem is the less costly of the two, it is the resource which is exchanged first. The older worker may attempt to exchange esteem for a lightened workload or his supervisor's tolerance of his decreased efficiency. However, esteem is a commodity the value of which decreases quickly in subsequent exchanges. Consequently, in exchanges of longer duration it is, as Mulkay (1971) indicates, "unlikely to prove an adequate incentive for those making particularly valuable contributions to the group." As a result, those exchange partners who are receiving valued benefits are obliged to reciprocate in some new and equally rewarding manner. It is at this stage that compliance, a very costly commodity, enters into the exchange ratio.

When the esteem offered by the older worker no longer is sufficiently rewarding, he must resort to compliance, as when, for example, the older executive is forced to comply with management's wishes for him to "step down" to a less prestigious and responsible position or to suffer a decrease in salary. Eventually, the older worker must comply with management's demands for his resignation in the guise of retirement. Over the years, as this scenario has been repeated countless times, the process has become routinized, institutionalized, and legitimated. Indeed, the actual event known as retirement more accurately refers to a series of events—or exchange relations—in which the power advantage favors the employer:

> In this exchange relationship . . . the employee is more dependent than is the employer and accordingly more effectively controlled by the threat of negative sanctions (Mulkay, 1971).

Disengagement as exchange

One answer, therefore, to why people disengage may not be because it is mutually satisfying for themselves and society to do so but rather because in the exchange relation between the aged and society, society enjoys a distinct power advantage. As to the question of how did this unbalanced exchange relation evolve with society as the more powerful partner, the answer is that by being in the enviable position of "providing unilateral benefits to others (read the aged), ...

(society) accumulates a capital of willing compliance on which he can draw whenever it is to his interest to impose his will . . . " (Blau, 1964).

Due to this legitimating function of social norms, the behavior of older persons is governed and restricted further by the sanctioning power of other older persons themselves. The older person who restricts his social life for fear of what his acquaintances would think is actually exchanging his compliance to their standards of acceptable conduct for their social approval. This exchange is interesting because it illustrates the double bind less powerful groups face when power is supported by social norms—they suffer possible reprisal not only from the group which possesses the power but also from within the boundaries of their own group as well. Mulkay (1971) explains:

> As power becomes mediated through legitimating norms, the processes of exchange involved become increasingly complex and indirect. Before power has been recognized as legitimate there is a relatively direct exchange between persons of high and low status. Those with high status provide valuable services while those with low status respond with esteem and compliance. Once power is supported by social norms, however, a new type of transaction develops among subordinates. For subordinates now receive approval from their peers, as well as from their leaders, for complying with the directives of those in authority. The act of compliance is no longer solely a means of rewarding one's superiors for valued services; it is also a request for approval from the collectivity at large. These transactions with peers introduce additional pressures for compliance. For they constrain individuals inclined to resist particular directives to submit rather than forego the approval of their colleagues.

The pressure from his peers, together with the tremendous costs incurred by remaining engaged, offers a possible explanation of why some older persons seemed resigned to, even welcome, the opportunity to disengage. Because of their limited power resources, the costs of remaining engaged—that is, the costs in compliance and self-respect—steadily increase. Finally the point is reached beyond which additional costs become prohibitive. This is the phenomenon of disengagement.

It has been noted that disengagement from certain social institutions is inversely related to disengagement from other institutions (Carp, 1968). So, for example, the retired couple who interact less with their former friends and acquaintances often increase their frequency of interaction with their family. The explanation offered by Carp is that disengagement from either family or other significant reference or membership groups requires an increased dependence on the group(s) remaining. This very dependence, however, places the aged family member in another unbalanced exchange relationship with his increased dependence serving to again limit his potential power in the relationship.

A recent study of retirees in France lends support to this analysis. Focusing on the changes in family relationships resulting from retirement, the authors posit a direct relationship between power resources and degree of autonomy within the family:

> . . . We should observe that the greater the retiree's economic and cultural patrimony to transmit to his children, the more he will actualize an organic and dominating familial solidarity. A situation of dispossession would lead him to contract organically solid familial exchanges, but which express a relation of dependence to the family. A medium level of resources would lead the retiree to maintain an autonomous relation with his family (Guillemard & Lenoir, 1974).

The cycle of exchange of esteem followed by compliance for the rewards of social acceptance, human interaction and the satisfaction of his other human needs is repeated, following closely the pattern of exchange of the older worker (cf., Nord, 1969). The observations of Blau (1973) illustrate this point:

> The appearance of "mellowness" in many older people is a tactic to win acceptance and support. To protest their marginality would only alienate others, and this the person without any socially useful role cannot do because he lacks the opportunities for finding alternative social resources to replace his remaining social ties.

Propositions

Two basic propositions can be drawn from this exchange theory analysis of aging in contemporary industrial society. From a macro-societal perspective, it can be observed that the amount of power resources possessed by the aged relative to other age strata is inversely related to the degree of societal modernization. Unlike the aged in more traditional societies, older people in industrialized societies have precious few power resources to exchange in daily social interaction. The net effect is an increased dependence upon others and the concomitant necessity to comply to their wishes. Mandatory retirement as a social policy is the most obvious result of this lack of power resources and consequent lack of power among the aged. A correlated hypothesis, stating an inverse relationship between societal modernization and status of the aged, has recently been tested and supported by various researchers (Palmore & Whittington, 1971; Cowgill & Holmes, 1972; Press & McKool, 1972; Bengtson, Dowd, & Smith, 1975).

The second proposition, reflecting a more micro-orientation, posits a curvilinear relationship between chronological age and the degree of power resources. Possession of power resources tends to be limited in youth, increasing through late middle age, and decreasing sharply in old age. More than any other social event, the phenomenon of retirement is directly related with the precipitous decline of power resources beyond middle age. A previous analysis by Abarbanel (1974) of ethnographic data from 47 societies supports the notion of a curvilinear relationship between age and control of power resources. Abarbanel found that control over most resources began before or immediately after marriage; peaked at the time termed middle family phase, that is, when the children are adolescents and the family labor force is most productive; and declined either in the latter part of the middle phase or in the late phase of the family cycle, when children marry and leave home. However, in terms of control of positions of political and spiritual leadership, Abarbanel reports that the peak control in preindustrial, nonurban societies is not reached until the late family phase.

The relationship stated here between age and power resources reflects current realities and need not, therefore, be characteristic of aging in the future. Several trends, if continued, may anticipate a much less drastic decline in power resources in old age. Higher levels of education predicted for future aged cohorts, for example, would constitute a power resource of considerable significance. So, too, the growing public concern over pension funds and social security financing may lead to legislation promoting greater economic autonomy of older persons through regulated pension plans, increased social security benefits and, even, the re-employment of the older worker in a part-time capacity. The point is that there is nothing inherent in the aging process itself that necessitates a decline in individual power resources. The nature and degree of power resources possessed by any group of older persons is a function of shared cohort experience in addition to individual attributes.

The relationship between chronological age and possession of power resources must be further specified as to individual socio-economic status and ethnicity. Those fortunate enough to possess con-

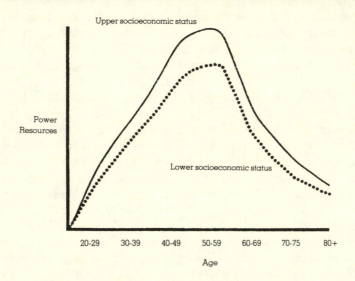

Figure 1. Hypothesized relationship between control of power resources and age, within categories of socioeconomic status

siderable economic capital beyond retirement possess a power resource of undeniable importance. Socioeconomic status constitutes, in effect, a critical control variable in the relationship between age and power resources. The nature of the relationship, except in those rare cases of extreme wealth, does not change markedly with increased SES; it is more a case that, within a particular age stratum, the higher SES individuals will generally possess the greater power resources. Across age strata, however, the curvilinear relationship will tend to hold. The effect of SES is represented in Fig. 1.

Summary and Conclusions

Exchange theory is a unique perspective of human behavior, one which views social interaction as basically an exchange of rewards between two social actors, be they individuals or groups of individuals. Similar to the economic transactions of, say, currency for either goods or services, it remains true in social exchange that "money talks." Whichever party in the exchange relation possesses the greater degree of social power (as with money) is the party which is able to control the rate of exchange and the distribution of rewards, or profits, among the parties to the exchange. So, unlike both disengagement and activity theories, an exchange theory of aging predicts outcomes of variable interaction and level of engagement in old age depending upon the relative power of the individual older person or group of older persons vis-à-vis the source of the rewarding interaction, society.

Activity theory assumes the need for continued involvement throughout life; disengagement theory assumes that decline in involvement may be a phenomenon mutually desired by both individual and society. Exchange theory assumes neither but posits that the degree of engagement in old age is an empirical question, an outcome of a specific exchange relationship between an individual or group of individuals and the society in which the more powerful exchange partner dictates the terms of the relationship.

A serious limitation of the exchange approach summarized here has been recognized by Emerson (1972) as an inability to predict which of the four balancing operations (Withdrawal, Network Extension, Status-giving, or Coalition Formation) will be adopted at any one time. Although coalition formation appears to be the most potent alternative (the possibility of the aged coalescing with younger age-groups is indeed intriguing, albeit improbable), the aged themselves have yet to develop any extensive awareness of their common social and economic plight which is a necessary prerequisite to entering into coalitions. The aged have yet to display the emotional response to distributive injustice that Homans (1961) has so carefully operationalized as "anger."

Yet the fact that distributive justice is not being realized in the daily lives of many older persons is readily apparent. After a lifetime of investment in the forms of career, family, reputation, community service, etc., the aged are forced to endure the ignominy of prestige loss, social and economic discrimination, poverty-level subsistence, and social isolation. Blau (1964) acknowledges that although common norms develop in most societies that stipulate fair rates of exchange between investments and rewards, the going rates in many groups nevertheless depart from the fair rates, "making it impossible for some individuals to realize a fair return on their investments." Blau goes on to state that some individuals

> cannot even realize the *going* rate in their exchange transactions because factors other than these social norms and standards also affect exchange processes, notably the conditions of supply and demand in particular groups and the power relations that have developed.

It is our contention that this has been the case with the aged.

References

Abarbanel, J. S. Prestige of the aged and their control over resources: A cross-cultural analysis. Paper presented at 1974 annual meeting of the Gerontological Society (Portland).

Adams, D. L. Correlates of satisfaction among the elderly. *Gerontologist*, 1971, *11*, 64-68.

Adams, F. M. The role of old people in Santo Tomas, Mazaltepec. In D. O. Cowgill & L. D. Holmes (Eds.), *Aging and modernization*. Appleton-Century-Crofts, New York, 1972.

Alston, J. P., & Dudley, C. J. Age, occupation, and life satisfaction. *Gerontologist*, 1973, *13*, 58-61.

Atchley, R. C. Disengagement among professors. *Journal of Gerontology*, 1971, *26*, 476-480.

Bengtson, V. L., Dowd, J. J., & Smith, D. H. Modernization, modernity and perceptions of aging. *Journal of Gerontology*, 1975.

Bierstedt, R. Review of Blau's exchange and power in social life. *American Sociological Review*, 1965, *30*, 789-790.

Blau, P. M. *Exchange and power in social life*. John Wiley & Sons, New York, 1964.

Blau, Z. S. *Old age in a changing society*. New Viewpoints, New York, 1973.

Byrne, J. J. Systematic analysis and exchange theory: A synthesis. *Pacific Sociological Review*, 1971, *14*, 137-146.

Carp, F. M. Some components of disengagement. *Journal of Gerontology*, 1968, *23*, 382-386.

Clark, M. Cultural values and dependency in later life. In D. O. Cowgill & L. Holmes (Eds.), *Aging and modernization*. Appleton-Century-Crofts, New York, 1972.

Cowgill, D. O., & Holmes, L. D. (Eds.), *Aging and modernization*. Appleton-Century-Crofts, New York, 1972.

Cumming, E. New thought on old age. In R. Kastenbaum (Ed.), *New thoughts on old age*. Springer, New York, 1964.

Cumming, E., Dean, L. R., Newell, D. S., & McCaffrey, I. Disengagement: A tentative theory of aging. *Sociometry*, 1960, *23*, 23-25.

Cumming, E., & Henry, W. E. *Growing old: The process of disengagement*. Basic Books, New York, 1961.

Cutler, N. E. Aging and generations in politics: The conflict of explanations and inference. In A. R. Wilcox (Ed.), *Public opinion and political attitudes*. Wiley, New York, 1974.

Cutler, S. J. Voluntary association participation and life satisfaction: A cautionary note. *Journal of Gerontology*, 1973, *28*, 96-100.

Edwards, J. N., & Klemmack, D. L. Correlates of life satisfaction: A reexamination. *Journal of Gerontology*, *28*, 497-502.

Emerson, R. M. Power-dependence relations. *American Sociological Review*, 1962, *27*, 31-41.

Emerson, R. M. Exchange theory, Parts 1 & 2. In J. Berger, M. Zelditch, & B. Anderson (Eds.), *Sociological theories in progress*, Vol. II. Houghton-Mifflin, Boston, 1972.

Glenn, N. D., & Zody, R. Cohort analysis with national survey data. *Gerontologist*, 1970, *10*, 233-240.

Guillemard, A. M., & Lenoir, R. *Retraite et échange social*. Centre d'Etude des Mouvements Sociaux, Paris, 1974.

Havighurst, R. J. Personality and patterns of aging. *Gerontologist*, 1968, *8*, 20-33.

Havighurst, R. J., Neugarten, B. L., & Tobin, S. S. Disengagement, personality, and life satisfaction in the later years. In P. From Hanson (Ed.), *Age with a future*. Munksgaard, Copenhagen, 1964.

Homans, G. C. *Social behavior: Its elementary forms*. Harcourt, Brace & World, New York, 1961.

Knipe, E. E. Attraction and exchange: Some temporal considerations. Paper presented at annual meeting of the Southern Sociological Society, Atlanta, 1971.

Lemon, B. W., Bengtson, V. L., & Peterson, J. A. An exploration of the activity theory of aging: Activity types and life satisfaction among in-movers to a retirement community. *Journal of Gerontology*, 1972, *27*, 511-523.

Lipman, A., & Smith, K. J. Functionality of disengagement in old age. *Journal of Gerontology*, 1969, *23*, 517-521.

Lowenthal, M. F., & Boler, D. Voluntary versus involuntary social withdrawal. *Journal of Gerontology*, 1965, *20*, 363-371.

Maddox, G. L. Activity and morale: A longitudinal study of selected elderly subjects. *Social Forces*, 1963, *42*, 195-204.

Martin, R. The concept of power: A critical defence. *British Journal of Sociology*, 1971, *22*, 240-257.

Martin, W. C. Activity and disengagement: Life satisfaction of in-movers into a retirement community. *Gerontologist*, 1973, *13*, 224-227.

Mulkay, M. J. *Functionalism, exchange, and theoretical strategy*. Schocken, New York, 1971.

Nord, W. R. Social exchange theory: An integrative approach to social conformity. *Psychological Bulletin*, 1969, *71*, 174-208.

Palmore, E., & Whittington, F. Trends in the relative status of the aged. *Social Forces*, 1971, *50*, 84-91.

Prasad, S. B. The retirement postulate of disengagement theory. *Gerontologist*, 1964, *4*, 20-23.

Press, I., & McKool, M., Jr. Social structure and status of the aged: Toward some valid cross-cultural generalizations. *Aging & Human Development*, 1972, *3*, 297-306.

Riley, M. W. Aging and cohort succession: Interpretations and mis-interpretations. *Public Opinion Quarterly*, 1973, *37*, 35-49.

Rose, A. A current theoretical issue in social gerontology. *Gerontologist*, 1964, *4*, 46-50.

Ryder, N. B. The cohort as a concept in the study of social change. *American Sociological Review*, 1965, *30*, 843-861.

Shaw, M. E., & Costanzo, P. R. Theories of social psychology. McGraw-Hill, New York, 1970.

Tallmer, M., & Kutner, B. Disengagement and morale. *Gerontologist*, 1970, *10*, 317-320.

Tissue, T. L. A Guttman scale of disengagement potential. *Journal of Gerontology*, 1968, *23*, 513-516.

Tobin, S. S., & Neugarten, B. L. Life satisfaction and social interaction in aging. *Journal of Gerontology*, 1961, *16*, 344-346.

Wallace, W. L. Sociological theory. Aldine, Chicago, 1969.

Youmans, E. G. Some perspectives on disengagement theory. *Gerontologist*, 1969, *9*, 254-258.

2.4

The Social Context of the Aging Self

Irving Rosow

People's mental health reflects not only their psychological state and the personality changes within them, but also events in the world around them—events that give pleasure, impose hardship and strain, create opportunities, make life easier or more exhilarating, and drive men to madness. Although the reaction to these events may vary from one person to another, individuals seldom govern their own destiny or their own equanimity and peace of mind. The social world sets the stage on which they must play whether they like it or not. Regardless of justice or of the individual's understanding, it presents him with most of his problems and sets the conditions for meeting them. The social world specifies the ground rules by which the game is played and defines the meaning of events which have such an impact on the mental health and well-being of old people. These social rules create the crisis that is so consequential for the aging self.

Role Loss

The most crucial single rule by far involves the progressive loss of roles and functions of the aged, for this change represents a critical introduction of stress. Role loss generates the pressures and sets the conditions for the emerging crisis, and taken together, these delineate the social context of the aging self. What does this involve?

Copyright 1973 by The Gerontological Society. Reprinted by permission. *The Gerontologist*, Vol. 3, No. 1, 1973, pp. 82-87.

First, *the loss of roles excludes the aged from significant social participation and devalues them.* It deprives them of vital functions that underlie their sense of worth, their self-conceptions and self-esteem. In a word, they are depreciated and become marginal, alienated from the larger society. Whatever their ability, they are judged invidiously, as if they have little of value to contribute to the world's work and affairs. In a society that rewards men mainly according to their economic utility, the aged are arbitrarily stigmatized as having little marginal utility of any kind, either economic or social. On the contrary, they tend to be tolerated, patronized, ignored, rejected, or viewed as a liability. They are first excluded from the mainstream of social existence, and because of this nonparticipation, they are then penalized and denied the rewards that earlier came to them routinely.

Second, *old age is the first stage of life with systematic status loss for an entire cohort.* All previous periods—childhood, adolescence, and various phases of adulthood; from education through marriage, parenthood, raising and educating a family; from modest occupational beginnings through successively higher positions—all are normally marked by steady social growth. This involves gains in competence, responsibility, authority, privilege, reward, and prestige. But the status loss of old age represents the first systematic break in this pattern of acquisition. Not only are the gains and perquisites disrupted, but the sheer loss of status actually reverses the trend. People pass through a vague period of transition in which they are redefined as old and obsolete. The norms applied to them change quickly from achievement to ascription, from criteria of performance to those of sheer age regardless of personal accomplishment. People who were formerly judged as individuals are then bewilderingly treated as members of an invidious category. They are dismissed as superannuated, peculiarly wanting in substance and consequence, almost in character, and thereby lacking any moral claim on the normal social values available for distribution.

To be sure, there are other patterned status losses in our society, but none uniquely connected with age. People do have illegitimate children, go to prison, get divorced, wind up in mental hospitals, or otherwise fall from grace. But they are deviants who are in the minority; age has nothing to do with their status. They are construed as personal failures in some fundamental sense. Yet the losses of old age ultimately overtake everybody, not because they have significantly failed, but only because they have survived. This raises perplexing problems of social justice for the aged: to comprehend a loss of status when there has been no personal failure.

Third, *persons in our society are not socialized to the fate of aging.* This, too, is a major discontinuity from previous experience. Usually people are rather systematically, if not always formally, trained for their next stage of life. They are indoctrinated about future roles and expectations, about the values and norms that will govern them. While the role losses of old age are institutionalized, the socialization to them is not. People must adapt to the strains and develop a way of life without clear definitions, expectations, and standards. Our society generally does not prepare people for defeats and losses of status and certainly not for those of old age.

Fourth, *because society does not specify an aged role, the lives of the elderly are socially unstructured.* Even though people are classified as old, they have almost no duties. Shorn of roles, their responsibilities and obligations are minimal. Their position is part of no division of social labor and does not mesh with any definite group of others that sociologists call a "role set" (Merton, 1957). Consequently, they tend to live in an imperfect role vacuum with few standards by which to judge themselves and their behavior. Others have few expectations of them and provide no guides to appropriate activity. They have no significant norms for restructuring their lives. There are no meaningful prescriptions for new goals and experience, no directions to salvation as occasionally accompany sin, loss, or failure at younger ages. There are only platitudes: take care of yourself, stay out of drafts, keep active, hold onto the banister, find a hobby, don't overdo, take your medicine, eat. The very triviality of these bromides simply documents the rolelessness of the aged, the general irreversibility of their losses, and their ultimate solitude in meeting their existential declines.

In this sense, it is virtually impossible for them to be literal role failures. This is not necessarily reassuring, however, for psychologists know that unstructured situations generate anxiety. Certainly with a broad horizon of leisure and few obligations, many old people feel oppressively useless and futile. They are simply bored—but not quite to death.

Although freedom from responsibility may sound heavenly to the young, it actually demands strong personal interests and motivation. In earlier periods, life is mainly structured by social duties. People's social positions and role obligations largely govern their general activities and time budgets. This is not true in old age for, within objective constraints, life is essentially shaped by individual choice and personal initiative. Because many people lack the interest and initiative to fashion a satisfying existence independently (Hunter & Maurice, 1953), life patterns range from the highly active and imaginative to passive vegetation. To be sure, almost the entire spectrum of possible styles is socially acceptable (Rosow, 1967). But this broad range of permissible alternatives simply documents the role vacuum: there are few prescriptions, norms, and expectations, weak definitions of what an old person should be like and how he should spend his time; and only a clouded picture of the good life in old age.

Finally, *role loss deprives people of their social identity*. This is almost axiomatic, for sociologists define the social self as the totality of a person's social roles. These roles identify and describe him as a social being and are central to his very self-conceptions. The process of role loss steadily eats away at these crucial elements of social personality and converts what is to what was—or transforms the present into the past. In psychological terms, this is a direct, sustained attack on the ego. If the social self consists of roles, then role loss erodes self-conceptions and sacrifices social identity.

These then are the social inputs of the crisis of aging. For the first time in life, the elderly are excluded from the central functions and social participation on which self-conceptions and self-esteem are based. They systematically lose perquisites and status solely on the basis of age. Social pressures that they are powerless to dispel result in invidious judgments of them, and their personal efforts cannot significantly affect their various losses. Because they lack major responsibilities, society does not specify a role for the aged, and their lives become socially unstructured. This is a gross discontinuity for which they are not socialized, and role loss deprives them of their very social identity. This is the social context of the aging self that psychologists must take into account when confronting the problems of mental illness in old age.

Personal Stress

There is ample evidence that these social inputs are not illusory, but extremely consequential; they generate significant personal pressure. Old age does impose severe if unobtrusive psychological stress, perhaps more than that of any earlier life stage. For old people show unmistakable signs of strain, with higher rates of suicide and mental illness than any other age group. These rates increase steadily in the course of life and reach their peak at the very end. For example, in 1967, the over-all suicide rate for American men was 15.7/100,000 (USHPS, 1969). But among old men, the rate progressed from 32.9 for those 65-74 to 41.3 for those 75-84 and 50.9 for those 85+ (USPHS, 1969). Between youths in their 20s and men in their late 80s, the frequency of suicide more than tripled, with the tempo quickening after 65. Similarly, the aged also contribute a disproportionate share of the mentally ill. In 1970, patients in state and county mental hospitals represented a rate of 166.2/100,000 population (Biometry Branch, 1970). But among older persons, the rates were drastically higher, rising to 446.9 for those 65-74 and to 571.3 for those 75+ (Biometry Branch, 1970). Among adults at least 25 years of age, those over 65 were more than twice as likely to be hospitalized as those younger (494.2 vs. 228.6). Thus, suicide and mental hospitalization occur between two and four times as frequently for old persons as all persons. This is genuine evidence of significant stress in old age.

Thus, the process of aging represents an actual life crisis, one that is both private and prolonged. Though it is punctuated by critical events such as widowhood or retirement, these signify new stages of loss that are cumulative and generally irreversible. However traumatic, these specific events serve as transitions to deeper levels of stress in which there is little prospect of effective relief. Hence, the strain of aging tends to be chronic, cumulative, and prolonged.

Yet it also tends to be intensely personal and private. Life may present old persons with many common problems and place them in a similar situation so that millions of contemporaries may undergo the same pressures. But they do not share the strains, for they *do not confront and survive the stresses as a group.* Typically, declining health, retirement, widowhood, and other losses strike the elderly individually and separately, not jointly and simultaneously. They do not go through a collective ordeal together, as an age-grade is initiated in puberty rites, or members of a combat team receive the same baptism of fire, or victims of a tornado or earthquake are exposed to the same catastrophe. The aged do not share their significant personal losses with the same immediacy, directness, and mutuality. They are essentially a social category rather than a viable group. Regardless of the sympathy they may evoke, they experience their common fate separately and alone, not with each other. In this sense, their stresses are deeply individual. Thus, from the personal perspective, the crisis of old age is not brief and public, but prolonged and private. This condition can have significant effect on the aging self.

If the social system exerts such strong social pressures, then one basic problem of the aging self concerns people's reactions to stress. This is not a simple issue. The response to various life crises is highly complex and extremely variable among individuals. Those exposed to strain do not react in the same way. Some hold up and cope, others crumple and give way, some simply withdraw, while others become psychotic. The annealing heat of stress toughens and even purifies some souls in a trial by ordeal (like Thomas à Becket) while it softens others to indecision and paralysis (like Hamlet) and even destroys still others (like Ophelia). The problem is to explain what governs such variations.

All stress situations are not the same, and we do not yet understand how to equate their effects. Are alienation and demoralization comparable for the old, the impoverished, unwed mothers, the crippled, the psychotic, and other marginal groups? Does the stigma of personal failure for which people are responsible have the same force as the stigma of aging for which the elderly are not responsible? Are people affected in the same way by specific traumatic incidents, such as accidents or natural catastrophes, and by prolonged emergencies, such as wars and depressions, which become corrosive burdens of attrition? Do they respond differently to strictly personal crises, such as the death of a child or spouse, and to public emergencies which simultaneously engulf large masses of people? Do private strains exact a greater or more enduring psychological toll than shared public stresses? Do group supports moderate significant depredations to the self? If so, how might group supports be strengthened so as to reduce the worst effects of old age?

We cannot yet answer all these questions definitively, but a valuable body of research on all kinds of stress clarifies some of the basic issues. In certain areas, the gross outlines of our present knowledge were beginning to be laid down in the mid-1930s; other areas required much longer. These studies are extremely heterogeneous and cover many diverse situations: not only aging itself, but also the psychological effects of military combat, in the air and on the ground (Grinker & Spiegel, 1945; Janis, 1951; Shils & Janowitz, 1948; Stouffer, 1949); such catastrophes as the Cocoanut Grove fire in Boston (Cobb & Lindemann, 1943; Lindemann, 1944); the road to the mental hospital (Lowenthal, 1964, 1965); adjustment to divorce (Goode, 1956); natural disasters of all types (Quarantelli, 1954; Tyhurst, 1951); bombardment during the war (US Strategic Bombing Survey, 1946a,b); imprisonment by the North Koreans during the Korean War (Hunter, 1956; Lifton, 1956, 1957; Schein, 1956, 1960, 1961; Shein, Hill, Williams, & Lubin, 1957; Segal, 1957; Strassman, Thaler, & Schein, 1956); the depression, poverty and extended unemployment (Bakke, 1934, 1940a,b; Ginzberg, 1943; Harrington, 1962; Jahoda, Lazarsfeld, & Zeisel, 1971; Komarovsky, 1940; Sletto & Rundquist, 1936); internment in concentration camps (Bettelheim, 1943; Cressey & Krassowski, 1957-1958; Gliksman, 1945; Kogon, 1950; Nirembeski, 1946; Shuval, 1957-1958); and so on. Obviously they include extreme crises of many kinds: short and long, natural and social, public and private, etc. Trauma appears in all possible degrees of severity.

Stress and Personality

Even cursory review of this work is revealing, for these studies unequivocally establish two major points. The first is that *people's response to stress varies according to factors of personality*. They react differentially to strain. Some will be more deeply, even permanently, affected by a situation than others who have different emotional characteristics. This is true in most settings, including concentration camps, military combat, etc. During the depression, many men in Europe and America went without work for several years, but in the process, some were transformed from the unemployed to the unemployable. Further, when Orson Welles frightened half the nation with his broadcast of the Martian invasion in the late 1930s, those people who hysterically jammed the New Jersey highways were emotionally less stable than those who stayed to enjoy the end of a good show (Cantril, 1940).

As far as aging is concerned, Townsend's (1957) sample of the elderly in London showed that it took women between 5 and 10 years on the average to adjust to widowhood, but the range of time varied considerably more than this. Presumably, a large part of the difference between those who needed only 3 years and those requiring 12 is attributable to personality differences, such as dependency, modes of ego defense, and so on. Further, Lowenthal (1964, 1965) has shown that old men who are ripe for psychiatric hospitalization are psychologically atypical, with distinctive life histories, patterns of relating to others and dealing with problems. By the same token, when the objective means are at hand, some elderly simply lack the personal initiative and self-confidence to establish friendships and gain desired new experience, even under optimal conditions (Hunter & Maurice, 1953; Rosow, 1967). Almost 20 years ago, Busse and his colleagues (Busse, Barnes, Silverman, Shy, Thaler, & Frost, 1954, 1955) at Duke University already indicated that, if there is no organic damage to the brain and nervous system, emotional states in later life are essentially similar to those that came before. They might be somewhat more intensified, but they are fundamentally consistent with previous personality functioning and an extension of it. If a person had been hysterical or depressive, he would tend to remain so or become worse. If he had functioned reasonably well and appropriately, he would probably continue to do so. In other words, there is a basic continuity in the mode of dealing with stress that probably does not change in old age. The underlying principle is clear: personality factors are significant determinates of people's reactions to stress, whether in a stunning invasion of Martians or the steady crisis of aging.

In personality terms, people can be ranged on a continuum in their ability to withstand stress. At one extreme are those with very high tolerance. They have unusual flexibility and stability, personality strengths which enable them to endure more pressure than others. They represent a low-risk group. At the other extreme is a high-risk group with an unusually low tolerance for strain. They have only limited personality resources on which to draw, so they tend to be quite brittle and ineffective in the face of crisis. Lowenthal's sample and mental hospital patients exemplify such casualties of limited personal reserves and high vulnerability. But between these extremes of unusually low- and high-risk groups lies the bulk of the population. This large middle group is the most problematic for the response to stress: they are neither as pathological as the high-risk nor as resilient as the low-risk group. They are simply average—which is to say, potentially quite sensitive to variations in the degree, nature, and conditions of stress in old age.

Stress and Group Support

The second major result of existing research substantiates Durkheim's classic study of suicide in 1897: *people effectively withstand stress to the extent that they have strong group supports.* This is abundantly clear in almost all contexts. Bettelheim's and others' reports of the concentration camps (*cf. supra.*), Shils and Janowitz' (1948) analysis of the disintegrating Wehrmacht, various studies of older people (Rosow, 1967, in press) and other research show that members of strong solidary groups cope with stress more effectively and with less personal damage than those without these supports. For example, in the Korean war (*cf. supra.*) the Turks were much more successful than Americans in resisting North Korean attempts to brainwash prisoners of war. The Turks met those efforts with exceptional group cohesion and strong support of their individual members while the Americans did not. Group support is generally vital in withstanding stress and probably crucial for the problematic middle-risk group.

We have seen that old age is stressful and its impact is largely private. But its effects can be moderated by strong group supports. Obviously then, in the face of major role loss, the fate of old people's other group memberships is significant for their mental health. Now, what actually happens to those memberships that might help them meet the pressures of aging? The evidence speaks out loud and clear (Babchuck & Booth, 1969; Booth, 1972; Dotson, 1951; Wright & Hyman, 1968). Their group memberships atrophy, declining sharply by the age of 65 and precipitously after 75. This holds true on all significant dimensions. They belong to fewer organizations, they hold fewer offices and participate less where they do belong. They also tend to have fewer friends and to see them less. Residential changes, deaths, declining health, and lower income combine to loosen the network of group ties. Their social world simply shrinks and, with it, the web of affiliations that support people psychologically. Thus, old age shows a major reduction in group memberships and the weakening of buffers against stress.

We have reviewed here some central variables in the response to the aging crisis. When they are taken together and refined, they should account in large measure for people's reactions. Old age is a stage of prolonged private stress that people meet with varying degrees of personal resources. Its detrimental effects can be significantly moderated by strong group supports. But the aged are not a viable group, and their various group memberships and solidary ties wither away. Consequently, there are few structural compensations for the social losses and personal stresses that are inevitable.

Policy Implications

The foregoing analysis contains some clear policy implications for the public arena. (1) To offset their loss of function in our society, we can use the skills of the aged in new service roles that many proliferating social programs require. (2) To reduce their isolation and promote group support, viable social groups of the elderly should be fostered where they are found, particularly within larger natural communities. (3) Because economic utility governs our voluntary distribution of values, the legitimate social claims of the aged can probably only be satisfied through their militant political action, both independently and in alliance with other aggrieved minorities.

References

Babchuck, N., & Booth, A. Voluntary association membership: A longitudinal analysis. *American Sociological Review*, 1969, *34*, 31-45.

Bakke, E. W. *Citizens without work*. New Haven: Yale University Press, 1940. (a)

Bakke, E. W. *The Unemployed man*. New York: E. P. Dutton, 1934.

Bakke, E. W. *The Unemployed worker*. New Haven: Yale University Press, 1940. (b)

Bettelheim, B. Individual and mass behavior in extreme situations. *Journal of Abnormal & Social Psychology*, 1943, *38*, 417-452.

Biometry Branch, National Institute of Mental Health. Unpublished material, 1969, 1970.

Booth, A. Sex and social participation. *American Sociological Review*, 1972, *37*, 183-193.

Busse, E. W., Barnes, R., Silverman, A., Shy, M., Thaler, M., & Frost, L. Studies of the process of aging: Factors that influenced the psyche of elderly persons. *American Journal of Psychiatry*, 1954, *110*, 897-903.

Busse, E. W., Barnes, R., Silverman, A., Thaler, M., & Frost, L. Studies of the processes of aging. X. Strengths and weaknesses of psychiatric functioning in the aged. *American Journal of Psychiatry*, 1955, *111*, 896-901.

Cantril, H. *The invasion from Mars*. Princeton: Princeton University Press, 1940.

Cobb, S., & Lindemann, E. Neuropsychiatric observations (after the Cocoanut Grove fire). *Annals of Surgery*, 1943, *117*, 814-824.

Cressey, D., & Krassowski, W. Inmate organization and anomie in American prisons and Soviet labor camps. *Social Problems*, 1957-1958, *5*, 217-230.

Dotson, F. Patterns of voluntary association among urban working class families. *American Sociological Review*, 1951, *16*, 687-693.

Ginzberg, E. *The unemployed*. New York: Harper & Bros., 1943.

Gliksman, J. *Tell the West*. New York: Gresham Press, 1945.

Goode, W. *After divorce*. New York: Free Press, 1956.

Grinker, R., & Spiegel, J. *Men under stress*. Philadelphia: Blakiston, 1945.

Harrington, M. *The other America*. New York: Macmillan, 1962.

Hunter, E. *Brainwashing*. New York: Farrar, Straus & Cudahy, 1956.

Hunter, W., & Maurice, H. *Older people tell their story*. Ann Arbor: Univ. of Michigan, Div. of Gerontology, 1953.

Jahoda, M., Lazarsfeld, P., & Zeisel, H. *Marienthal: The sociography of an unemployed community*. Chicago: Aldine-Atherton, 1971.

Janis, I. *Air war and emotional stress*. New York: McGraw-Hill, 1951.

Kogon, E. *The theory and practice of hell*. London: Secker & Warburg, 1950.

Komarovsky, M. *The unemployed man and his family*. New York: Dryden Press, 1940.

Lifton, R. Thought reform of Chinese intellectuals: A psychiatric evaluation. *Journal of Social Issues*, 1957, *13*, 5-20.

Lifton, R. 'Thought reform' of Western civilians in Chinese Communist prisons. *Psychiatry*, 1956, *19*, 173-195.

Lindemann, E. Symptomatology and management of acute grief. *American Journal of Psychiatry*, 1944, *101*, 141-148.

Lowenthal, M. Antecedents of isolation and mental illness in old age. *Archives of General Psychiatry*, 1965, *12*, 245-254.

Lowenthal, M. *Lives in distress*. New York: Basic Books, 1964.

Merton, R. *Social theory and social structure* (Rev. ed.). New York: Free Press, 1957.

Nirembeski, N. Psychological investigation of a group of internees at Belsen camp. *Journal of Mental Science*, 1946, *92*, 60-74.

Quarantelli, E. L. The nature and conditions of panic. *American Journal of Sociology*, 1954, *60*, 267-275.

Rosow, I. *Social integration of the aged*. New York: Free Press, 1967.

Schein, E. The Chinese indoctrination program for prisoners of war. *Psychiatry*, 1956, *19*, 149-172.

Schein, E. *Coercive persuasion*. New York: W. W. Norton, 1961.

Schein, E. Interpersonal communication, group solidarity, and social influence. *Sociometry*, 1960, *23*, 148-161.

Schein, E., Hill, W., Williams, H., & Lubin, A. Distinguishing characteristics of collaborators and resisters among American prisoners of war. *Journal of Abnormal & Social Psychology*, 1957, *55*, 197-201.

Segal, J. Correlates of collaboration and resistance behavior among U.S. Army POWs in Korea. *Journal of Social Issues*, 1957, *13*, 31-40.

Shils, E., & Janowitz, M. Cohesion and disintegration in the Wehrmacht in World War II. *Public Opinion Quarterly*, 1948, *12*, 280-315.

Shuval, J. Some persistent effects of trauma five years after the Nazi concentration camps. *Social Problems*, 1957-1958, *5*, 230-243.

Sletto R., & Rundquist, E. *Personality in the depression*. Minneapolis: Univ. of Minnesota Press, 1936.

Stouffer, S. *The American soldier* (2 vols.). Princeton: Princeton Univ. Press, 1949.

Strassman, H., Thaler, M., & Schein, E. A prisoner of war syndrome: apathy as a reaction to severe stress. *American Journal of Psychiatry*, 1956, *112*, 998-1003.

Townsend, P. *Family life of old people*. London: Routledge & Kegan Paul, 1957.

Tyhurst, J. Individual reactions to community disaster. *American Journal of Psychiatry*, 1951, *107*, 764-769.

U S Public Health Service. *Vital statistics of the United States, 1967. Vol. II—Mortality, Part A*. Washington: National Center for Health Statistics, 1969.

U S Strategic Bombing Survey, Morale Division. *Effects of strategic bombing on German morale* (2 vols.). Washington: 1946. (a)

U S Strategic Bombing Survey, Morale Division. *Effects of strategic bombing on Japanese morale*. Washington: 1946. (b)

Wright, C., & Hyman, H. Voluntary association memberships of American adults. *American Sociological Review*, 1958, *23*, 284-294.

CHAPTER III

TRANSITIONS

A developmental approach to aging rests on the principle that all lives go through a similar sequence of stages and transformations, and that each of these stages—infancy, adolescence, young adulthood, etc.—carries with it a set of crises to be dealt with, as well as its own opportunities for growth and fulfillment. Furthermore, it assumes that each stage is dependent on the preceding one for mastering the skills needed to cope with the contingencies of life.

Aging, as the last stage of the life cycle, is no exception to the above premises, and some of the theories reviewed in the previous chapter characterized it negatively in terms of its cumulative traumas of depletion, power and role loss. Some of the changes occurring in aging have been, in fact, incubated in middle age, one of the least studied segments of the life cycle. Some others, like retirement, have been universally instituted through formal policy decisions. While certain changes respond to intrinsic, developmental processes, others are the predictable effect of social and environmental circumstances.

It would go beyond the scope of this volume to inventory all the transitions and transformations that occur in later life. This chapter will focus on only three of them: middle age, retirement, and relocation.

Rosenberg and Farrell in their paper, "Identity and Crisis in Middle Aged Men," contend with the frustrating paucity of data on middle age and summarize their bibliographic probe with the conclusion that male middle agers are susceptible to undergo a crisis. Moreover, the majority is unable to introject, or properly deal with, the disturbing connotations of their age.

After drawing from relevant findings in sociological, social, and clinical research, plus the often incisive contributions of popular fiction, they attempt to spell out their own model or typology. Two variables or dimensions are taken into account: open confrontation or denial of crisis and satisfaction or alienation. The resulting patterns or "stereotypes" are: first, a sort of satisfied, successful coper, the "hero" of the middle age story; second, an overtly satisfied authoritarian who denies his covert depressions and anxiety; third, a highly alienated or repressed depressive; and finally, the punitive, disenchanted type. Rosenberg and Farrell have re-exhumated Adorno's authoritarian personality syndrome and skillfully linked it to crisis theory constructs. The authors regard this model as being of heuristic value in that it specifies a number of dimensions to be operationalized for social intervention and may provide a more holistic view of the middle age "frontier."

The next paper by William Withers brings an economic and manpower perspective to the analysis of retirement. He starts from the empirical contention that for many people, retirement is a traumatic experience and concludes that the American retirement system is simply irrational and arbitrary. The trauma of retirement stems not only from decreased income, but also from the multiple institutions and values that turn the retiree into a social reject. Withers does away with some of the erroneous assumptions about older or middle aged and older workers: that they are nonproductive, that they can manage with less income, that they are not needed, etc. In searching for the basis of these irrational assumptions, the author again blames "youthism," the glamorization of everything associated with being young. This is a rather simplistic conclusion, but it does not invalidate the otherwise correct assessment of the inconsistencies of retirement. Published in 1974, this paper anticipated the national legislative debates of 1977 on mandatory retirement.

Yawney and Slover summarize the research that has been done on relocation of the elderly and use their findings to suggest environmental and counseling strategies for helping older persons who are moving. Most Americans change residence for a better job or a better home, but when an older person moves, it is likely to be a disruptive and even a devastating experience, commonly associated with financial or health setbacks, widowhood, or loss of work.

The paper reviews four types of relocation: from one community setting to another; from one community to an institution; from one institution to another; and finally, from an institution to the community. Relocation involves a complex sequence of experiences and emotional responses, including some extreme forms of stress and feelings of helplessness. The risks involved in relocation have been emphasized too often, but its potential benefits are not mentioned. The authors, in their roles as social planners, are confident that much can be done to increase the likelihood of a successful outcome. They prescribe environmental manipulation, encouragement, support, and concrete aid as effective therapy for elderly relocatees.

3.1

Identity and Crisis
in Middle Aged Men

Stanley D. Rosenberg and Michael P. Farrell

Introduction

A mounting number of studies indicate that middle aged males in American society exhibit a striking incidence and prevalence of many of the signs of personal disorganization: neurotic and psychotic disorder (Pasamanick, 1962; Leighton et al., 1963; Srole, Langner, Michael, Oppler, & Rennie, 1962), alcoholism (Moon & Palton, 1963), marital dissatisfaction (Pineo, 1968), psychosomatic and hypochondriacal complaints (Vital and Health Statistics, Series 11, Nos. 1-15, 37; Blumenthal, 1959). These findings, although consistent and clear cut, continue to be puzzling. On the one hand, they are congruent with a number of clinical and conceptual formulations as well as widespread cultural stereotypes. The common explanatory or descriptive construct which emerges in these perspectives is the "mid-life crisis." More systematic attempts to confirm or disconfirm the existence and impact of such a crisis have provided no evidence in support of the construct and have, in fact, tended to promote opposite conclusions, seeing middle age as a relatively non-stressful period of life. To add further ambiguity, these recent investigators have themselves exhibited some sense of suspicion about their findings (Lowenthal & Chiriboga, 1972).

Copyright 1976 by Baywood Publishing Co., Inc. Reprinted by permission. *International Journal of Aging and Human Development*, Vol. 7, No. 2, 1976, pp. 153-170.

If middle age is associated with a reduction in external pressures and tends to be relatively non-problematic in terms of the organization of the self system, how do we account for its associated disorders? The cultural stereotypes and clinical commentary on the middle aged identity crisis would have to be dismissed as almost entirely fantastic or diametrically opposed to reality if the more direct, systematic findings are to be granted total credibility. Such a negative relation between fictional literature, theoretical speculation, and fact is not entirely improbable, but in the context of the data available, it gives one grounds for skepticism, or at least confusion.

Despite some recent efforts, there remains a paucity of adequate descriptions or substantiated conceptualizations of middle age as a life stage, existentially meaningful event or even as a social category. Nevertheless, the available data may provide a basis for a working model and a set of hypotheses which can help to ameliorate the existent confusion.

In reviewing some of the significant work that has emerged from several disciplines, we shall attempt to outline a new working model which can subsume much of the seemingly contradictory data and thus serve to more sharply focus investigation in this area.

Relevant Data

As stated above, much of the social science data on the middle aged seems to undercut the notion of a "mid-life crisis" as a common event. Indeed, results often indicate that the middle aged themselves view this part of their lives as a "golden period" characterized by security, diminishing external pressures and the maturity and good judgement to enjoy what life has to offer.

For example, Neugarten's study of 100 successful middle aged persons of both sexes conclude:

> These people feel that they effectively manipulate their social environments on the basis of prestige and expertise; and that they create many of their own rules and norms. There is a sense of increased control over impulse life. The successful middle-aged person often describes himself as no longer "driven," but as now the "driver"—in short, "in command" (Neugarten, 1968).

Similarly, Deutscher's study concludes that the great majority of respondents finds the post-parental phase of life as good as, if not better than, "preceeding phases" (Deutscher, 1968).

In a more recent study, Lowenthal and Chiriboga find that when men entering the "empty nest" phase are asked to rate the "high points" in their lives, choices seem to fall pretty evenly in all stages, including middle age. When asked to designate low points, male respondents pointed to adolescence and young adulthood as being at least as difficult as the present. Further, when asked to rate themselves on how happy they were, empty nest males described themselves as "very happy" and "pretty happy" as often as a comparable group of high school seniors, with 8 per cent more of them describing themselves as "very happy" (Lowenthal & Chiriboga, 1972). The middle aged male also reports fewer unwanted characteristics in a self-ideal comparison than does his adolescent counterpart (Lowenthal & Chiriboga, 1972).

Gurin, Veroff and Feld, in a 1957 study of 2,500 adults, showed a slight decline in those reporting themselves as "very happy" associated with age, and a concomitant increase of those indicating they were "not too happy," but the middle aged individual also reports less worry than the younger person (Gurin, Veroff, & Feld, 1960).

This data might lead one, at first glance, to conclude that the mid-life or middle age crisis is no more than a figment of the overactive literary imagination, but other evidence would indicate that such a conclusion may be too hasty. Psychoanalysts and psychiatrists in our culture, for example, tend to see the middle age crisis as universal, a developmental inevitability (Jacques, 1965; Pearce & Newton, 1963; Bergler, 1954). Such assertions are often dismissed on the grounds that the clinician does not see a representative sample of the population, but rather the affluent, verbal and discontent. At any rate, the psychoanalysts do not assert that they see overt, conscious confrontation with this issue, but rather a myriad set of pathological reactions to it. Denial of the crisis and subsequent attempts at escape (e.g., frantic activity or sexual adventures which prove burdensome) are often noted, along with more general forms of decompensation such as anxiety states, depression and diffuse rage.

Whether or not such conclusions are artifacts of the clinicians' narrow world view, it would seem obvious that simply asking individuals how happy they are can't adequately tap into the phenomenon of middle age crisis as they describe it or as it is portrayed in literature. Furthermore, a number of indices are available which lend inferential support to the position that middle age—and especially the initial state of entering it—is peculiarly stressful.

Lowenthal and Chiriboga are themselves suspicious of the high expressed satisfaction of their middle aged male respondents. The authors report that the subjects " . . . seem rather to have a conscious reluctance to report negative circumstances or affect to repress them altogether" (1972). Yet Lowenthal and Chiriboga seem to be left with the impression that such negative affect persists and finds less direct modes of expression. "The cost of this effort to live up to a strong male image may be great . . . it is the men who have serious difficulties in mid-life, as reflected by . . . alcoholism rates, admission to mental hospitals, suicide rates and serious physical illness" (1972). Men in the study, for example, report greater satisfaction with sex in marriage in middle age, while their wives report a decline in both frequency and satisfaction. The men appear to reach a kind of equilibrium by lowering their own expectations for themselves while ignoring their mates' dissatisfactions. Cuber, in a study of 437 upper middle class Americans between the ages of thirty-five and fifty, finds widespread disillusionment and cynicism among his respondents (Cuber & Harnoff, 1965). His lengthy, in depth interviews demonstrate a strong tendency on the part of the subjects to rationalize away the disturbing aspects of their existences, both in terms of living with themselves and maintaining a front for others. Many continue in marriage arrangements which are described as "conflict-habituated," "devitalized," or "passive-congenital" (1965). Husbands tend to describe such arrangements as workable or convenient while some wives tend to be more vocal in describing these patterns as a disappointing and deadening mode of existence. Cuber also cites instances in which respondents imply that they would not have revealed their true feelings about such intimate and significant areas if the researchers had simply asked them to respond to a brief question about how satisfactory they found marriage or life. Cuber's findings cannot, of course, be considered definitive, even for this specific sector of the population. They do, however, stand in clear opposition to the findings reported by such researchers as Neugarten, Deutscher, and Lowenthal. Such contradictory results point up a need for clarification in this area.

Is the surface calm exhibited by the middle aged male an accurate representation, a reflection perhaps of the security of knowing himself and his own capabilities as Neugarten (1968) suggests? To what extent can it represent a veneer overlaying interpersonal difficulties or inner turmoil which he cannot face?

A number of indices would seem to lend greater weight to the latter alternative than would the recent social psychological literature. To list a few of these:

A longitudinal study reported by Pineo indicates that marital satisfaction for both men and women in fact declines in middle age (Pineo, 1968).

A study in Baltimore indicated a sharp increase in the rate of psychoses in the middle aged as opposed to the young (Pasamanick, 1962).

Leighton reports on initial peaking of psychoneurosis in late thirties through the mid forties in his study of Sterling County (Leighton et al., 1963).

The Midtown study of Srole and his colleagues also uncovered greater symptom formation in the middle aged group than the younger adults (Srole, Langner, Oppler, & Rennie, 1962).

First admissions for alcoholism to state hospitals peak for the age group 45-57, as do mental hospitalizations for other reasons (Jaffe & Gordon, 1968).

Less severe psychological symptoms appear to follow the same pattern. Middle age is associated with the "feeling of impending nervous breakdown" in several studies (Vital and Health Statistics, Series II, No. 37). It also shows a positive relation with general "nervousness" and headaches.

The incidence of a number of psychosomatic ailments also shows sharp increase for the middle aged. Peptic ulcer, in most studies, has its highest incidence in the 40-50 age group, with those in the 30-40 age group showing the next highest rate (Blumenthal, 1959). Hypertension and heart disease also show an increasing incidence in middle age as compared with young adulthood (Vital and Health Statistics, Series II, Nos. 1-15).

The ambiguous and somewhat paradoxical nature of the data not only points to a need for further investigation, but is also suggestive of a tentative model which may be more adequate than the simple either/or approach.

Rather than simply asking whether or not middle age is a time of crisis, we might more profitably ask:

What is the range of response to reaching this developmental plateau? To what degree is the term crisis, as it has been outlined in clinical and popular literature, a useful and accurate construct for understanding these life changes and their associated disorders? In what ways do more general social and psychological variables (such as social class, ethnicity and the structure of personal defenses) contribute to the mid-life crisis and individual response to it?

Addressing these questions requires us to clarify what we mean by the terms "crisis" and "response to crisis." This clarification and the generation of our working model can be expedited by the use of a different sort of data: Images of middle age as they appear in contemporary literature.

Middle Age in Popular Culture

In contemporary culture, widespread interest is focused on the issue of transition into middle age, particularly as it effects the middle class male. In the past years, for example, several popular publications (*Look* Magazine & The *New York Times*) have featured portrayals of successful but essentially bored businessmen and professionals abandoning their secure and desirable niches to find new challenges and reinfuse their lives with a sense of meaningfulness and adventure. Interestingly, they were not presented as malcontents or neurotics, but rather seemed to take on an aura of culture heroes, manifesting the courage to act out common fantasies and aspirations. Many recent novels and films have presented a less benign picture in which the approach of middle age precipitates a profound existential crisis and is associated with malaise, alienation from one's milieu and personal disorganization. At best, this crisis is seen as liberating, enabling the protagonist to take a fresh look at himself and his environment and emerge with a kind of wisdom, maturity and insight which are beyond the grasp of youthful capability. At worst, the crisis is kept from becoming fully conscious and results in destructiveness toward both the self and others, attitudinal rigidification and a dominating need for others to confirm the very mode of being that is experienced as painful. We shall try to briefly encapsulate the themes which have commonly appeared in many of the recent novels and movies dealing with a subject.

The dissenter: open confrontation with crisis

A consistent and explicit view of middle age recurs in a particular vein of contemporary literature. In these works, the transition into middle age is viewed as inextricably bound up with a sense of frenzy if not a total crisis in identity. Time and again, the aging protagonist emerges as anti-hero, trying to recapture some lost sense of wholeness or integrity by denouncing the existent value schema. The previous adult period of his life is not only seen as mismanaged, but also as a kind of malignant fantasy; a fog of self-deception in which the individual has given up the potential vividness of experience and life. Herzog, one of contemporary fictions most notable characterizations, provides a case in point.

> Late in spring, Herzog had been overcome by the need to explain, to have it out, to justify, to put in perspective, to clarify, to make amends . . . he sometimes imagined he was an industry that manufactured personal history, and saw himself from birth to death. . . .
> Considering his entire life, he realized that he had mismanaged everything—everything. His life was, as the phrase goes, ruined. But since it had not been much to begin with, there was not much to grieve about. . . . He went on taking

stock, lying face down on the sofa. Was he a clever man or an idiot? . . . Resuming his self-examination, he admitted that he had been a bad husband—twice. Daisy, his first wife, he had treated miserably. Madeleine, his second, had tried to do him in. To his son and his daughter he was a loving but bad father. To his own parents he had been an ungrateful child. To his country, an indifferent citizen. To his brothers and sister, affectionate but remote. With his friends, an egotist. With love, lazy. With brightness, dull. With power, passive. With his own soul, evasive. . . . Herzog himself had no small amount of charm. But his sexual power had been damaged by Madeleine. And without the ability to attract women, how was he to recover? It was in this respect he felt most like a convalescent (Bellow, 1964).

Vonnegut's Billy Pilgrim leaves the reader with little doubt that his life experience has only left him with a sense of futility, absurdity and staleness (Vonnegut, 1969). In trying to review what retrospectively appears as the central experience of his life, the protagonist writes:

> I think of how useless the Dresden part of my memory has been, and yet how tempting Dresden has been to write about, and I am reminded of the famous limerick:
>
> There was a young man from Stamboul,
> Who soliloquized thus to his tool:
> "You took all my wealth
> And you ruined my health,
> And now you won't pee, you old fool."
>
> And I'm reminded, too, of the song that goes:
>
> My name is Yon Yonson,
> I work in Wisconsin,
> I work in a lumbermill there.
> The people I meet when I walk down the street,
>   They say, "What's your name?"
>   And I say,
>   "My name is Yon Yonson,
>   I work in Wisconsin . . . "
>
> And so on to infinity (Vonnegut, 1969).

Billy's entire existence is portrayed as such a "nightmare of meaninglessness."

And we were flown to a rest camp in France, where we were fed chocolate malted milkshakes and other rich foods until we were all covered with baby fat. Then we were sent home, and I married a pretty girl who was covered with baby fat too.

And we had babies.

And they're all grown up now, and I'm an old fart with memories and his Pall Malls. My name is Yon Yonson, I work in Wisconsin, I work in a lumbermill there (Vonnegut, 1969).

Nor is the situation seen as rectifiable; there is really no one other than one's self to blame. Ultimately, Vonnegut's hero, like Bellow's, penetrates his being to sense that his own rationalizations and fears are the basis of his dilemma. While they totally renounce the values of society, they come to recognize that they have not been misled by the flawed wisdom of the culture so much as that they have eagerly embraced and even helped to generate it, finding it a convenient device for temporarily escaping the basic issues of their existence. Formulations vary here: The protagonist may be escaping from freedom, from fear, from desire or some combination of these.

While details and conclusions may differ, there is an extensive and popular literature which portrays the mid-life crisis in substantially similar terms: Wheelis' *The Seeker*, Kazan's *The Arrangement* (1967), several of Miller's plays, Friedman's *Stern* (1962) and *The Dick* (1970), and the ubiquitous *Portnoy* (Roth, 1969) are representative. In all of them the middle-scent must experience a new identity crisis and, in so doing, realize that his "maturity" was not based on the successful resolution of the issues of childhood, but rather on their denial. The "rational" goal seeking of their adulthood comes to be reinterpreted as largely compulsive and meaningless.

Several recent movies treat this issue in similar terms. The protagonist in "Faces," a successful businessman, finds himself increasingly bitter and desperate as his youth slips away. Utterly dissatisfied with the wealth, power and possessions he has worked so hard to accumulate, he seeks to find some gratification with a young prostitute, while his equally troubled wife seduces a stranger. Another Cassavetes' movie, "Husbands," centers on the reaction of three forty-year-old suburbanites to the death of a fourth member of their group. As the film evolves, it becomes apparent that the event is no more than a precipitant which pushes them to recognize the meaninglessness of their own existences. Like Laing's schizoid (1960), they live a life which is dead so as to ward off the fear of death. They attempt to break loose by going on a binge, but find that they can not escape from that part of themselves which impels them towards the dull, routinized existence of middle class life: A sham more fantastic than their wildest dreams of escape.

The dissenter–anti-hero may thus engage in a variety of behaviors, but tends to experience a given variety of emotions and to perceive himself in fairly regular terms. As he arrives at "successful" middle age, he seems to evince a sense of shock and disbelief, as if to ask, "is this all there is?" Finally released from the pressure of achievement striving in the quest for status and material comfort, he finds that "having it made" is in no sense the gratifying state of affairs he foresaw when he gave up the freedom of youth to enter the "system." In one way or another, he strives to look into himself and find a way out of the box of his intolerable, self-chosen existence.

The reactive modality

Less commonly, the middle aged male is portrayed as depressed, suffering with a sense of declining potency and preoccupied with themes of death. Instead of attempting to reverse his life course, he turns his despair outward, directing his rage at those who would repudiate the very mode of life that constitutes his misery. The protagonist in the reactive modality needs confirmation that he has chosen an inevitable path, that his basic assumptions remain correct. He must thus struggle to repress and deny many of his feelings and consequently project onto and hate out-groups, particularly deviants and dissenters who would overthrow the system which is the object of his own ambivalent rage and need. For example, in *Joe*, a strange alliance develops between an affluent advertising executive and a factory worker—both fathers of adolescent children—who review their existences and confide to one another: "Didn't you ever get the feeling that it's all a crock of shit?" This revelation is portrayed as intimately tied to attitudes toward youth, who are seen as representing erotic expression. After participating in an orgy with several hippies, and subsequently being rebuffed by them, the two men go on a rampage and kill the residents of a commune. Their erotic release—although an emotional high point—makes them hate the hippies even more for having the youthful potential and tolerance for nonstructure which the men themselves have wasted.

This type of treatment, like Vonnegut's, is clearly not in the genre of realism but rather are attempts to highlight latent anxieties and fantasies and their relation to overt behavior and beliefs. More commonly, the reactive modality is dealt with in terms of recognizable intra-familial conflict. The father becomes more rigid, authoritarian and punitive as he senses his son's maturation and potential for choice while also experiencing himself as becoming impotent and trapped.

The emergent literary model

To abstract briefly, there is a growing body of work in popular culture
that provides us with a set of hypotheses and beliefs about middle age.
Its approach seems to involve internal upheaval, which may or may
not be precipitated by such external events as job crisis, children's
maturation or marital difficulty. Often, these are portrayed as symptoms, rather than causes, of the crisis. This crisis is not always experienced consciously, but may lead to alterations in behavior or attitudes
on several fronts, or escape into psychosomatic illness, alcoholism,
and psychiatric disturbance. Although extreme reactions such as
divorce or "chucking it all" to run off with the younger woman may be
relatively rare behaviorally, they are portrayed as common thematic
concerns and salient fantasy material for the middle aged male. The
themes of rebellion, rebirth and erotic release are heavily emphasized. Those who have succeeded within the system find themselves
nonetheless bitterly disappointed, while those who have failed tend to
be miserable about both their striving and its meager results.

There are a number of possible explanations for the increasing
prevalence and popularity of these cultural stereotypes of the mid-life
crisis. On the one hand, we might take them to be essentially accurate,
at least for important segments of the society. In this case, the treatment of the middle-aged identity crisis in the mass media might be
seen as a means of vocalizing common discontents in a controlled
sphere. Such literature would thus serve as a releasing mechanism,
relieving the pressure to express felt needs in a non-disruptive manner.

An alternative interpretation of the rise of this particular alienated
vein of literature might be advanced. To a large extent, it is the young
who are the major consumers of this type of culture. Seeing the middle
aged in terms discussed above is a convenient myth. It is a way of
expressing one's own doubts and alienation by attributing them to
others, while it is also confirmatory of a rebellious or reformist stance
toward the "system." While not all of the young adopt these stances,
the affluent and educated (those who read such novels and see such
movies) largely identify with them. Finally, in many of these works,
youth itself gets resurrected as an ideal. Those who are just contem-
plating or beginning to compete within the social structure can see
themselves as essentially better off, more potent, and freer than those
who, in many ways, control their futures. The extent to which this
factor accounts for emergence of the mid-life crisis stereotype can only
be assessed in the light of more systematic evidence.

Progress in clarifying these issues would, however, seem to be
dependent on the generation of a working model which points the way
to appropriate variables and levels of analysis. From the operational

indices which they select, it would almost appear, for example, that clinicians and social-psychological researchers are discussing entirely different phenomena under a common rubric. What, for example, is the assumed or demonstrated relationship between expressed satisfaction in a survey response and underlying depression, existential doubt or identity disruption? What is required is a more general conceptualization which suggests relationships between physical, psychological, interpersonal and cultural variables.

Suggested Working Model

In this section, we shall attempt to draw together an integrated picture of the life changes associated with middle age in our society and the kinds of adaptational patterns they evoke. Since the problems of confronting middle age must be ubiquitous (although the mid-life crisis may or may not be), we would clearly expect the generation of cultural images which can serve to reassure and reanchor the individual caught in such upheaval. These cultural images and stereotypes both reflect certain personal realities in our society and also help, by their availability, to encourage and legitimate the dissemination of these patterns.

It may be reasonable to surmise that, as men in our culture approach middle age, there are a number of forces operating which make an assessment of one's major commitments in life highly probable. Perhaps the primary precipitant is in the area of career.

> Men perceive a close relationship between life-line and career-line. Middle age is the time to take stock. Any disparity noted between career-expectations and career-achievements—that is, whether one is "on time" or "late" in reaching career goals—adds to the heightened awareness of age. One 47-year-old lawyer said, "I moved at age forty-five from a large corporation to a law firm. I got out at the last possible moment, becuse after forty-five it is too difficult to find the job you want. If you haven't made it by then, you had better make it fast, or you are stuck" (Neugarten, 1968).

Research findings would thus tend to reinforce literary insight. Reaching or approaching the optimal point on one's career does not simply occur, it is also experientially relevant. While men do not necessarily reach peak earnings, highest rung on the organizational ladder, or maximum recognition until later middle age, indicators of how far they will go in these dimensions tend to appear much earlier.

Those slated for top management have been separated from middle managers; there are very few academics or scientists who make major contributions after the onset of middle age who have not made contributions of equal magnitude earlier in their careers (Fried, 1967). These facts appear to be part of the common lore within the organizations and professions and tend to reduce the expectations that one is any longer in the running for dramatic or unexpected career advances. The changes in life chances associated with age must also be felt in the working class. Those for whom physical vigor and agility are important elements of work can only expect diminution in productivity.

Within the nuclear family, middle age is also associated with a major turnabout; children are maturing and about to leave home. The ascendency of male offspring may be particularly threatening to the middle aged male, who is experiencing a decline in his own sense of physical potency (Fried, 1967).

He must go through the process of "giving up" his daughter, and act with good grace as her maturational needs and role demands lead her to find another male to act as protector and love object. The inherent difficulties of this rupture may well be exacerbated by the state of narcissistic vulnerability associated with his own life stage.

There appears to be a shift in the locus of power within the nuclear family at this stage, as well as high role differentiation on the affectivity dimension. In a TAT study of familial relations (Neugarten & Guttman, 1968), it is found that the assertion of authority within the family was problematic for the middle aged male, who experienced guilt around his own aggressiveness. He attempted to deal with this by recourse to either passivity (which was sometimes rationalized as a passive "cerebral" control, particularly by the white middle class males) or by justifying his control on moral grounds, as a force for "good" within the family. The wife on the other hand, comes to be seen as the central figure in the family constellation. She exhibits high affectivity and impulsiveness. Among the earlier periods of middle age, she is "checked" by the husband, but her hostility and nurturance are nonetheless central to the family's emotional life and fantasies. The limits of these fantasies may become more apparent in older age groups, who perceive continuing ascendency of the mother—eventually to the point where she pushes the father from the stage and seems to draw strength from his decline.

In general, the researchers see both middle age and older males as using woman as the focus for much projected material. "The woman is the figure of 'unchecked' impulse (which) breaks into a scene otherwise peopled by more restrained or affiliative figures. She is a figure of primal omnipotence and wrath—'a devil' . . .'" (Neugarten & Guttman, 1968).

This projective modality seems to also operate in the males' perception of the younger generation, and the social environment in general. As a group, middle aged men tend to deny their own aggressiveness and impulsivity. They simultaneously tend to attribute these characteristics increasingly to others, while also becoming more strident in their demands for conformity and more punitive and less forgiving towards deviance (Gergen & Back, 1966). The younger male becomes a particular receptacle for such projective attribution (Lowenthal & Chiriboga, 1972).

Given both the concrete and suggestive findings available on the mid-life experience, the following model appears to us a parsimonious way of ordering what is known or suspected and directing further systematic research.

Several major precipitants converge at around the age of forty[1] which predispose the man in contemporary culture to redefine his self; his life undergoes a qualitative shift. The simultaneous encroachment of these major changes creates a condition of vulnerability. Past modes of personal organization and relating to the social environment become less appropriate and useful. In the context of cultural values, many of the changes undergone are negative ones. Furthermore, the individual has an opportunity previously unavailable to him. He can, particularly if he has been successful by external criteria, gauge the extent to which his commitments to career and/or family have been worthwhile in the sense of providing the sense of gratification he had expected.

These potentially crisis inducing elements in the life space of the middle aged male are made even more difficult to manage by the matrix of social demands in which he is generally embedded. He is often in the position of having to be a role model and socializing force vis-à-vis his maturing children. Witnessing their adolescent struggles may reawaken or threaten his own identity conflicts, yet he is not nearly so free as the adolescent to work through or express his problems. While his physical strength may be declining, he is just approaching the height of his symbolic and social power. In work, community, and family social structure, he is expected to provide strength and commitment commensurate with his status. Thus, expression of the doubts and conflicts inherent in reaching middle age would be mitigated against by both the need for internal integration and by cultural expectations.

Thus, the personal sense of vulnerability and decline is sharply juxtaposed with the unfolding shift in status. It occurs in a context where the middle aged male is being thrust into the symbolic position of patriarchal leader. His own father is nearing death and is being progressively stripped of the roles and statuses which had reflected his dominance. The middle aged man is called upon to symbolically become his father: To assume responsibility for the "family" vis-à-vis the larger culture, to be the rock upon which the interpersonal network rests. (The fact that his dominance becomes a point of contention with his wife and children—and perhaps even with his aging parents—does not mitigate the latent expectation that he assume the position successfully. It becomes the ideal against which his potency is measured, both by himself and others.) This displacement of the father presumably evokes stress and internal conflict. While supplanting or out-achieving the father may have been a central project for the maturing adult, his actual ascendency is over a now weakened and sympathetic figure. Guilt and depression would intermingle with any potential elation. To the degree that the middle aged male's identification with the father is strengthened by the role shift, it functions to emphasize the sense of deterioration and mortality associated with his own physiological changes. Finally, looking to the father or cultural "elders" as a source of strength, control and wisdom, becomes a mechanism no longer available to the middle aged. As the source of control, one becomes less free to express vulnerability or find external agents to lean on, in either fantasy or reality.

Like the adolescent, the middle aged male is confronted by biological, status, and role changes that precipitate efforts to redefine who he is; but unlike the adolescent he is not granted an institutionalized moratorium for exploring identities. Instead he is more constrained than ever by the expectations of others, his obligations to them and his concern for his already established identity, which is a known if not entirely satisfactory commodity.

However, there are some culturally legitimate identities open to him that allow for stabilization (if not resolution) of the crisis. By providing intra- and extra-familial roles as well as modes of self perceptions and self-system organization, these cultural stereotypes can be seen as providing congruent "solutions" to the myriad problems of transition to middle age. These solutions may themselves be more or less problematic and are subsumed in our typology.

While we recognize the pitfalls inherent in attempting to extrapolate personal modes of response from group data, some general characteristics of the middle aged male and a tentative typology of response types or syndromes might be hypothesized. We advance this set of assumptions and typology as a potential structuring device for future research. They have the properties of being:

1. a logical way of integrating the findings bearing on the topic,
2. consistent with many of the persuasive portrayals which abound in popular culture,
3. the basis for specifying the major dimensions of variables associated with the mid-life crisis and reactions to it.

The stereotypes and clinical portrayals available are probably neither exhaustive nor mutually exclusive. What is remarkable about them is that they are all derived from the interplay of a limited number of themes and concerns and portray personal responses as being built around a relatively few devices. Since the stereotypes represent the extreme points along these dimensions, they help to highlight the focus of variables for investigation and to generate firmer expectations about the relations between variables.

For the purposes of illustrations, the typology might be arranged on the two dimensions given in the table below.

	Open Confrontation with Crisis	Denial of Crisis
Satisfied	Assess past and present with conscious sense of satisfaction. Few symptoms of distress. Open to own feelings. Acceptance of out-groups. Feels in control of fate.	Overtly satisfied. Attitudinally rigid. Denies feelings. High authoritarianism. High or covert depressions and anxiety. High in symptom formation. Merton's Ritualistic Conformer.
Dissatisfied	High alienation. Active identity struggle. Ego-oriented, uninvolved interpersonally. Low authoritarianism.	Highest in authoritarianism. Conflict with children. Dissatisfaction associated with environmental factors.

One working assumption underlying the typology is that, while the problematic aspects of entering middle age are often denied under direct questioning, the issue appears to have a greater degree of emotional saliency than is overtly recognized or admitted.

Direct confrontation with the issues of middle age appears to be a privilege of the affluent. Those who have consciously confronted the issues as outlined would fall into two categories, the overtly satisfied and the overtly dissatisfied. The former type might be characterized as transcendent-generative. In Erickson's terms (1956), they are able to assess their past and present and match them to inner feelings with a positive sense of satisfaction. The transcendent-generative would tend to exhibit few symptoms of psychological and psychosomatic distress, have positive feelings toward work and marriage, have a definite and satisfactory sense of self, be open to his own feelings, have good relations with his children, tend to be non-punitive and accepting of out-groups, feel in control of his fate and have high tolerance for ambiguity.

Those who are self-reflective and overtly dissatisfied with life and work would tend toward the image of the struggling anti-hero discussed above. They would be expected to be somewhat more symptomatic than the first group, but to be distinguished primarily by a strong sense of alienation and an active identity struggle. Being highly ego-oriented in his concerns, the anti-hero would be basically uninvolved interpersonally and hence show relatively little concern about controlling his children. He would be neither ethnocentric nor authoritarian attitudinally. This would be the true or active middle aged identity crisis and would be overrepresented in the middle or upper middle class, especially in individuals who have undergone extreme status mobility.

The third and fourth types might be characterized as the repressed-depressive and the punitive-disenchanted or "authoritarian" syndrome. The former would tend to represent themselves—in response to overt questioning—as similar to the transcendent-generative. In fact, they would embody many of the characteristics attributed to the faceless American in existential writing (Laing, 1967), black humor literature (Vonnegut, 1969; Friedman, 1962 & 1970), and similar critiques of modern mass culture (Cleaver, 1968). The repressed-depressive is beset by concerns about potency and death which he cannot confront, is attitudinally rigid, more punitive and ethnocentric than groups one and two and is constantly engaged in the struggle to deny his own feelings. His discontent might find expression in religion, alcoholism, hypochondriasis or psychosomatic ailment, and he tends to exhibit unrecognized depression and anxiety. Overall, there is a large gap between his presentation on self-report measures and the way he appears on indicators less amenable to conscious or preconscious manipulation.

There is also suggestive evidence that, in the paternal role, this group's ambivalence may lead not only to repressive rigidity, but also to covert reinforcement of the son's tendency to rebel and "act out." Such reinforcement would obviously serve the function of permitting the father, in the name of innocence, to vicariously enjoy expressive release and aggression against a system which he overtly supports but which he may experience as oppressive. That is, the father may indirectly communicate to the son a sense of his own dissatisfaction and impotence, making the son's emulation of him highly improbable. Kenniston's study of alienated youth seems strongly to indicate that the "uncommitted" perceive their fathers—who tend to be successful by external criteria—as in reality acquiescent to an alien external system. They describe their fathers as having "sold out" something within themselves, thereby killing off a most important part of themselves.

And in the implicit descriptions of their parents' relationship with each other, we have noted how alienated subjects describe their mothers as the more vigorous, decisive and strong. But the most specific instance of father's defeat by life comes in these subjects' account of their fathers' vocations. Here they emphasize the abandonment of early hopes and youthful dreams, and the attendant breaking of their fathers' spirits.

The subjects imply a certain sympathy for the abandoned dreams of their fathers, and perhaps for their image of the youthful fathers themselves; but toward their fathers as they are now, they feel (or communicate) a lack of basic respect. Their sympathy for their fathers is more attached to their fantasy of what their fathers were like twenty-five years ago (Kenniston, n/d).

Such perceptions of the father are thus not themselves without ambivalence. Rebellion seems to be linked to love of the father, at least some part of him now lost. A crucial question is to what extent the father indicated to the son that this is the only lovable part of himself. The father can espouse any number of ideologies while acting out his rebellion indirectly.

The fourth type combines his denial of inner feelings with projection, turning his anger and self-hatred toward dissidents and outgroups. This stereotype is, of course, congruent with Adorno's characterization of the "authoritarian personality" whose need for controls is expressed in a paranoid world view, a denial of aggressive impulses within the self and the adoption of a rigid and punitive sociomoral code (Adorno, Frenkel-Brunswick, Levinson, & Sanford, 1950). While Adorno's work had obvious methodological shortcomings, his conceptualization may nonetheless be useful in ordering the particular phenomenon of reaction to middle age. Those approaching the authoritarian stereotype may openly express discontent, but it is couched in terms of the necessity of controlling the environment ("this country is falling apart," "kids don't have enough respect for their parents") or altering one's circumstances in terms of income and status. It would be associated with the working or lower middle class. This kind of discontent is thus vocalized and experienced in system confirming terms.

We would expect the two types of response based on denial to be preponderant among those for whom middle age is, in fact, problematic. The individual's tendency to deny this issue and its associated affect is socially reinforced. By reaffirming those values by which he has lived, the middle aged male can both justify himself and support normative integration. In so doing, he is enabled to retain symbolic potency as recompense for his declining physical and emotional vigor. To denounce the meaningfulness of the normative structure in which he has gained (or at least sought after) some measure of power, prestige, and respectability would be to admit, like Vonnegut's and Bellow's heroes, the meaninglessness of their own existence. The middle aged have, by and large, established a behavioral commitment to the value system of self denial, striving, and conformity to social norms which may be most difficult to undo (Festinger). In fact, as an existence based on these organizing principles becomes more problematic, the need to reaffirm them becomes more urgent.

As we have attempted to show, these four primary stereotypes are not only common in the culture, they are also congruent with both the direct and tangential findings on middle age. Each can be seen as representing an integrated mode of response to a common set of role and psychological pressures associated with a major status shift. Individuals may tend to move out of one mode of response on a transitory basis (as when the repressed go on a "binge" and move closer to the perceptions and behavior of the anti-hero) and, perhaps, show a combination of responses. The repressed-depressives, for example, are sometimes portrayed as being amenable to adopting the authoritarian response when under sufficient stress. In general, however, we might suspect that individuals move toward one mode or another as an overall means of ego-defense and as an accepted way of dealing with the social environment. Culture provides well delineated role models for each type of response, increasing the probability of such movement. That is, the existence and popularity of the stereotypes themselves represents a socializing force which works in just this direction.

Summary and Discussion

We can summarize our working assumptions as follows. Men entering middle age, as a group, confront a common set of life space alterations which predispose them to undergo a crisis; that is, their relation to self and social environment tends to become problematic in a way that represents a qualitative shift from earlier adulthood. For some, these changes are minimally disturbing or even viewed positively, and new modes to integration are easily forged or old ones perpetuated.

More commonly, we would hypothesize, the problem is not so easily resolved. Relatively few men tend to openly recognize and confront the disturbing issues associated with middle age in our culture. For those who do, a total reopening of assumptions and reexamination of self and society may be likely to ensue. Such a reaction tends to be associated—at least initially—with a dissatisfaction with one's life, one's commitments and socially approved values. For many more, it would seem, the stress associated with the issue is seen in other terms or totally repressed and denied. It may remain, nonetheless, an underlying factor and predisposes him toward a number of symptom formations and reactive behavior patterns and attitudes. The strength and consistency of the denial operate to make the reaction to the crisis even more extreme and personally damaging, and may have important implications for those who share the interpersonal matrix of the middle aged male (Levi, Stierlin, & Savark, 1972).

Past research in the area of middle age has not, we would contend, been highly productive because it has not combined methodological rigor with a holistic and depth view of the phenomena. The biological and role changes which occur around middle age can best be interpreted as experiential rather than literal impingements on the self. That is, their major impact comes about through the endowment of meaning on these changes by the individual and by his culture. The processes by which these changes are recognized (or avoided) assessed and adapted to by the individual thus become crucial areas for examination.

Notes

1. This chronological estimate obviously varies with social class as well as individual life circumstances.

References

Adorno, T. W., Frenkel-Brunswick, E. F., Levinson, D. J., & Sanford, R. N. *The Authoritarian Personality*. New York: Harper & Row, 1970.

Bellow, S. *Herzog*. New York: Viking, 1964.

Bergler, E. N. *The Revolt of the Middle Aged Man*. New York: A. A. Wyn, 1954.

Blumenthal, I. S. *Research and the Ulcer Problem*. Rand Corp., June 1959.

Cleaver, E. *Soul on Ice*. New York: Delta, 1968.

Cuber, J. F. & Harroff, P. B. *The Significant Americans*. New York: Appleton-Century, 1965.

Deutscher, I. The Quality of Postparental Life. *Middle Age and Aging*. B. Neugarten (ed.) Chicago: The University of Chicago Press, 1968, pp. 255-269.

Erickson, E. The Problem of Ego Identity. *Journal of the American Psychoanalytic Association* IV: 1, pp. 58-121, 1956.

Festinger, L. *A Theory of Cognitive Dissonance*. Stanford, CA: Stanford University Press, 1957.

Fried, B. *The Middle Age Crisis*. New York: Harper & Row, 1967.

Friedman, B. J. *Stern*. New York: Simon & Schuster, 1962.

———. *The Dick*. New York: Knopf, 1970.

Gergen & Back, 1966, as cited in Riley, M. W. & Foner, A. *Aging and Society*, Vol. 1. New York: Russell Sage, 1968, p. 325.

Gurin, G., Veroff, J., & Feld, S. *Americans View their Mental Health.* New York: Basic Books, 1960, pp. 19-20.

Hyman, H. & Sheatsley, P. B. The Authoritarian Personality—A Methodological Critique, in *Continuities in Social Research,* Jalnda and Christie (eds.) New York: Free Press, 1964.

Jacques, E. Death and the Midlife Crisis. *International Journal of Psychoanalysis,* 46, October 1965, pp. 502-514.

Jaffe, A. J. & Gordon, J. B. *Demography of the Middle Years: an Interim Report of the Highlights.* New York: Bureau of Applied Social Research, January 1968.

Kazan, E. *The Arrangement.* New York: Stein & Day, 1967.

Laing, R. D. *The Divided Self.* London: Tavistock, 1960.

———. *The Politics of Experience.* New York: Ballantine, 1967.

Leighton et al. 1963, as cited in Riley, M. W. & Foner, A. *Aging and Society,* Vol. 1. New York: Russell Sage, 1968, p. 373.

Levi, L. D., Stierlin, H. & Savark, R. J. Fathers and Sons: The Interlocking Crisis of Integrity and Identity. *Psychiatry,* 35, February 1972.

Look Magazine and The *New York Times.*

Lowenthal, M. F. & Chiriboga, D. Transition to the Empty Nest: Crisis, Challenge or Belief. *Archives of General Psychiatry,* 26, p. 14, January 1972.

Miller, A. *Collected Papers.* Viking, 1957.

Moon, L. E. & Palton, R. F. The Alcoholic Psychotic in New York State Mental Hospitals, 1951-1960. *Quarterly Journal of Studies in Alcohol* 24: 4. December 1963, pp. 664-681.

Neugarten, B. The Awareness of Middle Age. *Middle Age and Aging,* B. Neugarten (ed.) Chicago: The University of Chicago Press, 1968.

Neugarten, B. L. & Guttman, D. L. Age-Sex Roles and Personality in the Middle Age: A TAT Study. *Middle Age and Aging.* B. Neugarten (ed.) Chicago: The University of Chicago Press, 1968.

Pasamanick, 1962, as cited in Riley, M. W. & Foner, A. *Aging and Society,* Vol 1. New York: Russell Sage, 1968, p. 370.

Pearce, V. & Newton, S. *The Condition of Human Growth.* New York: Citadel Press, 1963.

Pineo, P. C. Disenchantment in Later Years in Marriage. *Middle Age and Aging.* B. Neugarten (ed.) Chicago: The University of Chicago Press, 1968.

Roth, P. *Portnoy's Complaint.* New York: Random House, 1969.

Slater, P. *The Pursuit of Loneliness.* Boston: Beacon, 1970.

Srole, L., Langner, T., Michael, S., Opler, M., & Rennie, A. C. *Mental Health in the Metropolis.* New York: McGraw Hill, 1962, p. 160.

Vital and Health Statistics—Selected Symptoms of Psychological Distress, Series 11, No. 37, U.S. Dept. of HEW, PHS, p. 8.

Vonnegut, K. *Slaughterhouse Five.* New York: Delta, 1969.

Wheelis, A. *The Seeker.*

3.2

Some Irrational Beliefs About Retirement in the United States

William Withers

For many people retirement is a traumatic experience. It usually occurs prematurely and involuntarily at ages well below the proverbial three score and ten. Income is drastically reduced when it happens. At least 40 percent of all employees are not covered by private pensions, and many who supposedly are never receive a penny: They change jobs prior to eligibility, or the funds are dissipated. Social Security benefits and savings seldom compensate for loss of the income they had when working or for the lack of a private pension.

But the trauma of retirement comes not simply from decreased income, although many regard it as the prime factor. Society has created institutions and values which make the retiree a social reject. Since he no longer works, he is relegated to an inferior social status. Such social downgrading was caused by the Industrial Revolution, which placed prime value on work rather than leisure (Jones, 1968).

Deprived of work, the social basis of self-respect, it becomes difficult for the individual to justify his leisure. Bravely he insists that his golf score, assisting his wife with the household chores and volunteering for work with the Red Cross are adequate substitutes for being a business executive or a well-paid, blue-collar worker. He tries to rebel against the mores, but the attempt is made at an age when he has lost much of his capacity for rebellion.

Reprinted from *Industrial Gerontology*, 1 (1) new series, 1974, pp. 23-32. Copyright by the National Council on Aging, Inc.

The arbitrariness of our retirement systems and the many irrational attitudes and mistaken beliefs about older workers make the problems of retirement difficult to solve. For example, consider the following assumptions for which there is little if any solid supporting evidence.

The right age for retirement is 65.

Work capacity always declines with age.

Older workers cannot be retrained.

It does not pay to retrain older workers, because they retire so soon afterward.

It is futile to retrain older workers, because no one will hire them.

Older workers cannot be hired by companies with insurance programs, because it is impossible to fit them into these programs.

It is undesirable to hire older workers as a group; they are so poorly educated.

In retirement, income can be greatly reduced because old people consume less per person and need less income than young people.

Older workers should be retired because in our advanced technological economy their labor is not needed. They should make room for younger workers.

The Sacrosanct Age

For many people, Age 65 has been regarded as the right age for retirement, at least for men. It was legally sanctified in 1935 by the Social Security law. One fails to uncover any significant reason for this choice, except the fact that by then 65 had become common as a cut-off point in business. Moreover, life expectancy was approaching 70, and a five-year prior retirement must have seemed logical.

It should not be implied here that a higher age should have been chosen due to the subsequent improvements in the health and productive capacity of older people. Rather, the difficulty with Age 65 comes from the rigidities it introduced into our retirement systems. An obvious illustration is the involuntary retirement of persons at 55 or less with no Social Security for seven or ten more years. At the upper end of the age scale, still-capable people are forced to retire at 65; if they go on working, their earnings are arbitrarily limited.

The meaninglessness of Age 65 is evinced by the deviations from it. In reducing the eligibility for Social Security to 62, first for women and then for men, even the Federal Government departed from the original plan. But the main deviation occurred in private business, seen in the decreasing participation rates for male workers in the labor force aged 55 to 64 from 83.4 percent to 80.5 percent between 1950 and 1973.

In many private and public pension systems, retirement may occur after 20 or 25 years of service without regard to age at the time of retirement, except that in many plans a person must be at least 55. Thus, in some pension systems age has become less of a qualification for retirement than years of employment. Where employees are not in jobs covered by pensions, separation from employment often occurs without a specific age related to it.

One man may be thrown out of work at 45 simply because the business that employed him failed and he cannot find other work for which he is suited. The age at which people are considered too old for a job varies widely. In one occupation it may be 45; in another, 60. In fact, age often is not so much a determining factor in the discharge of older workers as the pressure to employ younger people or management's effort to reduce or avoid large pension obligations.

Systems more flexible in Europe

In some European countries, age requirements in public and private pension systems are more flexible than in the United States. Specific ages do not have the sanctity we bestow on age 65. Public insurance plans are less uniform and varied to suit different types of employment. Austria, for example, has separate systems for wage earners, farmers, self-employed workers and miners. Although the normal retirement ages for men and women are usually 60 to 65, pensions may be received as much as five years earlier (Organisation of Economic Cooperation and Development, 1970).

Also in European systems, a variety of circumstances permits workers to receive pensions prior to the specified retirement age. Austria, Italy and Luxembourg allow a lower pensionable age when insurance payments have been made for 35 or 40 years. In Austria and West Germany, the pensionable age may be reduced if a worker is currently unemployed and has been involuntarily so for one year. In Greece, Spain and Italy, earlier retirement is allowed in unusually tiring or unhealthful employment. Austria, Denmark and Turkey permit earlier retirement in case of chronic illness. In 12 countries, workers receiving pensions may continue to work and earn any amount. (These countries include France, Germany, Iceland, Ireland, Italy, Luxembourg, the Netherlands, Norway, Sweden and Switzerland.)

Only three countries, Belgium, Greece and Sweden, follow our practice of limiting the amount of pensions granted before a fixed retirement age to the reduced actuarial value of contributions, and only the United States and Great Britain restrict the amount a pensioner can earn after retirement.

Fixing retirement universally at a given age is irrational because it (1) bears no strict relationship to work capacity; (2) is not adapted to the conditions or practices of different industries or occupations; (3) limits older peoples' potential earnings even though security benefits fail to supply them with enough income; (4) creates an artificial reason for the premature discharge of older workers; and (5) if the pension system is based strictly on an actuarial basis, the number of years worked and contributions made, *not the retirement age*, should determine the eligibility of an employee to receive a pension.

Productivity assumptions are erroneous

Irrationality about retirement age is closely associated with irrationality about older-worker productivity. If workers produce progressively less as they grow older, surely by 65 they should be put out to pasture. If the regression in capacity accelerates due to technological advancement, the argument for retirement at 65 becomes stronger. Closely related is the lesser degree of formal schooling of the present 45-to-65 group, since it is assumed that the kinds of jobs that become available as technology advances require more education. If true, can the older worker be retrained as he is forced out of the labor market by technology? The answer is often negative, on the assumption that aging causes a decline in learning capacity.

Let us first consider the relevance of formal schooling. To begin, it is largely irrelevant except for a few professional occupations. Modern technology, by and large, does not require that the average worker have more formal schooling (Berg, 1970; Jaffe and Froomkin, 1968).

Secondly, older workers in the next couple of decades will have much more formal schooling than at present. For persons aged 25 to 34, the median number of years of school completed will increase from about 12.5 in 1970 to 13.0 in 1990; for those aged 45 to 54 the median will rise from 12.1 to about 12.6; and for the age group 55 to 64, from 10.6 to 12.5 (Johnston, 1973).

As to retraining, available evidence indicates that (1) older people can be retrained as readily as the young provided the training methods are suitable to them (McFarland, 1973), and (2) that intelligence, a factor in retraining, does not decline with age (Jamieson, 1968; Haberlandt, 1973). Longevity studies of intelligence, which at one time tended to prove its decline with age, more recently have demonstrated the opposite when tested groups are differentiated by educational and environmental background (Green and Reimanis, 1970).

Contentions such as the inadvisability of training older workers because they will soon retire, or that no one will hire them after retraining, are also fallacious (Mullan and Gorman, 1972). They assume inhibiting conditions which do not necessarily exist. If a worker, age 60, is retrained at a cost of $1,000, this expenditure is similar to a capital investment. If the annual yield on an investment is high enough and spread over sufficient time, the pay-back point is reached and profits are earned. If the worker in our example were retired in a year, obviously it might not pay to retrain him, but why retire him in a year? Contradictory reasoning is involved in the no-hiring assumption.

As for the argument that labor productivity decreases with age, the evidence is contradictory; it depends on the individual and the job (Arvey and Mussio, 1973).

Do old people need less income?

Pensions and retirement income, including Social Security benefits, are far less on the average than preretirement incomes. Lower retirement income is rationalized by the assumption that people 65 and over need less to live on, explicitly stated in the U.S. Department of Labor's Retired Couple's Budget for a Moderate Living Standard (1966). They have no go-to-work expenses; they need less entertainment money; less clothes replacement; less furniture, and so on. But a percentage decrease in need is seldom cited, nor are most fully aware of the amount of the decrease in income that occurs.

Jaffe (1972), found that the median annual income of families with 65-year-old heads were 49 percent of those with heads 55 to 64. The percentage has declined steadily from 56 percent in the period 1950 to 1954. Those over 65 living alone, in 1969 about two-fifths of the upper-age population, had an even greater percentage of income reductions.

But the assumption that "need is less" is wrong. A number of investigations reveal that older people's consumption needs increase. Even with such belt-tightening as they can and do manage, their legitimate needs cannot be reduced by 50 percent. Jaffe compared *per capita* expenditures of cohorts of family heads of the same income class at ages 65 to 74 with those 55 to 64. Total expenditures of the older heads were nine percent higher. Clothing expenses were five percent less, but all other types of spending were greater.

In recent years, the areas where old age expenditures increase, such as rent and medical care, have been inflated most. Notions about the reduced consumption of old people are a throwback to the early 19th century rural life, when grandmother lived at home with her children and grandchildren in the family farmhouse and ate only porridge because she had lost her teeth. The landlord did not raise her rent, and her clothing and medical costs were negligible.

Even if we could assume that old people are able to reduce their standard of living drastically, the question remains, why should they? Are they not entitled to live as well as anyone else? One suspects social rejection of the aged or a belief that only the young can enjoy life. Also involved is the work ethic labeling persons who don't make money inferior and unworthy of much income. They should be happy to get anything; they are "through," and society is through with them.

Aren't older workers needed?

Has technology so increased productivity that we can produce all we need with a smaller and smaller labor force? A common belief is that we can. If true, there *is* a strong case for retiring people earlier.

We have been producing much more from year to year, with shorter hours and longer vacations. In real terms, the Gross National Product (GNP) has increased greatly since World War II; we are still growing, although at a rather slow rate. Thus, mathematical calculations can be made which seem to prove that fewer and fewer workers are needed, that older workers will find it increasingly difficult to obtain jobs and that the average retirement age will be further reduced.

Jaffe (1972) makes such calculations. He estimates, for example, that with a work year of 1,560 hours, a three percent average annual increase in output per man-hour and an average annual increase in the GNP of four percent, only 106 million workers will be needed in the year 2000, although the total minimum labor force will amount to 123 million in that year. His projections may come true because of our economic system's restrictive character, but his method of projection may be incorrect.

Output per man-hour is a physical figure which cannot really be compared with GNP growth, a monetary figure, even if converted for price change. In modern income flow analysis, full employment equilibrium is a parity of consumption and investment spending with incomes (wages, interest, rent and profits) at a level that will employ everyone seeking work, whatever the output per man-hour. At income levels near full employment, output per man-hour declines. Whether we can or will employ everyone in the labor force depends on our willingness *to pay everyone*, and this in turn depends upon what we are willing *to pay for*.

Millions of citizens impoverished

If we consider our present economic system, we find millions of people at or below the poverty level. They lack adequate food, clothing, housing, education, social services, recreational facilities and medical care. If we set aside all theoretical and statistical analysis, we are bound to conclude that we still have too much poverty. We do not produce enough despite our great economic progress; much of what we need to produce requires more manpower. It cannot be produced through machines that increase output per man-hour alone.

Can we mechanize doctors, teachers, entertainers, social workers so that one worker produces as much as three or four did before? The future picture of labor needs would seem different if seen from the standpoint of physical input and output. In money terms, we may need less labor; in physical terms, we need more.

The immediate question is: Can we expect the future economy to shift money demands so that it results in a fuller satisfaction of our physical needs? Though no one knows, must we assume that it cannot or will not? Ever since the New Deal, the distribution of income has been altered in the direction of greater public welfare.

The future need for older workers will depend in part on the population's age distribution and its absolute size. A stationary population appears to be in the offing; the chart of age distribution is changing from a pyramid into an oblong (U.S. Bureau of the Census, 1972). Assuming a stationary population and a growing economy, is it not reasonable to expect an increase in the demand for labor? If there will not be enough 21-to-44 year-old workers in the labor force to meet the accelerating demand for labor, employers will be forced to turn to those in the 45-to-65 age group.

Irrationality bases are multiple

The programs to cope with old age problems in this country amount to a confused and jerry-built structure of Social Security and public assistance, resulting from conflicts with older beliefs and new social values which have emerged since World War II. In the early days of the New Deal, when the Federal Government assumed great responsibility for relief through the Federal Emergency Relief Administration (FERA) and the Works Progress Administration (WPA), a controversy developed in Washington over *need* and *right*. The FERA distributed millions of dollars in terms of need, but a public reaction soon developed against giving money "for nothing." In part, the WPA was a response to this objection by making token work the basis of relief. Subsequently, the Social Security system was established to provide pensions after 65 *as a right* created through payroll tax deductions from wages during the working lives of the claimants.

Aid to those with low incomes continued and also increased on both the local and national government levels. We compromised. Persons with insufficient income receive supplements partly based on need and partly on right. Since neither is enough to eliminate poverty in old age, it continues to be a serious national problem.

The concept of *right* stems from the 19th century work ethic. Payment is made for work, and one has a right to an old-age income only if he has worked and saved for it. He saves either voluntarily or through compulsion in the Social Security system of saving. Consequently, to give people in their old age, or at any age, money which they have not earned or saved seriously violates the work ethic. Our Social Security system, originally (and which largely remains) actuarial in theory, is founded on the work ethic. Every major increase in benefits requires an increase in payroll deductions.[1]

The concept of right may be questioned now just as it was in the early New Deal days. If a person works hard all his life, does he have a right only to a substandard living merely because he could not save enough to provide an annuity that will pay better? Many of our public pension systems for teachers, policemen, firemen and other civil servants have abandoned the actuarial basis. If civil servants have a right to a reasonable pension whether or not their payroll deductions are adequate to pay for it, why is the same not true for the great mass of Social Security recipients? What, then, is meant by *right*? Is it the right to receive what an individual saved or the right to a decent standard of living in his old age?

Several objections have been raised to discarding the actuarial basis for Social Security. Some say it would cost too much, but actually the country could afford it. The fact is we are not sure that we want to discard it. Basically that *is* the reason, and it leads us right back to the work ethic and to another element in the situation—derogation of age. In our time, Youth is King.

A wave of Youthism has had a counterpart in the derogation of age since World War II. Few societies today place such high value on youth and so little value on age as does the United States. No doubt the results of studies by sociologists and anthropologists will show the value system is due partly to the war which caused a veneration of power and youth and widespread rejection of older ways of thinking. Its emergent attitudes and values were related to youth. Emphasis on strength and the "looks" of things are all associated with youth. As youth was upgraded, naturally age went down. So, some of our irrationalities about retirement and older workers are the rationalizations used to derogate age.

We cannot solve the problems of older workers, retirement and old-age poverty unless we think straight about these matters. The removal of old-age poverty should be a prime national objective. Higher incomes for older people should be mandated. They can be provided if we have a higher rate of economic growth, fuller employment of those over 45 and public and private pensions based on need, far higher than those we have now.

Admittedly, all this will require more careful national planning than we now have and also basic revisions in our social values and priorities. But fundamental changes will not be possible if we cling to our retirement irrationalities.

Notes

1. See Book Review of Brown's *An American Philosophy of Social Security: Evolution and Issues*, p. 90.

References

Arvey, R. D. and Mussio, S. J. Test Discrimination, Job Performance and Age. *Industrial Gerontology*, No. 16, pp. 20-29, Winter 1973.

Berg, I. *Education and Jobs: The Great Training Robbery*, New York, Praeger Publishers for Urban Education, 1970.

Green, R. F. and Reimanis, G. The Age-Intelligence Relationship— Longitudinal Studies Can Mislead. *Industrial Gerontology*, No. 6, pp. 1-16, Summer 1970.

Haberlandt, K. F. Learning, Memory and Age. *Industrial Gerontology*, No. 19, pp. 20-37, Fall 1973.

Jaffe, A. J. Retirement: A Cloudy Future. *Industrial Gerontology*, No. 14, pp. 1-88, Summer 1972.

———. and Froomkin, J. *Technology and Jobs*, New York, Praeger Publishers, 1968.

Jamieson, G. H. Age, Speed, and Accuracy: A Study in Industrial Retraining. *Occupational Psychology*, 40 (4): 237-242, 1968.

Johnston, D. F. Education of Workers: Projections to 1990. *Monthly Labor Review*, 96 (11): 22-31, 1973.

Jones, H. A. The Elderly Person. *Quarterly Journal of the National Old Peoples Welfare Council*, 81: 2-8, June 1968.

McFarland, Ross A. The Need for Functional Age Measurements in Industrial Gerontology. *Industrial Gerontology*, No. 19, pp. 1-19, Fall 1973.

Mullan, C. and Gorman, L. Facilitating Adaptation to Change: A Case Study in Retraining Middle-Aged and Older Workers at *Aer Lingus. Industrial Gerontology*, No. 15, pp. 20-39, Fall 1972.

Organisation for Economic Cooperation and Development. *Flexibility of Retirement Age*, Paris, 1970.

U.S. Bureau of the Census. Projections of the Population of the United States by Age and Sex: 1972 to 2020, *Population Estimates and Projections*, Series P-25, No. 493, December 1972.

U.S. Department of Labor, Bureau of Labor Statistics. *Retired Couple's Budget for a Moderate Living Standard*, Bulletin No. 1570-A, Autumn 1966.

3.3

Relocation of the Elderly

Beverly A. Yawney and Darrell L. Slover

Most people change their residence for a better job or a better home. But when an elderly person moves, it is likely to be the result of financial or medical setbacks, loss of spouse, or the termination of a career. It may have a wide range of effects, some beneficial and others detrimental, even lethal. This article summarizes the research that has been done on relocation of the elderly and uses the findings to recommend strategies for helping older persons who are moving.

Moving is disruptive at any age, and for the older person it is often compounded by social isolation, intergenerational conflict, or the feeling of imposing upon someone or being imposed upon. A major illness, bereavement, financial difficulty, or perceptual-motor impairment may be interfering with the tasks of daily living. These problems are usually interdependent, and the move is imbedded in the complex.

Older people move to apartments, to low-income public housing, retirement villages, age-segregated housing, homes of family or children, and nursing homes or hospitals. When they move, their life-style changes. Some become totally dependent; others increase their independence. Most older people move more than once as age-related needs and circumstances change.

Reprinted with permission of the National Association of Social Workers, from *Social Work*, Vol. 18, No. 3 (May 1973), pp. 86-95.

The effects of moving are sometimes salutary. Moves to new age-segregated apartment complexes have resulted in improved health, morale, and social relations (Carp, 1967; Lawton & Jaffe, 1967; Havens, 1966). Moving from an institution to the community may also result in improvements in functioning and morale (Stotsky, 1967; Jasnau, 1967; Cohen & Kraft, 1967). A growing body of research suggests, however, that relocation of the elderly entails considerable risk. In many cases, disruption of social relations, decline in morale, disorientation, and increase in mortality and morbidity rates have occurred after relocation. Aldrich's and Mendkoff's follow-up of 182 residents of a home for the chronically disabled, all of whom were moved to new residences after the home's closing, revealed a significantly higher mortality rate in the three months following the move. Many residents responded with anger, anxiety, and depression (Aldrich & Mendkoff, 1963).

Miller and Lieberman have described another situation in which residents of an old-age home were moved for administrative reasons. Twenty-three of the forty-five subjects in their study were judged to have shown serious physical or psychological deterioration soon after the move (Miller & Lieberman, 1965). A study of the results of transfers of patients from one ward to another within a mental hospital revealed a 35 percent increase in the mortality rate among geriatric patients (Jasnau, 1967). This pattern has been repeated in a number of instances (Aleksandrowicz, 1961; Killian, 1970; Blenkner, 1967; Fried, 1963; Shahimian, Goldfarb & Turner, 1966).

Types of Relocation

Relocation takes four basic directions: (1) from one community setting to another, (2) from the community to an institution, (3) from one institution to another, and (4) from an institution to the community. A move in any of these directions may disrupt relationships with the past and the present, may fragment routines, change expectations, and disrupt spatiotemporal orientation. Individual attitudes about different moves will vary from happy anticipation to dread.

Moves from one community setting to another may be made at the time of retirement or when the children leave home and smaller quarters seem more suitable. The death of a spouse is another occasion for such a move. For many elderly people a small apartment in the immediate locale offers the best solution; others prefer to move to warmer climates or retirement villages and seek the companionship of persons their own age.

Crisis situations—emotional problems or failing health—frequently prompt a move to an institution. The individual has little control over the situation in such a crisis, and the move is involuntary and often traumatic.

Many older persons already in institutions have no one to care for them after discharge. The usual solution is a move from that institution to another one—a nursing home, an old-age home, or a foster home in the community (Stotsky, 1966; Flynn, 1966). In other cases, the individual may be sufficiently improved to return to independent community living.

Stages

Relocation is a complex sequence of experiences and emotional responses, culminating in various levels of psychosocial well-being. To help clarify the variety of situations and demands that face the older person, the relocation process can be divided into three stages: (1) decision and preparation, (2) impact, and (3) settling in (Lieberman, 1965).

The decision and preparation stage.   Deciding that a move is necessary and choosing the destination are only the first of many decisions that must be made. Emotional reactions to the problems that precipitated the move must be resolved (Brody). The older person has to cope with the entry procedures of the new environment, make decisions about the disposition of his belongings, deal with the institutions involved in his business and legal affairs, and overcome his regrets about leaving familiar surroundings and friends. At the same time he is trying to anticipate the changes that will be required in his daily living patterns.

There is a high level of mobilization during this stage. A sense of helplessness and powerlessness mixed with anxiety has been observed more frequently among older people awaiting institutionalization than among long-term institutional residents. In many cases, there is a tendency toward depression, withdrawal, and lowered self-esteem. Crises relating to separation, loss, and rejection have also been observed during this stage (Lieberman, Prock & Tobin, 1968). Apparently there is no significant increase in mortality or physical and psychiatric disabilities, but it does seem that the prerelocation stress may precipitate such disabilities later (Lieberman, 1965). Even when the move is anticipated with pleasure, there are still many decisions to be made, and uncertainty about the new environment arises at a time when the individual may be least able to cope with it.

The impact stage.   The impact stage, during and immediately after the actual move, is the period when the most adverse psychological effects of relocation have been observed. There are wide variations in the success of relocation adjustment and in the depth and quality of the experience, but most people express some degree of grief (Fried, 1963). A sense of helplessness, direct or misplaced anger, and depressive affect are evident. Disorientation, serious ego disabilities, role diffusion, and personal distress often appear. These reactions can be caused to some degree by the strange environment and disruption of familiar daily routines.

There is a tendency to idealize and long for the lost environment. It has been noted that those who enter institutions spend the first 1½ to 6 months shifting emphasis from the community to the task of mastering the new institutional environment. If unsuccessful, the older person may later withdraw and become insulated from the new environment. There are indications that most elderly residents never completely accept their new world (Lieberman, 1965).

Increased mortality and morbidity are most likely to occur during the impact stage. Mortality rates during the first year of actual residence average more than double the rate during the decision and preparation period (Lieberman, 1961). Some mortality studies show an increased death rate throughout the entire first year of residence, with the most crucial period occurring during the first three months (Aldrich, 1964; Aleksandrowicz, 1961).

The settling-in stage.   Once the initial shock of relocation has diminished, the individual is faced with the task of adapting to the new environment. Disrupted social patterns need to be reestablished, as do spatial and temporal ones. Inability or unwillingness to make new friends can be a major factor in unsuccessful relocation. Research suggests that loss of positive relationships with other people contributes to grief reactions during relocation (Fried, 1963).

Social-class membership may serve to mediate the individual's relationship to his environment. The urban poor tend to view the entire neighborhood—shopping areas, church, park, friends, merchants—as home. A move means developing a new spatial identity related to a wholly unfamiliar milieu. Members of the middle class, on the other hand, appear to be less dependent on external stability of place, on local social patterns, relationships, and routines. They are more likely to have developed flexible spatial patterns that are more functional in unfamiliar situations and surroundings. Thus a marked relationship has been found between social class and the depth of grief experienced during relocation: the higher the status, the smaller the likelihood of severe grief. It is primarily because external stability is so important to the working class that dislocation from a familiar residential area has a particularly disruptive effect on their spatial identity (Fried, 1963).

In a familiar neighborhood, an older person can devise ways of continuing to function independently through the support of neighbors, arrangements with shopkeepers and landlords, and supportive assistance from clergy and friends. A study of small towns found older people enmeshed in a network of close and intimate personal relations which prevent isolation and alienation. This condition appears to exist in older urban neighborhoods as well (Rose & Peterson, 1965).

The relocated older person no longer has the support of familiar surroundings, friends, church, and other organizations to help him. He is faced with the dual task of familiarizing himself with a new environment and developing a network of social relations. All this may be complicated by a decline in functional abilities and by the limited opportunities and status offered to the aged in our society.

The Relocatee

Although it has been difficult in research on relocation to measure the factors related to success and risk, there have been some findings with potential value for application by practitioners. These findings can be classified into three types of predictive relationships: (1) characteristics of the relocatee, (2) preparations for the move, and (3) the quality of the postrelocation environment.

Much research has been devoted to finding out which types of persons are more vulnerable to the stress of relocation. Increased mortality and declines in health, the outcome variables most commonly used in this research, have frequently been associated with organic brain damage (Aldrich & Mendkoff, 1973; Shahinian, Goldfarb & Turner, 1966; Guze & Cantwell, 1964; Miller & Lieberman, n/d).

> [The] senile psychotic person, although not sufficiently in contact to understand advance explanations of a move, is nevertheless sufficiently aware of familiar environmental cues to become disturbed when the cues are no longer at hand. According to this hypothesis, the senile psychotic individual cannot prepare for a change, and when the change occurs, he lacks the adaptive capacity to cope with it (Aldrich, 1964).

Measures are available to help the practitioner identify elderly persons who might be vulnerable to relocation stress because of organic brain damage (Goldfarb, 1964).

Ability to cope with the disruptions associated with relocation may also reflect the more general capacities of the organism to withstand stress. Poor health or advanced degenerative changes in physical functioning due to the aging process may prevent the older organism from marshaling its resources to withstand and recover from stress. The older person's equilibrium is more easily disrupted, and homeostatic processes tend to be slower. A combination of poor health and organic brain damage would call for a particularly poor prognosis for adaptation to stress, yet frequently this is just when relocation occurs: the person is hospitalized for medical reasons, enters a nursing home, or is admitted to a mental hospital.

Depression or the absence of hope is another factor that has been related to negative outcomes in mass transfers from one institution to another. Residents who were depressed before the transfer may feel they were deprived throughout their lives and that they accomplished little. Because their life lacks meaning, they seem unable to envision a future for themselves. They tend to suffer adverse physical or psychological reactions in the new environment (Lieberman, 1965).

In addition to assessing the relocatee's capacity to withstand stress, the worker should examine the person's *style* of adapting to new situations. One of the major factors found to affect ability to adjust is the pattern of the individual's prior mastery (Lieberman, 1965). Turner suggests that persons who coped well in the past can usually cope well in future stress situations *if* they are able to appraise the situation realistically. Among a sample of entrants to homes for the aged, she found that those who were generally more aggressive, distrustful, and hostile toward others adjusted more satisfactorily. Although these characteristics might be seen as dysfunctional for community living, they appear desirable or necessary for adapting to the demands of an institutional environment (Turner, 1968).

Throughout the life cycle, one develops basic psychological anchorages such as a positive body image, an acceptable home, socioeconomic security, patterns of satisfying activities, and a meaningful purpose in life. The older person would like to maintain these anchorages, but failing health or a changing environment may make the task difficult, and he may increasingly rely on defenses. Depression and psychoneurosis in later life can be precipitated when a person's security is threatened by fear of death or disability, financial problems, retirement, breaking up a home, becoming a burden, or moving to a strange location (Butler, 1967; Clow & Allen, 1951). The relocation experience is a prime threat to older persons since it often involves all of these stresses. Furthermore, the reaction of each person to the event and his subsequent adjustment are unique. The social worker must be sensitive to the wide individual differences among the elderly.

In short, the social worker's role in relocation should begin with a thorough assessment of the psychosocial functioning of each relocatee to determine his capacity to withstand stress, his readiness to cope with the event, his unique constellation of needs, and his suitability to the new environment. Poor health or severe disorientation often precipitate a decision to relocate but also minimize the person's ability to survive the relocation. In such cases, alternatives to relocation should be explored. If possible, the move might be delayed while the relocatee's readiness is strengthened through therapeutic intervention.

Preparation

There are means of intervention available to the worker assisting the relocatee through the stressful waiting period. However,

> practical measures . . . are, to a large extent, frustrated by the lack of community services (such as day-care, homemaker, or temporary care facilities), and by the unavailibility of financial aid which would enable the family to procure service for the amelioration of acute pressures (Brody).

Access to an interested counselor may provide psychological security during this period. Periodic telephone or personal contact by a social worker or paraprofessional aide provides assurance that the institution remains aware of the need for admission and will offer help with new emergencies. The Philadelphia Geriatric Center uses the following procedures during the waiting and admission periods:

1. Continuing social work services are given during the decision-making process for evaluation of psychological and social appropriateness of admission.
2. Help is offered with interim planning during the waiting period.
3. Visits and tours of the facilities are offered to the applicant.
4. Meals in the dining room help provide a realistic view of the institution.
5. Available community resources are mobilized, such as clinics, family agencies, nursing homes, and so on.
6. Referrals are made to public agencies for financial assistance.
7. Diagnostic medical studies are scheduled when necessary.
8. A portfolio is assembled that presents a comprehensive view of the individual and his life-style to the staff of the center (Brody).

A home for retired teachers maintains a room that prospective residents are invited to use for a day or so before making their decision to move in. When they become residents, the initial period is under a temporary contract which they can easily cancel. In two months, many of them say they are ready to leave. The predominant reason seems to be loneliness. Often they change their minds after visiting old acquaintances; the retirement home looks good in comparison with the noise, bustle, and lack of privacy in the home of family or friends (Posenauer, 1971).[1]

As a rule, older people move to smaller quarters; many personal possessions must be disposed of. If the relocation occurs at a time of crisis and considerable confusion, the person does not have a chance to consider what to do with his treasured possessions. In many cases someone else must make the decisions. Then the person feels grieved and resentful over the lost articles. It is "something *they* did to me." Families should be encouraged to discuss the disposal of possessions with the older person *before* a crisis develops. In this way the older person can maintain a central role in the process. He might derive pleasure and satisfaction from giving possessions to friends or donating them to charities. At times there will be a need for some of the person's things in the new environment; a public housing project, for example, may have a library with many empty shelves. Knowing that one's former possessions will be used and appreciated is not as traumatic as not knowing what happened to them.

In general, families place elderly relatives in institutions only as a last resort. Workers should recognize and understand their emotional struggles, and should use family ties by actively involving the children and helping them to appraise realistically the needs and capacities of the older person. The older person himself should play a central role in all decisions. This helps him maintain his identity during the period of disruption. Families and workers must avoid infantilizing or stereotyping the old person; instead they should build upon his strengths and hopes. By acting as an advocate and offering patience, kindness, and respect, the workers and the agency can help to minimize or prevent severe stress or deterioration.

Two concentrated rehabilitation programs aimed at returning aged mental hospital residents to the community or to geriatric centers have achieved instructive results. Both programs concentrated on improving the resident's physical condition and restoring self-care abilities such as grooming, housekeeping, and other functions needed to maintain oneself successfully in the new environment. The goal of the programs, to have the patient remain successfully in the new location, was achieved in 70-80 percent of the cases. To be placed successfully in a residential community, the patient needed to develop a high degree of self-sufficiency, exhibit no bizarre behavior, be cooperative, and have good orientation to time, place, and person. The patients who moved to nursing homes or county institutions could be more dependent (Cohen & Kraft, 1967).[2] Another major factor found to affect adjustment after discharge was the ability of persons living with the patient to tolerate unusual behavior (Boureston, Wolff & Davis, 1961; Stotsky, 1970).

Increased death rates have been linked to involuntary relocation for which no preparation was made. In a study of individual and mass transfers of nonpsychotic patients, mass moves with little or no preparation were followed by a 35 percent increase in death rate as compared with the rate one year before relocation. Among relocated patients participating in educational programs and emotional preparation prior to the move, however, the death rate was substantially below the baseline rate. In the latter group no patient was moved against his will (Jasnau, 1967).

Among a sample of voluntary entrants to new apartments, the mortality rate remained low. It was comparable to a nonrelocated control group of older people matched for age, sex, and initial functional health status (Lawton & Jaffe, 1967).

There are indications that the ability to envision the move realistically in advance can be helpful in coping with it when it happens (Turner, 1968). This hypothesis receives support from the finding that denial or repression of the event is related to mortality among aged residents (Aldrich, 1964). Since relocation is often far from voluntary, the least traumatic approach would seem to be a realistic appraisal of it in advance with maximum opportunity for choices in how it will be done.

The postrelocation environment.   The quality of the environment may be the most critical factor in the success of a relocation. In a follow-up study of discharged geriatric mental patients, the characteristics of postdischarge environments emerged as more powerful predictors of adjustment than did the predischarge characteristics—the coping styles, orientation, mood, and activity patterns—of the patients (Lieberman, Tobin & Slover, 1971). A custodial environment or one unsuited to the particular needs of the new resident might reverse the gains resulting from intensive prerelocation preparatory efforts. In institutional settings, when the social worker may have some influence over the quality of the environment, efforts can be made to create a more supportive and therapeutic milieu. Elsewhere, however, efforts are limited to assessing the characteristics of the relocatee and trying to find a new environment to match.

Locating a new environment that meets the needs of the resident, however, can be difficult for several reasons. First, ideal accommodations are seldom available. Second, the choice of suitable environments may be restricted by the resident's mental or physical impairment. Third, many problems in the environment are not apparent until a person lives with them—noise, for example, or lack of safety factors, or inconvenient location. The beautiful new apartment may seem ideal until one moves in and finds the walls are thin and the neighbor plays acid rock at midnight. Shopping facilities may be near, but fire sirens, trains, or the chiming of the town clock may prove annoying.

Younger family members are frequent sources of contact, support, and assistance for the older person in times of stress, and adult children may invite the aging parent to live with them (Sussman & Burchinal, 1962). The three-generational family can live together successfully, but this arrangement has a potential for considerable strain. To help predict family relations in a three-generational setting, the following factors have been suggested: (1) degree to which friendly contacts have been maintained; (2) role adjustment within the household; (3) authority assignments in the family; (4) grandparent role—lenient or authoritarian; (5) adult child's attitude toward the older parent—condescending, respectful, resentful; (6) older person's adjustment to newer social trends—drinking, divorce, parties, music (Cavan, 1965).

There are indications that the elderly often adapt more successfully in areas where there are higher concentrations of other elderly people (Carp, 1967). Older persons tend to form new friendships at a rate proportionate to the number of old people living near them. There is also a tendency for those in the same age group to help each other in time of need (Havighurst, Neugarten, & Tobin, 1968). In any event, the relocatee should be assisted in maintaining some relationship with his old home ground. This might be accomplished through visits to or from previous acquaintances. Retaining some treasured possessions, such as a favorite bed, chair, radio, and pictures, should be encouraged.

When a move to a hospital, county home, or nursing home is required, the problem of institutionalization is added to those already present. There is considerable risk of fostering passivity and dependence. Morale, social relations, contact with the environment, and the ability to take care of oneself may rapidly deteriorate. The amount of trauma experienced during relocation and the degree to which the resident becomes institutionalized seem to depend on admission practices, staff attitudes, and the custodial/therapeutic orientation to providing care. In environments where the strengths, interests, and remaining skills of the resident are not assessed, respected, and developed, the result may be a decline in social and psychological functioning (Slover, 1973).

The outside world loses its meaning for the institutional resident. He may feel less capable of functioning in that setting. Instead, he invests himself in the institutional milieu, thus decreasing prospects for overall improvement and ultimate return to the community. Close personal relationships are infrequent, and there is increased distrust and

Table 1.   Stages in the Development of Institutionalization[a]

Stages of development	Symptoms	Prognosis
Stage of uncertainty	Loss of identity	Readily reversible
Deprived of cultural and social reinforcement	Looks for success and adaptation; hypersuggestible	
Doubts about physical and mental condition	Questioning; faltering	
Feels relieved of responsibility because he is receiving message: "something is wrong with you"	Less interest in personal care; resents being treated as incompetent	Therapy is increasingly difficult
Compliant but still feels more competent than other residents		
Loss of contact with family and friends	Fewer letters and visits; socially awkward	
Identifies self with others in · institution	Complete psychosocial degradation	Not readily reversible

[a]Adapted from Maurice E. Linden, "You Won't Believe It." Paper presented at State of Delaware Governors' Conference on Aging, 1967. Mimeograph copy available from New Jersey Department of Community Affairs, Division on Aging, Trenton, N.J.

minimum expectation of receiving gratification from others (Lieberman & Lakin, 1963).

Table 1 outlines the symptoms, development, and prognosis of the institutionalization process (also referred to as the social breakdown syndrome or syndrome of psychosocial degradation). It may occur not only in hospitals and other institutions, but perhaps in community environments as well.

Linden has used the analogy of a traveler entering a foreign country where the language and customs are unfamiliar. Uncertain of his identity in relation to the new setting, the traveler experiences the first phase of the syndrome, change in identity and self-image. Ensuing experiences may then encourage or prevent the development of the next six stages (Linden, 1967). It seems likely that the patronizing attitudes and discrimination that older people encounter in the community often produce the same degradation that is created by the restrictions and dependency-producing practices of institutions.

Social workers, family members, and the older person himself may be impressed by the quality of the physical plant of the institution and its listed medical and recreational facilities. For influencing long-range adjustment, however, these characteristics are likely to weigh less than staff orientation to the provision of care. These factors should be explored in interviews with staff members, informal observations of the institutional milieu, and conversations with present residents of the facility.

When the move results from deinstitutionalization, rehabilitation programs aimed at restoring deteriorated cognitive functioning can enhance personal ability to cope with the new environment. Efforts should not be directed toward altering the individual's long-established needs and patterns of coping to suit the environment. Instead, manipulation of the environment or matching the environment to the needs of the individual is more effective in promoting a successful return to the community. Although it will be difficult to achieve a perfect match of person to environment, knowledge of adaptive patterns of the elderly and results of past relocation experiences, as well as adequate information about available environments, can lead to a viable postrelocation adjustment. In a setting that is rich in social and cultural opportunities and that provides security and encouragement, the adjustment of older persons can frequently be maintained or improved. This is born out by findings suggesting that although chronic geriatric patients adjust as adequately in nursing homes as in hospitals, they prefer the warmer atmosphere and greater freedom of movement that they find in the nursing home (Dobson & Paterson, 1961).

The risks involved in relocation must be emphasized, but when the potential benefits appear to outweigh the risks, much can be done to increase the likelihood of a successful outcome. Manipulating the environment to provide support, acceptance, encouragement, and aid will likely prove to be more effective and feasible therapy for elderly relocatees than one-to-one therapy aimed at resolving specific personal conflicts.

More Research Needed

The suggestions presented in this article may be of some use to social workers aiding in the relocation of the elderly, but additional information and direction are needed in this relatively new and urgent area of study. Testable hypotheses and replicable research must be developed as bases for new directions. Thus social work intervention in this area has two goals: (1) to use existing knowledge to manipulate environments and assist older people and (2) to promote accumulation of new knowledge.

Notes

1. From an interview with Doris Posenauer, York Manor, Syracuse, N.Y., March 1971.
2. Negative results from relocation preparation efforts have also been reported. Maximum service programs involving considerable "living arrangement" services for institutionalized residents were conducted by nursing and social work services. The resulting death rate was four times higher than when minimal services were offered. See Blenkner, op. cit., p. 101.

References

Aldrich, C. K. & Mendkoff, E. Relocation of the Aged and Disabled: A Mortality Study. *Journal of the American Geriatrics Society*, 11 (March 1963), p. 190.

Aldrich, C. K. Personality Factors and Mortality in the Relocation of the Aged. *The Gerontologist*, 5, No. 2, Part 1 (June 1964), p. 92.

Aleksandrowicz, D. R. Fire and its Aftermath on a Geriatric Ward. *Bulletin: Menninger Clinic*, 25 (January 1961).

Blenkner, M. Environmental Change and the Aging Individual. *The Gerontologist*, 7, No. 2, Part 1 (June 1967).

Boureston, N. C., Wolff, R. J. & Davis, H. R. Prognostic Factors in Elderly Mental Patients. *Journal of Gerontology*, 16 (April 1961), p. 150.

Brody, E. M. Congregate Care Facilities and Mental Health of the Elderly.

Butler, R. N. Aspects of Survival and Adaptation in Human Aging. *American Journal of Psychiatry*, 123 (April 1967), p. 1233.

Carp, F. M. The Impact of Environmental Setting on the Lives of Older People. *The Gerontologist*, 7, No. 2, Part 1 (June 1967).

Cavan. R. S. A Sociologist Looks at the Role of the Older Person In the Family. In H. Lee Jacobs, ed. *The Older Person in the Family: Challenges and Conflicts*. Proceedings of the Conference on Gerontology, Institute of Gerontology, University of Iowa, Iowa City, June 1965, pp. 42-44.

Cohen, E. S. & Kraft, A. C. The Restorative Potential of Elderly Long Term Residents of Mental Hospitals. Paper presented at the 20th Annual Meeting, Gerontological Society, St. Petersburg, Florida, November 9, 1967.

Dobson, W. R. & Paterson, T. W. A Behavioral Evaluation of Geriatric Patients Living in Nursing Homes as Compared to a Hospitalized Group. *The Gerontologist*, 1 (September 1961), p. 139.

Flynn, John P. Accidental Findings in Providing Foster Care for the Aging. Unpublished paper available from Family Homes for the Aging, 120 Main Street, Rochester, N.Y. 1966.

Fried, M. Grieving for a Lost Home. In Leonard Duhl, ed. *The Urban Condition*. New York: Basic Books, 1963.

Glow, H. E. & Allen, E. B. Manifestations of Psychoneuroses Occurring in Later Life. *Geriatrics*, 6 (January 1951), p. 31.

Goldfarb, A. L. The Evaluation of Geriatric Patients Following Treatment. In Hoch, P. H. & Zubin, Joseph (eds.) *The Evaluation of Psychiatric Treatment*. New York: Grune & Stratton, 1964.

Guze, S. B. & Cantwell, D. P. The Prognosis in Organic Brain Syndromes. *American Journal of Pyschiatry*, 120 (September 1964) p. 88.

Havens, B. J. An Investigation of Activity Patterns and Adjustment in an Aging Population. Paper presented at the 19th Annual Meeting of the Gerontological Society, New York, New York, November 5, 1966.

Havighurst, R. J., Neugarten, B. L., & Tobin S. S. Disengagement and Patterns of Aging. In Neugarten, B. (ed.) *Middle Age and Aging*. Chicago: The University of Chicago Press, 1968, pp. 161-172.

Jasnau, K. F. Individualized versus Mass Transfer of Non Psychotic Geriatric Patients from Mental Hospitals to Nursing Homes with Special Reference to Death Rate. *Journal of the American Geriatrics Society*, 15 (March 1967), p. 280.

Killian, E. C. Effect of Geriatric Transfers on Mortality Rates. *Social Work*, 15 (January 1970), p. 19.

Lawton, M. P. & Jaffe, S. Mortality, Morbidity and Voluntary Change of Residence by Older People. Paper presented at the Annual Meeting of the American Psychological Association, Washington, D.C., September 2, 1967.

Lieberman, M. A. Depressive Affect and Vulnerability to Environmental Change in the Aged. *Proceedings of Seminars*, April 1965, Duke University, Council on Gerontology.

————. Factors in Environmental Change. Paper presented at the Conference on Patterns of Living and Housing for the Middle Aged and Aged. Washington, D.C., March 1965.

————. Relationship of Mortality Rates to Entrance to a Home for the Aged. *Geriatrics*, 16 (October 1961), p. 517.

———— & Lakin, M. On Becoming an Institutionalized Aged Person. *Processes of Aging*. Williams, R. H., Tibbits, C., & Donahue, W., eds., Vol. 1. New York: Atherton Press, 1963.

————, Prock, V. N. & Tobin, S. S. Psychological Effects of Institutionalization. *Journal of Gerontology*, 3 (July 1968), p. 343.

————, Tobin, S. S. & Slover, D. L. Effects of Relocation on Long-Term Geriatric Patients. Unpublished project report, University of Chicago, Committee on Human Development, June 1971.

Linden, M. E. You Won't Believe It. Paper presented at State of Delaware Governors' Conference on Aging, 1967. Mimeographed copy available from New Jersey Department of Community Affairs, Division on Aging, Trenton, New Jersey.

Miller, D. & Lieberman, M. A. The Relationship of Affect State and Adaptive Capacity to Reactions of Stress. *Journal of Gerontology*, 20 (October 1965), p. 494.

Rose, A. M. & Peterson, W. A. *Older People and Their Social World*. Philadelphia: F. A. Davis, 1965.

Shahinian, S. E., Goldfarb, A. I., & Turner, H. Death Rate in Relocated Residents of Nursing Homes. Paper presented at the 19th Annual Meeting of the Gerontological Society, New York, New York, November 4, 1966.

Slover, D. L. *Relocation of Selected Long-Term Elderly Mental Patients*. Unpublished doctoral dissertation. University of Chicago, 1973.

Stotsky, B. A. Is the Hospital Back Ward Being Moved to the Nursing Home? *Psychological Reports*, 19 (October 1966), p. 602.

————. A Controlled Study of Factors in the Successful Adjustment of Mental Patients to Nursing Homes. *American Journal of Psychiatry*, 123 (April 1967), p. 1243.

————. *The Nursing Home and the Aged Patient*. New York: Appleton-Century-Crofts, 1970.

Sussman, M. B. & Burchinal, L. Kin Family Network: Unheralded Structure in Current Conceptualizations of Family Functioning. *Marriage and Family Living*, 24 (August 1962), p. 231.

Turner, B. R. *Psychological Predictors of Adaptation to Institutionalization in the Aged*. Unpublished dissertation abstract, Committee on Human Development, University of Chicago, 1968.

CHAPTER IV

THE AGING EXPERIENCE: LIFE STYLES AND LIFE EVENTS

Each generation of older persons has lived through a unique set of historical circumstances and shaped a profile of its own. Generalizations about its life experiences may therefore not be applicable to successive cohorts. New generations enter the aging stage with their own developmental stakes and are exposed to unprecedented realities.

The way each generation ages and how generations follow each other is, however, both intriguing and problematic. There are few, if any, givens about the transferability of their experiences or their reciprocal obligations. The study of the profile of each aging cohort seldom proceeds in holistic terms, and both the popular media and the social sciences find it instead more manageable to handle them piecemeal. Such experiences are made, after all, of myriads of behavioral patterns, life events, and environmental variables impinging upon the members of each cohort. This is precisely the course followed in this chapter. We realize that by extrapolating issues such as family interactions, kinship, sex and intimacy, widowhood, loneliness, victimization, urban life, and ethnicity,

etc., we are far from exhausting the aging experience; but
a composite presentation may well provide a better
glimpse, a more revealing approximation of such a complex and elusive reality.

The family life of the aging is a perplexing theme that
reappears in most chapters of this book. Several authors
may arrive at different conclusions even when starting
from similar premises and analogous empirical founda-
tions. Cowgill, in our first chapter, felt confident in the resilience and continuity of viable family supports in old age.
Judith Treas in her "Family Support Systems for the Aged"
arrives now at less encouraging conclusions, when aiming
to reconcile the paradox of the reiterated importance of
intergenerational kinship with the overwhelming evidence
of its historical decline. Demographic change has reduced
the number of descendents to whom an older person can
resort for assistance. Growing numbers of middle aged
women are confronted with the choice between attending
to their frail parents or working to support themselves and
insure a better education for their children. Treas has no
illusions about the alleged renewal and viability of
primary support systems: she finds instead that both grown
children and their aged parents will become liberated
from economic dependence on one another. Publicly
sponsored services, she concludes, will have to ultimately
take over the care of the aged.

Judith Brier and Dan Rubinstein in "Sex for the Elderly?
Why Not?" denounce the conspiracy of silence, the professional evasiveness, and the pejorative conventionalisms
that inhibit sexual expression in old age. Drawing from
recent research contributions, they assert the potential
continuity of sexual prowess beyond the menopausal
years. They discuss sex, however, in more than physiological terms, as a part of a larger gestalt of intimacy and
human interaction. Three major sociological issues are
raised in this paper. The first is the inequality of roles in
later years and the "double standard" that oppresses
women, but also enhances the vulnerability of men, by
demanding that they measure up to ridiculously aggres-

sive standards of *machismo*. Second, the inequities of
Social Security payments and its adverse economic ramifications affect remarriage in old age. The authors claim
that unwed cohabitation is spreading among the aged, in
order to retain a higher income. This statement may be
exaggerated, but it calls proper attention to a tangle of
intergenerational attitudes and inconsistent policy regulations, not to mention the vestiges of a Victorian heritage
laden with censure and guilt. Finally, changes for the
widowed and institutionalized older persons are viewed as
social role disruptions. Widows are constrained into a
restrictive existence and expected to disavow and repress
all sexual desires. The institutionalized aged, even those
who are married, are often segregated, denied privacy,
and literally forbidden from any show of affection and
sensuality, let alone sexual contact. Widows and the institutionalized aged are literally forced into a sexless role at a
stage in life when the need for love and human warmth is
as pressing as in younger years.

Helena Lopata reviews the life experiences of widows
and widowers within the context of urbanization and
changes in kinship network relations.

Widows and widowers have certain problems in
common: economic loss of income for women, and hardships for men having to pay for services formerly supplied
by their now deceased wives; however, grief and loneliness are the foremost problems. Because there are five
times more widows than widowers in America, it's only
natural that this paper should give primacy to their specific
change of status. Lopata finds that there are no automatically engaging primary support systems, such as nearby
family and neighbors, who will assist the widow through
her initial crisis and take over the duties of her late husband. Primary support systems, as observed in the preceding paper by Judith Treas, cannot be taken for granted.
They often break up or lose their effectiveness. Formal
specialized services are in turn in abundant supply, but
they require skills in voluntaristic engagement and
familiarity with organizational systems, for which present

cohorts of older women have never been trained. Only the more versatile, cosmopolitan, and affluent ones are capable of taking advantage of these resources.

Loneliness appears as the main correlate of widowhood; it is partly attributed to the couple companionate world that refuses to incorporate the single person. But it is also a form of existential affirmation, the price the widow must pay for independence, when she refuses to become a babysitter or housekeeper for her offspring.

Loneliness reappears as the central theme in Joyce Stephens's "Society of the Alone: Freedom, Privacy, and Utilitarianism as Dominant Norms in the SRO." Reference is made to the elderly living in single room occupancy (SRO) hotels, usually slum and decaying residences in the core cities of America. The author describes the impoverishment of social relations in this type of society. It is an atomistic world of strangers, lacking in mutual involvement or group shared ideals. Whatever interaction does occur is purely utilitarian, and aimed at satisfying private objectives. It is mistaken to assume, however, that these extreme forms of isolation are inevitable correlates of the aging process. The SRO residents were lifelong isolates who simply continue their life style into old age. They wish to retain a peculiar form of freedom characterized by the avoidance of intimacy and the enthronization of mutual suspicion.

Fear of crime is a more pervasive form of suspicion often overlooked in gerontological research. Frank Clemente and Michael B. Kleiman find that the fear of victimization among the aged is more of a problem than crime itself. Drawing from several national studies, they conclude that the elderly have, in fact, lower victimization rates than the rest of society, even when considering that many elderly do not report crimes for fear of future retaliation by their victimizers.

The fact remains, however, that the fear itself intimidates older persons into a self-imposed "house arrest," a life style characterized by forced reclusion that limits further human contact. National survey data indicates that female, black, or metropolitan residents are the most vulnerable, because they possess higher fear rates. On the whole, the aged appear as a very heterogeneous population and while some of its segments are excessively fearful, others are relatively free of anxiety.

This chapter concludes with Marjorie H. Cantor's analysis of the life experience of urban elderly residing in poor, high-risk, and deteriorating neighborhoods. In "Effect of Ethnicity on Life Styles of the Inner-City Elderly" she aims to determine the effects of ethnic identification on the aging process among white, Spanish and black elderly, and to highlight areas of convergence or disparity.

She found the Spanish elderly to be the youngest group. They are economically the worst off, but they enjoy a closer knit family life. However, this picture is being eroded among the younger, more acculturated Spanish adults. More than one-fourth of the Spanish elderly already live alone. The black elderly face many of the same economic and minority discrimination problems as their Spanish counterparts, without, however, the compensations of extended family supports. Fewer blacks in old age are still married and living with a spouse than among the other two subgroups. Among blacks, increasing numbers are living alone in old age, with less supportive intervention on the part of their offspring.

The white elderly present a more conflicting picture. Role losses, economic demotions, and social discontinuities are for them more extreme and traumatic. While they are objectively slightly better off than their Spanish and black peers, they are more reluctant to accept help and services. Cantor concludes that problems of isolation from relatives and kin and the incidence of living alone will continue for the three ethnic groups.

Primary support networks, as Treas implied at the beginning of this chapter, are not universally available. Supportive community services need to be, therefore, improved and expanded. This is precisely the main thrust of our next chapter.

4.1

Family Support Systems for the Aged: Some Social and Demographic Considerations

Judith Treas

At a time when gerontologists are hailing the family as the linchpin in support systems for the aged, a discordant lament is heard for the passing of filial piety in America. An oft-voiced sentiment holds that younger people no longer accord the parental generation the respect, love, and help which are traditionally its due. Indeed, some would blame the indifference of kin for the social isolation and economic insecurity confronting so many of the aged. Researchers, on the other hand, have documented generational solidarity in shared values and beliefs (Bengtson, Olander, & Haddad, 1976) and have described the affection, attention, and assistance which children routinely provide to elderly family members (Hill, 1970; Shanas, 1968; Streib, 1968). Generational relations undoubtably have undergone historical change. However, it is not altogether clear that societal transformations have undermined family structure or weakened family ties. Sussman (1976) has argued that Social Security, nutrition programs, and Medicare (rather than usurping family responsibilities for the care of the aged) have created a new role for kin as mediators between institutional bureaucracies and elderly relations. Shorter (1975) contends that the historical emergence of the "modern family" has been marked by unprecedented demands on kin for intimacy and affection.

Copyright 1977 by The Gerontological Society. Reprinted by permission. *The Gerontologist*, Vol. 17, No. 6, 1977, pp. 486–491.

This paper attempts to reconcile the paradox of the continuing importance of intergenerational kinship with the widespread notion of its historical decline. This effort demands a consideration of change in population patterns, in social roles, and in the economic organization of society. This comparison of the past and the present yields insights on the extent to which the family can serve as an effective vehicle for the physical, psychological, and economic support of aged Americans.

The Demography of Intergenerational Relations

Long-run trends in demographic processes of mortality and fertility have had startling consequences for the kin network. Survival into old age, a commonplace occurrence today, was a rarity in a past characterized by higher death rates. Under mortality regimes prevailing in the United States in 1900, only 63 percent of women surviving to childbearing years (e.g., age 20) could expect to reach a 60th birthday (Preston, Keyfitz, & Schoen, 1972). The mortality schedule of 1973 implies that fully 88 percent of women living to age 20 will reach this threshold of old age (National Center on Health Statistics, 1975). The survival of those born in the high fertility era of the late 19th and early 20th centuries has swelled the ranks of the older population, thus increasing the likelihood of having a living parent.

In addition, the aged's share of the population has grown relative to younger age groups. In 1975, 14.8 percent of the U.S. population was 60 years or older compared to only 6.4 percent in 1900 (U.S. Bureau of the Census, 1976). This proportionate growth owes less to improved health and survival than to the historical trend toward smaller families. Because successive cohorts of women bore fewer children than did their mothers and grandmothers, the ratio of older "dependents" to younger "producers" has risen. As Table 1 illustrates, 1900 saw 13 Americans aged 60 and over for every 100 adults aged 20–59; by 1975, there were 29. Projections by the U.S. Bureau of the Census (1976) suggest this figure could rise to 44 by the year 2030.

The implications for Social Security financing of such shifts in the societal age structure have been widely publicized. The consequences for support systems within families have received less attention. Today's middle-aged adult is more likely to have a living parent than his counterpart in the past. Despite the improved survival chances of offspring, the aging parent, having raised fewer children, will have fewer descendents to call upon for assistance than did his own parent. The increasing mobility of American society

**Table 1.   Old Age Dependency and Sex Ratios:
United States, 1900 to 1975**

	Population 60 years and Older per 100 Persons Aged 20-59	Males per 100 Females 65 Years and Older
1900	.13	102.0
1930	.16	100.4
1960	.27	82.6
1970	.29	72.0
1975	.29	69.3

Source: U.S. Bureau of the Census, Demographic Aspects of Aging in the United States, *Current population reports* Series PC-23, No. 59, USGPO, 1976, Tables 3-1 and 6-10.

has been indicted for restricting the older generation's day-to-day access to younger kin, but declining fertility is the demographic process more profoundly affecting the availability of younger family members. Improvements in communications and transportation may have worked to overcome family barriers of distance, but the dearth of descendents poses greater problems.

Clearly, kin networks can offer fewer options and resources when there are fewer members of the younger generations. All things considered, an aging couple will fare better when several children can contribute to its support. Certainly, it is easier for an aging widow to find a home with offspring when there are a number of grown children who might accommodate her. Indeed, Soldo and Myers (1976) confirm that childless or low fertility women have a 15 percent higher chance of institutionalization before age 75 than do women who bore 3 or more children. In explaining the growing propensity of older women to live alone, Kobrin (1976) eloquently argues the intergenerational implications of demographic change: although 1910 saw almost 3 women aged 35–44 for every widow and divorcee 55 or older, there were by 1973 only 1.2 such "daughters" for each such "mother."

These illustrations suggest another aspect of the demographic dilemma confronting kin networks. The older population has experienced not only growth but also changes in composition. An older relative today is more likely to be a woman, a widow, and very old. Table 1 demonstrates that as recently as 1930, there were about as many men as women in the population 65 and older; by 1975, there were only 69 men for every 100 women in this age group. While three-fourths of the men lived with spouses, only one-third of the women did (U.S. Bureau of the Census, 1976). This reflects the fact that women typically survive their husbands both because they tend to be younger and because they enjoy lower death rates. Furthermore, older women remarry less readily than do men (Treas & VanHilst, 1976).

It is widows who traditionally have called on the resources of family support systems. Older couples can maintain considerable independence in the face of infirmities by nursing one another or reallocating housekeeping chores. The woman who has outlived her husband lacks this flexibility. What with her lower income, the widow may require greater attention from family and is more likely to live in an offspring's home.

Another compositional change is seen in the aging of the older population itself. At the turn of the century, 4 percent of those 65 years and over were actually age 85 or older. By 1975, the figure was 8 percent (U.S. Bureau of the Census, 1976). We might question whether the extreme aged today are not healthier, more vigorous, or less needy than their counterparts in other eras. Nonetheless, advancing years are associated with the decrements which make assistance by others more necessary. We have noted that demographic shifts have meant fewer brothers and sisters with whom to share the sometimes considerable burden of physical, financial, and emotional support of aging parents. This burden is made more poignant by the realization that some of the aged are very old. No longer are the children of these "frail elderly" prime-age adults. The very old in greatest need of care have offspring who are the "young-old" with their declining energy, health, and finances.

If family support systems are now taxed by the high ratio of aged to younger family members, the future promises little relief. Now moving into old age are cohorts for whom the Depression cut short marital aspirations and childbearing plans. About 7 percent of women 60–64 in 1970 had never married, and, of those who had wed, an unprecedented 20 percent bore no children (U.S. Bureau of the Census, 1972, 1973a). A present-day return to the high fertility that characterized much of the past is unlikely. Had the U.S. vital rates for 1967 continued indefinitely, each 65-year-old woman would average 1.2 living daughters (Goodman, Keyfitz, & Pullum, 1974). The chances would be 85 in 100 that a 35-year-old woman would have a mother alive and 28 in 100 that she would have a grandmother still living. In fact, current fertility has fallen below 1967 rates to a level which, if sustained, eventually could achieve zero population growth. Shanas and Hauser (1974) explore the implications for the aged of such a population possibility and conclude "those aspects of housing, recreation, health care, and income maintenance now provided by younger generations for their elderly parents and grandparents will need to be provided by society at large."

Women's Changing Social Roles

Children routinely provide to aging parents services, companionship, financial aid, gifts, advice, and counsel. These family exchanges often reveal a sexual division of labor in the care of older kin. Lopata (1973), for example, reports that Chicago-area widows found their sons helpful in managing funeral arrangements and financial matters while their daughters fostered closer emotional ties by giving services and visiting. As the mainstay of family support systems, it is daughters who have taken widowed mothers into their homes, have run errands, and have provided custodial care. Devoted though sons may be, it is clear that the major responsibility for psychological sustenance and physical maintenance of the aged has fallen traditionally to female members of the family. Current enthusiasms for alternatives to institutionalized care of the aged must be tempered by realistic expectations of the willingness and ability of modern American women to provide continued services for aging kin.

The care of the aging parents is but one of a number of competing responsibilities confronting mature women. Children and spouses also pose demands, and today a higher proportion of middle-aged women are married and have offspring than in earlier eras. Comparing the 1890–1894 birth cohort of white women with its counterpart born 1930–1934, Uhlenberg (1974) estimates that spinsterhood will have declined from 10 to 4.5 percent for those surviving from ages 20 to 50. The percentage of white women with childless marriages declined from 22.5 to 5.5. To a greater extent than their predecessors, this younger cohort of women, aged 41 to 45 in 1975, have husbands and children whose interests must be balanced against those of aging kin. We now face a shortage of "maiden aunts" to devote themselves to parents who are in their last years. Currently, young women are entering first marriages at a slower pace than in the postwar era. However, it is too early to tell whether marriage is being foregone or merely postponed by current generations. If more women never marry, it may mean that more women will be available to care for aging kin, although they themselves will lack offspring to call upon in old age.

Postwar years have witnessed dramatic changes in the social roles of women in the United States. Increasingly, women work for pay outside the home. Middle-aged wives have benefited especially from an economy which has created new job opportunities for women

(Oppenheimer, 1970). If we consider married women, 45 to 54, living with their husbands, we find 47.8 percent were working in 1970 compared with only 11.1 percent in 1940 (U.S. Bureau of the Census, 1973b). Although their jobs may offer personal satisfaction in terms of career accomplishment, social contacts, or just keeping busy, most women admit that they work because they need the money.

Few can fault the middle-aged woman for wanting to contribute to children's college education or savings for retirement. Inflation has made the second income increasingly necessary to maintain family living standards. However, working hours cut into the time available to shop for shut-in kin or to perform nursing functions. Work in the labor force has come about at the expense of women's leisure and even sleep, since working women enjoy neither reduced housekeeping chores nor increased assistance from husbands in domestic tasks (Vanek, 1973). Although vigorous older people who live with grown children may provide welcome help with household chores, resident parents who need care can require considerable attention. For example, one study found two-fifths of children caring for aged parents in their homes spent the equivalent of a full-time job in this custodial activity (Newman, 1976).

It is uncertain how many working women might quit their jobs in order to furnish daily care to older kin who are sick or senile. We do know that 30.8 percent of the mothers of preschool children were in the labor force in 1970 (U.S. Bureau of the Census, 1973b). If so many mothers are willing to trust the care of small children to others in order to work, women are probably willing to delegate responsibility for the maintenance of aging parents as well. Likely, their jobs provide wherewithal to pay for such care. These trends in women's roles outside the home portend a future in which the family can no longer offer day-to-day care to aged who can no longer care for themselves.

The Changing Currency of Intergenerational Exchanges

Much of our understanding of our less affluent past suggests that the historical cement between generations of family members has been economic interdependence. There is evidence that children in less developed societies have been regarded as insurance policies against the hardships of old age (Hohm, 1975). This trust in filial piety is well placed wherever parents in their last years still exercise control over their offsprings' futures. In agricultural economies, day-to-day subsistence as well as the chance to marry have been contingent on parents' willingness to provide doweries to daughters and to turn over family farms to sons. The terms of the transfer of property to children in exchange for support in retirement have depended not only on custom and affection but also on legal contract between generations (Arensberg & Kimball, 1968; Berkner, 1972). In his study of 17th century farming families in Andover, Massachusetts, Greven (1973) documents the way in which aging fathers perpetuated control of grown sons. Although a son might marry and settle upon family land, a father retained the property deed until his death. Lacking clear title to sell the land, offspring couldn't leave Andover without parental approval. Even the last will and testament which transferred land ownership might bind the heir to his filial responsibilities, since wills typically stipulated the conditions of support for the surviving widow—a room in the house, a garden, firewood. Parental control of potential heirs was insured by the ultimate threat—disinheritance.

Dowd (1975) has suggested that generational relations might be characterized aptly as a situation of exchange in which the aged have diminishing power resources with which to effect the compliance of others. Historical changes in the economic organization of society have operated to reduce the economic clout which aged parents can exercise over grown children, because material legacies are of lessened importance to the financial success and security of offspring. Today, one's livelihood commonly derives from a job rather than from the family farm or business enterprise, and occupational opportunities usually depend on educational credentials (Blau & Duncan, 1967). Although parents may make substantial investments in children's schooling, they do so in the prime of life. By the time parents reach old age, children have established careers and independent lives and, hence, are in a position to resist whatever economic threats or inducements parents might muster. It is hardly surprising that Becker's (1976) study of Israeli and American high school students found the Americans both more eager to establish their own independence and less inclined to support a hypothetical law requiring children to support aging parents.

This is not to argue that the familial status of the aged has declined historically. Evidence remains too limited to merit sweeping generalizations (Laslett, 1976). With the lessening importance of economic transfers within families, emotional ties have supplanted economic bonds as the currency upon which family members trade in exchanges with one another (Shorter, 1975). Even Becker's American adolescents acknowledged that it is to family they would turn for help, and it is family whom they would help first should disaster strike. Rather than being motivated by economic coercion, assistance to aging kin rests on delicate sentiments such as affection, gratitude, guilt, or a desire for parental approval. This changing basis for intergenerational relations may be seen in the growing importance of symbolic bequests. As Rosenfeld (1974) notes, the treasured memento or family heirloom—items of sentimental as opposed to monetary value—may now serve to reward faithful children while disinheritance may carry the threat of public and final rejection by parents.

Of course, the success of parents' emotional claims on attention, affection, and assistance of kin reflects their own economic independence from family. Financial support of the aged no longer rests solely with younger family members—a fact which limits the control that kin can exercise over the aged. The transfer of resources from the young to the old is now accomplished through such societal mechanisms as Social Security so the elderly can count on at least minimal subsistence regardless of the closeness of their own family ties. In short, historical transformations of the economic structure have diminished the power of the aged to insure their support by family while reducing the dependence of the old on family support systems.

The Future of Family Support Systems for the Aged

Forces of societal change are insuring that the family will not be the end-all-and-be-all of care for the aged. On a collision course with the declining number of descendents are the surer survival and lengthening life-span of the aged parent. Kin resources readily become overextended in the day-to-day care of aging relations, because there are fewer adult children to share the responsibility. Increasingly, other obligations and constraints compete with duties toward elderly family members. Growing numbers of middle-aged women are asked to choose between nursing frail parents or working to support themselves, their families, their own children. Futhermore, the extreme aged now pose an impediment to aging offsprings' aspirations for a retirement free of financial cares or demands on their time.

As we inch toward a post-industrial society and a welfare state, both grown children and aged parents have been liberated from economic dependence on one another. If the old can no longer wield financial power over descendents, neither are they abjectly dependent upon them for financial support. Most would agree that emotional bonds are more desirable as an intergenerational tie than is economic necessity. However, it is unreasonable to assume that family sentiment can insure adequate day-to-day supervision, housekeeping, personal maintenance, or nursing of older Americans. Some families thrive on affection while others are marked by disaffection. Alienated children hardly can be expected to take on these daily ministrations, and even well-meaning kin may find that custodial care is simply too much for them.

Just as Social Security shifted economic support of the aged from the family to a broader societal base so do support services for the sick or senile require a societal response. Already the limitations of the family support system are spawning a service industry and a professional corps to provide regular meals, housekeeping services, and institutionalized care. This trend can be expected to continue. We can also expect that public opinion will be increasingly disposed in favor of the inevitable—the growth of governmental and private intervention in the care of the aged.

Today, unfortunately, the aged's institutionalization (and even their independent living) is stigmatized by widely held stereotypes of their abandonment by kin. Although the adult offspring of institutionalized parents may labor under culturally imposed guilt about their inability to meet parents' needs, society offers few direct supports for the exercise of filial responsibility. Home aides, day care centers, meals-on-wheels, and dial-a-ride trams may offer ready relief to overburdened family support systems. However, state and federal programs might consider the wisdom of direct subsidies to families who participate in the day-to-day care of aging relatives. Families who overcome the many obstacles to home care of the aged would seem to warrant direct payments as surely as do strangers providing less personalized services. Tax breaks, special allowances, and direct reimbursements to family caretakers promise to promote those kin ties so threatened by social and demographic change.

References

Arensberg, C. M., & Kimball, S. T. Family and community in Ireland. Harvard Univ. Press, Cambridge, 1968.

Becker, T. Self, family, and community: A cross-cultural comparison of American and Israeli youth. *Youth & Society*, 1976, *8*, 45-66.

Bengtson, V. L., Olander, E. B., & Haddad, A. A. The "generation gap" and aging family members: Toward a conceptual model. In J. E. Gubrium (Ed.), *Time, roles, and self in old age*. Human Sciences Press, New York, 1976.

Berkner, L. K. The Stem Family and the developmental cycle of the peasant household: An 18th-century Austrian example. *American Historical Review*, 1972, *77*, 398-418.

Blau, P. M., & Duncan, O. D. *The American occupational structure*. John Wiley, New York, 1967.

Dowd, J. J. Aging as exchange: A preface to theory. *Journal of Gerontology*, 1975, *30*, 585-94.

Goodman, L., Keyfitz, N., & Pullum, T. Family formation and the frequency of various kinship relationships. *Theoretical Population Biology*, 1974, 5, 1-27.

Greven, P. J., Jr. Family structure in seventeenth century Andover, Massachusetts. In M. Gordon (Ed.), *The American family in social historical perspective*. St. Martin's Press, New York. 1973.

Hill, R. *Family development in three generations*. Schenkman, Cambridge, 1970.

Hohm, C. F. Social Security and fertility: An international perspective. *Demography*, 1975, *12*, 629-44.

Kobrin, F. E. The fall of household size and the rise of the primary individual in the United States. *Demography*, 1976, *13*, 127-38.

Laslett, P. Societal development and aging. In R. H. Binstock & E. Shanas (Eds.), *Handbook of social sciences and aging*. Van Nostrand, Reinhold, New York, 1976.

Lopata, H. *Widowhood in an American City*. Schenkman, Cambridge, 1973.

National Center on Health Statistics. *Vital statistic of the United States, 1973, life tables*. Rockville, MD, 1975.

Newman, S. *Housing adjustments of older people: A report from the second phase*. Institute for Social Research, Ann Arbor, 1976.

Oppenheimer, V. K. *The female labor force in the United States.* Institute of International Studies, Univ. of California, Berkeley, 1970.

Preston, S. H., Keyfitz, N., & Schoen, R. *Causes of death: Life tables for national populations*. Seminar Press, New York, 1972.

Rosenfeld, J. P. Inheritance: A sex-related system of exchanges. In R. L. Coser (Ed.), *The family: Its structure and functions*. St. Martin's Press, New York, 1974.

Schorr, A. L. *Filial responsibility in the American Family*. Social Security Administration, 1960.

Shanas, E. *Old people in three industrial societies*. Routledge & Kegan Paul, London, 1968.

Shanas, E., & Hauser, P. M. Zero population growth and the family life of older people. *Journal of Social Issues*, 1974, *30*, 79-92.

Shorter, E. *The making of the modern family*. Basic Books, New York, 1975.

Soldo, B. J., & Myers, G. C. The effects of total fertility on living arrangements among the elderly women: 1970. Paper presented at Annual meetings of Gerontological Society, New York, 1976.

Streib, G. Family patterns in retirement. In M. B. Sussman (Ed.), *Sourcebook in marriage and the family*. Houghton, Mifflin, New York, 1968.

Sussman, M. B. The family life of older people. In R. H. Binstock & E. Shanas (Eds.), *Handbook of aging and the social sciences*. Van Nostrand Reinhold, New York, 1976.

Treas, J., & VanHilst, A. Marriage and remarriage rates among older Americans. *Gerontologist*, 1976, *16*, 132-6.

Uhlenberg, P. Cohort variations in family life cycle experiences of U.S. females. *Journal of Marriage & the Family*, 1974, *36*, 284-92.

U.S. Bureau of the Census. Census of population: 1970. Subject reports, Final Report PC(2)-4C. *Marital Status*. USGPO, Washington, 1972.

U.S. Bureau of the Census. Census of population: 1970. Subject reports, final report PC(2)-3A. *Women by Number of Children Ever Born*. USGPO, Washington, 1973(a).

U.S. Bureau of the Census. Census of population: 1970. Subject reports, final report PC(2)-6A. *Employment status and work experience*. USGPO, Washington, 1973(b).

U.S. Bureau of the Census. Demographic aspects of aging and the older population in the United States. *Current population report series PC-23*, No. 59, USGPO, Washington, 1976.

Vanek, J. *Keeping busy: Time spent in housework, United States, 1920-1970*. Dissertation, Dept. of Sociology, Univ. Michigan, 1973.

4.2

Sex for the Elderly? Why Not?

Judith Brier and Dan Rubenstein

Latent or manifest, in reality or in mythology, there appears to be an ardent expression for the fulfillment of the human sexual response in the later years. King David of Israel hoped to maintain his sexual vigor by sleeping between two virgins (the story is also reported as sleeping *with*) to imbibe the youthful vapors they supposedly exuded.

French surgeon Serge Voronoff, in 1926, claimed that sexual vitality could be restored by transplanting the sex organs of young animals in the bodies of aging humans. The practices of bathing in or imbibing youthful blood and other secretions are recounted again and again in literature. Descriptions of the procedures of injection, ingestion or transplant of fluids, powders, tissues or organs from animals, fowl or fish in the desire to maintain youth and virile sexuality are legion.

Aristophanes, in his play, "Ecclesiazusae," describes a social utopia where, if any young man was attracted to a girl, he could not possess her until he had satisfied an old woman first. The old women were authorized to seize any youth who refused and to insist on their sexual rights also.

Reprinted from *Perspective on Aging*, November/December 1976, pp. 5-10, and January/February 1977, pp. 7-11. Copyright by The National Council on the Aging, Inc.

Now we have the conclusive findings of the Masters and Johnson 1968 study of sex in the elderly, maintaining that "regularity of sexual expression coupled with adequate physical well-being and healthy mental orientation to the aging process will combine to provide a sexually stimulative marriage [and/or relationships]. This climate will, in turn, improve sexual tension and provide a capacity for sexual performance that frequently may extend . . . beyond the 80-year level."

This acknowledgment may have heralded the beginning of freedom from the shackles of sexual repression. The consensus that sex stops at sixty is being challenged; knowledge and attitudes of the human sexual condition in later life are being affected and modified. Sex is being seen as a natural physiological function; aging itself does not cause cessation of sexual activity.

No time limit drawn

There is a growing acceptance of the fact that there "is no time limit drawn by the advancing years to female sexuality and for the male, too, there is a capacity for sexual performance that frequently may extend beyond the eighty-year age level" (Rubin, 1966). The potential for erotic pleasure seems to begin with birth and does not need to end until death. Apparently, the sexual capacity of aging females is unlimited, and the male changes that do occur do not reduce the need for satisfactory expression.

However, the capacity to enjoy sex may slow down naturally in the later years, as do most organic functions with age. Physical changes in the male and female do take place. In the female, vaginal lubrication occurs more slowly and the mucosa thicken; contractions in orgasm are less vigorous and frequent, and the shrinking vagina may cause a tender condition. In the male, penile erection becomes less frequent and more difficult to sustain, and ejaculatory squirt diminishes in both volume and pressure. Orgasm becomes less frequent, and more direct physical stimulation is needed to produce erection. This gradual sexual waning need not culminate in impotency, though there is no special anomaly in the spermatozoa of the aged man. Theoretically, the fertilization of the ovule by the male sperm remains indefinitely possible.

There seems to be no indication that there is a diminution of the sexual drive's intensity. Factors such as boredom; preoccupation with career or other pursuits; physical and mental fatigue; fear of failure; feelings of sin, shame and other social, cultural or religious rejection may well affect the sexual drive. However, the strength of the sexual drive (libido) can be most powerful, even to the point where it can persist in impotency.

Impotency can be reversible

Physical or psychological disorders can cause a temporary loss of sexual interest, but these disorders could cause disinterest in the young and middle-aged as well. Some of the conditions are myocardial infarction (heart attack); aging of the diencephalon (forepart of the brain); depression; obesity (a common contributor to impotence); alcohol (a powerful sedative), and sexual disuse atrophy. Such conditions are generally reversible.

The capability and capacity for sexual response in the later years have been well-substantiated in the research literature in the past half-century. Sustained interest, desire and performance are reported in numerous studies. The most current studies (and those most often referred to) are Masters and Johnson and the Duke University longitudinal study (Pfeiffer *et al*), both published in 1968. The Masters and Johnson work has been referred to as dealing with "the amatory prelude, the mechanisms of the love machine, the *modus operandi* of the coital act," while the Duke study deals with the socio-psychological-physiological problems of sexual activity. Alex Comfort is regarded as the expert on the removal of inhibitions and constraints and the making of sex more appetizing and enjoyable.

The human sexual response, as we know it, is a mental, social and physical condition that can perform as a maintainer and preserver of our position and status in life. But it is a status and condition that is in flux and must overcome the many constraints pitted against it.

Why the role is lost

Research has clearly established that, under proper physical and psychological conditions, the capacity to enjoy sex is not lost. Yet there is a strong feeling that, because of the derision, denial and despair brought on by misinformation, misapprehension and prejudice, older people are "hocused" out of continuing sexual activity by a society that seemingly has little use for the aged. The common beliefs are that women are asexual or nonsexual; they are not expected to have any sexual feelings and surely not to participate in any sexual expression. Many could well believe and readily subscribe to the statement that "sexual activity, enjoyable as it may seem in itself, still has as its natural aim the propagation of the species, and this activity belongs to the second, not the third act of life's drama" (de Ropp, 1962).

This concept of sexuality in later life reflects the way our culture has structured marriage and its sexual component around the child-raising purpose. Since this is true of marital roles, it then follows that it would carry over into social roles. Socially, it has not been appropriate for a woman to have sex after the child-bearing years. Any sex interest and activity after that time has been considered inappropriate, improper or deviant.[1]

The older male fares no better in the social perspective. While he is not perceived as asexual, he too is not expected to be sexual. Should he exhibit sexual desire or interest, he is a dirty old man, a lecher or some other form of deviant. Dickenson (1974) tells of an incident where an elderly person inquired of a knowledgable source, "How much sex should a person over sixty have?" The answer was "nothing. Rosary beads and go to church."

Our social mores perceive sex only for the young. "Society does not take well to grandparents cavorting in bed," says Gochros (1972). That children get uncomfortable or upset with the thought of their parents' participating in sexual activity may well be the result of the parents' own attitudes and teaching. Many of today's grandparents were born around 1900, when sexual attitudes were Victorian and restrictive, and sex was considered by many to be a biological duty that ceased after menopause. It is not unlikely that their guilt and shame about sexual feelings and activity in the later years instilled similar values in their children.

Rationale has cultural seeds

The belief of the general populace that human sexual response cannot be retained and that it is not normal or appropriate may well have its rationale in inappropriate cultural accumulations. One author explained that many persons now over age sixty were at the peak of their sexual potential during the Depression years of the thirties, an era of "economic contraception" to limit the number of children in a given family. The inhibitions on sexual performance because of fear of pregnancy may have contributed to a habit pattern of continence which tended to weaken the libidinal drive that many carried into the aging years.

Some people assume that the sexual desire (libido) just fades away. Others believe that males have a limited number of sperm cells, so that either intercourse or masturbation will use them up, causing impotence, loss of drive and energy in later years or even death. Some feel it sinful or evil to have sexual desire or activity in older age. Many believe sex is for the physically attractive, and that the elderly are not. Some believe sexual activity in old age causes insanity; that it uses up one's blood (a drop of semen is equal to forty drops of blood).

To still others, hysterectomy and menopause cause impotence and lack of desire; sexually active men over sixty will most likely molest children or, if they have sex with younger women, precipitate and encourage an oedipal type of intercourse. And, to some, the elderly are too fragile for sexual activity; anyway, their juices have all dried up.

With a cultural heritage of fear and anxiety, asexual women and dirty old men, it becomes credible to believe that, as we age, sex is either unacceptable, dangerous or taboo, inevitably to be completed by "x" date on the calendar. However, this heritage has a secondary affect; these expressions of disgust, dysfunction and disapproval have brought about a self-fulfilling prophecy.

Stated simply, the self-fulfilling prophecy postulates that, in many if not most situations, people tend to do what is expected of them—so much so, in fact, that even a false expectation may evoke the behavior that makes it seem true. We can readily understand why it is so difficult to convince the elderly that all humans are sexual beings and that they can retain the same deed till they die. It is most difficult for them to comprehend that loving and being loved physically is appropriate, not contemptible.

The Climacterium

The socio-psycho-physiological condition known as the climacterium has significant social implications for the human sexual response in old age, since it signifies a period of time[2] in one's life where a dramatic (or traumatic) change of life style takes place, with its subsequent ramifications for one's behavior with others. It has been called that critical moment in the female's life where the balance of the mind and body is on the brink. The climacteric condition of menopause, associated physically with the decline in ovarian function, cessation of menses and the termination of reproductive life, have been, initially, the basis of study and reports of the aging female's sexual activity.

Early studies of female sexuality were mainly limited to the menopausal or immediate postmenopausal years. This sexual tension state stimulated the 45-to-55-year-old woman to seek relief from the physical and psychosocial problems inherent in the condition. Comfort (1974 tapes), in his enlightening and jocular manner, has said "women have a *men*-o-pause," but "men do not have a *women*-o-pause." The allusion to the fact that men do not have a corresponding phenomenon has been noted time and time again. Nevertheless, there is a continuous desire for sexual equality and the so-called male menopause. Some studies note the gonadal functional diminution, vasomotor symptoms that might parallel female menopause. As Dr. Harry Benjamin sums it up, "It would thus seem justified to speak of this period in a man's life as 'male climacteric,' provided one does not expect it to resume too closely its female counterpart."

Our concern with climacteria relates to its social significance as a ceremony indicating the rites of passage from sexuality to asexuality, thus constraining the human sexual response in the later years. For the male, it portends the loss of prestige, self-confidence and manhood (*macho*) and, for the women, the fears of loss of attractiveness, usefulness and desirability.

The change of life, a vernacular expression symbolizing the demise of sexual expression as a social constraint, has a more serious ramification in that it initiates the premature cessation of sexual function. This may well accelerate physiological and psychological aging, since disuse of any function usually leads to concomitant changes in other capacities. Regular, continuing sexual activity is generally agreed to be essential to maintain both the interest and capacity for effective sexual performance.

It has been noted that some women, who have been unhappy with the sexual experience in marriage, find in the menopause a respectable rationale for ending an activity (or duty) that has been uncomfortable or distasteful to them. The myths and ignorances about menopause have caused abstinence and sometimes suffering in other women.

Yet there is more than adequate evidence that sexual activity need not be constrained by the onset of the climacterium. To the contrary, Kaplan (1974) notes that "from a purely physiological standpoint, libido should theoretically increase at menopause, because the action of the androgens, which is not materially affected by menopause, is now unopposed by estrogen." It should also be evident that the termination of the reproductive function liberates both the male and female from the constraints of bothersome, cumbersome birth-control mechanisms, thus free to be more efficacious in sexual expression.

Our current cultural expectations of the menopause are of a period of physical discomfort and mental anguish, but it is now apparent that these conditions need not persist. In the near future, it is likely that we will hardly note or miss this landmark social event, much to the furtherance of sexual expression.

The Double Standard

The inequality of roles in human sexuality is quite pronounced; de-Beauvoir (1972) states it succinctly:

> I have never come across one single woman, either in life or in books, who has looked upon her old age cheerfully. In the

same way no one ever speaks of a "beautiful old woman"; the most one might say would be a "charming old woman." Some "handsome old man" may be admired, but the male is not a quarry; neither bloom, gentleness nor grace are required of him but rather the strength and intelligence of the conquering subject: white hair and wrinkles are not in conflict with this manly ideal.

The norms determining femininity and masculinity in this society assign preoccupation with one's physical appearance to the female sex role and little attention for one's looks in the case of males. Traditionally, women are more intimately concerned with aging than men, since their status attainment depends largely on the ability to maintain sexual attractiveness. Sontag (1972) feels that "the double standard about aging sets women up as property, as objects whose value depreciates rapidly with the march of the calendar."

Thus the female role as sexual partner and sexually desirable object is strained for many middle-aged and older women; often a woman's primary role as mother ends at approximately the same period of time. With the loss of these important assets, an identification crisis and a corresponding degree of prestige loss may arise out of this ambivalent rolelessness.

This double standard is a socialization process that starts early in life. *Masculinity* is identified with competence, autonomy and self-control, qualities that improve with age; *femininity* is identified with weakness, incompetence, dependence, passivity and compliance, pejorative qualities not expected to improve with age. The aging man may, as he grows old, become "dignified" and "venerable," while the woman can become "ugly" and "wasted." Sontag calls this social convention an "instrument of oppression" that enhances a man but progressively destroys a woman. "A man doesn't need to tamper with his face. A woman's face is the canvas on which she paints a revised portrait of herself."

Genevay's concept of "Ageism and Sexism = Old, Ugly and Worthless" (unpublished) is reinforced by numerous life situations, taking a heavy toll of a woman's self-identity. This denigrating attitude, poor image and unacceptance are often manifested in the loss of sexual interest and activity, social and physical withdrawal, anxiety and/or alcohol and drugs.

'Machismo' expected in males

This double standard, while most oppressive to women, often can cause identity crises in the male. He is expected to carry and maintain *machismo*, the masculine traits of dominance, aggressiveness and physical prowess. In the socialization process of boyhood to manhood, there is little emphasis on the sexual relationship as a meaningful, shared experience. The aggressive component in male sex has always been strongly emphasized, and it has become even more so today with the continual reification of machismo.

What then of the elderly male, who has long subscribed to this culturally defined male sex role, when he experiences in his sex life the need for more direct physical stimulation to produce an erection, when orgasm becomes less frequent and ejaculation is at a slower rate? Even though these physical changes are functionally minimal (and even if he understands that the involutionary processes are to be expected), he worries about his "macho," or natural function.

Masters and Johnson (1974 tapes) note "the moment any male says to himself, even in a joking manner, 'What's wrong?' he's 50 percent on the way to impotence, because he is beginning to question himself. [The doubtful machismo or less a man.] It is inevitably true that, as a natural physiologic function, we should expect to take longer to achieve erections past the ages of 45 or 50, and most of us do."

Not understanding the natural debilitations of the aging process, the man worries and becomes anxious. "The wife or partner has no frame of reference as to the fact that diminutions occur, [who] helps him as she says, 'Well, John, it doesn't matter, we have all night.' In truth, she is very little equipped to deal with this natural phenomenon. The first thing that would occur to her as she covers up her feelings is the possibility that something is wrong with her, that she is no longer stimulating or attractive or . . . is failing to inspire her husband sufficiently to respond." The interrelated process of misunderstanding and confusion may well contribute to a growing human sexual inadequacy.

The ascription of sexual status over the life cycle is fraught with many hazards for identity in the growing-old process. How, and in what way, these antiquated social conventions could be removed or ignored may well be the questions that need resolving if the elderly are to be freed to continue in the human sexual response.

Economic Security and Sexual Response

It would appear a terrible paradox if one had to deny oneself intimate sexual relations as an either/or choice of economic survival. Yet this is the situation that confronts many elderly. After experiencing in marriage the intimacy that supports and sustains a meaningful life, an elderly person, on the loss of a spouse, may wish to remarry and recapture that good experience. Values carried from Victorian times may well be set in the elderly of today, and these attitudes spell out marriage as the only condition for engaging in human sexual interaction.

Since marriage is both required by one's set-values and for possessing the opportunity for emotional and sexual satisfaction, it is the most desired state, and often occurs in later years. (In 1968, 13,210 brides and 28,554 grooms over 65 were reported. Less than 10 percent were first marriages.) Woodruff and Birren (1975) note that, after age 65, less than half the women are living with a spouse, a fact that portends that living together could readily be perceived as a great need for fulfillment in the later years.

But marriage for the elderly may have grave economic ramifications, even to deprivation. Benefits from pensions, Social Security, Supplemental Security Income (SSI) and public welfare (Food Stamps) are affected when the recipient's status is formally changed by marriage; incomes (when joint) are reassessed and benefits most likely recalculated, with the beneficiaries getting less. Those 65 and over in financial need are eligible for economic support through monthly SSI cash payments from the Federal Government.

Marriage carries penalties

In New York state, such an individual, living alone, would receive a monthly check for $218.55; two individuals living separately would receive a total of $437.10. If they marry, they would receive a combined $312.54 (a deficiency of $124.56), presumably on the premise that two can live cheaper than one.

Obviously, the Social Security Administration does not encourage marriage or remarriage in the later years. Its general laws are structured to inhibit the meaningfulness of the marital state or the change to a new marital partner. For instance, payments to an aged wife or aged, dependent husband are ended if a divorce occurs before 20 years or more of marriage.

If a widow's Social Security benefit depends exclusively on her late husband's primary accrued insurance, remarriage could have drastic effects. Remarriage before age 60 precludes any entitlement; after age 60, her benefit rate is reduced by half. Widows remarrying under specifications of many private pension plans may also sustain losses.

For the current generation of elderly, living together out of wedlock is a major decision. The social, ethical, moral and psychological implications are disturbing at a time when coping to maintain some sense of equilibrium is a major preoccupation, and the pressures from family, peers and conscience are strong. It assuredly takes a strong, willful individual to defy convention in order to reap the sexual and emotional benefits of an "unblessed" union.

Unwed cohabitation spreading

Yet not all elderly are bound by their Victorian heritage, fearful of censure and constrained by guilt. Some feel that the expression of cohabitation without marriage in youth is spreading to the elderly, that many are now establishing such relationships to retain higher income as well as for companionship and possibly sex. Glick (*New York Times*, February 20, 1974) reported that the U.S. Census Bureau listed more than 18,000 couples over 65 as unmarried and living together; undoubtedly, there are many others.

The overt or covert attitudes of children or other kin are also a strong socioeconomic constraint to marriage or remarriage in the later years. Overtly, they may perceive revived sexual interest as inappropriate, foolish and self-denigrating, or that the elderly are being duped or seduced; covertly, they may feel that, with a formal marriage arrangement, they may stand to lose money or property to which they feel entitled.

Under these conditions, little interest or concern is directed toward the older person's social/sexual needs and desires. Unless the elderly themselves change their value orientation, our society's structured social constraints will continue to impose economic sanctions on the elderly who wish to marry or remarry.

The Widowed Condition

With more women than men in the population (140 women to 100 men in 1973), a sizable proportion may not have the opportunity to be sexually intimate with a man. With their higher life expectancy at age 65 (16 years or more for women, 13 years for men) and their tendency to marry older men (almost two-fifths of older men have wives under 65), the proportion of women who marry in later life drops significantly.

Only a small proportion of the elderly (7.3 percent ment, 9.1 percent women) have been divorced, separated or never married. Heavier proportions of older women are widowed, rising from 20 percent at ages 55-64 to about 66 percent at 65 and over; slightly more than 70 percent of men are married at 65 and over. More than a third of all older persons live alone or with nonrelatives (41 percent of all older women but only 17 percent of older men).

Beyond these skewed population factors is another demographic problem denying the opportunity for sex, that of living arrangements. To naturally and comfortably engage in the human sexual response, it needs to be expressed in an atmosphere of privacy. In the later years, this may not be possible for many.

With approaching old age, individual roles are subject to drastic changes. In adult socialization, various persons and groups attempt to influence the adult's overt behavior, an action that may clash with the individual's personality conceptions. The basic roles of spouse, parent and wage earner are taken for granted to such an extent by the adults conditioned to performing them that they are seldom conscious of the degree to which self-identity and the patterns of everyday interactions are dependent upon a mere handful of significant roles. It is only with alteration of accustomed positions in society during old age that full manifestation of these roles are realized.

Changes in or loss of meaningful roles are problematic for either the elderly man or woman. Often, modification or alteration of significant roles and self-concepts is required. Such is the case for the widowed or institutionalized elderly person.

Widowhood disrupts social role

The social state of widowhood disrupts the networks of social relationships, militating against the ongoing continuation of rewarding and fulfilling sexual activity for men and women in the later years. Lopata (1973) overviews this general condition by explaining that "The social space of each person is dependent upon his or her location in the social system and . . . ability to use the resources offered by society . . . understanding of the social system and knowledge of how to mobilize the environment to meet needs. In our heterogeneous society, many members are restricted in the life styles available to them . . . particularly older widows."

Widows, a large part of the elderly population, in their later years lead constricting restrictive lives. We assume that widowhood will not come as a sudden shock to the older woman, since she is generally younger than her husband and knows that her life expectancy is greater. Despite the expectation and anticipatory socialization, grief and loss take heavy tolls on the psyche.

And what of the new socialization? For some who have been unhappy and burdened in marriage, it may offer relief and opportunities for freedom and new life styles. For most, it means loss, necessitating reorganization and acquisition of new social roles. While new or adaptive social roles are varied, some contribute to well-being in old age, and some do not. Most assuredly, the roles relating to human sexual activity are the ones most strained or abandoned. In a survey by Newman and Nichols, only seven of 101 single, divorced or widowed subjects reported any sexual activity with partners.

Social mores set patterns

Refraining from sex by elderly widows is socially expected and followed. Repression of sexual desires and the disavowal of sexual interest become a way of life, a life of denial, not necessarily to be perceived as an intrapsychic weakness on the woman's part. She depends on her man's survival or the availability of other men. Since women outlive men and are in greater number, they are frequently denied the opportunity.

It is also worth noting that, on being widowed, living arrangements may be altered. More than a third of elderly widows, unwilling or unable to live alone, now live with their children, thus sacrificing privacy and opportunities for sexual involvement. The obstacles are horrendous. Women without a socially acceptable partner have little, if any, sexual activity.

To solve the conundrum of achieving the emotionally, socially and sexually satisfying state of remarriage (most desired and most unobtainable, limited as it is by demography, economics and protesting kin), alternative life styles are being proposed. Along with the opportunity to live out of wedlock, other arrangements are appearing, such as women living together, polygamy, group marriage and communes. Polygamy seems to be the most promising form for providing a sexual partner.

Widows and widowers and the never-marrieds, without sexual partners, still have sex needs. It would appear that some solitary sexual expression (particularly masturbation) may be practiced. Beginning with the Kinsey research, many studies have indicated a practice of masturbation far exceeding popular expectations. (Expectations are probably inordinately low, since little attention is paid to sex in later life.)

Myths rampant, die hard

The elderly may well be accustomed to think of masturbation as childish and outgrown (some have never accepted it at any time). Others find masturbation an alternative release from sexual tension—an outlet when needs persist and other opportunities for gratification are not available. While support for acceptance of this sexual act may be improving, the elderly are still troubled by learned cultural behavior;

the myths of "self-abuse" die hard. Should they engage in the practice, it would probably be accompanied by guilt.

Though the loss of a mate is more problematic for women and less for the widower (his opportunities for sex are greater), the male may develop a debilitating sexual condition. This "widower's syndrome," as named by observers Masters and Johnson, is manifested in the man married for many years, who has a satisfactory sex life until his wife's terminal illness. During the illness, intercourse stops; when his wife dies, the cessation continues. A few months later, a neighborhood lady makes an acquaintance that leads to the bedroom. The man, who had been without prior sexual dysfunction, cannot achieve an erection.

Such a situation may lead to tension and alcoholism, certainly to great emotional strain. The man, or both partners, may well be unaware that his inability to function is due to the sustained period of disuse and of the significance of continuity in sexual potency. If the widower's syndrome is approached with understanding (and sometimes therapy), it is reversible.

The widowed or widower state, as a social condition, is unwanted; it creates much concern for those desiring continuance and fulfillment through the human sexual response.

Congregate Care: Setting of Constraints

At this stage of life, who is competent to assume the authority to draw the fine, sensitive line in deciding for others what is moral or immoral, or whether a door must remain open despite a longing for the privacy that those in control take for granted themselves? (Dickenson, 1974)

There comes a time in the later years when, no longer self-sustaining, one may have to seek a congregate care facility for a short or extended period. Homes for the aging, nursing homes, extended care facilities, mental hospitals and other total-care institutions tend to perceive the elderly as sexless. In one study of congregate care facilities, it was found that, in a major state home for the elderly, married couples were separated at admission, the man going into one building and the woman into another.

Because the segregated facilities existed, the authorities did not perceive the policy as violating a natural personal right. (Subsequent Federal Medicaid regulations—spelling out patient's rights—now guarantee a married couple's right to be housed together. Even so, it is doubtful if the regulations are observed.)

Rigid segregation of men from women with no visiting in each other's rooms or quarters is normative practice. Administrators fear sex and sexual activity, concerned lest they lose control, so they desocialize, forbid, discourage, make sinful, punish and dissuade from any display of compassion and sensuality among institutional residents. Institutional employees may also have problems with sexuality, since they, too, may not be comfortable with their own attitudes toward its expression. More concerned with their own functioning, they are frequently distressed and uncertain; lack of knowledge leads to prohibition, avoidance or a rationale that sex is unneeded or deviant.

Some activities 'unusual'

In institutions, ignorance and confusion about elderly people's thoughts and feelings about sex are manifested in unusual activities, ranging from prohibition to permissiveness. Some have strict rules forbidding social or physical contacts. Some furnish petting rooms, while some staff members direct residents to "secret" spots on the grounds (probably behind bushes) and/or conjugal visiting rooms.

Residents often develop their own programs (unauthorized by the institutions), including surreptitious room occupancy, guards and monitors. Comfort, seeing liberal and permissive opportunities as well-meaning and patronizing, wonders when institutional personnel will "stop mocking, governessing and segregating the old and the aging, for it is to their sexuality we owe our existence."

The fault is also with relatives; family and kin rarely address themselves to the elderly's sterile sexual conditions. They seemingly acquiesce, as if ashamed that a parent or grandparent should still be human enough for sexual loneliness.

The institution's lack of privacy is as effective in limiting sexual activity as are the rules and practices of the facilities. There are seldom any provisions for privacy or for opportunities of conjugal relations. This lack of privacy may also be enforced by inappropriate physical settings. Institutional atmospheres deindividualize people, discouraging identity and self-serving activity. Room and facility usage preclude privacy and deny opportunity.

In most cases, concerns for economy or insensitivity to the need for sex in the later years may well be the cause for antisex environments.

Erwin (Syracuse University, unpublished manuscript) stated it most succinctly when he wrote, "Many inappropriate environments are a direct result of poor architectural understanding and stem from initial facility design. Even where best architectural designs are produced, they are often rendered ineffective by a staff which does not properly maintain the behavioral intentions of the original concept."

The needs and desires of older people for human warmth and contact tend to be greater as their conditions and opportunities diminish, as they do in the inverse condition of the boundaries of behavior in congregate care facilities. Where the requirement for love and affection is in great demand and need, the institution mobilizes its strengths and resources to prevent or prohibit such activity. It appears that the only ones who care are the dependent and powerless, the ones unable to fulfill their natural desires. The need for change in conditions and environments of the congregate care facilities is critical.

Summary

> Old people stop having sex for the same reason they stop riding a bicycle. General infirmity, because someone told them they looked ridiculous, and because they haven't got a bicycle . . . Most people can and should expect to have sex long after they no longer wish to ride bicycles. (Comfort, 1974)

The social constraints affecting human sexual response in the later years are many and effective. "Aging," says Sontag, "is much more a social judgment than a biological eventuality." The cumulative practices of our cultures and mores have socialized[3] the elderly out of the natural sexual functions that could contribute to their well-being in the later years.

Our examination has shown that effective sexual functioning can play an important role in the elderly's lives and can continue well into the later years. Only two factors need be present: A reasonably good state of general health and an interested and interesting partner. Continuity, we find, is another critical factor. Most studies find that the likelihood of continued sexual expression in the later years is substantially greater for individuals who were highly interested and had maintained regular, active sexual practice throughout their lives. To the contrary, discontinuity and abstinence are deterrents to one's ability to maintain sexual function. It *is* true that, if you "don't use it," you may "lose it."

Even if you don't lose it, lack of expression will surely affect sexual performance. With regard to the physical condition, there is a need to overcome the myths and realities affecting sexual activity. We now know that the physiological act of sexual intercourse need not be demanding and debilitating; it has been found to be the physical equivalent of walking up two flights of stairs (Butler, 1975).

It must be fully accepted some day that sexual activity sustains intimate social relations and can be a source of pleasant recreation, long after the biological functions of reproduction are over. Since the later years are periods of losses (job, friends, income, status, spouse, etc.) it must be recognized that the sexual needs of older persons may not only continue but actually be heightened in other areas of their lives (a compensatory phenomenon).

The conspiracy of silence about sexuality in the later years must be overcome. As it is being overcome, we may see new ideas that change attitudes and lead to greater freedom in sexual expression. This education and awareness can overcome avoidance and enable problematic issues to be confronted; issues, such as *professional indifference* (what do you expect—it's old age), *social pejorative reinforcement* (reifying negative aspects as a condition of aging), *social rejection and loss of status* (noncontributive and no longer needed—the youth culture is in, old age is out), *provision of sexual outlets* (being less condemning and more permitting) and *resensitizing the basic hangups* of "asexual women" and "dirty old men."

Closeness serves for expression

Other realities must also be faced. The aging process is physically, socially and psychologically debilitating. Notwithstanding our new discoveries of sexual proclivities, we cannot expect every sexual encounter to possess mutual orgasm, flashing lights and clanging bells; elderly persons may find that coitus is not the only possible vehicle for expression. Expression may be found in some of the gentler and less specifically genital forms of sensuality and self-expression.

Without diminishing the romance of sex, it must be perceived as a part of the larger gestalt of human interaction: Of touch, of stroke, of emotion, of support, of affectionate and caring relationships. It may be tactile or not tactile; it may be genital or not genital, but it will be some form of togetherness. This reminder is especially relevant at the onset of handicap or disability, when intercourse is no longer feasible. The need for other aspects of social relationship, such as closeness, security, sensuality and being valued will persist. Felstein (1975) sums it up in a phrase he borrowed from Schubert's "Quartet in D minor, Second Movement," where the tempo is marked *andante, con variazoni:* "A steady pace, with variations on the theme."

That maintenance of the human sexual response in the later years is conducive to well-being and a more fulfilled life is most evident, well-documented in the studies and inquiries reported earlier. However, there is a growing contention that sexual activity and interest increase in the later years. This is not such a radical thought in the "early" stages of aging, where freedom from child-rearing roles, post-menopausal incapacity to become pregnant and the return to the privacy of the nuclear family may well be conducive to the resurgence of sexual desire and activity. Environments of freedom, abandonment and privacy are strong factors leading to the acceptance of sexual increase. But when we examine the sexual interest and activity of persons over 60, we are well past the climacterium and the onset of the empty nest.

Pfeiffer, *et al* (1968) claim, in their Duke longitudinal study, that "a *significant* portion of elderly subjects, when followed over a period of years, may show rising patterns of sexual activity and of sexual interest." This finding has been quoted and heralded time and time again as a discovery supporting the contention of increased sexual activity in the later years.

More critical look needed

On closer scrutiny, we observe very little data to support such a conclusive finding. The study included 116 subjects (nonrandom); of those showing increased activity, there were 13 percent of one category and 15 percent of another. In calculating this usage, we find the documentation is substantiated on approximately 21 subjects of a residual population of 116 from an original longitudinally intended population of 254.

There is a need to be more critical and open in our examination of sex attitudes and practices. The overzealous elaboration of some of the new sexual findings has produced studies with poor samples, biased inquiry and conclusions with little or no statistical significance. Rubin (1968) confirms this observation, noting that "No studies of sexual behavior and attitudes of the aging have been done on a sufficiently representative sample to provide us with norms."

Not all sex survey findings are positive and indicative of prolonged sex practice. Gilmore (1973), in a study of 66 healthy elderly couples (65-68) living in their own homes, found that the majority slept in the same room, with some tendency toward separate rooms and beds. Thirty-nine of the 66 stated they were no longer sexually intimate; the majority agreed that the frequency of intercourse lessened with age, which had reduced the need for it.

In the heightened activity of sexual inquiry, the "inquisitors" often forget that, in the examination of elderly people, one needs to be aware of the particular era in which they have lived to gain an appropriate understanding of the forces and factors affecting their conduct. All people are sum and substance of all their living. This must be understood. Many questions and questionnaires are embarrassing and offensive to the elderly, as well as misunderstood.

Many researchers report that interviews or self-reporting studies of human sexual response behavior may be less than candid if not truthful, or both. Others caution the acceptance without reservation of statements from other people about sexual relations; male vanity and female shyness often distort the facts.

We also find that exploration in the realm of human sexual responses among the elderly can have a stimulating effect. In the positive vein, it serves as an introduction, creating a climate of renewed sexual interest in a socially acceptable way. This interest can be transferred to an atmosphere of sexual enrichment. One rarely sees the enrichment process in operation, so such claims may only be illusions.

Can cause overreaction

On the negative side, the sex inquiry may tend to stimulate older people into overreactions of sexual guilt or more activity than they are prepared for. The sex survey may also stimulate the surveyor. The survey, as an instrument, may follow Kaplan's Law of the Instrument (1964) that says "Give a small boy a hammer, and he will find that everything he encounters needs pounding."

The sex inquiry is gaining impetus, regardless of the legitimacy of its intent or the quality of its methodology. It is hoped that, through the inquiry, contributory information will add to the further understanding of sexual desire and sexual activity in the later years.

The opportunity for a full life is a basic entitlement at any time in one's life. The opportunity to meet the potential of human sexual response is, more and more, becoming more established as a right. However, the need for sex is an individual choice, and the importance of individual difference must never be overlooked. Assuredly, we can expect a best-seller if Alex Comfort ever publishes "The Joy of Sex in the Later Years."

Notes

1. Freud perceived a functional need for socialization to regulate and repress sexual expression. He considered sexual control essential for creation of the family unit, that it is the parents' role to socialize and maintain a disciplined expression of the libido; energies should be diverted from sexual activities and allocated to economic production as a prerequisite for the preservance of the social structure, thus of civilization itself.

2. In *Adaptations and the Life Cycle*, Neugarten expresses this concept as "periodicity," a "socially prescribed timetable for the ordering of major life events."

3. A definition of socialization might include acquisition of status, assumption of socially accepted roles and social participation. When one is "socialized in," one performs as above. However, on being "socialized out," one loses status, roles and social participation.

References

Butler, R. N. Sex after Sixty-five. *The Later Years: Quality of Life*. Publishing Science Group, MA. 1965.

Comfort, A. *Topics in Aging*. (video cassette tapes), Sandoz Pharmaceutical Co., East Hanover, N.J., 1974.

deBeauvoir, S. *The Coming of Age*. New York: Putnam, 1972.

de Ropp, R. S. *Man Against Aging*. New York: Grove Press, 1962.

Dickinson, P. A. *The Fires of Autumn*. New York: Drakes Publishers, Inc., 1974.

Felstein, I. *Sex in Later Life*. Baltimore: Penguin Books, 1973.

Gilmore, A. Attitudes of Elderly in Marriage. *Gerontologicia Clinica* (Basel) 15 (2), 1973.

Gochros, H. L. The Sexually Repressed. *Social Work*, March 1972.

Kaplan, A. *The Conduct of Inquiry*. San Francisco, CA: Chandler Publishing Co., 1964.

Kaplan, H. S. *The New Sex Therapy*. New York: Bruner/Mazek Publishing Co., 1974.

Lopata, H. Z. Couple-Companionate Relationships in Marriage and Widowhood. *Old Family/New Family*. New York: D. VanNostrand, 1975.

Masters, W. E. & Johnson, V. E. *Topics in Aging*. tapes (see Comfort).

Pfeiffer, E. et al. Sexual Behavior in Aged Men and Women. *Archives of General Psychiatry*, December 1968.

Rubin, I. *Sex Life after Sixty*. New York: Basic Books, 1965.

———. Sex After Forty and After Seventy. *An Analysis of Human Sexual Response*. New York: New American Library, 1966.

Sontag, S. *The Saturday Review of Society*, September 23, 1972.

Woodruff, D. & Birren, J. *Aging: Scientific Perspectives and Social Issues*. New York: D. VanNostrand, 1975.

4.3

Widows and Widowers

Helena Lopata

The lifestyles of widows and widowers in modern urban America are quite different from those of past centuries and of the present time in some parts of the world, for several reasons. The main factor contributing to these unique lifestyles in this location is the relative independence of the nuclear family unit and the looseness of its ties to the extended family or kinship network and to the community. Another factor is the use of "secondary" sources, that is, nonpersonal ones such as a job or social security, for economic maintenance by men and the economic dependence of the wife upon her husband's sources of income. The situation of women is beginning to change in America, but most widows currently living here depend for the money they need on their husbands' social security, pension, insurance, and similar resources. A third factor is the importance our society attaches to the marital relation, placing it close to, if not higher than, the role of mother for the wife, and just below the occupational role for the husband.

What is unique in the American situation is the economic and social independence of the husband and wife from the male (and in the few cases of matriarchy, the female) family line and the strong mutual dependence upon each other.

Reprinted with permission from *The Humanist*, September/October 1977.

Widowhood in America

In 1975, there were less than two million widowers and over ten million widows in America. The few studies of widowers conducted thus far indicate that their two main problems are loneliness and discomfort over self-maintenance. These problems are a consequence of the breakup of the extended family, or at least the loosening of its day-to-day contact and controls, as well as of increased mobility. The loosening began when men became economically independent of their family line, being able to migrate and develop their own land or to obtain training for an occupation away from home and to market themselves for a wage sufficient to support themselves and a family. This revolutionary change, combined with modifications occurring in the lives of women and in the structures and cultures of the centralizing European and American societies, led to marital relations completely different from those of past times. Husbands and wives began selecting each other on the basis of emotional attachment and setting up their own households independently of either family of orientation. Such independence of each nuclear unit, with help during crises or transitional periods but self-maintained for the most part, contributed to a movement toward increasingly egalitarian marital relations, although patriarchal traditions have definitely not been eliminated altogether.

Attempts at creating a more democratic setting within the American family have been complicated by the division of labor between husband and wife that began in the eighteenth century as work was moved out of the home. Cottage and entrepreneurial industry became converted to paid employment in large organizations. At first, all family members, including the children, worked in the factories, but by the mid-1880s in England, and at different times in other societies, reformist protest led to the removal of children from paid employment. Deprived of relatives and other people, such as servants, in private households, European and American societies evolved a solution to the care of the no-longer-employed children by assigning this function exclusively to the mother and insisting that she remain in the home without income-producing activity from the time she bore her first child. Various historians have offered alternative explanations of why other forms of household formation and child care were not developed by those societies, but the fact remains that the home became a small, private dwelling with the husband supporting it economically, and containing, in addition to him, the housebound wife and preadult children. Interestingly enough, the wife in all but recent decades of American society was expected to remain in the household until her death, not venturing again into the occupational world, even after the children were grown. It has only been in recent times that she outlived an active motherhood role.

This division of labor in the family means that the husband becomes totally dependent upon the wife for most activities pertaining to the home and even his own maintenance, except for a few "male" tasks. In addition, the woman has been assigned, or took upon herself, the function of maintaining the couple's social relations, not only with her family and other couples but even with the husband's family. Felix Berardo found widowers in the state of Washington frequently incapable of adequate self-maintenance and socially isolated because they did not know how to retain social relations outside of work. *U.S. News and World Report*, in "The Plight of America's Two Million Widowers" (April 15, 1974), reported that American widowers have a much higher rate of mental breakdown, physical illness, alcoholism, suicide, and accidents than do widows or married men. However, the demographic composition of the widowed population and the cultural norm allowing men to marry down in age, make it easy for widowers to remarry; the rate for this solution to the problems of widowerhood is very high.

The case of widows is quite different, although there are changes taking place that will modify their lifestyles in the future. Most widows living in America were socialized in childhood and early marriage to a world quite different from that of today. They were brought up to be passive vis-à-vis the world outside of the home, with automatically involving support systems within the family and a stable village or neighborhood. As a result, many are living very restricted lives, in spite of the abundance of resources outside of their home, in a society requiring voluntaristic engagement in these resources. The creation of an isolated, though independent, nuclear family, financially dependent upon the husband's salary or social security, with a strong emphasis on marriage and motherhood as the main occupations of women, has resulted in social isolation for those women who do not have personal resources for reengagement when their life is disorganized by the death of the husband. Traditional support resources in the form of children, neighbors, and lifelong friends are dispersed, and many widows do not have the personal resources needed to get a job, join a group, make friends, or otherwise reengage in relational networks when a voluntary or involuntary event cuts off a prior relation.

A study was made recently in metropolitan Chicago of 1,169 widows who were former or current beneficiaries of social security. The women described above are not the only types of widows living in metropolitan Chicago, but they are highly representative of the older women and the ones most needful of societal intervention. There are also widows who are strongly involved with adult children and their families who live nearby or even with the mother; and there are widows who still live in unchanging neighborhoods and continue to be embedded in multileveled interaction with them and in local groups. Finally there are the truly "urban" or "cosmopolitan" women, able to take advantage of many of the resources of the society in order to develop complex support systems and lifestyles encompassing a multiplicity of social relations. They are pleased with their independence, as are their somewhat more restricted counterparts who are busy working or taking care of younger children as their main form of social engagement.

Even more important than age, income left from the late husband's work, or the presence and age of children as an influence on lifestyle of a widow is the combination of her education and urbanization. The Chicago study strongly points to this conclusion. Of course, the amount of schooling a woman achieves influences her selection of a husband, most white women marrying a man with the same or slightly more education, many black women still having to marry men with somewhat less schooling. The man's education influences his occupation and the income he earns. This means that the nonemployed wife builds the family lifestyle within definite income parameters. However, it is increasingly apparent that this lifestyle is heavily dependent upon the abilities, world view, and self-confidence the woman has and that these characteristics come mainly from her background, especially from her schooling. There is a family history to this schooling, even in upwardly mobile America. The more educated woman is apt to come from parents with only somewhat less education, who provide her with the background resources with which to better utilize the knowledge and planning skills she gains in school. The more educated the woman, the more apt she is to have returned to paid employment after the children reach a certain age or, in widowhood, to belong to voluntary associations and to have developed friendships.

Urbanization history is also important and strongly associated with schooling. One of the reasons so many of the widows are restricted in their personal resources is that they were reared either in rural, or at least nonurban, areas by parents who had been so reared. Most of the parents of the widows we studied had been born on farms, in villages, or in small towns. Many came from other countries or from states in America in which the schooling system was minimal and did not prepare them to provide a home environment with a breadth of perspectives. Many of the daughters who had themselves been urban-born of such parents, some of whom do not even speak English, grew up in ghettolike areas in which rural, agriculturally trained people are apt to locate when they migrate to the city. The in-depth interviews conducted with some of the widows during the exploratory stage of the research indicate that they lack knowledge and understanding of the city within which they live. They have no "map" of it and of its resources and are even unaware of services that they could use to their great advantage. They are frightened of the city and of the agencies that could help them. In addition, they have a negative self-image that precludes any efforts at friendship formation or engagement in voluntary associations.

Problems in Widowhood

Although there are great variations among widows and widowers in their lifestyles, depending on some of the factors discussed above, there are certain problems they have in common as a result of the death of their mates. The women usually face a drop in income. Three-quarters of the Chicago-area widows experienced the death of the husband when the wife was still less than sixty-five years old. The white women had a greater drop in income than did the blacks, because the latter were already living on a low budget. As of now, almost half of the women report an income falling below the poverty line for their size family. The widowers reportedly face an economic hardship mainly because they have to pay for services formerly supplied by their late wives. If they are left with small chidren, this cost can create an especially heavy burden.

The second major problem is emotional. Regardless of how conflict-ridden or minimally engaging the marriage, widowhood brings an involuntary end to it and to a whole style of life, leaving the survivors bereaved. In modern America, any marriage that survives into widowhood is assumed by those involved and by observers to be sufficiently rewarding to continue. Grief for a spouse is culturally prescribed, and most studies find that it is actually experienced, though in varying degrees and for different lengths of time. One of the difficulties with grieving in American society is the lack of adequate ritual and permissiveness for its public and emotional expression. Stoic self-control is idealized, especially for men. The process, which is psychologically necessary, is called by psychiatrists "grief work," and it refers to both the grieving and obsessional reviews and reconstruction of the self as a partnerless person.

One of the interesting consequences of grieving that became apparent in the study of the Chicago-area widows is their tendency to idealize the late husband, often to the point of sanctification. Other observers have referred to the idealization process, and I finally constructed a scale to measure the sanctification extremes. The bottom statement of the scale reads, "My husband had no irritating habits." Anyone agreeing strongly with that statement seems to have reconstructed the reality of the past; few wives of living husbands circle that response. The sanctification process performs many functions for the widows, and undoubtedly for any other survivors who go through it. In making the late husband into a near saint, the widow removes from his spirit any mortal sentiments of jealousy or irritation over not being mourned forever. He becomes a good, protective spirit. In addition, the fact that such a good man married her brings her feelings of self-worth, at a time when his death and consequent events increase her need for such emotional supports. Since the marriage was ongoing, and since the major adjustments had been made early in its history, or at least since it is not likely that major changes were still taking place, the idealization process undoubtedly did not have to work through a great deal of unfinished business. At least, we found that the younger women are much less apt to sanctify their late husbands than are older ones.

Another reason that a woman tends to idealize her late husband, even to the point of sanctification, is the drop of status and lifestyle she often experiences with his death. This is especially true of middle- and upper-class women who were heavily dependent upon the position the husband had in the community and who are traditionalists as far as gender roles are concerned. Many of the older women feel hesitant in going out alone without a male escort, and the likelihood of finding a replacement for the late husband is low. Several of the women I talked with who have the money to do so refuse to go on a vacation, or to a restaurant alone or with other women. The feminist movement will change this attitude but having a man as a partner away from home was important to many traditionalists.

There is another aspect of widowhood that leads both to sanctification of the late husband and to loneliness. Middle-class Americans tend to live in a couple-companionate world. Widows report feeling like a "fifth wheel," or that they are ignored by their friends in any situations in which the living husband is present. Married friends will visit them during the day, but dinners, parties, or excursions to public places are primarily undertaken with couples, and the widow is simply not invited. One of the problems with this situation is definitely sexual. Widows report that their married women friends are fearful that their husband may enter into a sexual relation with the widow. Some widows report that some husbands do offer their services, but fewer experience such propositioning than report jealousy from the wives. When such propositioning occurs, and it is reported mostly by women in their fifties—possibly because the younger women find escorts and the older ones are less apt to have contacts with married friends' husbands—it is met with anger. What the widow wants, if she is interested in a relationship with a man, is a combination of companionship, sharing of public activities, and sexual intercourse, but without fear of jealousy by friends or of being in a relation with no future. The culturally and self-imposed fears and uncertainties result in a considerable change in the social life of a woman who loses her husband through death, and, as I understand it from colleagues who are studying divorce, from that method of marriage dissolution. On the other hand, there are women who report a much more active social life than before, either because of the long illness of the late husband or because of his constraining personality. In fact, they do not want to lose their freedom and independence through remarriage, even when offered the opportunity.

However, these women are already over the grief period and have, for the most part, resolved their loneliness problems. Loneliness itself is a complicated set of feelings and its form and content vary by person. Robert Weiss, in *Loneliness: The Experience of Emotional and Social Isolation*, separates emotional from social loneliness, and the Chicago-area widows report missing the person for whom they are grieving, having a love object, being a love object, the only person to whom they had been an important human being, a companion with whom activities were shared, a partner in couple-companionate interaction, an escort at public events, a father to the children, someone around whom work and time were organized, a presence in the home, and so on. In addition, they are lonely for the whole past lifestyle, daily and special, that the husband's presence made possible.

Widows devise various methods of coping with loneliness, which is usually felt most keenly in evenings and on weekends. Television is a great help, and many women eat their meals while watching it. Activities with other no-longer-married women sometimes cover periods previously taken up in couple-companionate interaction; some widows still see their couple friends, usually hoping that an event such as a dinner does not include matchmaking behavior by the hostess. Others simply get used to spending much of their time alone and learn to enjoy it. Interestingly enough, very few widows live with people other than their never- or no-longer-married children. If previously married offspring are in the home, they are likely to be living with the mother rather than she with them. Eighty percent of the widows in the Chicago-area study are heads of their own households, and those who do not have young children still at home live alone. They do so mainly out of choice, not wanting to give up the independence of their own home management and being unwilling to face anticipated conflicts and work in the home of their married offspring. As one reported, "My daughter invited me to live with her and her family, but she added, 'Ma, you'll have to keep your mouth shut.' Now tell me, what is the fun of living if I have to keep my mouth shut?" Visits to the homes of offspring provide enough evidence to the widow that she is going to find something, usually many things, of which she is critical and that moving there would produce serious problems. Besides, she now feels independent and life is easier than it has been in the past. She does not want to give this up to be a baby-sitter and a housekeeper in someone else's home.

Summary and Implications

All in all, the few pieces of evidence about the lifestyles of widowers and the expanding knowledge about widows in urban America indicate that the isolated nuclear family in today's mobile society, with its dependence upon the income earned by the husband, its looser ties to the extended family, and the stronger dependence of the husband and wife on each other, makes the early stages of widowhood very difficult. There are no automatically engaging support systems, such as nearby family and neighbors known for a lifetime, who help grief work, prevent or decrease loneliness, and take over the duties of the late husband. Urban American society provides an enormous amount of resources for social interaction and social relations, but these resources call for voluntaristic engagement. Each member must define her or his needs, determine which resources can best meet them, plan action to reach and utilize these resources, and turn to new activities when prior forms of engagement are voluntarily or involuntarily disorganized. Unfortunately, the recent changes in social structure away from ascribed social engagement have not been matched by changes in the socialization or by constant updating of the personal resources of most people that is needed to voluntaristically involve themselves in the system. Traditional European and American societies discouraged voluntaristic behavior of any but their tiny upper class, for both men and women. Democratization, particularly of American society, and changes in the economic sphere of life pushed more and more men into training for voluntaristic engagement outside of the home, with varying degrees of success depending on background, but with strong encouragement for upward mobility, as did the migration to American urban centers of its own rural people and of foreigners. However, it is only recently that American women have begun pushing for flexible and voluntaristic social engagement. New generations of women and men will build their lives with flexibility of entrance and movement within a variety of social roles. However, present widowers are still uncomfortable in the home, in planning social interaction considered the "woman's domain" in America, and in seeking help when needed.

There are also millions of women who are not able to function in a manner utilizing societal resources at different stages in their lives.

Hopefully, some societal action can be developed that will help those members of the two or so generations of women and men who are not satisfactorily socially engaged to find new social roles and relations after their lives are disorganized by such an event as the death of a spouse. These people, moreover, are not the only ones experiencing transitional events. Others might benefit from societal help, while new generations are training to solve their problems more voluntaristically. The study of Chicago-area widows leads to a recommendation from the formation of *neighborhood networks* designed to locate problem situations among local residents, provide immediate resources to meet acute needs, and serve as a connecting link to community resources. Such networks can be organized from existing voluntary or paid resources, which abound in most communities. The study of widows dramatically pointed up the absence of these "helping" agencies or groups in their support systems. Most groups help only their own members, but often not even knowing when they are in trouble. The networks would have to cut across organizational boundaries and help the invisible residents not being reached. These people needing help can be new residents, women whose lives are changed with the birth of a child, those experiencing a major illness in the family, others facing problems, and especially the widowed. Many of the people facing these events may not need resource information or connecting links to the neighborhood, but as of now, few neighborhood members even know if there are unmet needs restricting the social engagement of people near them. Future generations will need automatically linking helpers much less, because of their personal resources; but our society would do well to invest in such neighborhood networks to help reengage those people who do not have them.

4.4

Society of the Alone:
Freedom, Privacy, and Utilitarianism
as Dominant Norms in the SRO

Joyce Stephens

Social gerontologists have seriously neglected one segment of the aged in American society—the elderly tenants of slum hotels. The SRO (single-room occupancy) hotel, although comprising the living arrangement for a significant number of the urban elderly, has received relatively little research attention. As a consequence, little is known of the sociological and psychological characteristics of the elderly tenants of these deteriorating hotels situated in the cores of our cities.

The present research concerns the findings of a sociological study of the elderly occupants of the "Guinevere" a SRO in a large midwestern city (Stephens, 1973). This study investigated the network of relationships and roles that had developed among the elderly "permanent guests" in the Guinevere and delineated characteristics of the interpersonal world of the elderly SRO tenant. Specifically, the salient features identified include dominant norms of freedom, privacy, and utilitarianism.

Previous studies have described the world of the elderly SRO tenant as marked by extreme degrees of isolation, impersonality, and freedom (Lawton & Kleban, 1971; Shapiro, 1966, 1969, 1970). They point

Copyright 1975 by The Gerontological Society. Reprinted by permission. *Journal of Gerontology*, Vol. 30, No. 2, pp. 230-235.

out that the elderly tenants of inner city hotels do not usually establish strong and viable relationships with their fellow tenants. A common shortcoming of earlier studies lies in their failure to evaluate the crucial influence of dominant SRO norms, which define both the types and frequency of social relationships which will be permitted to develop among tenants.

Various authors have attested to the overall social isolation of the elderly in American society (Bell, 1967; Blau, 1961; Heilbrun and Lair, 1964; Maddox & Eisdorfer, 1962; Rosow, 1973). Indeed, a major framework for the analysis of the relationship between aging and adjustment is the theory of disengagement (Cumming & Henry, 1961) which posits that decreasing social integration is an identifying characteristic of the later years.

However, relatively few studies have made a distinction between voluntary and involuntary isolation. Townsend's (1957) study of elderly persons in a London district pointed out the difference between isolation as an objective condition and loneliness as a subjective state. Lowenthal (1964) noted that most studies of increasing isolation in relation to aging have left open the question of voluntary vs. involuntary disengagement. In a study of hospitalized and nonhospitalized elderly (Lowenthal, 1964; Lowenthal & Haven, 1968) three classifications of degree of isolation were developed: life-long extreme isolates, life-long marginal isolates, and late isolates. The presumed correlation between increasing isolation and low morale was not supported in the case of the life-long extreme isolates. Rather, the data suggested that for some elderly persons voluntary isolation has been a life-long pattern and is not to be attributed to the aging process.

It is clear that a critical theoretical and research issue in social gerontology is the importance of social isolation and decreased role consistency for the adjustment and morale of the elderly individual. Recent studies strongly suggest that the relationship between isolation and adjustment may not be a simple one. The intervening factor of degree of voluntariness, that is, the extent to which isolation is imposed and resented or, on the other hand, embraced and preferred as a life-long pattern, is a major related issue which must be taken into account.

Sampling and methodology

Approximately 100 elderly permanent tenants in the Guinevere Hotel were observed and interviewed by the researcher during the course of this study. Males greatly outnumbered females (97 and 11, respectively), which is characteristic of the SRO population. The average age was 67, with the oldest individual being 91. The length of residence ranged from 2 to 51 years, with a mean of 9.75 years.

The data for this study were gathered over a period of 9 months. For the first half of the study, the researcher lived in the Guinevere as a tenant and utilized participant observation as the major data-gathering method. The researcher assumed the participant-as-observer role and supplemented observations and participation in SRO society with a variety of other research techniques, including document analysis, unobtrusive measures, trace analysis, and informant and respondent interviewing.

Reactions to the researcher evolved through a discernible pattern—from initial skepticism to the frequently expressed concern on the part of the subjects that, "she get everything and tell it all, without leaving out anything."

From the analysis of data gathered during the participant observation stage, the researcher constructed an interview schedule, and the last half of the study was spent interviewing residents of the Guinevere, hotel staff, social workers with clients in the hotel, and residents of neighboring SROs.

Transients and Permanents

There are two categories of people with whom the elderly SRO tenants must deal on a day-to-day basis and with whom reciprocal expectations and norms must be worked out. The first category includes those individuals connected with the operation of the hotel, *viz.*, the manager, desk clerks, porters, maintenance people, switchboard operators, room maids. The second category consists of other SRO tenants and includes both transients and permanents in the Guinevere or neighboring SROs. Except for some peripheral groups (social workers, police officers, prostitutes, owners of nearby cafes and bars), it is these individuals who form the core of the hotel society and with whom the network of interpersonal bonds is established.

The division of the hotel tenants into two groups—transients and permanents—is essential to an understanding of the social world of the elderly SRO tenant. The transients are those tenants who are living temporarily in the hotel, pay by the day or week, and do not look upon the Guinevere as their permanent "home." Also, they are considerably younger as a group than the permanents. In contrast, the elderly permanents have lived in the hotel for several years and define the Guinevere as their permanent "home." There exists a definite gap between these two groups and, in almost all ways, they constitute separate societies. They rarely have anything to do with each other and despite their close spatial proximity and overlapping activities (eating at the same restaurants, drinking in the hotel bar, using the hotel elevators, congregating in the hotel lobby, etc.), they are for the most part, disinterested in establishing relationships with each other.

A partial explanation for this finding lies in the attitudes of the permanent guests toward the transients. These attitudes are distinctly negative and resentful. No long-term resident was encountered who did not clearly distinguish between the transients and the permanent guests. The transients are defined by the permanents as intruders. The permanents look upon the hotel as their home, and in their eyes, the transients merely view the hotel as a place where they can get cheap lodging for a day or week. There is a strong feeling among the permanents that the transients do not belong there and are interlopers in the private domain of the elderly tenants, many of whom have lived in the Guinevere for years.

Other differences between the transients and the permanents are: the transients are younger; more likely to be in couples or small family groupings; are more likely to have been born in another state; spend considerably less time in the hotel (thus, use the hotel primarily as a place to sleep); rarely stay longer than a few days or weeks at the hotel; and are less likely to use the public areas of the hotel for socializing. In contrast, the permanents are elderly; spend the major portion of their time within the hotel; are dependent upon the public areas of the hotel (lobby, front stoop, bar) for socializing; are not within the family constellation; define the Guinevere as their home; and do not anticipate moving to any other residence.

Although the majority of the elderly permanents insist that the Guinevere is their home and believe that they will die there, as the following comments reveal, they feel a considerable ambivalency over this fact:

> The Guinevere is the road of no return. Old timers come to this point of their life. This is the last place they'll ever stay. When they get here, they don't never leave.

> A lot of us come down here to do this or that with the intention of leaving, but we kept coming back and at last, we never leave.

> This is a place where people come to die.

The permanents maintain that the transients lower the standards of the hotel. They refer contemptuously to the transients as being on the welfare rolls. They contrast the youth and health of the transients with their own advanced years and chronic illnesses and conclude that, for the elderly permanents, receiving state aid is forgivable, whereas for "those others," being on the "dole" is a shameful commentary to the effect that "they could work but don't want to."

The most resented aspect of the transients lies in their behavior, which the permanents view as causing trouble. Complaints about the transients for disturbing the orderly lives of the permanents and damaging the reputation of the hotel are common:

> Those others upset the permanent guests. We need privacy, to be left alone. They're always causing trouble. Before you know it, here come the police. He's (manager) on the phone, calling the police. Well, he's got to, you see.

> They don't respect nothing, nothing at all, and these here are the worst of the lot.

Thus, the elderly tenants define the transients as endangering their life-style, with the importation into the hotel of a variety of bothersome activities, such as, violence, quarreling leading to fights, drugs, mixing with street rowdies. This opinion is shared at least partially by the manager, who sees these problems as attendant to renting to a transient clientele; however, he also sees the permanents as generating problems, just different ones. Social ties between the transients and the permanents are, then, sparse, as the elderly permanents tend to avoid and resent these interlopers in what they define as their home.

Relationships with Other Permanents

Close ties between long-term residents are uncommon; intimate relationships are a rarity. The impoverished relationships that do develop are sustained on two bases—economic activities and interests and leisure-time activities and interests. Over-all, the pattern of social interaction which emerges is one of a minimal and utilitarian nature.

Over 80% of the elderly tenants are receiving some form of state aid. The average monthly income per individual is less than $150.00. The necessity for many of these elderly individuals to supplement their meager finances results in a large proportion who are more or less continuously seeking a means to earn money. The hotel occasionally has an opening that can be filled by one of these elderly tenants, but this is not common. By and large, the most relied upon source of additional income is some variant of hustling. Hustling comes in myriad forms in the Guinevere, ranging from delivering coffee, cigarettes, liquor ("go-fors"), to selling stolen merchandise, to renting out the backseat of one's car to vagrants, to street peddling.

In particular, the street peddlers have coalesced into a group with identifying characteristics. The primary source of cohesion is the exigencies that arise in the course of arranging for the hustle, with secondary sources of cohesion being generated from the common experience, interests, and often times backgrounds (many have worked previously with carnivals and circuses) surrounding the hustle. The street vendors are referred to as "carnies" by the tenants, and enjoy a certain prestige in that they are still working and actively maintaining their independence (Stephens, 1974).

The solidarity among the carnies is based upon their recognition of mutual economic need and resembles the other relational bonds formed in this hotel society, *i.e.*, tends to be instrumental and non-intimate. The carnies who may work together eleven hours a day and afterwards sit together in the bar drinking, do not consider themselves friends, rather, they define the association as a business partnership. When falling-outs occur, and they occur with predictable regularity, the cause will be money or job-related disagreements.

Nevertheless, the carnies constitute the most distinct social grouping to be found among these tenants and they display the most solidarity and group identification.

The second basis for social groupings is the use of leisure-time. Most of these elderly people spend the greater part of their time in the hotel. Certain leisure activities and interests head the list at the Guinevere—they are drinking, betting (the horses and sports events), and socializing in the public areas of the hotel. Relationships which emerge in the course of pursual of these activities are fairly transitory, superficial, and nonintimate. There is considerable overlapping, and attempts to delineate distinct leisure groups were not feasible, as they would ignore the fluidity of boundaries that is characteristic. Leisure groupings are considerably more evanescent and transitory than the work groups of the carnies.

Leisure-time is spent either in one's room, in which case it is not a social affair (with the exception of sexual contacts), or in a public area, in which case it may remain a private activity or may become the stage for interaction. There is a strictly adhered-to line of demarcation which defines certain areas of the hotel as private and not suitable for social intercourse and other areas as public and open to interaction. The more singularly private areas are the rooms of the tenants: the tenants guard the privacy of their rooms with a definiteness that doesn't bear challenge. There is no visiting in each other's rooms.

The proper areas for visiting and socializing are those areas of the hotel defined by the tenants as public. Socializing and visiting take the form of congregating in these areas, e.g., the hotel lobby, the hotel bar, the front stoop. On warm evenings some will gather in small groups of two or three on the front stoop; during the afternoon and evening, small groups will drink together in the bar; and the hotel lobby is always available to anyone who wishes to spend some time standing and watching as people come and go.

The topics of conversation most often center around events at the hotel. Among the elderly men, the principal subjects of interest are betting, drinking, sex, and possible hustles. Checking up on each other commands a major share of the conversation. Thus, it is noted when a tenant is untidy, unshaven, or in some way deteriorated looking. It is popular to make comparisons that are favorable to oneself. Gossip is pervasive and there are no loyalties. There are frequent falling-outs over gossip which gets back to the target. Some vendettas of several years' vintage exist that originated over gossip. Danger is also a favorite topic—danger as personified in the black—the black addict, the black mugger, the black rapist.

The hotel bar is the scene of much visiting among these elderly tenants. Some of the elderly men drink here on a daily basis; some drink alone; others have drinking companions. These drinking companions part company outside the bar: their "friendship" does not survive outside the common interest of drinking. The bar is also an important center for many of the business deals of the carnies; hustles are arranged, and money changes hands. Finally, the bar is the setting for sexual contacts. Prostitutes from the area work the elderly men in the bar, particularly on the first of the month when social security checks arrive.

Although the hotel bar is a natural locale for interaction; nevertheless, at all times, a goodly proportion of the drinkers will be sitting alone. The fact of the matter is that, over-all, a major portion of the activities of these people is carried out alone: they eat alone; they drink alone; they leave the hotel alone; they do not telephone each other; they do not visit in each other's rooms; they do not commemorate special occasions, such as birthdays, holidays, deaths, or the like.

Looking at the society of these elderly people we are forcefully struck by the pervasive strictures against attempts to become too intimate with one another. Relationships that permit mutual concern or the sharing of deeply personal matters are not encouraged by these individuals. It is common for them to say that in the Guinevere there are no real friendships:

I don't have any friends, *real* friends here. I don't get too thick because they'll be prying into my business.

If you get friendly with them, they start telling you about their problems and I don't want to hear it.

Nobody's friends. Why, they'd give a dollar to a prossie (prostitute) than to one who thinks he's a friend and needs it.

Listen, the only one here everybody talks to is Jerry (the book-maker).

As for mutual aid, there are occasional instances of it; but in gene-ral, their belief that one could be sick for days and perhaps even die without anyone knowing or caring, is an accurate appraisal of the situation. Even individuals who interact frequently with each other become psychologically unavailable when confronted with the option of moving toward a closer, more demanding relationship. Several elderly tenants summed up the situation in their remarks that, "here, it's everyone for himself."

The dominant values of privacy and autonomy operate to inhibit the forming of either deeply personal or enduring relationships. Be-havior that reflects contradictory assumptions is met with reactions ranging from suspicion to icy aloofness to alarm. Real intimacy is neither expected nor encouraged.

Related to the pattern of avoidance of close relationships is the mutual suspicion they display toward one another. In this society of the alone, suspicion is institutionalized. The avoidance of intimate contacts is related to the taken-for-granted meanings that attach to their identifi-cation of each other as untrustworthy and exploitative. Thus, it is taken-for-granted in their society that the motives of the other are al-ways suspect, and the appropriate response is caution and distrust.

The routinizing of suspicion is facilitated by the maintenance of a hotel "mystique." By mystique is meant a core of commonly held be-liefs about the supposed "type" who lives in hotels. For many of these elderly tenants, their personal biographies reflect failure to fulfill to varying degrees cultural and social mandates. Many of them have had checkered careers, often with histories of involvement in petty crime, incarceration in prisons or mental hospitals, etc. A conse-quence of this knowledge is the ubiquity of face-saving maneuvers. The most widely used technique for saving face is the remaking of one's personal past. Thus, one can never be sure that the story the other is telling is true or manufactured for the audience. Not surpris-ingly, attitudes of cynicism and suspicion predominate. In the Guine-vere, individuals, in their own need to conceal and refurbish social identity, must jealously guard their own secrets, on the one hand, and be cynical about the stories of others, on the other hand. It is presumed that the other is doing the same reconstructing of his past. Although this suspicion pervades all aspects of the ways in which they do (and do not) relate to one another, it is nowhere more manifest than in their routine assumption that everyone has something to hide. Consequent-ly, it is assumed that most explanations of background are false. As a core belief of the mystique, everyone is at the Guinevere for a "reason" and chances are, this reason is shameful or reprehensible.

The coming together of independence and mutual distrust is vividly revealed in the words of an 80-year-old widow who lives in the Guinevere:

> I take care of me, because no one else is going to. I don't trust anybody. I look for the angle. I tabulate them and then I get their number. It's best to keep them guessing, than to go whining and crying to the manager when something goes wrong.

In the face of accumulating losses—physical, mental, social, and financial—these elderly slum dwellers sustain a determined autonomy and a fierce sense of privacy. Their mode of adjustment means that they pay a heavy price in terms of social isolation, and indeed, many of them identify loneliness as one of the generic features of their old age:

> The biggest problem of old people anywhere in the world is loneliness. Yes, I could show you how old, retired men go from bar to bar because they haven't anything to do, anywhere to go, anybody who cares.

> It's (the hotel) full of strangers who come and go. I shared the bath with this man. Never saw him for three months. Then, one night, his room caught on fire. It was the first time I ever saw him. It's very lonely, especially for the women.

Nevertheless, loneliness is a price that they are willing to pay to maintain themselves independently. The evidence of this study supports the finding that these individuals eschew and avoid relationships and have always done so. Theirs was and is a world of the alone. For these elderly, the SRO is not the end result of changes in social integration, they have spent a life-time in SROs and similar environments. The situated features of the hotel mitigate against the building of close interpersonal ties. These elderly people have limited resources that reduce their capacity to make the compromises attendant to sustaining intimate relationships. Relationships are prescribed in this hotel society that are nonintimate and instrumental, that is, vehicles for getting what one needs. Other forms of relatedness which would involve mutual trust are not to be found within the world of the elderly SRO tenant.

Summary

The findings of this study emphasize the highly atomistic character of the society of the elderly SRO tenant. With the exception of the carnies, little in the way of group solidarity is present. The world of the SRO tenant is atomistic; the fabric of social relationships is not dense and possesses a certain fragility. The lack of group cohesiveness creates a world of strangers interacting in terms of their individual goals rather than groups acting for shared goals. These elderly individuals are able to sustain social bonds that are relatively impoverished and whose primary function is the attainment of goods and services. These are, then, fundamentally economic relationships. Supporting these instrumental relationships are the dominant SRO norms of privacy, freedom, and utilitarianism.

In their characteristic ways of relating to each other, these elderly may be classified in terms of Lowenthal's typology. The majority of the elderly SRO tenants are life-long social isolates. Indeed, they have sought out the impersonal world of the SRO as an environment in which they can live a life style of their choosing. The SRO encourages freedom, privacy, and utilitarianism to extreme degrees.

The avoidance of intimacy and the routinization of suspicion that are endemic features of the SRO can be seen to be compatible with the voluntary self-isolation of these elderly. They are life-long isolates and for them, the SRO is a familiar environment. Though some of these individuals may pay lip service to feeling "lonely," nevertheless, we are understandably skeptical as to the intensity of this feeling when confronted with individuals whose personal biographies reveal life-long choices that avoided and even precluded any strong degree of social integration.

Thus, in considering the SRO elderly, we see a converging of individual (psychological) and situational (social) forces which operate to maintain life-long patterns. For these elderly, isolation has been life-long and to a marked degree voluntary, and is not adequately explained as a consequence of age-related changes.

References

Bell, T. The relationships between social involvement and feeling old among residents in homes for the aged. *Journal of Gerontology*, 1967, 22, 17-22.

Blau, Z. S. Structural constraints on friendship in old age. *American Sociological Review*, 1961, 26, 429-439.

Cumming, E., & Henry, W. E. *Growing Old*. Basic Books, New York, 1961.

Heilbrun, A., & Lair, C. Decreased role consistency in the aged: Implications for behavioral pathology. *Journal of Gerontology*, 1964, 19, 325-329.

Lawton, M. P., & Kleban, M. H. The aged resident of the inner city. *Gerontologist*, 1971, *11*, 277-283.

Lowenthal, M. F. Social isolation and mental illness in old age. *American Sociological Review*, 1964, *29*, 54-70.

Lowenthal, M. F., & Haven, C. Interaction and adaptation: Intimacy as a critical variable. *American Sociological Review*, 1968, *33*, 20-30.

Maddox, G., & Eisdorfer, C. Some correlates of activity and morale among the elderly. *Social Forces*, 1962, *40*, 254-260.

Rosow, I. The social context of the aging self. *Gerontologist*, 1973, *13*, 82-87.

Shapiro, J. H. Single-room occupancy: Community of the alone. *Social Work*, 1966, *11*, 24-33.

Shapiro, J. H. Dominant leaders among slum hotel residents. *American Journal of Orthopsychiatry*, 1969, *39*, 644-650.

Shapiro, J. H. Reciprocal dependence between single-room occupancy managers and tenants. *Social Work*, 1970, *15*, 67-73.

Stephens, J. Loners, losers, and lovers: A sociological study of the aged tenants of a slum hotel. PhD dissertation, Wayne State Univ., 1973.

Stephens, J. Carnies and marks: The sociology of elderly street peddlers. *Sociological Symposium*, 1974, *11*, 25-41.

Townsend, P. The family life of old people. Free Press, Glencoe, IL, 1957.

4.5

Fear of Crime Among the Aged

Frank Clemente and Michael B. Kleiman

As Gubrium (1974) recently pointed out, one of the most neglected areas of empirical investigation in social gerontology is the impact of crime upon the aged. There have been very few attempts to examine the effect of crime, fear of victimization, or other aspects of criminal behavior on the elderly (see Goldsmith & Tomas, 1974, for an important exception). In fact, even criminologists have generally ignored the problem. Our review of 5 years (1970-1974) of *Crime and Delinquency Abstracts* indicated that of literally thousands of studies on crime only a handful dealt specifically with the elderly.

Given this neglect of the impact of crime on the aged it is not surprising that discussions of the topic are laden with questionable assumptions and untested hypotheses (Gubrium, 1974). Even more important, however, as Goldsmith and Tomas (1974) have noted, the paucity of research and data has severely inhibited the development of viable programs to reduce the effect of crime on the aged. Our research attempts to at least partially alleviate this situation by focusing upon an important aspect of the problem—fear of crime among older people. Systematic research along these lines will provide an empirical background for practitioners seeking to control fear of crime among the aged segment of the population.

Copyright 1976 by The Gerontological Society. Reprinted by permission. *The Gerontologist*, Vol. 16, No. 3, 1976, pp. 207-210.

Fear as a Problem

While there are many facets to the impact of crime on the elderly, one of the most important relates to fear of victimization. In fact, it is reasonable to argue that for older people fear of crime is even more of a problem than crime itself. Despite popular assumptions to the contrary, the victimization rates for crimes against the person are *lower* for the elderly than for any other age group over 12. This pattern holds regardless of whether victimization data come merely from crimes reported to the police or from surveys of the general population. We emphasize this point because some commentators have suggested that the lower victimization rates among the elderly are due to their reluctance to report crimes (cf. Goldsmith & Tomas, 1974). All national survey data we have seen, however, clearly indicate that the aged have low victimization rates. For example, the most recent survey by the U.S. Dept. of Justice, *Criminal Victimization in the United States* (1974), indicated that for the age group 65 and over the victimization rate of crimes against the person was 4.4 per thousand. This compares with 10.9 in the 35-49 group and 31.3 in the 20-24 age category. These survey data demonstrate that even when the problem of nonreporting by the elderly is taken into account they have low victimization rates.

On the other hand, these low victimization rates notwithstanding, fear of crime among the aged is a harsh reality. Two recent statements from the social gerontology literature yield insight into the situation:

> . . . criminal behavior has a chilling effect upon the freedom of older Americans. Fear of victimization causes self-imposed "house arrest" among older people . . . (Goldsmith & Tomas, 1974).
>
> crime has . . . become increasingly a source of public fear . . . I don't believe that such effects are anywhere more apparent than among the segment of aging persons in the United States . . . (Cunningham, 1974).

Simply put, fear among the elderly is real and pervasive. It matters little whether this fear is out of proportion to the objective probability of being victimized. As Goldsmith and Tomas (1974) correctly point out, even though such fears may be largely unwarranted by local conditions, the effect is just as severe as when the fears are justified. The rate of elderly women being attacked on the street may be only one per thousand population. But if 80% of such women are afraid to leave their homes fear of crime has become a major social problem.

In essence, then, there is solid documentation that the elderly suffer from a substantial fear of crime. To date, however, little empirical work has been done to assess which segments of the aged population are the most fearful. The elderly are not a uniform group with monolithic attitudes. Rather, they are a heterogenous aggregation. This diversity raises important questions in regard to fear. For example, are the black aged more afraid of crime than the white aged? Are the rural elderly less afraid than those who live in large cities? These and related questions demand careful attention before policy decisions can be made and effective programs can be developed and implemented. To this end, our analysis breaks down fear of crime among the aged by four variables which previous research has shown to be important for the general population. These four explanatory variables are: (1) sex, (2) race, (3) socioeconomic status, and (4) size of community.

A National Data Set

Data were drawn from the 1973 and 1974 General Social Surveys conducted by the National Opinion Research Center (NORC) at the University of Chicago. Both were national multistage area probability samples designed to represent the noninstitutionalized adult population of the continental United States (see Davis, 1973 & 1974 for details). We combined the samples in order to insure an analytically sufficient number of older people. This procedure yielded a total sample of 461 individuals age 65 and over. For comparative purposes we will present parallel data from the non-aged respondents (N = 2,488).

Fear of crime was ascertained via the question, "Is there any area right around here, that is, within a mile—where you would be afraid to walk alone at night?" Responses were dichotomized as either "yes" or "no."

This question is useful for our analysis for several reasons. First, it was asked in identical form in both years. Second, it clearly gets at fear of crime rather than concern over the crime rate. As Furstenberg (1971) has emphasized, it is important not to confuse these phenomena. A person may be quite concerned over rising crime but not in the least afraid to walk about his own neighborhood. Third, the question has conceptual relevance because it brings the fear of crime down to the personal level. Our specific concern is whether or not people are afraid of crime. It seems reasonable that being afraid to walk about one's own neighborhood is a useful indicator of that concept.

Explanatory variables were operationalized along traditional lines. Sex and race are natural dichotomies. Socioeconomic status was measured along two dimensions. First, income—family dollar income per year, coded as either (a) less than $7,000 or (b) $7,000 and over. Second, education, coded as (a) less than high school, (b) high school, and (c) more than high school.

Community size was measured in the NORC surveys on the following five-category scale:

(1) large city (250,000 plus),
(2) medium size city (50,000-250,000),
(3) suburb of large city,
(4) small town (2,500-50,000),
(5) rural (under 2,500).

The Fearful

The first task is to assess the difference in fear between the aged and non-aged. Our data strongly support the assumption that the elderly are more afraid of crime than their younger counterparts. While 51% of those respondents age 65 and over said they were afraid, only 41% of the under-65 group said so. Given this significant difference, we now turn to the disaggregation of the data by the explanatory variables.

Sex. Virtually all surveys on the fear of crime have indicated that women are far more likely to express fear than men (cf. Erskine, 1974). This reluctance of men to admit fear is readily apparent in our data but is less prevalent among the elderly than among the non-aged. For example, while only 19% of the non-aged males said they were afraid, over one-third (34%) of the elderly men admitted fear. These figures compare to 60% of non-aged women and 69% of aged females. In other words, while men of all ages were less likely to express fear than women, this pattern was considerably less profound among elderly men.

Race. Blacks are more afraid of crime than whites. This holds true for all age categories and is especially evident in the aged. Our data indicated that about 47% of the white elderly were afraid to walk their neighborhoods alone at night. This compared to 69% of the black aged. More specifically, while less than half of the white aged expressed fear, over two-thirds of the black elderly did so.

Socioeconomic status (SES). People at the higher SES levels generally express less fear of personal crime than people at the lower levels (cf. Ennis, 1967). In terms of income, our data fit this pattern for both age groups. Among the elderly with incomes less than $7,000 per year, 51% expressed fear. This compares to 43% of those with an annual income of more than $7,000.

A slightly larger difference by income existed in the under 65 group. For the non-aged, 47% of those with incomes under $7,000 said they were afraid as opposed to only 36% of those above $7,000. Thus, while in both age groups income emerges as a specifying factor, it is more important for the non-aged than the aged.

In regard to education and fear, however, there are minimal differences among the aged. For example, of elderly respondents with more than high school education 49% expressed fear. This compares to 53% of those with high school and 49% of those with less than high school. In short, for the aged, education makes little difference as to fear of crime.

For the non-aged, however, the situation is somewhat different. Of the respondents under 65 with more than high school education only 37% said they were afraid to walk alone at night within a mile of their home. For the high school and less than high school groups this percentage was 44 and 43, respectively. Thus, while education did not emerge as an important specifying factor in regard to fear among the elderly, it did have a slight effect for the non-aged with the more educated respondents expressing less fear.

Community size.   Community size has typically been found to be directly related to fear of crime (cf. Erskine, 1974). That is, residents of large cities tend to be more fearful of victimization than people in smaller towns and rural areas. Our data regarding the elderly parallel these findings. The percentages of the aged showing fear decrease in a clear step pattern as one moves from large cities to rural areas: 76% for large cities, 68% for medium size cities, 48% for suburbs, 43% for small towns, and 24% for rural locations. In other words, while over three out of four elderly respondents were afraid, only one in four of the rural elderly indicated fear. This result provides strong support for the necessity of developing programs to reduce the effect of crime upon aged residents of large metropolitan areas.

The poor position of the aged residents of large cities in regard to fear of crime is even further highlighted when we turn to responses of the non-aged. The percentages of respondents under 65 who indicated fear are 57 in large cities, 47 in medium size cities, 39 in suburbs, 40 in small towns, and 25 in rural areas. Note the large difference in fear between aged and non-aged residents of metropolitan cities (76% and 68% versus 57% and 47%). These findings dramatically underscore the deteriorating quality of life of the metropolitan elderly in the United States.

As noted above, low income respondents in our national sample express substantially greater fear of crime than do respondents earning more than $7,000 annually. In addition, the NORC data indicate that such poor persons are disproportionately concentrated in urban areas. For example, while 26% of small town respondents had an annual income of less than $7,000, 38% of large city residents fell into this low income category. To assess the effects of the disproportionate urban concentration of poor persons on the relationship between city size and fear of crime, then, we utilized income as a control variable in the analysis.

The results of partialing on income indicate that even when the fact that low income respondents are more prevalent in cities is taken into account, the clear decrease in fear among the aged as one moves from large cities to rural areas remains in force. In other words, urban residents are more afraid than their rural counterparts regardless of income. For example, the percentages of low income elderly showing fear in each of our size categories are: 71 for large cities, 70 for medium cities, 56 for suburbs, 48 for small towns, and 24 for rural areas. For the aged earning more than $7,000 a year, these respective figures are 77%, 75%, 27%, and 14%.

The extent of the metropolitan elderly's fear is further substantiated when we look at the results for the non-aged. The percentages of low income respondents under 65 who indicated fear are 62 in large cities, 43 in suburbs, 38 in small towns, and 28 in rural areas. The corresponding percentages for the high income non-aged are 55, 46, 38, 38, and 23. Again, note the large differences in fear between aged and non-aged residents of cities over 50,000 (71% and 70% versus 62% and 54% for the less than $7,000 income bracket; 77% and 75% versus 55% and 46% for the $7,000 or greater income group). These differences are yet another indication of the widespread fear of victimization among the urban elderly regardless of income.

In sum, then, the aged residents of cities over 50,000 show significantly greater fear of crime than either their younger counterparts or older inhabitants of suburbs, small towns, and rural areas. It is among these metropolitan elderly that fear of crime takes the most heavy toll. It is this group that stays behind locked doors subject to what Goldsmith and Tomas (1974) accurately term "house arrest." It is this group that is forced to curtail social activities, stay home from church, or abandon shopping trips for fear of being robbed. It is this group that is afraid of a strange adult, terrified of two or three youths on the street, and frightened by a dimly lit elevator. And, clearly, it is this group which deserves and merits the development and implementation of programs designed to control the fear of crime.

Implications

Several important implications can be drawn from this analysis of a national data set. First, the results strongly support the argument that the aged are not a homogeneous group in regard to fear of crime (or, we suspect, most other attitudinal states). Rather, there are important specifying factors in regard to fear of victimization. Clearly, it is not sufficient to merely conclude that the aged are more afraid of crime than the non-aged. Our findings, for example, indicated that sex, race, and city size were very important in specifying the relationship between age and fear. Socioeconomic status generally failed to emerge as an important factor for the aged.

Hopefully, our findings will serve as a useful point of departure of future research in the area. One line of investigation which would seem to merit careful consideration revolves around the "socio-environmental" perspective advanced by Gubrium (1974). He has suggested, for example, that fear of crime among the aged is likely to be greater in age-heterogeneous housing than in age-concentrated housing. Unfortunately, the NORC data were not amenable to a test of this interesting hypothesis. There seems to be a surge of interest in social gerontology regarding the impact of crime on the aged (for example, the national conference held at American University in June, 1975). Further, various programs have been developed in several large cities to alleviate the fear of crime among the aged. In Philadelphia, for example, a pilot program of block organization to report crimes and quell rumors has received both federal and state funding.

References

Cunningham, C. The scenario of crimes against the aged. In N. E. Tomas (Ed.), *Reducing crimes against aged persons.* USDHEW, Philadelphia, 1974.

Davis, J. A. *National data program for the social sciences.* Univ. of Chicago, Chicago, 1973.

David, J. A. *National data program for the social sciences.* Univ. of Chicago, Chicago, 1974.

Ennis, P. H. *Criminal victimization in the United States.* USGPO, Washington, 1967.

Erskine, H. The polls: Fear of violence and crime. *Public Opinion Quarterly,* 1974, *38,* 131-145.

Furstenberg, F. Public reaction to crime in the streets. *American Scholar,* 1971, *51,* 601-610.

Goldsmith, J., & Tomas, N. E. Crimes against the elderly: A continuing national crisis. *Aging,* 1974, *236,* 10-13.

Gubrium, J. Victimization in old age. *Crime & Delinquency,* 1974, *29,* 245-250.

U.S. Dept. of Justice. *Criminal victimization in the United States.* USGPO, Washington, 1974.

4.6

Effect of Ethnicity on Life Styles of the Inner-City Elderly

Marjorie H. Cantor

Just as individuals are clearly distinguished from one another by physical, social, and psychological characteristics, so aggregates of people in our society can be differentiated by virtue of their shared culture, ethnicity, and socioeconomic status. As we move toward greater acceptance of the value of a pluralistic society, the importance of understanding differences becomes even more critical for environmental or social planning. Increasingly, decision makers are faced with the need for subgroup analysis as they attempt to fairly balance the competing interests of various ethnic and nationality groups. Nowhere is this need more evident than in large urban areas characterized not only by high density of population but by wide diversity of the backgrounds of its citizens.

Yet in planning services for the elderly there has been a tendency to view older people as a homogeneous group, set off from the rest of society by virtue of a single determinant, age.

But older people on reaching 65 (or whatever arbitrary figure a society chooses to signify as old age) do not shed their identity as members of racial, ethnic, or socioeconomic subgroups. Rather, it may

Reprinted, with permission, from *Community Planning for An Aging Society: Designing Services and Facilities*, M. Powell Lawton et al., editors. Copyright © by Dowden, Hutchinson and Ross, Inc., Stroudsburg, Pa.

well be that this subgroup membership is the crucial factor in conditioning how older people grow old and in determining the social, physical, and psychological needs to which the planning process should be addressed.

In all stages of life, morale and well-being are related to an individual's ability to successfully perform the tasks set forth for his age group by society. In childhood, control and mastery of environment is a gradual process, with considerable dependency upon adults as mediating agents. Adulthood presumes the ability, skills, and competence to effectively control environment and determine the course of one's own daily existence. The degree to which this is possible determines to a considerable extent the individual's mental health and integrity of personality. A sense of powerlessness is anathema to successful adulthood in industrialized societies.

Similarly, in old age, although social roles change, the basic drives for independence, competence, and mastery of environment remain. At the same time, with deteriorating health and reduced income, frequent concomitants of old age in our society, a countertrend of gradual diminution of mastery occurs. To the extent that an older person can continue to exercise considerable freedom of choice and control, morale will be high and aging successful.

But the form in which the basic needs of all older people are expressed and the relative role of the family and community in providing the necessary assistance for independent living are heavily conditioned by cultural, economic, and kinship patterns. When family structure continues to be strong and cohesive, more help from that source can be expected. When family is dispersed or nonexistent, the community role is of increasing importance. Meaningful social planning requires precise knowledge of both the extent to which the aging process is similar for all older people and the degree to which racial, ethnic, and socioeconomic differences require varying types of community facilities and services to sustain older people independently in the community for as long as possible.

The urban elderly poor

A review of the gerontological literature confirms the paucity of data about the urban poor and particularly the minority-group elderly. In general, much stress has been placed (not inappropriately) on discovering the broad patterns of the aging process. Where subgroups of elderly have been singled out for study, the sample too often consists of white middle-class respondents in medium-sized or suburban communities. Yet, increasingly, the concentration of elderly in all industrialized societies is in the largest cities—most frequently in the older central or inner city where poverty and social and environmental blight are common conditions of life.

New York City is the home of three major racial ethnic subgroups—white, black, and Spanish-speaking (mainly Puerto Rican). Although at present the vast majority of older New Yorkers are white, there are growing numbers of black and Puerto Rican elderly; this trend is expected to continue. In an attempt to document the basic similarities, but more importantly the differences, in the life styles and needs of the three major groups of elderly and thereby provide the specificity of data needed for immediate and long-range physical and social planning, the New York City Office for the Aging undertook in 1970 one of the first and most comprehensive cross-cultural studies of the urban elderly poor living in the inner city (Cantor et al., 1975). Findings in several major areas of particular interest to planners will be discussed and the social policy implications highlighted.

Although New York City is in many ways *sui generis*, particularly with respect to size and complexity, the findings have considerable implications for other major urban areas. Perhaps more important than any specific findings, the New York City study provides a case history in the use of subgroup analysis as a tool for meaningful planning.

Study goals, population, and methodology

The study goals were as follows:

1. To describe the life of urban elderly residing in neighborhoods characterized by poverty, decay, and high risk. Highlighted were problems of income maintenance, social isolation, the unique nature of housing and environmental conditions, and patterns of mobility.
2. To determine the effects of subgroup membership on the aging process among white, Spanish, and black elderly and to document areas of similarity and difference.

    Particular emphasis was placed on identifying the factors that enable the elderly to cope with and effectively control their environment. The relative roles of the individual, family, and community were considered for the population as a whole and for each subgroup.
3. To document the needs of the three major subgroups of elderly for supportive community services with a view toward enhancing mastery over environment. Where possible, differential needs were identified and related to the desirability for new services or the improved delivery of existing services.

4. To explore the degree to which positive feelings of mastery over environment are related to the concepts of high morale and successful aging as presently employed in the gerontological literature.

The focal point of the study was the elderly of the inner city rather than a citywide sample for three major reasons:

1. First, much is known about middle-class older people but little about the life styles and support systems of the urban elderly poor. Yet it is among the urban poor that one would expect to find the greatest need for community assistance.
2. A principal goal of the study was to document the effects of subgroup membership on aging and identify the commonalities and differences among the life styles and coping mechanisms of the three major ethnic subgroups found in New York. Most of the black and Spanish elderly reside in the inner city, yet the majority of older people in these core neighborhoods are white, as is the case for the rest of the city.
3. In the belief that environment was a key variable in life styles, it was desirable to limit the universe to older people living in similar conditions of neighborhood blight and deterioration.

Defining the inner city in New York was somewhat more difficult than in other urban areas of the country. Typically, a central city is an easily identifiable geographic entity with all the classic attributes of environmental and social decline, surrounded by concentric rings of middle-class communities to which the more affluent have fled. In New York, on the contrary, each borough has its blighted areas interspersed amid middle- or upper-class neighborhoods. Sometimes, even on a single block, tenements stand next to luxury apartments.

The central city of New York was, therefore, defined operationally to be the 26 neighborhoods designated as poverty areas by the Human Resources Administration. These areas have the highest incidence of crime, infant mortality, welfare case load, and deteriorated housing, and clearly duplicate the objective conditions found in the inner city of other urban centers in the United States.

The criterion of aging was purposely set at 60, rather than at the more usual 65 years, to enable the gathering of information about the life styles and needs of those entering the aged cohort as compared with the "older" elderly. The sample was limited to noninstitutional elderly living in the community.

A replicated probability sample was employed, that embodied five randomly selected, stratified, interpenetrating matched samples. Through a two-step enumeration process, 2,180 households were identified as having one or more older persons. Six callbacks ultimately yielded 1,552 interviews, a completion rate of 71 percent—quite good considering the areas in which the study was conducted and the possible fears of older people about opening doors to strangers.

The final sample of 1,552 respondents proved to be highly representative of the approximately 400,000 older persons living in the 26 neighborhoods in 1970 when interviewing took place. The ethnic distribution of the sample is remarkably accurate with, if anything, a slight overrepresentation of black and Spanish elderly—the very groups usually underrepresented in most studies. Where possible, any discrepancies arising from sample selection or interviewing were compensated for through weighting. Interviews were held in the home, ran from 1 to 2 hours, and elicited information on virtually all aspects of the lives of older New Yorkers.

Findings

An aging population can be subdivided in many ways: well versus sick, the young elderly versus the older elderly, or institutionalized versus community based. From the beginning the cross-cultural approach was chosen. It was hypothesized that the influence of ethnicity and culture on the life styles of older people is crucial, particularly in the areas of greatest interest to us—the support system and the relative roles of family and community in enhancing the lives of older people. Furthermore, little or nothing is known about the similarities and differences in life styles of the aged among the major ethnic groups in urban society. Finally, inasmuch as New York City contains the largest number of white, black, and Spanish elderly in the country, it seemed most appropriate to place our initial stress on ethnicity and culture.

However, not unmindful of the importance of socioeconomic class, the final study report will attempt to identify the relative importances of ethnicity, culture, and class. The fact that the study population is limited to poverty-area elderly acts to narrow the range of socioeconomic class. But particularly in the case of the white elderly, social-class status prior to old age may be unrelated to current income and may well be a determining factor in attitudes and life style. In addition, the white population is not as homogeneous with respect to culture as the black and Spanish. Finally, ethnicity and culture are used interchangeably in this discussion of the findings.

Table 1.   Major Demographic Characteristics of Inner-City Elderly Respondents (percentages)

	Total	White	Black	Spanish
Age				
60-64	22.0	15.2	26.2	35.8
65-69	28.2	25.1	31.8	30.0
70-74	22.1	22.3	23.5	17.2
75+	27.2	36.9	17.9	17.0
Sex				
Male	41.0	45.2	35.2	41.9
Female.................	59.0	54.8	64.8	58.1
Ethnicity				
White	49.4	49.4		
Black....................	37.4		37.4	
Spanish	13.2			13.2
Religious affiliation				
Protestant	43.5	18.3	86.0	17.4
Catholic	35.3	43.2	9.6	78.7
Jewish...................	14.9	29.5	0.8	0.4
Socioeconomic status				
Hollingshead's ISP (IV and V: working and lower class)	74.7	63.8	85.3	85.3
Income: under $2,500/yr. (est. per capita)	63.8	55.6	71.3	73.6
Occupation: manual......	67.6	57.3	79.4	72.4
Education: 8th grade or less .	59.9	50.1	65.3	80.4

A brief profile of the inner-city elderly

Who then are the inner-city elderly, what are their general characteristics, and to what extent does ethnicity affect these characteristics? (See Table 1.)

First the inner-city elderly are clearly not a homogeneous middle-class white population. Rather, the study population is a low-income, urban elderly sample encompassing three distinct ethnic groups. Although inner-city neighborhoods are increasingly nonwhite, at the present time whites still predominate among both young and old alike. Thus, in the sample, 49 percent of the respondents were white, 37 percent black, and 13 percent Spanish-speaking, principally of Puerto Rican origin.

Table 1.   (continued)

	Total	White	Black	Spanish
Marital status				
Married	34.3	35.9	29.3	42.6
Widowed	42.0	39.9	45.2	41.1
Never married	13.4	17.3	10.8	6.1
Separated or divorced	10.3	6.8	14.8	10.3
Living arrangements				
Live alone	39.2	47.4	33.1	26.2
Live with spouse	33.4	34.7	29.0	41.0
Live with others (not				
spouse)...............	27.4	17.9	37.9	32.8
Health				
Have health problem(s) ...	67.3	62.8	72.1	70.6
Self-perceived health as				
poor)	23.8	20.6	25.2	31.4
Incapacity index: severely				
impaired or incapaci-				
tated	15.4	13.6	15.5	22.2
Nativity: born on U.S. main-				
land	53.3	46.5	80.2	3.4
Total respondents	1.552	766	580	205

Source: Cantor et al., *The Elderly in the Inner City*, New York City Office for the Aging, in press.

Ethnicity has a considerable effect on age distribution. If old age is conceptualized as a continuum having a beginning, middle, and ending period, the Spanish elderly are the youngest, tending to cluster in the initial period. Two thirds of the Spanish elderly were under 70. Black elderly tended to be more in the middle, older than the Spanish but younger than whites. Nearly 60 percent of the blacks were under 70; among white respondents, the oldest of the three groups, 40 percent were under 70 and 60 percent were 70 or older. Several cultural factors contribute to these age differences. The most important is differential longevity. Black life expectancy is 7 years less than that of whites; although exact data with respect to mainland Puerto Ricans are lacking, it is believed that a similar differential exists. In the past, another factor contributed to ethnic differences in age distribution in the city—the tendency for blacks and Puerto Ricans to return "home" upon reaching old age. This out-migration factor is expected to fade in succeeding generations of black and Spanish elderly.

With respect to the presence of a spouse, more Spanish married originally and as the youngest group more were still married and living with spouse (43 percent). Whites were next most likely to still be married (36 percent). Although blacks had the second highest rate of marriage originally and were younger than the white respondents, at this point in their lives they were least likely of the three subgroups to report still being married and living with spouse. Persons who reported never having been married were most likely to be found among the whites.

The health of the inner-city elderly is poorer than older people generally, as measured both by self assessed health and the Townsend Index of Functional Ability (Shanas et al., 1968). Although younger, Spanish and black elderly appeared to have significantly more health problems than whites, and a higher proportion was found to be severely impaired or incapacitated (see Table 1). However, although most respondents reported at least one chronic illness, they were not homebound and were able to get around. (Only approximately 7 percent were in wheelchairs or bedridden.)

The inner-city elderly, like all older New Yorkers, had lived in the city and in their immediate neighborhoods for a long time. They had deep roots and considerable feelings of belonging, although they recognized the urban blight around them and were often very fearful of the "strangers in the neighborhood." As expected, whites had the longest tenure in the city (mean residency of 52 years), followed by blacks (mean residency of 39 years). Relatively recent arrival was characteristic only of the Spanish elderly, most of whom came to the mainland when they were 40 years old or more. But even the Spanish in the sample had lived in New York an average of 25 years.

The late arrival of the Spanish has had serious implications affecting their ability to learn English, their employment opportunities, and their Social Security coverage, to say nothing of the psychological problems attendant upon uprooting and moving to an alien culture in the middle and later years of life. It is noteworthy that 86 percent of the Spanish elderly spoke Spanish at home. In the case of most other foreign-born elderly, whether white or black, English was the language in the home.

Although it is common to think of the present generation of white elderly in big cities like New York as largely foreign born, this was far from the case. Almost half the white respondents were native-born, and of this group 40 percent were at least second-generation Americans. The inner city is apparently the home of a substantial number of white Americans of old stock, mainly Protestant, who are living in hidden "genteel" poverty.

Because they grew up during the period when higher education, including high school, was mainly for the well-to-do, it is not surprising to find little formal education among the inner-city urban poor. Most of the sample had a grade school education or less, with the least amount of formal education being reported by the Spanish. (This lack of education coupled with minority-group status has severely limited the job opportunities available to most black and Spanish elderly during their adult years.)

Although there is considerable occupational and social-class spread among the inner-city elderly, particularly in the case of the whites, 64 percent of the sample was classified according to the Hollingshead Index of Social Position (Hollingshead and Redlich, 1958) as being in the two lowest categories (i.e., working or lower class), and most respondents were involved in skilled or unskilled occupations during their working years. Spanish and black elderly almost exclusively held unskilled or semiskilled jobs, with only a handful reporting employment in skilled or clerical/sales occupations. White elderly showed a somewhat greater occupational spread. Although the bulk were skilled workers during their adult years, 15 percent held managerial or professional positions and 20 percent were owners of small businesses or held sales or clerical jobs. As is to be expected, there were relatively few upper-middle- or upper-class elderly living in the inner city, no matter what their ethnic backgrounds.

Retirement and income

If older people, regardless of their ethnicity, are to live independently in the community, two essential requirements are the ability to buy what they need and the physical strength necessary to permit an adequate level of functioning. Since poverty areas contain more families with lower earnings, lower Social Security coverage, and less savings, one might expect that economic pressures would operate to keep more poverty area elderly at work than is usual among older people in general. This was not so. Inner-city elderly were far less likely to be working after 65 than their peers nationally.

Even though all males and 70 percent of the female respondents reported gainful employment sometime during their adult years, 78 percent of the inner-city elderly sample were retired. Ethnicity clearly influences the point at which an older person leaves the labor market. The Spanish were forced out of the labor market earliest. Among Spanish males 60 to 64, 61 percent were no longer working. With respect to black males the picture was slightly better than among the Spanish but still very bad; 50 percent of black male respondents in the 60 to 64 age cohort were no longer working.

Among whites in our sample the picture was very different and corresponded to the national labor force participation statistics for the age group. Only a relatively small proportion (25 percent) of those 60 to 64 were retired. Whites continued to work much longer. Of those in the 65 to 69 age cohort, over 25 percent were still working, as compared with only a very small proportion of black and Spanish males. Even among whites 70 and over, 13 percent of the sample were still working.

These patterns clearly reflect the close link between ethnicity and work status; persons in professional, managerial, and higher-skilled jobs tended to continue working longer than the less skilled. Thus a greater proportion of white male respondents was still working in their late sixties and the early seventies than was true for the other two groups. Sadly enough, the very groups in the elderly population with the lowest incomes during adult working years, and therefore the lowest Social Security benefits in old age, were, because of lack of skill and minority-group status, the first groups forced out of the labor market.

It has been pointed out that poor health may also be a cause of early retirement. In our sample, Spanish reported the greatest health deficiencies, followed by blacks; whites reported the best health. Health of course was related to low income.

It is interesting that among nonworking men in the 60 to 64 age group, black and Spanish elderly were two and one-half times more likely to consider themselves retired rather than unemployed as compared with similar-aged white men. This undoubtedly represents a reality orientation. Black and Spanish males are more likely to experience chronic unemployment in their adult working years and, therefore, correctly consider themselves out of the labor market by age 60.

Whereas black men tended to be out of the labor market earlier, black women continued to work longer, certainly through their sixties. Of the black women 60 to 64, 39 percent were still working; in the 65 to 69 age cohort, 20 percent of the black women still worked as compared with only 9 percent of the black men.

From this picture of work status, it is no surprise to learn that the income levels of the inner-city elderly were far below those required for adequate living in a city of high costs. Respondents' incomes were abysmally low, significantly below the citywide levels for older people, and sharp ethnic differences existed. In 1970, the median income for white respondents was $2,746, for blacks, $2,166, and for the Spanish, $1,946. Increases in Social Security since 1970 do not appear to have altered the relative income positions of the inner-city elderly or of the three subgroups.

If these figures do not fully convey how poor the inner-city elderly are, New York City's rent increase exemption program set $5,000 as the upper income eligibility limit for elderly households, and the Bureau of Labor Statistics (U.S. Department of Labor, 1969-1970) considered that a retired couple in 1970 needed $3,080 to maintain a minimum living standard and close to $4,700 for a moderate living standard in New York City.

Although Social Security was the principal source of income for all inner-city elderly (73 percent were receiving Social Security), what was less expected was the extent to which Social Security was the *only* source of income. Relatively few elderly received income from pensions, investments, or savings (30 percent), and fewer still, as we have already mentioned, from employment. Despite the low income levels, only 20 percent received Old Age Assistance and only 11 percent reported financial aid from families.

There were major differences among ethnic groups in regard to income sources, which reflect differential occupational history and minority-group status. White elderly were more likely to receive income from Social Security than either of the other two groups—82 percent as compared with 70 percent of the blacks and 50 percent of the Spanish elderly. And the benefit received by whites was larger in the fall of 1970—$139 monthly for white elderly, $118 for blacks, and $107 for Spanish. Inasmuch as some of the elderly (or their spouses) were still working, the proportion receiving income from Social Security is not necessarily identical with coverage. But similar differentials were found with respect to coverage; 93 percent of the whites reported being covered by Social Security compared to only 87 percent of the blacks and 73 percent of the Spanish. The study data raise the question as to whether Social Security should not begin at age 55 for Spanish and black elderly, especially since so many are out of the labor market earlier and their life expectancy is so much shorter than whites.

Far fewer black and Spanish elderly received retirement pensions than did whites. One third of the whites reported pensions compared to only 25 percent of the blacks and 11 percent of the Spanish elderly. Whites were far more likely to have income-producing savings and investments (43 percent) as compared to black (8 percent) or Spanish elderly (9 percent). However, this income was rarely a large amount or a substantial part of the total income of the poverty-area respondent.

In view of the lower coverage of black and Spanish elderly by Social Security and pensions, the fact that more of these two groups received Old Age Assistance (OAA) than did whites is not surprising. Forty-five percent of the Spanish respondents received OAA as compared with 25 percent among blacks and only 9 percent among whites. Considering the low level of income, it is indeed surprising that more of the respondents were not recipients of OAA.

The question of Old Age Assistance and by the same token the newer Supplemental Security Income (SSI) program appears fraught with cultural implications. Spanish elderly, whose incomes were lowest, seemed to have the least hesitation accepting OAA—most of those eligible in our sample were covered. Among the black elderly, although a large proportion (60 percent) of those estimated to be eligible were covered, there was a sizable group of apparent eligibles, 40 percent, still uncovered. Some of these undoubtedly were still working, and in answer to a question on whether or not they would turn to OAA in case of need, most blacks indicated a willingness to use the program.

It is among the white elderly that one finds the greatest resistance to entitlement such as OAA or SSI. Thus only 30 percent of the white respondents estimated to be eligible actually used the OAA program, and almost 25 percent flatly said they would never turn to such a program even if in need. In the case of white respondents, some small few may be precluded from OAA because of unwillingness to surrender meager savings, but far more important seems to be the culturally conditioned feeling of lack of dignity and surrender of independence involved in turning to welfare. Early reports on SSI enrollment indicate that this new program also is having difficulty in attracting many of the white elderly who so desperately need the assistance. As long as such programs are seen as based on means tests and as welfare handouts, the potential for reaching the needy eligible of the inner city appears severely limited.

Living arrangements

A crucial factor affecting an older person's sense of independence and personal integrity is his or her living arrangements. Does the older person live in his own household or is the older person living in the home of a child or other family member? Certainly, in our culture to give up one's home is viewed as a move away from independence toward dependency. Whether or not one lives alone affects the need for support in time of crisis and the potential for social isolation. What is the picture in the inner city today and what trends are discernible?

First, whose household is it? The vast majority of older persons in the poverty areas, as in the rest of the city, live independently in their own homes; 91 percent of the sample reported that they or their spouse were head of household; only 8 percent lived in the household of another, usually a child. However, a higher proportion of the inner-city sample maintained their own homes than is true in the city as a whole, and fewer have moved in with families. Thus, although 84 percent of noninstitutionalized elderly 65 and older in the city live in their own homes, 91 percent live independently in our sample. Some part of the differential is due to the presence of 60- 64-years-olds in the study sample, but not much. More important is the changing nature of the populations of these areas, with considerable out-migration of younger white families and replacement by blacks and Puerto Ricans. As noted previously, the older population is, however, still predominantly white. This white population appears to consist of fiercely independent elderly who prefer to remain in their own homes rather than move in with their children, as well as older persons who have no choice in the matter, either because they can't afford homes elsewhere or have no families with whom to live.

The strong desire of older people to maintain their own homes is compatible with the cultural norms of the nuclear family so cherished by the dominant white population. Among ethnic groups more accustomed to extended family patterns, one would expect to find a higher proportion of older people giving up their independent residences and moving in with their families. Such was the case among the respondents of Spanish background and to some, although lesser, extent among blacks; 95 percent of the whites and 89 percent of the blacks continued to maintain their own homes. But the proportion of Spanish living independently dropped significantly to 82 percent, in spite of the fact that the Spanish were the youngest of the three groups and more still had a living spouse.

Although Spanish and blacks were less likely to maintain their own homes than their white peers, the proportion who cling to independence was higher than might be expected, given the extended family tradition and the pressures of poverty. With the continuing acculturation of the younger Spanish population and the difficulties of finding suitable apartments for large families, it is likely that in the future few if any older people will live with children, no matter what their ethnic background. As will be noted later, there is evidence of considerable interaction between older people and children despite the existence of separate households. Perhaps urbanized society is developing a new kind of extended family based on mutual help rather than joint domicile.

But living in one's own household is not the whole question. Whether or not an older person lives entirely alone without anyone else in the household has implications for assistance in time of crisis as well as for morale and degree of social isolation. Although a live-alone is not necessarily an isolate, the likelihood of isolation is greater and the potential need for community intervention is increased.

New York City has more older people living alone than is the case throughout the country (30 percent as compared with 22 percent nationally), and the problems of live-alones are particularly acute in the inner-city neighborhoods.

Among persons 65 and over in New York City as a whole, 30 percent live alone; in the inner city the proportion was 41 percent. The proportion of live-alones in the sample as a whole was 39 percent, but this included younger elderly 60 to 64, who are far more likely to be still married. Thus 4 out of 10 of New York's inner-city elderly 65 and over had no one else in the dwelling unit with them. This is a much greater proportion of live-alones than found in two other urban poverty samples; only 26 percent lived alone in the low-income areas of Philadelphia (Kent and Hirsch, 1971), and in the model-city neighborhoods of Los Angeles the proportion was 28 percent (Gelwicks et al., 1971). Although age and sex affected the likelihood of living alone (women were more apt to live alone than men and the oldest elderly were more often found alone), ethnicity was perhaps the most decisive factor. As noted previously, white elderly were far less inclined to move in with their children and, instead, cling to independent living in their own households, even when loss of spouse occurs. Thus many more white than black or Spanish elderly in the inner city were found living alone. Among white respondents, 47 percent lived alone as compared with 37 percent among blacks and 27 percent among Spanish. The highest incidence of single-person households was found among the frailest segment of the white population, older people in their seventies and eighties, particularly among widowed or single women. For such elderly the changing ethnic composition of their neighborhoods only compounds the objective conditions of aloneness and isolation. But even among black and Spanish, where the pattern of living alone was not yet as prevalent, a surprisingly high proportion were alone—27 percent among the Spanish and 34 percent among the blacks. It is, therefore, likely that large numbers of older persons living alone will characterize inner-city neighborhoods, even if there should be a continued decline in white residents. Providing support for these live-alones, many of whom are the oldest, frailest, and most isolated elderly, will continue to be a challenging community responsibility.

Family relationships in the inner city: Extent of contact between elderly and children

In urban industrial society, the support system of the elderly increasingly involves an amalgam of services provided by the family and significant others and services offered by large-scale governmental or voluntary organizations. As kinship structure evolves from the extended family to the modified extended family (i.e., a coalition of separately housed semi-autonomous nuclear families in a state of partial dependency; Litwak, 1965), the importance of the familial versus societal role shifts. Thus today it is government that provides the floor of basic services for older people in such crucial areas as income maintenance, health, and transportation. But the family and significant others still retain considerable importance, particularly in meeting the more idiosyncratic human needs of the individual. An elder person without a circle of significant others can be severely disadvantaged.

In most societies, children and immediate kin are looked to as the first line of support in time of crisis. Particularly as freedom of movement is curtailed owing to increased frailty, poorer health, and the resultant lessened capacity to manage one's own life wholly independently, the circle of significant others—children, siblings, friends, and neighbors—becomes increasingly significant. It is, therefore, important to know to what extent older inner-city residents have living children, how close they are to these children, and the degree to which relationships are maintained. And, perhaps most crucial, if there are relationships, what is the quality and form that they take?

Contrary to myths that circulate widely about today's parent-child relationships, most inner-city elderly had children and had not been abandoned by their children. Two out of three had at least one living child. Spanish elderly were significantly more likely than either black or white to have had children in the first place, to still have a child in the household, and to have larger families. (Spanish mean number of children was 4.7 as compared with 3.2 for blacks and 2.7 for whites.)

The majority of the children of all three ethnic subgroups lived relatively near their parents, and the two generations had frequent face-to-face and telephone contact with each other. In view of the frequently described flight of children to suburbia, it is significant that 28 percent of all chidren were within walking distance, living either in the building or immediate neighborhood, while 26 percent lived elsewhere in the five boroughs of New York. Only 13 percent resided in the suburbs, and 32 percent were beyond the metropolitan area. (It should be noted that the sample was heavily weighted toward the working and lower-middle classes. It is likely that among older people in the city as a whole the proportion of children living in suburbia would be greater. Even in our more limited sample there was a significant difference between the proportion of children in suburbia among the highest-income elderly and the lower-income groups.)

According to the respondents, they see half of their children at least once a week and two thirds at least monthly. Even though more white children live in the suburbs (19 percent white, 11 percent Spanish, and 8 percent black), while the children of Spanish and black elderly tend to reside more frequently in the neighborhood or within city limits (47 percent white, 62 percent black, 55 percent Spanish), there was little difference with respect to the proportions of the three groups of children who saw their parents regularly (50 percent white, 48 percent black, 53 percent Spanish). Apparently, the greater affluence and mobility of white children enabled them to keep in contact with parents even though they lived farther away.

But although children as a group may have lived in relatively close proximity and had a high level of interaction with parents, this does not go to the heart of the question of availability of familial support in time of need. The crucial question is how many older people in the inner city are in contact with at least one or more children on a frequent and regular basis.

The study data indicate that the majority of respondents with children (68 percent) saw at least one child once or more per week. In the case of the Spanish elderly, whose children live the closest, the proportion seeing at least one child weekly was over 80 percent; among blacks the figure was 70 percent, and among whites, 62 percent. At this point we do not know whether the frequent visitor was the same child, perhaps a daughter, or whether the responsibility for the weekly or biweekly visitation was shared among all the children. Whatever the case, the majority of all older persons in the sample had a regular weekly visit from at least one child. In addition, face-to-face contact was supplemented by frequent telephoning, especially between white parents and children, who used telephone contact more frequently than Spanish and black families. The greater frequency of telephoning among white respondents and their children was probably a matter of both greater affluence and greater distance rather than availability of telephones, since 87 percent of the whites and blacks in the sample had a phone in their own household, as did 76 percent of the Spanish.

Although most of the sample had considerable contact with living children, one cannot overlook the fact that there was a sizable minority of older people without living children for whom primary support may have had to be from neighbors or the community. One third of both the white and black poverty-area respondents indicated that they were without children. Among the Spanish elderly, more of whom initially married and had larger families, there was only 18 percent who were childless.

Type of relationship

An older person can see children frequently and not have close, meaningful relationships. When the respondents were asked to evaluate the closeness of their relationships with their children and to delineate what closenesss means behaviorally, a fascinating system of mutual assistance emerged. Although many older people may find it difficult to state to an interviewer that they are not close to a child, and favorable responses may, therefore, be somewhat inflated, white and

Spanish respondents felt very close to somewhat more than 75 percent of their children and not fairly close to most of the remainder. Black respondents reported somewhat less closeness, indicating that they felt very close to 66 percent of their children, fairly close to 17 percent, and not too close to 16 percent. Here it is likely that the strains of long-term poverty and institutionalized racism have had their effects on the family.

Contact between parents and children is not limited to mere visiting or "checking up," valuable as this type of support may be psychologically. In attitudinal questions the respondents expressed strong feelings about the appropriateness of assistance within the kinship structure and the desirability of mutual interdependency between parents and children. The behavior of the generations appears consonant with these attitudes and involves concrete patterns of mutual help between generations, but clear cultural differences in kinds of assistance emerge.

Respondents were given a series of common types of assistance and asked which they performed for their children, which their children did for them, and the frequency of assistance. Four broad categories of help were involved: (1) ongoing assistance in chores of daily living; (2) advice giving, (3) crisis intervention, and (4) gift giving (see Table 2).

Over 75 percent of the elderly reported helping children in some manner, and this type of involvement of children with parents was even greater; 87 percent of the respondents reported that their children helped in some way.

Looking first at the flow of assistance from parents to children, among all three ethnic groups, the giving of gifts, baby-sitting, and helping in times of illness were the most often reported forms of parent-child assistance. Spanish parents less frequently gave gifts involving money than did white and black parents, reflecting unquestionably to some degree their lower income. But, more importantly, the Spanish elderly still appeared to have a more direct role in the family than their black or white peers, and were far more often involved in giving advice with respect to running the home, child rearing, and making major decisions on such things as jobs or substantial purchases. They were also involved in helping to raise grandchildren than were white or black grandparents. Whites and blacks, on the other hand, although available for help to children in times of illness and for occasional baby-sitting, appeared to play a more passive role with respect to family operations. Their main form of assistance on a regular basis appeared to be gift giving.

A similar pattern with respect to degree of actual involvement in day-to-day chores of life is seen when we look at what children did for parents (as reported by the parents). Help from children was, if any-

Table 2.　Patterns of Mutual Assistance Between Inner-City Elderly of New York and Their Children (percentages)

	Parents to Children				Children to Parents			
	Total	White	Black	Spanish	Total	White	Black	Spanish
Crisis intervention	50.7[a]	50.5	49.2	54.8	67.8	67.4	67.7	69.1
Assistance in chores of daily living	38.3	35.2	40.9	41.7	65.1	63.1	66.6	67.7
Baby-sit	22.7	21.0	21.9	29.2	—	—	—	—
Shop, errands	17.6	14.0	21.4	19.4	50.5	42.3	57.9	57.5
Fix things in house	11.3	9.5	10.9	17.5	39.4	38.3	42.1	42.1
Keep house	13.0	8.1	17.8	16.0	21.7	13.9	25.9	34.4
Meal preparation	—	—	—	—	16.1	11.5	21.6	17.1
Take away in summer	—	—	—	—	19.2	23.3	10.2	27.2
Drive to store, doctor	—	—	—	—	28.5	33.3	22.1	29.3
Giving advice	35.5	26.7	36.3	52.8	26.0	24.6	27.0	27.9
On child rearing/home management	27.3	20.2	29.2	43.5	—	—	—	—
On major purchases	9.4	9.0	8.5	12.8	12.2	15.1	8.7	11.9
On jobs, business, money matters	17.1	13.8	18.2	24.3	21.7	17.5	26.0	23.8
Gifts and giving	66.6	72.3	64.0	55.2	81.6	83.7	77.9	82.7
Gifts (nonmonetary)	65.0	70.2	63.1	54.1	79.1	82.2	76.5	76.1
Money	19.9	20.6	21.2	14.9	29.0	20.1	33.4	44.8
No assistance	21.6	19.1	23.2	24.9	13.3	10.5	16.1	15.1
Total respondents	1,020	480	374	166	1,020	480	374	166

[a]Respondents could give more than one response in a category. Totals of subcategories are therefore greater than that for the category itself.
Source: Cantor et al., *The Elderly in the Inner City*, New York City Office for the Aging, in press.

thing, even more extensive than parents helping children. Almost 9 out of 10 older people having children reported such help (see Table 2).

As one might expect, gift giving and crisis assistance were the principal forms of assistance reported by respondents of all three ethnic groups. Among all three ethnic subgroups similarly high proportions of respondents received gifts from children (78 percent black elderly, 84 percent white and Spanish). There were, however, some significant differences in the form of gift. Spanish elderly, with the lowest incomes, more frequently received monetary gifts, followed by blacks. Among the white respondents, gifts were generally in the form of objects (a coat or refrigerator) rather than money.

The difference in type of gift may well reflect the greater need for money on the part of Spanish and black elderly, and a reluctance on the part of white elderly to accept monetary gifts that connote greater dependency.

Children of all three ethnic subgroups assisted equally in time of illness; the proportions of respondents receiving crisis intervention were virtually identical (67 percent white, 68 percent black, 69 percent Spanish) (see Table 2).

Although a similarly high proportion (appproximately two-thirds) of each subgroup reported receiving some assistance from children in the chores of daily living, there were noticeable differences in the form of assistance. Spanish and black children appeared to be significantly more involved than white children in such things as shopping and running errands, keeping house, and preparing meals. This greater involvement undoubtedly is partially a reflection of the closer geographic proximity of black and Spanish parents to children, but it is probably also a manifestation of the continuing influence of the extended family structure.

Even more significant with respect to the nuclear family and independence, far fewer white respondents reported that children gave advice in matters of daily living than was the case among the black and Spanish elderly. Among blacks and Spanish, at least one quarter received advice regularly from their children.

Our data clearly indicate that the Spanish elderly, and to some extent the black elderly, are still part of an extended family network encompassing frequent contact and much direct mutual assistance. White elderly, although involved with their children, are less directly involved in day-to-day household activities and have a less time-consuming, a less specified, and a less direct role with respect to the lives of their children. It is, of course, impossible to predict how long this extended protective family system will continue for the Spanish and black elderly. From the attitudinal material in our study, it would appear that the impact of the dominant culture is already having its effect and that the Spanish elderly more than any other group are feeling the strains of attempting to bridge two cultures.

Discussion and Implications

The foregoing findings point to the important strengths held and difficulties faced by the inner-city elderly of New York.

First, with respect to the newest arrivals, the Spanish elderly as a group are at the younger end of the elderly continuum and have fewer years of residency in the city, although still a substantial amount. Spanish elderly tend to be still married and living with a spouse and may even have a younger child still in the household. Economically, they are the worst off, both with respect to when they leave the labor force and to their level of job skills. Because of relative lack of skill and education they held the lowest paying jobs during their adult years and, if covered by Social Security, receive only minimum benefits. Many, however, are not even covered by Social Security, and they are less likely to be covered by Medicare. However, the Spanish elderly, although suffering from communication difficulties (many still speak only Spanish), have turned to Old Age Assistance and, therefore, Medicaid to a much greater degree than either their black or white peers. The municipal hospitals tend to function as their doctors, and without Medicare coverage they use private physicians to a lesser degree than do the black and white elderly. Low incomes and poor nutrition have undoubtedly contributed to their self-assessed poorer health, but here cultural factors are important, for illness is not considered something to hide but rather to talk about widely (especially among the women). But balanced against severe handicaps of language, economic privation, and lack of Social Security coverage is the fact that the Spanish elderly, more than their peers, are still functioning within the protective environment of the extended family. Many indicate that they still have rights as elders, and they tend to interact strongly with their children in giving both advice and assistance in a variety of tasks from baby-sitting to shopping to fixing things in their childrens' homes. With less money, they are not as apt to give children material gifts but appear to have outlets for giving of themselves and a role to play within the family circle. However, this picture is being eroded as the younger generation of Spanish-background adults becomes more acculturated. Already 27 percent of the Spanish elderly live alone rather than within the extended family, and Spanish elderly show signs of mental stress and worry to a far greater degree than do black or white elderly. The very thing they worry most about—children and family matters—is indicative of the strains that are evident in the changing family situation among New Yorkers of Spanish background. It would appear that the future holds considerable uncertainty for the Spanish elderly, who in coming generations will probably be caught up in the same dilemma of role crisis presently faced by their peers.

The black elderly are facing many of the same economic and minority-group problems as the Spanish elderly without some of the redeeming features of close-knit, extended family life. Although slightly better off economically than their Spanish peers, they too suffer from extremely low incomes, job discrimination, and forced early retirement for the men. Social Security coverage is far from complete, particularly among women, many of whom continue to work into their late sixties and early seventies. Like the Spanish, black elderly tend to receive minimum or near-minimum Social Security benefits. They are more likely to be covered by Medicare and when ill tend to use private physicians or the clinics of the voluntary hospitals.

Because of poverty and discrimination in childhood and adulthood, blacks have 7 years less life expectancy than whites and report poorer health and a greater incidence of chronic illness than white elderly. A somewhat different family pattern is evident among the black elderly. Although most married at one time, fewer blacks in old age are still married and living with a spouse than among the other two subgroups. The incidence of divorce and/or separation is more frequent among blacks, and widowhood is as prevalent as among whites. As a result, there are more female-headed homes with younger family members living in the households of the grandmother. Blacks report slightly less emotional closeness to children, although the majority of their children live within the city limits or in the immediate neighborhoods of the elderly and there is contact between the generations. Black parents help children out somewhat less often than Spanish elderly but seem to play a more direct role in the functioning of their childrens' households than do white elderly. They give gifts as freely as their white peers, although they have less income, and in turn children are available for assistance in time of crisis. However, intervention on the part of children on a day-to-day basis is not as frequent as among Spanish families. Black elderly in need seem more willing than whites to accept Old Age Assistance, but not all black respondents estimated as eligible for income maintenance assistance are getting such help. Among the blacks, increasing numbers appear to be living alone in old age, and it is likely that in the future the problem of live-alones will reach proportions similar to that found among the white population.

Of the three subgroups, black elderly express the greatest satisfaction with their lives in old age and worry the least. It is impossible to determine the exact meaning of this higher level of life satisfaction. Are such attitudes genuinely indicative of present happiness or are they perhaps a reaction formed in reponse to the discrimination suffered by blacks in this country, a psychologically protective stance adapted early in childhood and carried over into old age? Certainly, black elderly face severe problems of low income, poor health, inadequate housing, and difficulty in obtaining supportive assistance from both the community and often from their families; their high scores on measures of life satisfaction must be accepted with some hesitation. However, just reaching 65 may indeed be a cause for considerable satisfaction.

The white elderly in the poverty areas of the inner city present a conflicting picture. Most have been lower-middle or middle class during their adult years; old age for them brings not only role loss but severe economic and often social discontinuity. Living longer, many more are found living alone; the incidence of live-alones is particularly high in the case of women, who far outnumber men and are not as likely to remarry upon loss of spouse. Residing in changing neighborhoods, often among hostile neighbors whom they cannot understand, there is considerable fear of crime and of persons different from one's self.

On the other hand, the white elderly have lived in New York a long time; they have strong feelings of belonging and are particularly appreciative of the easily accessible neighborhood facilities and the richness and variety of city life. They are staunch New Yorkers and speak out about the city with considerable affection, although recognizing the problems inherent in deteriorating neighborhoods.

The white elderly, although slightly better off than their Spanish and black peers, are truly New York's hidden poor. They have strong feelings of pride and are unwilling to accept easily the help available, such as Old Age Assistance, if it means any loss of independence or dignity. Although most have living children in the area with whom they feel close and are in contact, the separation between the generations is complete in most cases. Children and parents help each other in times of crisis, but involvement in the details of daily living is neither expected nor desired on the part of white elderly nor does it appear to be forthcoming from children, many of whom live outside the immediate neighborhood. Love and affection is shown through gifts, money, visiting, phoning, and emergency help or occasional baby sitting; other types of more direct intervention, including advice giving, are rare. Parents and adult children function as two separate nuclear families, and this separation is both accepted and real.

For the black and Spanish elderly the community must be prepared to accept considerable financial responsibility to compensate for low retirement incomes and poor work histories. The entire cost of adequate housing, health, nutrition, and the variety of services needed by older people certainly cannot be assumed by most black or Spanish elderly, given their low incomes. White elderly, given rising Social Security benefits and pensions, may in the future be better able to assume a greater part of the cost of their needs. But problems of greater isolation from family and higher incidence of living alone will continue to require supportive community services for them as well; particularly in the case of the older and more frail elderly and the unattached women, the two groups of white elderly most often found living alone and with the lowest incomes. In addition, many white elderly need economic assistance, but it must be given in a way that does not strip pride and destroy independence. Hopefully, the assumption of Old Age Assistance by the Social Security system will mean greater economic security for the elderly of all three ethnic groups, coupled with a consideration for personal feelings and for a sense of personal dignity. The elderly of the inner city and their peers throughout the city have contributed long hard years of work and they deserve an old age of respect, dignity, and freedom from want. If today's older New Yorkers fail to realize such a life, neither will coming generations.

Acknowledgment

The research reported here was supported by Administration on Aging Grant AA-4-70-089-02.

Marjorie H. Cantor is Brookdale Professor of Gerontology, Fordham University, and a faculty member of the School of Social Work. She formerly was Director of Research of the New York City Department for the Aging, under whose auspices the research report was conducted.

References

Blau, Z. S. *Old Age in a Changing Society, New Viewpoints.* New York: Franklin Watts Press, 1973.

Cantor, M. H., and Mayer, M. *Health Crisis of Older New Yorkers.* New York: New York City Office for the Aging, 1972.

———. et al. *The Elderly in the Inner City.* New York: New York City Office for the Aging, 1975.

Clark, M., and Anderson, B. G. *Culture and Aging.* Springfield, Ill.: Charles C. Thomas, 1967.

Gelwicks, L., Feldman, A., and Newcomer, R. J. *Report on Older Population: Needs, Resources and Services.* Los Angeles: Los Angeles Gerontology Center, University of Southern California, 1971.

Hollingshead, A. B., and Redlich, F. C. *Social Class and Mental Illness.* New York: Wiley, 1958.

Kent, D., and Hirsch, C. *Needs and Use of Services Among Negro and White Aged,* Vols. I and XI. University Park, Pa.: Pennsylvania State University, July 1971 and October 1972.

Litwak, E. Extended kin relations in an industrial democratic society. In E. Shanas and G. Streib (eds.), *Social Structure and the Family.* Englewood Cliffs, N.J.: Prentice-Hall, 1965.

Rose, A., and Peterson, W. A. (eds.). *Older People and Their Social World.* Philadelphia: F. A. Davis, 1965.

Rosow, I. *Social Integration of the Aged.* New York: Free Press, 1967.

Shanas, E., Townsend, P., Wedderburn, D., Friis, H., Milhoj, P., and Stehouwer, J. *Old People in Three Industrial Societies.* New York: Atherton Press, 1968.

Townsend, P. *The Family Life of Old People.* London: Routledge & Kegan Paul Ltd., 1957.

U.S. Bureau of the Census, 1970 Census of Population. Washington, D.C.: Government Printing Office.

U.S. Department of Labor, Bureau of Labor Statistics. *Three Budgets for A Retired Couple in Urban Areas of the United States, 1969-70.* Washington, D.C.: Government Printing Office.

CHAPTER V

THE INTERVENTIONS

As people live longer, their needs for health and social services are also likely to expand. An increase in life expectancy rates, epidemiologists remind us, may be accompanied by higher morbidity rates. The number of vulnerable, frail persons of advanced old age—the likely consumers of multiple service resources—is already multiplying at an unprecedented rate.

This chapter aims to precisely focus on those service resources. It is designed, however, to highlight some extreme service categories rather than cataloguing the whole services continuum. It, therefore, begins with a primary or preventive level of service for middle agers, such as preretirement planning, and it then proceeds to the other end of the spectrum, with tertiary level, protective services for the frail and disabled.

The hypothetical linkage between primary support networks and formal community services, and finally, the legal aspects of the aging life experience complete this chapter.

Retirement, regardless of whether it is flexible or mandatory, is a universal institution. Although the average middle aged worker may anticipate to live between fifteen and twenty years after his or her exit from the labor force, no adequate expectations or role definitions have been yet spelled out for the particular status of retiree. Society has prescribed anticipatory socialization resources for practically every age-related transition, but not for the sensitive passage into retirement.

Monk deals precisely with some of the programs for preretirement planning and systematizes their central themes into five models. They are: 1) rational-economic, centered on the deflection of productivity into activity engaging routines; 2) social, sensitive to the person's affiliative urgings and his potentialities for resocialization; 3) humanistic, responsive to the existential need for self-fulfillment; 4) complex-systemic, attending to the singularity of each person's life experience; and 5) crisis oriented, focused on the reality of loss that occurs at retirement, the subsequent grieving process, and the possible restitutions and compensations for the loss experience. A review of the literature on the effectiveness of these programs shows modestly encouraging results, but the author warns about the possibility of a built-in selective bias: people enlisting in preretirement preparation programs may be those who are already mindful and positively inclined toward retirement. Monk states what constitutes a full-fledged, legitimate program and spells out its essential structural ingredients. Preretirement preparation programs are evolving into a preventive service for middle agers, a facilitating device for one of the least understood transitions in the life cycle.

In "Protective Practice in Serving the Mentally Impaired Aged" Edna Wasser reports the operation of a protective service for a severely disabled and frail category of older persons. These are a high risk population because of their limited capacity to manage alone, but they are not institutionalized. A central problem in servicing these elderly, therefore, consists in developing and organizing the much needed services at the local community level.

Wasser begins by defining the profile of the frail and disorganized clientele, and then proceeds to present a model for the delivery of service. She emphasizes the role of the practitioner as change agent and convener of a community wide system of services. She also values institutional facilities as an essential component in the continuum of care, but anticipates that a well-orchestrated community system of protective services would make the former far less necessary. Protective services are described as a tertiary level of intervention, practically the end of the line and followed only by institutional care. Prevention at earlier levels must be developed, in order to anticipate and neutralize those problems and conditions of the aged that made protective services such a critical imperative.

In "Will You Still Need Me, Will You Still Feed Me When I'm 64?" Sussman, Vanderwyst, and Williams present the results of study about the viability of primary support networks and the willingness of American families to house and care for their aging relatives. The researchers began pondering what kind of inducements would be necessary to encourage relatives to take in those elderly kin and provide them with more than custodial environment.

The problematic nature of intergenerational supports became more than apparent when findings showed that a small majority would welcome cash incentives and accept their aging relatives. A recalcitrant 20 percent of the respondents would not accept these relatives under any circumstances. Incentives made it easier for the already committed to state their positive response but did very little to change the minds of the refusers. Even those who responded affirmatively had some qualifications: they were likely to accept female relatives but resisted solitary males.

The study ends, however, with some favorable conclusions as the possibility of combining family and community services is not discarded. Given policy incentives such as tax rebates, cash payments, and personal care or home health services, it would be feasible to keep many frail elderly in the community, rather than confining them in large custodial institutions.

The lives of the aged are enmeshed in complex legal provisions that regulate their income, the health services they receive under Medicare and Medicaid provisions, their rent supplements and tax rebates, the institutions they resort to for nursing care, etc. They enjoy numerous age categorical entitlements, but their actual benefits are often limited by unintelligible definitions of eligibility. Their access to universal entitlements may be also blocked by subtle discriminatory practices. Finally, and as they grow more vulnerable, they may require certain levels of protection which remain subject to what Nathanson in his paper, "Legal Aspects of Aging," calls "the vagaries of the law of guardianship, conservatorship, and involuntary commitment." The author begins by unscrambling the interrelationship of legislative, judicial, and administrative processes affecting the aged and then isolates a handful of relevant issues. Age discrimination in employment, protective services, the status of women, and access to services were selected for a more specific analysis. Nathanson is not very confident in the effectiveness of the legal system and would prefer to see it removed altogether in certain instances, such as the resolution of disputes. Because the elderly do not have the several years necessary to pursue a litigation through the courts, Nathanson would rather see that consumer advocacy and ombudsmen programs play a wider role, instead of the lawyers and judges.

Services for the aged are still in the making. For the moment they constitute a disjointed and often irrational system, plagued with duplications, unjustified gaps, and insensitive eligibility requirements.

Our next chapter includes several recommendations for the future improvement of this system.

5.1

Models for Preretirement Planning

Abraham Monk

Preretirement preparation programs (PRPPs) are usually designed to neutralize or at least reduce the trauma that older workers may suffer at the time of their withdrawal from the labor force. In a more positive vein, and even in the absence of such crises, PRPPs are intended to also bring a higher sense of life satisfaction in the later years.

PRPPs are still in their experimental stage. Federal legislation has timidly fostered their development only recently, with the 1973 Amendments to Title III of the Older Americans Act, but we are still far from any semblance of universal mandate concerning their adoption. PRPPs have moved from a limited informational format into the wider personal constellation of the impending retiree. The former "restricted" programs were characteristic of management sponsored initiatives, while the latter evolved from adult education, counseling, and andragogical inputs.

PRPPs, far from having achieved generalized acceptance, have lately become the focus of some criticism and even disenchantment. It is claimed that:

1. They tend to pay too much attention to the impending retirement "event," or at best to the first year of retirement, but neglect the subsequent "recoil" phase, when the honeymoon with fishing and ceramics is over. The individual is suddenly faced with his loneliness, nostalgia for his past but unable to relate to his future.

Paper presented at the Fifth Professional Symposium of the National Association of Social Workers, San Diego, California, November 20, 1977.

2. They give excessive weight to needed compensations for the loss of work related roles to the detriment of other more expressive aspects of later life, such as family relationships, widowhood, or age identity.

An additional source of criticism is more ideological in nature. It attacks retirement itself as an unfair solution to the endemic problem of unemployment. It regards retirement as an expeditious way to make room for the young at the expense of the old, without even the graciousness of adequate compensation. PRPPs, accordingly, are the brainwashing device meant "to sugarcoat the bitter pill of retirement." They are accessories to an outrageous infringement of the right to work. Retirement as a universal institution is here to stay, regardless of whether it remains mandatory or becomes chronologically flexible. Programs preparing for retirement have multiplied in recent years, but attempts to systematize them are rather few in number.

The anatomy of PRPPs is pretty much universal. The main objective is to provide information and planning tools that will enable individuals to make right decisions concerning their impending retirement. Programs invariably include content on changing roles and attitudes, financial planning, health maintenance, nutrition, continuing education, housing alternatives, second careers or part-time employment, volunteer roles, and leisure time activities. The structural similarity of all programs obscures, however, the more substantive underlying philosophical differences. Preretirement Preparation Programs do not emerge in a vacuum and they do not respond to the corporate or personal idiosyncracies of their designers only. They instead reflect philosophical outlooks on the nature of man, the same basic assumptions about people that have served to legitimize policies and dominant directions in our society. At risk of engaging in some overgeneralizations, five types or models of PRPPs will be presented in this paper, roughly corresponding to Edgar Schein's formulation of four sets of images of man: rational-economic, social, self-actualizing, and complex (1970). A fifth type, centered around crisis theory, has been added here.

Model 1: Rational-Economic

This category or model assumes that people are primarily motivated by economic self-interest and that life remains pretty much the same after retirement, focused on work-oriented values. PRPPs must contend with the achievement motive and assuage it by deflecting it into two areas: hobbies and voluntarism. Prospective retirees must be kept "active" in the productive sense, by way of enhancing their functional efficiency. New rewards systems must be found, usually in civic or community oriented volunteer roles, because they offer a sense of partial restitution of power or control deficits. Too often, however, some of these volunteer roles are low status service jobs, usually shunned by other age groups, a fact that occasionally leads to charges of camouflaged exploitation of older people. Model 1 programs rather excelled in the development of functional coping skills. Their main thrust has been in the training for adjustment to a framework of diminishing resources. Typical titles of booklets and lectures are "How to stretch your health dollar," "How to eat nutritiously on 'X' dollars a day," "How couple 'Z' eats as good as couple 'Y' while spending twelve dollars less weekly," etc. These are responsible programs, methodically prepared by reliable nutritionists, homemaking specialists, tax advisors, and economists. They contain worthy instructional elements but they also foster excessive conformity, a sense of fatalistic acceptance of the status quo. Their message is: We will help you do your best within your present means. Nothing is said about improving those means and life conditions.

Model 2: Social

The social perspective claims that man's need to belong, to be accepted by others, overrides all other motives, including the financial one. PRPPs of this category are sensitive to the shrinkage of man's social world after retirement and consider it a serious threat to his personal identity. Loneliness is the number one enemy to contend with. *"Ready or Not,"* one of the commercially most popular programs, written by Arnold et al. (1974), starts by giving comfort to the potential retiree stating:

> *"You are Not Alone"*
> However you feel, it should not be lonely.
> Do you know that over 300,000 people enter the ranks of the aged every year?

Model 2 PRPPs rely primarily on group activities as the dominant media. Groups are assumed to be a more economical form of transmitting information, but their primary value lies in the fact that they help the reticent, the shy, and the confused to receive support from his peers. These programs exalt the development of special gerontological environments, such as multiservice centers, professional clubs, unions, clubs, etc. Some of these centers are totally open, of the "drop-in" or "store-front" variety; others are more exclusive and their membership is carefully screened, tested, and thereafter limited to a ceiling number.

Content wise, Model 2 programs emphasize:

A. *Role flexibility*, the capacity to take on new life roles, in situations which were not typical of the middle years. A very successful program in the USA is RSVP that trains older persons, who had never volunteered, to serve in teams—as volunteers—in services for the retarded, children of broken families, disabled, etc. Emphasis is also placed on tapping latent leadership qualities in those who seldom exercised them and put them in front of new organizations for the aged. By preparing the older person to reinvolve himself with new types of groups, he may acquire a new social identity. The ultimate criteria of success is given when the older person is not only an active participant of self-directed groups but is able to reinvolve himself, to circulate or to fit in new groupings, if the circumstances so demand it.

B. *Interpersonal competence*. Some programs, particularly those espousing a deeper commitment to leadership and social service, include laboratory training techniques, group dynamics, sensitivity training, encounter groups, and transactional analysis; these are nontherapeutic methods, but they do seek to effect personality changes in the form of better self-awareness, communication skills, the ability to handle conflicts, and tolerance for ambiguity and dissidence. These are all essential requirements for good organizational leadership in complex societies.

The best contribution of Model 2 PRPPs is that they brought about a special awareness of the impending social deficits at the retirement stage. Primary groups crumble with the death of spouse, relatives, and friends, or with children marrying and moving elsewhere. These programs are predicated not only on the creation of new social environments as mentioned earlier, but also on the development of social linkage systems, such as information and referral services that document, register, and evaluate all social contexts in a given community and refer older persons to those that suit them best. Model 2 PRPPs have to initially contend with the aversion of the preretiree to join peer group centers or environments. They have to bring about a measure of attitudinal change and overcome such resistances.

Model 3: Humanistic-Existential

It underscores that man has an urge for meaning, and that the worker's sense of pride and self-esteem is enhanced when they can free their creative capacities. Unfortunately, most people go through life without ever realizing what their latent competences are. They are thus alienated and psychologically oppressed even amidst free political systems. Model 3 PRPPs conceive retirement as a great opportunity for human liberation. Yet in order to make it work, man has to first conquer himself through learning, self-awareness, and the full realization of his potentialities. Andragogy, a theory and method of adult learning, has made an interesting contribution to this effect and it is therefore worth examining it in more detail.

Andragogy centers around the adult individual's experience as a learning resource. It is concerned with the paralyzing effects exerted by the "overabundance of choice," as Toffler characterized the acceleration of change today, and seeks to overcome it by problem finding in the "here and now" time dimension (1970). Andragogy is defined as the "pedagogy for adults." It seeks to enhance collaborative skill development toward concurrent aims: the definition of problems and their resolution through interpersonal work, and the reassessment of the individual's learning needs as they keep changing. Andragogy therefore implies two major processes: reeducation and self-directed learning. Malcom Knowles stated to this effect that:

> The important implication for adult education practice of the fact that learning is an internal process is that those methods and techniques which involve the individual most deeply in self-directed inquiry will produce the greatest learning. This principle of ego involvement lies at the heart of the adult educator's art. In fact, the main thrust of modern educational technology is in the direction of inventing techniques for involving adults in ever deeper processes of self-diagnosis of their own needs for continuing learning, in formulating their own objectives for learning, in sharing responsibility for designing and carrying out their learning activities, and in evaluating their progress toward their objectives (1970).

The individual's movement toward those ends happens in a mutual planning framework, in a group atmosphere of warmth and closeness that helps discover what individual differences and needs are. Needs assessment is, in fact, the fundamental prerequisite for effective planning, and it is conducted through "competence model building." These are analytic inventories of individual potential capacities in given fields. You start finding out what you can do, what you would like to do, and what is the gap between the two. It is assumed that the awareness of such a gap, between that which *I can do* and that which *I would like to do*, acts as a formidable motivator for individual reeducation and development. The exercise in itself constitutes an expansion of self-diagnostic skills. When coupled with the group climate setting, it leads to a more intense personal commitment to carry out the planning objectives. It is here where "decision-making models" succeed the preceding "competence models." They are not different from the planning or problem-solving designs widely used in the behavioral disciplines, from group dynamics to casework and management. Andragogical designs are predicated, however, on shared experience, on mutuality, and the group opportunity to identify the learning residue from the experience. The group task is more than an analytic exercise as it helps to identify both blocking and facilitating behaviors and to establish time horizons for action.

Andragogy sounds a bit esoteric and it runs the risk of being confounded with an ideological fad, a doctrinal bandwagon. Its advocates consequently insist on retaining the low profile of a mere experimental process approach. Because potentialities are explored, levels of growth and achievement spelled out, and results tested for their potential usefulness in a group context, andragogy cushions the risk-taking aspect of individual endeavors. Preparation for retirement, in its andragogical version, is education—the capacity for coping effectively with interpersonal relationships. It is not enough to enlighten the prospective retiree with his pension plan's fine print or have him acquire a few hobbies. It basically calls for developing a greater sense of self-acceptance, better communication skills, and more reliance on effective problem-solving social contexts.

Andragogically inspired preretirement programs are still sporadic and sketchy. There is hardly a model blueprint that could be presented here. It is, for the moment, a humanistic trend that is at variance with more rationalist approaches. It affirms growth and self-exploration. To continue to learn, however, is to keep risking failure. Exploration for self-realization requires a measure of insecurity, living with danger and excitement. Andragogy precisely affirms growth and self-renewal while keeping risk and uncertainty at a minimum. There are, however, many unconvincing aspects to andragogy. When is the group framework an auxiliary support, and when does it become a crutch that fosters dependence? When does the individual actually begin risk taking by making decisions on his own? What should be the duration of groups, and how are they reconstituted? There are many obscure angles, but the ground work is ready for further explorations.

As a humanistic strategy, this third model may ultimately overcome, according to Moody (1976), the "social services model" in education and substitute it with a "participation advocacy and self-sufficiency model."

Model 4: Complex-Systemic

This model starts from the premise that all preceding models are simplistic in nature and that they fail to perceive man as a complex, highly variable system. His interests and concerns are subject to continuous change and combine in motivational patterns that have meaning only to him. It also follows that new individual interests emerge at different points of life, displacing and substituting those that preceded them. It does not, therefore, make sense to box people into static categories. There is no such thing in reality as people who like or dislike work, or for that matter, retirement in the absolute sense. There are some aspects of either work and retirement that provide more fulfillment than others, and the preretirement planning counselor ought to be a good diagnostician. He must sense and appreciate individual differences. He must be flexible and expect that changes will occur to an individual. There are not, therefore, two individuals alike, even if they have strikingly similar careers and backgrounds: their retirement needs may be different and no standardized program will do them justice or adequately handle their needs.

Simpson, Back, and McKinney (1966) found that the attitude and response towards the prospect of retirement are in part a function of the type of work performed prior to retirement. Monk (1970) found that attitudes toward retirement and PRPPs differed even within the same occupational group, according to a "people" or "things" orientation in their job routines. Those who had more direct dealings with publics, colleagues, or subordinates were more positively inclined to retirement than those who dealt with the strict research and technological aspects of their professions. We could add the numerous personality typologies to support the contention that universal preretirement programs are not defensible. Like a single size shoe, they cannot fit everyone. Model 4 PRPPs advocate individualized retirement counseling. This individual case diagnosis and planning is supplemented by a more general type of counseling, again individual, but informational in nature. It aims to cover finances, recreational activities, home relocation, family problems, etc., in a sort of person-to-person exchange that assures immediate feedback to the prospective retiree. Needless to say, this is a rather expensive form of service. Its supporters claim however that it has a substantial preventative effect, as it helps detect and avert impending crises at an early stage. The effectiveness of counseling, it is added, is a function of the time when the program begins. The earlier the better, and some advocate that it be offered fifteen years before actual retirement.

Model 4 programs have underscored the relationship between the "career" concept of retirement, as a series of progressive stages of adaptation, and the preceding "work" career ladders. Counseling at fifty, for instance, is not only future-retirement related, it also detects problems that need immediate action. We are referring here to the worker's realization that he may have already reached the end of the road, caught in a dead alley with nowhere else to go, that his skills are no longer needed. It is therefore not surprising that Model 4 counselors have established "mid-career clinics" to guide middle aged workers into new occupational activities and retraining them. They also engage in job analysis by which current occupations are restructured or redesigned, new career ladders created, and bridges toward new career escalators built. They are doing the same with the postretirement stage by defining how old age employment and even volunteer roles should be structured. It was found, for instance, that the great turnover of volunteers is linked precisely to their role immobility and the lack of promotion to more sophisticated levels of service. Volunteers and employed retirees do not want to keep doing the same thing for the rest of their lives either.

Model 5: Crisis Orientation

In a sense the crisis model is not independent, as there is a crisis component permeating the four previous archetypes. They all have to contend with the eventuality of emotional disturbances, of anxiety, and fear. Yet there are programs that separately center around crisis as the inevitable accompaniment of retirement. They view the latter as a source of stress that disorganizes the individual's coping mechanisms. The worker senses the actual loss of control over crucial life variables and may fall prey to helplessness and even despair. The model does not necessarily suggest an irreversible course downhill toward psychopathological syndromes. The contrary may well happen: hardened by the crisis the individual may come out with greater moral strength and fortitude. Yet in the majority of cases, Model 5 PRPPs expect to contend with the injury that ego sustains in the face of loss and the resulting high risks of depressive states.

In terms of service delivery, Model 5 programs range from public community education and lecture series offered in community mental health centers, to more definitive therapeutic interventions. Again, their one commonality is the reality of loss and some sort of acceptance of this reality. While other models exalt growth, change, adaptation, self-realization, etc., here there is a candid reconciliation with the fact that we no longer can do or expect from life what we did or received in younger days. Rather than avoiding the issue or painting fake rosy images of better things to come, counselors and therapists encourage the preretiree to prepare to grieve. After all, grieving is a form of giving up intense emotional ties to something or someone that is being lost. There is a great deal of probing into the worker's past, making him aware of all his achievements and contributions to life. It is taking pride in their children, their occupational successes, or whatever strengths and assets they have. When confronted with the fact that their lives have not been wasted, it is easier to accept the forthcoming losses with a sense of fortitude rather than resignation, and to define some realistic objectives, such as the acceptance of a somewhat more dependent status as a natural concomitant of old age. This does not preclude continued or renewed involvement with life. It affirms that not all losses can be compensated but that the self is not lost or that the self-esteem is not irreparably damaged when an important loss does occur.

These five models are an attempt to introduce some order into a fast growing and intriguing field of human services. Like all typologies in science, their main flow is that of oversimplification and abstraction. They do not do justice to the richness and originality of some individual programs. Moreover, there are no "pure" model programs, as they usually incorporate features and attributes of more than one model. Perhaps it would be more appropriate to speak here of trends, of central or dominant ideas.

We cannot, therefore, suggest that any of the above models is better than another. They all have their strengths and weaknesses. There are, however, good and bad programs within each model and we wish we could measure them in terms of their impact and long range effectiveness, but we do not usually have the time horizon or adequate tools for it.

Do these programs work?

Evaluations of retirement preparation programs give evidence, however, of some promising gains. Mack (1958), after reviewing eighteen programs in the Chicago area, concluded that PRPPs alleviate the fears about retirement, increase positive attitudes toward it, and elicit desirable behavioral changes in actual preparations for retirement.

Don Charles from the Drake University Preretirement Planning Center assessed some 368 subjects that went through such programs and found an increasing apprehension concerning Social Security benefits, health, life styles, and less of a preoccupation about employment (1971). There was also more expressed interest in social involvement and social activities. These, however, were just attitudinal changes; they constituted an increase in awareness but gave no evidence of actual behavioral changes. Scheibe found better adjustment to postretirement life among workers that went through PRPPs (1968). Ash did a study of blue collar workers in England (1966). He compared a sample of graduates of a PRPP and a comparable group of retirees who did not go through such programs. The former had a better disposition towards postretirement life and three years after retirement they retained a higher sense of purposefulness. Only 8 percent of the former group, as compared to 22 percent of the second, said they had nothing to do or did not know what to do with themselves.

Greene et al., of the University of Oregon, assessed eight companies in Southern California and found that their retirees were better adjusted and showed a higher overall life adjustment, a higher activity level, and a better subjective rating of health and income, after undergoing a PRPP (1969).

There is, indeed, a danger of selective bias in these studies. While most studies indicate a positive relationship between planning for retirement and favorable attitudinal dispositions toward retirement, these may only demonstrate that persons already mindful, alert, and positively inclined are those who may start planning first. PRPPs have limitations or liabilities worth considering before one embarks on their implementation.

First, they tend to come in standardized packages and the industrial social workers or personnel counselors who use them may overlook the individual's plastic and richly experienced capacity for adjusting to change. Such programs also overlook the requirement that whatever adaptation occurs must be consistent with the person's previous life style.

Second, they may start too late, thus opening a Pandora's box of anxieties and concerns that are too late to resolve.

Third, it is claimed that less than 50 percent of the American workers receive some limited form of PRPPs. This is rather misleading because in reality most programs do not merit such designation. They probably do not go beyond a succinct one-shot presentation of the company's pension or Social Security benefits and some sort of ceremonial farewell. Most employers are even reluctant to go into any depth because, as they claim, it will constitute an incursion into the employee's private life. Companies with poor pension plans are the most reluctant to offer PRPPs for obvious reasons: they might be creating awareness about those deficiencies, thus inviting internal trouble. Comprehensive PRPPs probably do not reach more than 10 percent of the American labor force, and we have no knowledge of any such programs for the rural workers. In planning our program we concluded that, to merit the designation of "comprehensive" it must include most of the following attributes:

1. Counseling or group activities, or both, as a method of program delivery.
2. A starting point at least five years prior to retirement.
3. It is mostly conducted on employers' time.
4. Employees are exposed to more than ten hours counseling.
5. The employer will foster consultation and will provide for counseling services.
6. The counseling program will provide coverage of all or most of the following issues:

   a. pension and Social Security matters;
   b. personal financial planning and consumer problems;
   c. health and personal care;
   d. housing and living arrangements;
   e. leisure and post retirement employment;
   f. legal aspects.

In chronological sequential terms, the program should encompass:

1. An initial introduction to the issue.
2. A series of "awareness-raising" stimuli.
3. Invitations to take part in the program.
4. Systematic provision of information such as indirect counseling.
5. Special preretirement supports (longer vacations, medical examinations, etc.).
6. Group discussions (preferably with spouses).
7. Formulation of personal plans and testing out plans when feasible (in simulations, short try-outs, etc.).
8. Personal review and firming up plans.
9. Follow-up, postretirement linkages, and supportive services.

Fourth, most programs do not distinguish between preparation for retirement and preparation for aging. Are they the same thing? The trend is to confound them. Most industrial counselors would lead us to believe that, while we could separate them conceptually, in practice they are indistinguishable. Most PRPPs, in this assessment, deal with preparation for aging rather than preparation for retirement. If the latter is related to cessation of occupational, paid employment status, PRPPs ought to give consideration to new career interests, to occupational retraining and the increasing demand for new career escalators, even the notion of leisure careers. In other words, to a series of activity patterns that might very well be incremental or decremental. Too much attention is given by PRPPs to psychological well-being and measures of social adjustment, to the detriment of those activity behavioral sets.

Fifth, and finally, there is a danger that PRPPs may advocate a normative image of the "good life" after retirement. We do not think that they ought to prescribe how each of us should live. If this were the case, they would lead people into fads and cults. Instead, they should prepare the retiree for making his own decisions as to how his "good life" should be constructed.

Are PRPPs programs really needed?

A young or middle aged adult can expect, on the average, a fifteen-to-twenty year period of retirement once he or she reaches age sixty-five. This means an individual average of 30,000 to 35,000 hours of free time. Multiplying that figure by the 25 to 30 million retired persons in 1995 yields the mind-boggling figure of about 800 billion—or close to one trillion—hours, for this particular cohort of people, freed up by the retirement event and for the duration of their life time.

Those figures may be too conservative. Nearly one-third of the 55 and older workers are leaving the labor force because of job market discouragement. Jobs are shrinking for this age group if they become unemployed. Age, as Rosenblum indicated, is a "market" variable rather than a personal one (1975). Slack employer demands, demographic shifts, and difficulties in relocating make employment opportunities scarce, and many middle aged workers simply withdraw from active search. It is this reality of discouragement that underlies to a great extent the trend toward early retirement. It has little to do with affluence or the ultimate triumph of a leisured life style.

Will all that time, and all those lives, be laid to waste? We are not referring to their economic potential only. If they will be spent in anomic lethargy and frustration, sooner or later they are bound to spill over and contaminate all other age groups with a pervasive sense of bitterness and defeat. This is what PRPPs seek to prevent.

References

Arnold, S., Brock, J., Ledford, L., and Richards, H. *Ready or Not: A Study Manual for Retirement*. New York: Manpower Education Institute, 1974.

Ash, P. Preretirement Counseling. *The Gerontologist*, 6 (2): 97-99, 1966.

Charles, D. C. Effect of Participation in a Retirement Program. *The Gerontologist*, 11 (1): 24-28, Part I, 1971.

Greene, M. R., Pyron, H. C., Manion, U. V., and Winkelvoss, H. Preretirement Counseling, Retirement Adjustment and the Older Employee. Graduate School of Management, University of Oregon, Eugene, Oregon: 1969.

Knowles, M. S. *The Modern Practice of Adult Education*. New York Association Press, 1970, p. 51.

Mack, M. J. An Evaluation of a Retirement Planning Program. *Journal of Gerontology*, 13 (2): 198-202, 1958.

Monk, A. The Meaning of Retirement: Role Disvaluation and Psychosocial Unfittedness. Paper presented at the 22nd Annual Convention of the New York State Sociological Association, 1974.

Moody, H. R. Philosophical Presuppositions of Education for Old Age. *Educational Gerontology: An International Quarterly*, 1, 1976, pp. 1-16.

Rosenblum, M. The Last Push: From Discouraged Worker to Involuntary Retirement. *Industrial Gerontology*, 2 (1), 1975, pp. 14-22.

Scheibe, Jr. R. A. *The Psychological Impact of Impending Retirement on Management Personnel*. Unpublished Dissertation. Case Western Reserve University, 1968.

Schein, E. H. *Organizational Psychology*. Englewood Cliffs, New Jersey: Prentice Hall, 1970, pp. 55-71.

Simpson, I. H., Back K., & McKinney, J. C. Work and Retirement. In I. H. Simpson & J. C. McKinney (editors), *Social Aspects of Aging*. Durham: Duke University Press, 1966, pp. 45-46.

Toffler, A. *Future Shock*. New York: Bantam Books, 1970.

5.2

Protective Practice in Serving the Mentally Impaired Aged

Edna Wasser

The problem of the aged person requiring protective services usually surfaces when his way of living and his incapacities arouse a mixture of concern and revulsion in others in his surroundings. Attempts to help and otherwise deal with the problem by many in the community—social agencies, police, church, health services, landlords, relatives—usually culminate in a stalemate. Individual situations are found to be highly complex and thwarting to solve. The aged person is usually fearful and wishes to avoid the entry of others into his life lest they disturb whatever equilibrium he has achieved despite his limitations.

Referral Data

Source: visiting nurse association. Seventy-four-year-old woman, never married, living in vermin-infested unsafe house, refuses to leave, begs food, had a fire, acts paranoid, is diabetic, forgets medication, refuses treatment for ulcers. Visiting nurse, minister, health center, housing and sanitation departments are involved.

Reprinted by permission. *Social Casework*, Vol. 52, No. 8, pp. 510-522.

Source: health center. Eighty-six-year-old woman and sixty-two-year-old unmarried son, both shaky physically and mentally. Son cares for mother, gives her animal medicines, works sporadically, claims he carries a gun, frightens away neighbors.

Source: family service agency. Eighty-year-old man, unmarried, blind, suspicious, demanding, evicted from hotel because of homosexual activity. Unacceptable in various settings—residences, shelter, rest home, home for aged—all attempted through efforts of referring agency.

Source: housing authority. Eighty-four-year-old man and eighty-three-year-old wife, formerly refined couple, deteriorating last two years in appearance, housekeeping. Use newspapers for curtains, confused, living on milk and ice cream. Have marginal income from Social Security and work pension. Refuse nursing home care.

This article reports the essentials of a direct protective service practice in social work with mentally impaired older people who are not institutionalized but are considered, primarily by others, to constitute a high-risk population because of their seriously limited level of functioning and inability to manage alone.[1] The article will also deal with considerations and concepts that have special applicability in work with such older individuals. Comments will be made in reaction to research findings in the study that are of special significance to practitioners and other providers of service.

Because the disorder of the aged person is manifested in his deteriorated social functioning and self-management, social work has been regarded as a logical, although not always welcoming, primary resource in the provision of protective service. Since the aged person is an individual whose needs require that he be dealt with directly in relation to his lessened coping capacity and his disturbed and disturbing relationship with his environment, casework has been regarded as a responsible, indeed, desirable modus operandi. In this report, the practitioner operates as change agent primarily in relation to the client system.

Background

Protective service has developed as part of the broad range of social services to older persons. Although most of the aged manage in a relatively independent way, largely connected with family or other associates, many need help. The aged clientele served by social work represents a continuum of those who are relatively healthy and well functioning but have some difficulties ultimately to the mentally impaired whose functional incapacities result in inability to care for themselves, who lack responsible, responsive relatives or friends, and who are highly vulnerable to exploitation.

Protective service for the aged represents society's way of caring for those of its aging members who have become limited in their capacity to care for themselves and who lack the personal associates who would usually provide care. The service can be viewed also as society's efforts to deal with what it may construe as deviant behavior.

The burgeoning interest in protective services for the aged, heightened during the past fifteen years, has yielded well-intentioned, sporadic, partly interrelated attempts to deal with a grave social problem. Efforts have been on an individual and on a community basis, within the voluntary and public welfare systems and on local, state, and federal levels. They have cut across such disciplines as social work, medicine (including psychiatry), law, and nursing. The literature on protective services reflects much more the concern with the nature of the problem, the person, and various individualized and organizational activities (Wasser, 1961; Lehmann & Mathiasen, 1963; Eckstein & Lindey, 1964; Bennett, 1965; Hall & Mathiasen, 1968; U.S. Dep., 1970; & Martin, 1970) than with a delineation of the casework practice in a direct service (Diamond et al., 1961; Hemmy & Farrar, 1961; Turner, 1966; Wasser, 1966). Literature about work with the mentally impaired aged person tends to deal with him as a patient or resident in an institution (Brody et al., 1971; Kleban, Brody, & Lawton, 1971; Bok, 1971).

The fact that there are twenty million persons over sixty-five years of age in the United States and that 4 to 5 percent of them are institutionalized is well known. Less well known is the reasonably developed, but still to be definitively ascertained, conjecture that there is an additional 7 to 10 percent of older urban population who are mentally impaired and in probable need of some form of protection (Blenkner, Bloom, & Nielsen, 1971).

A central problem of the local community in providing help to aged protective persons is the organization—or lack of organization—and lack of services to meet their needs. The locus for a service, a source that will assume responsibility for carrying through until some reasonable solution is achieved, is troublesome to secure and a function resisted by many established agencies. A limited number of communities are experimenting with different forms of organizational responses. Illustrative solutions include experimenting with geriatric screening units (Levy, Asbury, & Lutovich, 1969; Rypins & Clark, 1968),[2] setting up an office of public guardian (Tri-County, 1970), developing emergency care facilities (Nat'l. Council on the Aging, 1970), creating "foster home" programs that can serve the elderly (State of Washington, 1970), and casework services within the court structure (University of Washington, n.d.).

The concerns on the federal and state levels have to do with the development of policy, legislation, funding, and the promotion of sound relationships with communities and practices in organization and delivery of services. The numerous endeavors within social work about protective services may suggest erroneously that definitive answers have been found concerning their provision. Rather, the range and intensity of activity may be considered a reflection of the complexity of the social problem it attempts to meet.

Casework with aged protective clients

Why is protective service practice with an aged person different from direct practice with one who is not considered to have a protective problem? Who is this person? What are the essential conceptual considerations in providing service? What is intrinsic to such practice? What are the ways of delivering services? What is the process in helping?

The caseworker who serves the older person having a protective problem derives his practice from what has been developed as sound casework with older persons (Diamond et al., 1961; Turner, 1966). He then clarifies additional aspects that are specific to this problem.

Nature of the clientele. Underlying all practice considerations is the nature of the clientele being served. The person with a protective problem has been clearly described and defined, with some variations (Weber, 1964).[3]

The finding that a person has a protective problem is based on the social judgment that he is suffering from a grave incapacity in social functioning manifested by his disorganized behavior and social disorientation. Such a condition can be caused not only by a person's mental incapability, but also interactionally by many social and environmental factors. Mental incapability in association with inadequacy for self-care, lack or inadequacy of others to help, and lack of situational control are focal. Not every person who has a mental disorder has a protective problem.

In the literature, frequent references are made to the person who is dependent and in need of care because of incapacitating physical illness. Many services, particularly medical and nursing, have been developed and generally are accessible to him. These services, however, are generally not accessible to the individual who is mentally incapable and seldom reaches out for care. A thin line separates these two kinds of persons. One who is severely ill organically and who is also unable to negotiate for himself is likely to need protective service. A person's mental capacities are inextricably interwoven with his physical limitations—a condition that results in varying degrees of physical, behavioral, and social dysfunctioning.

The caseworker's practice is bound to be affected by the way in which he understands and deals with behavior. Cognitive processes in aging have been coming under increasing scrutiny (Botwinick, 1967). Traditional methods of assessing a client's personality and ability to function based solely on theories from psychoanalysis and ego psychology limit the practitioner in understanding and working with the aged client who is suffering from thinking deficits that are so largely derived from organic changes and associated with the aging process. When disintegration of the person becomes evident, it is manifested not only by personality changes but also by a breakdown in mentation (memory, orientation, perception, and judgment), which is central to his behavior and inability to perform.

The nature of this older person's pathology is such that an expectation about client motivation for service requires revision. If the client has such serious need, why is there no reaching out for help or effort expended by him to take or use help even when offered?

First, the level of energy available to such a client is very low, and organic failures are likely to drain and limit him. In addition, the caseworker is confronted with ravages in client ego functions, most particularly in the person's mentation and problem-solving processes. Ordinarily a caseworker can assume that a nonpsychotic, nonprotective client who is reacting emotionally to stress, nevertheless has thinking abilities at least potentially in good working order. An aged person also reacts emotionally to his situation, but his thinking processes are likely to be intrinsically affected. How can a person who is drained of energy and is no longer capable of a good level of thought think through the moves to solve a problem in some consistent way? Failure by an aged client to keep appointments or to take his medications may be due not to emotional resistance or lack of wish, but to sheer inability to recall. A lack of impulse control can result not only from lack of control of emotions or a breakthrough of primitive id forces, but from organic senile changes. For diagnosis and treatment, therefore, a reorientation is required to identify specifically the cognitive capacities and limitations that have an overriding effect upon behavior and personality.

The concept of motivation in regard to casework can be reviewed concerning whose responsibility it is to instigate service and under what circumstances. Must the client always be motivated to seek service, or are there times when the worker should provide service so that the client—motivated or not—is cared for and comes to use the service because his need for it is great?

The aged person's failure to seek help or his refusal of help as an intrusion does not represent a measure of his need. Rather, it may cover up his underlying desperation. His will to seek help may have become paralyzed, and his judgment and perception about the very deteriorated conditions in which he lives have diminished along with his strength. Although he cannot reach out for help, his relief can be enormous if a helper succeeds in breaking through these barriers that are defended by his mistrust. Mistrust can be a reaction to previous efforts by others, however well meaning, who try to direct and control him. Mistrust can also be caused by his own increasing sense of vulnerability and diminishing grasp on his selfhood.

Those who would help may be inclined to withdraw from the aged person's mistrust, considering it a refusal. Yet behind a manifest resistance is likely to lie a latent wish to be cared for, protected, and helped. The aged person's anxiety that the refusal represents emphasizes the fear of loss of control and identity.

Intervention and the voluntary and involuntary client. Intervention has become an increasingly familiar concept to social workers (Bartlett, 1970; Briar, 1971). Protective intervention is a dominant component of protective casework practice. It is justified, insofar as intervention in the life of any individual can be justified, by the assumption that self-destructive and dangerous behavior of the aged adult comes not from his free choice but from deteriorating organic and personality changes and that failure to intervene constitutes social neglect.

Aged protective persons who are living alone are, at least to start with, not voluntary but involuntary clients who seldom if ever seek service. If the caseworker is to gain access, to maintain contact, and some control of the individual problem is to be achieved, a central characteristic of the practice is the use of professional authority as expressed in intervention (Wasser, 1971; Bernstein, 1971). Intervention may range all the way from the simple entry of a caseworker into the situation to decision making and decisive action undertaken on behalf of a client. The intervention per se, however narrowly or broadly conceived, is essential to the agency's treatment. Protective intervention with the aged is socially and professionally based. Conceivably, it could become legally based, as in the child protective agency or mental hospital. It can always proceed beyond its own limits to call on legal intervention or genuine power to act.

These elements are different from casework practice with the adult who voluntarily seeks service and does not suffer from such extreme social and mental pathology. When a person ordinarily applies for help, he gives implicit consent for the procedures to follow. He is encouraged to participate in the interactional helping process and to initiate his own planning. The emphasis is on the voluntary agreement of the client even though he is affected and influenced by the contact. In the protective service situation, the agency and worker move away from the relative safety of serving the applying, motivated, voluntary client, to the converse, the nonmotivated and apparently nonvoluntary client.

An important insight from protective practice is that once responsibility is taken for entering into the home and situation and for responding to the obvious need of the client rather than to his inability to ask for help or refusal through fear, the worker is likely to find voluntary clients in many apparently uninterested, unmotivated aged persons. Hence, the first step is to help the aged person become a voluntary client and accept those services that are offered and instituted, regardless of whether he asks for them. When he agrees with or can be influenced to accept the caseworker's judgment about necessary care, he has in essence become a voluntary client whose wishes can guide needed changes. It is possible to work on a voluntary basis with most clients having protective problems.

Nevertheless, a client may continue to resist help. His unwillingness may be only partial and related to one or another aspect of his situation and behavior. He may refuse to accept lifesaving medical advice or attention or to stop eating foods that are harmful, or he may be incapable of doing so. An intervention that is introduced may appear superficially helpful, and yet it may turn out to be intolerable. The worker needs to understand and evaluate the basis for the person's resistive behavior. For example, an elderly blind man with a history of homosexuality is known to have made it unbearable for a series of women home aides, or an ill woman who needs to be helped desperately and who resists a placement plan, nevertheless cannot yield control in any way and accept a home aide. Compromises to enable a client to pursue his wishes often become necessary with a yielding of the seemingly desirable course.

Infrequently, for some aged persons the most critical point may be reached when a decision must be made that the risks and dangers have become too great in following their inclinations and that a step must be taken toward placement against their wishes. It is with such involuntary clients that legal authority is called on, and, for example, guardianship or commitment proceedings are instituted through court procedures.

An older person may at times accept the idea of guardianship quite voluntarily when he has experienced some positive relationship with and trust in the worker, and such an arrangement may be made while the client is enabled to remain at home. Another older person— even one having a fairly good relationship with the agency staff—may take the step to which he has the right and resist the court action. A legal requirement that incompetency be established for guardianship can have devastating impact in humiliation and loss of civil rights, and any ameliorating steps that can help a person retain his sense of control over his own destiny are desirable. Adaptations of the existing system of guardianship have been reviewed considerably.[4]

The securing of guardianship in relation to an involuntary client, however, in no way lessens the difficulty of enforcing legal decisions even though these have been deemed essential for the client's survival. There is no magic in guardianship. How does one proceed to get a completely negativistic, ill, frightened, and helpless person to leave a foul setting that he prefers, although he cannot be cared for adequately there? After all, if the purpose of moving a recalcitrant human being to another setting—even a hospital—is to help him survive, the caseworker must be acutely aware that the client not be destroyed in the process.

The service. The model for the delivery of service that is being reported here uses casework as the core service, complemented by extensive ancillary services, within the structure of a voluntary social agency. The reinforcements provide financial aid, home aide service, medical care, psychiatric consultation and examination, legal consultation and service, fiduciary and guardianship service, and placement service.

The caseworker represents the fulcrum of the service to the individual client, drawing heavily on ancillary services as needs are perceived. The worker carries primary responsibility for serving the client and directing the course of activities with him and with community resources. Values are those that are rooted in individual worth and building trust, that maximize the client's decision-making capacities and sense of mastery, and that are well contained by a circumscribed use of influence. Efforts are strongly directed to enable the client to remain in his familiar surroundings if at all possible and to engage the concern and support of relatives and friends on a disinterested nonexploiting basis. The central dictum is that the caseworker is prepared to do or get others to do whatever is necessary to meet the demands of the situation.

General service goals and areas of sought-for improvement can be considered in relation to the client's welfare, survival, contentment, behavioral or affective signs and symptoms, functional competence, environmental protection, and collateral stress.[5] Although upward change is sought, arrest of deterioration and relief of suffering and stress are valued (Simon, 1970).[6] Although the central emphasis is on direct service to the aged person and treatment of individual situations, inevitably the worker becomes engaged in lesser measure with other persons and institutional structures in the community impinging on or being impinged upon by the client.

The phases in protective intervention and control can be identified as follows:

1. Entering into the situation, whether invited or acceded to by the client. This action means gaining and holding access. The caseworker determines if the client is willing to be helped once he becomes reassured and acquainted with the possibility of assistance. If he is unwilling, the worker attempts to turn the resistive, involuntary client into a voluntary client and helps him to accept assistance. This process entails reaching out to the client, if necessary persistently and repeatedly with tact and understanding of his fears; it means relating, communicating, interacting with, and influencing him.

2. Interposing a variety of supports and services. The worker does not wait to be asked, but deftly introduces what is needed, assuming agreement unless there is marked rejection. The worker presumes that the client develops a taste for service by tasting it.

3. Developing a stand-by plan when unable to effect change. When the situation seems frozen and unchangeable, the worker takes steps deliberately to stand by with a plan in the event of a crisis, which may provide a point of entry for resolution.

4. Determining the advisability of securing legal control if unable to resolve a grave situation. Control over the client's affairs and way of living in some or many aspects may be indicated when such a procedure offers the sole potential for a solution and suitable safeguards and accountability are set up.

Diagnostically, in relation to the specifics for each person, the caseworker arrives at an understanding of the nature of his mental and physical condition, at a working social diagnosis about the need for intervention and supports, and the possibility of stabilizing the situation and effecting some balance in his relationship with his environment. The worker concentrates, usually under community pressure and his own impulses to bring rapid relief, on a functional rather than on an etiological concept (Bennis, Benne, & Chin, eds., 1966), [7] that is, the capacity of the individual to function (Gaitz & Baer, 1970)[8] rather than on the origins of his condition. Acute diagnostic acumen is required for differentiation about what aspects of the client's mental and psychological processes are still relatively intact. These aspects then suggest the areas of functioning and decision making in which the person is still capable and which may be supported and enhanced. Medical evaluation is of overriding importance.

The practitioner's assessment is based on a sound comprehension of the health of the client, his ailments, and his positive physical attributes as they affect his physical and mental functioning; his cognitive capacities and deficiencies; his ego capacities and functioning; his quality as an individual and what he appears to have valued most in his way of living; what meaning his behavior conveys as well as what he can convey orally; the type and nature of his personality structure to the extent it is revealed by his behavior; his libidinal needs and manifestations; the severity and possible reversibility of some aspects of the pathology; his adaptability and in what areas of functioning it appears; the quality of any underlying wish to be helped—even if unexpressed—in juxtaposition with fears of losing control of the directing of his life; his vulnerability to exploitation or his harmful exploitation of others; his possible resistance to intervention; and the sources of deprivation and stress in his environment.

The disorganized person, his way of living, and frequently the great differences in cultural values can have a marked impact on the worker. Dealing with his own reacting negative feelings makes for additional heavy demands on the worker.

Often the severity and critical character of the problems force the worker into making rapid judgments as a basis for quick actions. Crisis theory and concepts offer leads for adaptation in work with aged clientele (Rapoport, n.d.; Oberleder, 1970).[9] The client's personal and social pathology create unusual predicaments and enormous need for help from some source. An interacting stressful impact between the older person and his environment cause a downward spiral, and a crisis or a series of crises tends to occur. The crisis may occur not only at the inception of the casework contact but also in the course of providing service.

Because information about the life history of the client frequently is not obtainable or is accumulated slowly and because casework judgments keep developing along with client reactions to the testing-out techniques used by the worker, the diagnostic process is a dynamically evolving one. In view of the character of the behavior and dysfunctioning of the older person, the diagnostic comprehension of the worker is likely to depend heavily on observations and judgments from ancillary disciplines and service personnel and collaterals. Because of the memory and verbal communication limitations in the client, the worker seeks other sources in the client's milieu for confirmation of data and his own intuitive judgments while he maintains confidentiality.

Simply stated, the caseworker makes an assessment of the activities necessary for the daily living of the client. He also determines whether his mental processes function well enough for him to continue in at least a quasi-independent way in the community if supports are introduced and some health improvement can be achieved.

Ordinarily, a caseworker assumes that a client is able to get to bed at night and arouse himself in the morning; toilet and cleanse himself; obtain, prepare, and eat some foods, however simple; take necessary medications; care for a home in some elementary fashion; and keep track of and spend his money, however little. Many aged persons, however, who have an intense will to remain in their own settings are incapable of carrying out one or many of these functions even unsatisfactorily. The caseworker is faced with determining the specific lacks and whether it is at all possible to create a prosthetic-like or even therapeutic environment within the home (Lindsley, 1964).[10] Practical devices and supports of various kinds, such as home aide service, visiting nurse service, and medical and paramedical services, can be introduced. It is intended that they lessen stress and stimulate the older person to keep whatever sense of wholeness his usual setting may provide, improve his self-image, and feel less depressed.

The treatment process is carried out with a full comprehension by the worker that a person's psychic (and perhaps physical) survival is likely to depend as much on retention of his sense of self, of which his will is central, as on the amelioration of the deteriorating forces in his person and social situation. It is particularly necessary to balance interventions intended for the very survival of the client against the negative impact that these can have on the client's sense of self, will, and control of his own life.

The purposes of treatment steps are the alleviation of the suffering of the client, the amelioration of the conditions under which he is living up to a minimum level of human decency, the improvement of his physical and mental health and sense of well-being, and the deterrence of further deterioration. To this end, the worker supplements client resources with agency funds and the ancillary resources. These add to what the worker is able to bring to the relationship with the client through supportive encouragement, persuasion, and the strength of his own ego—which, it may be said, needs to be strong indeed.

The referring individual may prepare the client for the worker's visit, although many clients may not comprehend explanations. The referrent may accompany the caseworker on the first visit to lessen client fears about a new person. The client may be asked to tell what is bothering and troublesome to him. Concern is shown by demonstration. For a person who has not eaten, is without food, or is unable to cook, food may be purchased and cooked on an emergency basis. An immediate action for hospitalization and medical care may be taken, or a rapid appraisal of the person may cause the worker to revisit, observe, evaluate slowly, gather knowledge about him, and test out what he can and may wish to do. Momentum is sustained by frequent visiting and continuing assessment as the client is given the opportunity to learn about the benign and helping intent of the worker.

The caseworker with good humor and a gentle, light touch suggests, persuades, and enables the client to act in his own home so that he may gradually achieve and maintain basic decent standards of self-care. Faced with varying degrees and kinds of resistance, the worker facilitates planning regarding problems of health, housing, money, basic conduct in daily living, relatives, and other persons.

Social treatment commences as judgments are made, often immediately. Imperceptible relational experiences introduced by the professional person set subtle forces of influence into motion. At times, even larger quite perceptible interventive actions may win client accord.

The caseworker frequently intervenes in the client's behalf with such outside environmental forces as neighbors, landlord, or other offended community representatives in order to lessen the impact and stress on the client and win them over to helpfulness. The caseworker may intervene by stimulating outside authorities, such as the health, fire, and police departments, to present realistic requirements to the client that he meet community standards. The aged person who gathers rubbish or collects wood but is careless about fire can seriously endanger himself and others. By using outside authorities, the caseworker can structure reality requirements, becoming not the enforcer but the assistant to the client in meeting standards.

Decision making weighs heavily on the caseworker as it looms larger than is usual in casework practice. Decisions must be made about when, how, to what degree, and, indeed, whether to act. The worker is constantly weighing alternatives and evaluating likely outcomes. How much risk should be tolerated for the sake of the client if the risk involves the opposing interests of others? Do the risks of remaining in his setting overbalance the gratifications for the client? At what point and on what basis is a decision made to help the client remain in his own setting or to influence him to change to a new one—most usually to a nursing home? If the client is unwilling, should legal recourse be sought and guardianship obtained? Is commitment indicated?

To the extent possible, the client can be encouraged to make decisions and act on his own, even if the choices are relatively simple, such as selecting his clothing, choosing his foods, or arranging his household. Acceptance of these choices conveys the worker's regard for him.

That an intervention may be great or of critical importance may not be felt by the client. Much depends on the way the intervention is handled by the worker. When the incapacity is crucial to life or safety and the person himself does nothing about it, the greater is the need for intervention. When a person needs to be persuaded or induced to stop some behavior, the simplest way is found. The worker acts himself or gets others to act.

For example, Mrs. B is a diabetic who can be impelled into a diabetic coma by her lack of self-control in eating sweets. The caseworker simply removes the sweets and encourages other sources of gratification. Mr. K lives in a third-rate hotel. His poor judgment in disregarding medical recommendations, medications, and diet are leading him to congestive heart failure. "How can eating ham hurt?" He cannot grasp the possible harmful results of salted foods. When he becomes gravely ill, it takes the combined activity of the caseworker and the visiting nurse to persuade the hotel manager, who is not eager to lose a paying customer but who has some influence with Mr. K, to take him to the hospital.

With the caseworker acting as a central regulator, ancillary services all play indispensable collaborative parts in varying degrees in the seeking of solutions and the meeting of needs. It is difficult for the caseworker to make quick decisions if no emergency funds are available. Collaboration with a particular member of a different profession is useful not only in the individual case but on pertinent broader issues affecting the larger social problem of protective services in the community.

Home aides are invaluable in the everyday living of the client and in the planning for his care. They can provide home care, cooking, shopping, companionship, personal care, and some simple nursing procedures. The introduction, continuance, and discontinuance of the service is integral to the casework planning. A preliminary evaluation of the kind and amount of service is made. Training and supervision of home aides make their service effective. In most instances, part-time service is sufficient.

Practical supportive devices can help. Memory aids can be built into a client's way of living, such as putting a sign on the kitchen counter that reminds him to take his pills or placing his medication in a familiar place. The worker's visit or a medical examination can be flagged by a telephone call the previous day. Since isolation may play into memory loss through sensory deprivation, it is useful to introduce the stimulation of other persons, such as a home aide, or to take the person out-of-doors to expose him to others.

Can the aged person's self-awareness about his limitations be used to build in protections? Do these limitations interfere with his well-being? How anxious is he? Is the client's memory poor? After all, defect of memory does not mean that a person is not able to eat, dress, or sleep. The nature of the client's incapacity is a clue to what needs to be built in or what substitutions have to be made.

Although improved nutrition, physical care, understanding, and stabilization of a situation may make for some improvement in behavior, it is difficult to judge if the pathological processes have been reversed or if that which is latently present thereby becomes more usable by the individual. The emotional support received from the concern and attention are bound to have a benign effect on the ego functions of many persons.

Frequently other individuals can be found who have some significant, if not always healthy, association with the client. Such persons may represent either substitute familial supports or drains upon the aged person and need to be included in the diagnostic assessment and planning. The involvement of the agency offers relief to many collaterals who may be finding the aged person an insoluble burden.

The beginning phase of treatment is likely to make the greatest demands on the time, planning, and activity of the caseworker. By its nature, care of the mentally impaired person is potentially long term, but once a situation is brought into some balance, the caseworker may be needed relatively little except at points of stress or change. Paraprofessional workers or home aides are able to meet client needs on a continuing basis (Farrar & Hemmy, 1963 & 1969).

If improvement or stabilization is not achieved, nursing home placement or mental hospital commitment are ultimate next steps. A basic principle in protective service is that when a crucial issue in the life of the client allows for no other solution and when all conceivable courses have been attempted, the most drastic step of calling in legal intervention be readily undertaken. When a legally based form of intervention and control is resorted to, the manifestations leading to it are (1) a medical problem of unusual gravity about which a client cannot, and will not, or fails to take the necessary steps for the treatment that is essential for life; (2) an emergency or direct threat to a client's life; and (3) the client's inability to make a decision on his own behalf in an aspect that is crucial to his life. Important is the fact that the person nevertheless may be able to be self-determining in some other aspects of his functioning.

But what will be the effect on the client who yields to persuasion to accept a change to a nursing home or a mental hospital? Will enforced placement create more trauma than continuance in a risky home setting? Does the fact that the worker, neighbors, relatives, or community agencies find an individual's way of living intolerable or unbearably risky mean that the changing must be solely by the aged person? Will the person do better if he must be moved by force to a sanitary, new place of good quality that may nevertheless have a disintegrating effect upon him? Whose needs is the move serving? It is most important to evaluate the danger of "transplantation shock" that may result from placement.

Perspectives on practice and research findings

The research finding of a higher death rate among those who received service in the project and of its possible link to institutionalization challenges review of the use of the institution, particularly the nursing home, in work with the aged protective client. In social welfare, the institutional solution for social problems has undergone reexamination and revision in one field of service after another—in child welfare for quite a time, in progressive corrections, and in mental health with its newer emphasis on community-based services. In each, the institution has come to be conceived less to serve the dilemma of society in its efforts to rid itself physically of the one who is disturbing and more to serve the needs of the troubled individual. For the aged protective individual and perhaps for the aged generally, the time has come for a reevaluation of whose purposes are served by the institutional solution.

It is especially noteworthy in a professional protective program so highly oriented toward noninstitutional solutions and rich in the many supporting services ordinarily not available, that service should nevertheless be associated with the likelihood of institutionalization at a rate higher than would occur even in the ordinary course of events. In another article on this issue, the authors suggest a societal and a practice ambivalence that treats the aged protective client as borderline between social deviance and social disorganization (Blenkner et al., 1971).

When the protective client is viewed by the society in which he lives as a social deviant, albeit one who may be unable to control his conduct without outside help, if at all, a practitioner, however well trained professionally, inevitably carries within himself as a member of this society some germ of such an attitude. Ambivalence is supported by the fact that the practitioner functions with a dual stream of opposing incentives, that of dealing with a protective client as a self-determining adult and, simultaneously, as one for whom serious interventions are required if he is to be helped to bring his disturbed and disturbing behaviors under control.

It is possible that even trained practitioners are unable to tolerate taking the risks involved in leaving alone many elderly people who prefer to continue in their unwholesome, marginal way of life. The frightening spectre remains of the occasional protective person who is consumed by fire in his own home or attacked by his starving animals. Yet interventions, especially institutionalization, may be felt deeply by an aged person to be contraventions of his will and his most cherished desires rather than care and protection. A throttling of his life force may occur and diminish his impulse to survive. This effect is likely to be as true for a mentally impaired person as for one considered normal. The impact may be magnified by the helplessness of the debilitated aged person to resist.

Removal from society is usually construed as a punitive action, even though the deviant behavior or conditions may not be within the individual's control. The aged person with a protective problem—like the carrier of contagious disease—has lived in society, absorbed the meanings of its constraints, and regards removal as punishment. The worker who often expends innumerable efforts unsuccessfully to avoid the institutionalization route may also consider it as punishment.

From another stance, survival may be reevaluated as a measure of treatment success. Is it the fact alone of survival or is it also the quality of survival that is important? The how of living and the meaning of dying and death raise important philosophical and ethical problems and are coming under increasingly intensive study (Kübler-Ross, 1969; Weisman & Kastenbaum, 1964; & Pearson, 1969). Is total death always associated with unfavorable status? With those who are in terminal decline, are there times when cessation of life may be considered favorable? If so, at what specific time in an individual's decline would it be? Theorists have conceptualized various aspects of death—psychological death, social death, physical death. Even the exact time that death is considered to occur physiologically is under medical scrutiny.

In addition to the results on survival, some notice should be taken of several other suggestive research findings significant to the practitioner. First, although the data were not as complete as desired for definitive conclusions, the reaction to the helpfulness of agency service by participant, collateral, and referring agency was highly favorable (Blenkner et al., 1971). Further, although the number of collaterals was limited by the nature of the sample under study, service was found to have the effect of relieving collateral stress. The implication is clear for the value of service to relatives and other associates who are under stress because of the aged person's problems.

In addition to that which appears pragmatically sound in the direct practice approach described herein, some leads are implicit for ongoing practice. The caseworker, whose roles are expanding in current practice reconceptualizations (Briar, 1967), emerges here as a kind of regulator, case manager or balance wheel in the intermeshing of the needed disciplines, or supporter of client strengths along with that of interviewer and decision maker, and of provider of services. The emphasis on behavior, on the cognitive as well as on the social functioning of the protective client, and on the provision of supportive means within the home setting suggests inquiry into use of behavior modification techniques (Thomas, 1970). Moreover, the way is open for adaptations of what is clearly an unusually expensive form of service if highly trained professional caseworkers are used exclusively. Instead, centralizing responsibility for leadership in a case situation and identifying the crucial points when expertise is required in the social planning can make it possible to provide sustaining adequate paraprofessional services in a much more extensive way so that many more needy aged can be reached.

In this article, the emphasis has been on the practitioner as change agent and intervenor in the client system. A more comprehensive community-wide systems approach to the social problem of protective services for the aging adult may well incorporate those direct service practices found to be desirable (Purvine & Billingsley, 1970; & Pincus & Minahan, 1970).

The kinds of needed community-based services to provide protection are fairly clearly known and require expansion. Institutional care that serves the needs of others than the aged protective client is far too costly in human values as well as in economics. Although institutional facilities that truly serve the genuine needs of the aged protective client are essential in the continuum of care, these could well be far less necessary if adequate community-based services are available and sensitively delivered.

Finally, as the protective syndrome in social welfare has been increasingly comprehended in mental health and public health terms, thoughts about prevention arise. In relation to the public health framework, the protective service described here represents the tertiary level in its efforts at disability limitation and rehabilitation. Prevention at earlier levels may be sought at critical points sooner in the lives of aging people when interventions and services may lessen the numbers and extreme conditions of the aged who develop problems that require protective services.

Notes

1. The direct practice was developed by the casework and ancillary service staff of the Benjamin Rose Institute, Cleveland, Ohio, who were involved in the protective service project. This article is based on the practice of Helen Cole, Helen Beggs, Jane Lenahan, and Margaret McGuire, caseworkers on the project. A more inclusive document on this practice is contained in the full report of the study.

2. The Baltimore Geriatric Evaluation Service of the Baltimore City Department of Health, Baltimore, MD. Lee Muth, director, also conducted experiments in geriatric screening.

3. Definition: "A non-institutionalized person sixty years of age or older, whose behavior indicates that he is mentally incapable of adequately caring for himself and his interests without serious consequences to himself or others; and has no relative or other private individual able and willing to assume the kind and degree of support and supervision required to control the situation." See also Hall and Mathiasen, *Overcoming Barriers*, op. cit., pp. 13-18.

4. For discussion of the idea of a "social guardian," see Helen Turner, Personality Functioning in Later Life. See also John B. Martin, Protective Services, on the need for surrogate and conservator services and recognition of the activities of the Office of Economic Opportunity and the American Bar Association in bringing about more desirable laws.

5. These items represent the variables under study in the Benjamin Rose Institute Project on Protective Services.

6. Simon states, "Inherent in the discussion of change permeation is a notion of prevention. And a kind of prevention—arrest or deterrence of continuing deterioration or disability development—has been implicit in the caseworker's goals of treatment throughout our history."

7. The editors draw particular attention to the etiological pitfall in which practitioners may become entrapped in searching for causes and a consequent effort to remedy the original causes. They suggest, "One way of avoiding this pitfall of extreme dependence upon 'etiology' is for the change-agent to start with scientific formulations of a strategy of action and intervention and then test the relevance of the diagnosis of origins or causes against the proposed plan."

8. The article deals with assessment based on functional capacity.

9. Rapoport discriminates between client groups for whom crisis intervention as defined by her may or may not be deemed effective. In responding to her own question—"When is a 'crisis' not a crisis?"—she alludes to those " . . . who live in a chronic state of crisis. For them, being in a state of crisis is a life style." For these people, emergency and first aid help is often needed. See also Muriel Oberleder, Crisis Therapy in Mental Breakdown of the Aging, *The Gerontologist*, 10:111-14 (Summer 1970).

10. Lindsley explains that the prosthetic environment compensates for the specific behavior deficit of the aged person so that the deficits are less debilitating. In contrast he says, "Therapeutic environments are essentially training or retraining centers for the generation of behavioral skills which maintain themselves once the patient has left the therapeutic environment."

References

Bartlett, H. H. *The Common Base of Social Work Practice.* New York: National Association of Social Workers, 1970, pp. 76-80; 161-90.

Bennett, L. L. Adult Protective Services and Law: Some Relevant Socio-Legal Considerations (Paper presented at the meeting on Protective Services for the Aging, American Public Welfare Association Northeast Regional Conference, New York, N.Y., September 13, 1965).

Bennis, Benne, & Chin (eds.), *The Planning of Change: Reading in the Applied Behavioral Sciences.* New York: Holt, Rinehart & Winston, 1966, pp. 196-197.

Bernstein, S. Self-Determination: King or Citizen in the Realm of Values. *Authority and Social Work: Concept and Use,* ed. Shankar A. Yelaja. Toronto: University of Toronto Press, 1971.

Blenkner, M., Bloom, M., & Nielsen, M. A Research and Demonstration Project of Protective Services. *Social Casework,* 52, October 1971, pp. 483-99.

Briar, S. The Current Crisis in Social Casework, *Social Work Practice, 1967: Selected Papers, 94th Annual Forum, National Conference on Social Welfare,* Dallas, Texas, May 21-26, 1967. New York: Columbia University Press, 1967, pp. 19-33.

Botwinick, J. *Cognitive Processes in Maturity and Old Age.* New York: Springer Publishing Co., 1967.

Brody, E. et al. Excess Disabilities of Mentally Impaired Aged: Impact of Individualized Treatment. *The Gerontologist,* II, Part 1, Summer 1971, pp. 124-33.

Diamond, B. et al. Casework with the Aging: Proceedings of a Seminar at Arden House, Harriman Campus of Columbia University, October 30-November 4, 1960. *Social Casework,* 42, May-June 1961, pp. 217-90.

Eckstein, R. & Lindey, E. eds. *Seminar on Protective Services for Older People: Proceedings of a Seminar Held at Arden House, Harriman, New York, March 10-15, 1963.* New York: National Council on Aging, 1964.

Farrar, M. & Hemmy, M. L. Use of Nonprofessional Staff in Work with the Aged. *Social Work* 8, July 1963; and Family Service Association of America, Social Work Team with Aging Family Service Clients: Third Summary Progress Report, submitted to the National Institute of Mental Health, mimeo. New York: Family Service Association of America, August 31, 1969.

Gaitz, C. M. & Baer, P. E. Diagnostic Assessment of the Elderly: A Multifunctional Model. *The Gerontologist,* Part 1, 10. Spring 1970, pp. 47-52.

Hall, G. H. & Mathiasen, G., eds. *Overcoming Barriers to Protective Services for the Aged: Report of a National Institute on Protective Services, Savoy Field Hotel, Houston, Texas, January 16-18, 1968.* New York: National Council on the Aging, 1968.

Hemmy, M. L. & Farrar, M. S. Protective Services for Older People. *Social Casework,* 42, January 1961, pp. 16-20.

Kleban, M. H., Brody, E. M., & Lawton, M. P. Personality Traits in the Mentally Impaired Aged and their Relationships to Improvements in Current Functioning. *The Gerontologist,* II, Part 1, Summer 1971, pp. 124-33.

Kübler-Ross, E. *On Death and Dying.* London: Macmillan & Co., 1969.

Lehman, V. & Mathiasen, G. *Guardianship and Protective Services for Older People.* Albany, NY: National Council on the Aging Press, 1963.

Levy, R. J., Asbury, D. M., & Lutovich, G. Inpatient and Emergency Services. *Handbook of Community Health Practice: The San Mateo Experience.* H. R. Lamb, D. Healy, & J. H. Downing, eds. San Francisco: Jossey-Bass, 1969, pp. 82-116.

Lindsley, O. R. Geriatric Behavioral Prosthetics. *New Thoughts on Old Age.* R. Kastenbaum, ed. New York: Springer, 1964, p. 46.

Martin, J. B. Protective Services. Position paper, Administration on Aging of U.S. Department of Health, Education, & Welfare, presented at the Conference on Protective Services, San Diego, CA, April 29-May 1, 1970.

National Council on the Aging. Progress Report on Project for Developing an Emergency Care Facility for Older Persons in Need of Protection, mimeo. New York: National Council on the Aging, 1970.

Oberleder, M. Crisis Therapy in Mental Breakdown of the Aging. *The Gerontologist,* 10, Summer 1970, pp. 111-14.

Pearson, L., ed. *Death and Dying: Current Issues in the Treatment of the Dying Person.* Cleveland: The Press of Case Western Reserve, 1969.

Pincus, A. & Minahan, A. Toward a Model for Teaching a Basic First-Year Course in Methods of Social Work Practice. *Innovations in Teaching Social Work Practice,* Lillian Ripple, ed. New York: Council on Social Work Education, 1970, pp. 34-57.

Purvine, M. & Billingsley, A. Protective Service as a Social System. *Journal of Public Social Services,* I, March 1970, pp. 34-45.

Rapoport, L. Crisis Intervention as a Mode of Brief Treatment. *Theories of Social Casework,* R. W. Roberts & R. H. Nee, eds. Chicago: The University of Chicago Press, 1970, p. 304.

Rypins, R. F. & Clark, M. L. A Screening Project for the Geriatric Mentally Ill. *California Medicine,* 109, October 1968, pp. 273-278.

Simon, B. K. Social Casework Theory: An Overview. *Theories of Social Casework*, Roberts & Nee, eds., op. cit., p. 392.

State of Washington, Department of Social and Health Services, Division of Public Assistance, Foster Family Homes for Adults (Progress Report 1115, Project No. 11-P-57021/0-03, December 31, 1970).

Thomas, E. J. Behavioral Modification and Casework. *Theories of Social Casework*, Roberts & Nee, eds., op. cit.

Tri-County Community Council. *Proposal for a Public Guardianship Project in Multnomah County.* Portland, OR: Tri-County Community Council, 1970.

Turner, H. Personality Functioning in Later Life: Implications for Practice. *Planning Welfare Services for Older People: Papers presented at the Training Institute for Public Welfare Specialists in Aging, Cleveland, Ohio, June 13-24, 1965.* Washington, D.C.: U.S. Dept. of HEW, Welfare Administration, Bureau of Family Services, 1966, pp. 59-65.

United States Department of Health, Education, and Welfare, *Project on Protective Services Interim Report*, prepared for the Social and Rehabilitation Service by J. J. Burr. Washington, D.C.: U.S. Dept. of HEW, 1970.

University of Washington, School of Social Work, Education and Development in Gerontological Service. Proposal for Grant no. 94-P-50072-9-01, Administration on Aging, U.S. Dept. of HEW.

Wasser, E. Responsibility, Self-Determination, and Authority in Casework Protection of Older Persons. *Social Casework*, 42, May-June 1961, pp. 258-66. Reprinted in *Authority and Social Work: Concept and Use*, op. cit., pp. 182-95.

———. *Casebook on Work with the Aging.* New York: Family Service Association of America, 1966.

———. *Creative Approaches in Casework with the Aging.* New York: Family Service Association of America, 1966.

———. Responsibility, Self-Determination, and Authority. *Authority and Social Work: Concept and Use*, op. cit.

Weber, R. E. Older Persons in Need of Protective Service Encountered by Thirteen Selected Cleveland Agencies in March, 1964: A Survey, mimeo. Cleveland, OH: Benjamin Rose Institute Protective Service Project Progress Report on Planning Phase, Supporting Document no. 3, September 1964.

Weisman, A. D., & Kastenbaum, R. The Psychological Autopsy: A Study of the Terminal Phase of Life. *Community Mental Health Journal.* Monograph Series, no. 4. New York: Behavioral Publications, 1964.

5.3

Will You Still Need Me, Will You Still Feed Me When I'm 64?

Marvin B. Sussman, Donna Vanderwyst, and Gwendolyn K. Williams

There was a period of time from 1910 to 1947 when, due to a housing shortage, 10 percent of American households were three generational. Since then the number has steadily decreased (Wake & Sporakowski, 1972). But lately with the continued increase in life expectancy, the prohibitive costs of nursing homes, the renewed interest in home health care as opposed to institutional care, and the prospects that persons over age 65, still in good health and able to contribute to the family materially and with services, has rekindled interest in the three generational family form. Members of the Congress have expressed similar concerns. Senator Buckley introduced a bill in the 1975 Congress which could provide a $1,000 income tax deduction for any household which provided a home for an aged member.

Government and social scientists are collecting data to try to determine if the American family is willing to house and care for their aged members. To date, the data do not indicate affirmative or negative conclusions on the American family's willingness to provide a creative environment for its aged members.

Presented at the 29th Annual Meeting, The Gerontological Society, October 13-17, 1976, New York City. This study was supported by funds from the Administration on Aging, DHEW, "Incentives and Family Environments for the Elderly," Grant #90-A-C16.

This study is one attempt to ascertain the conditions and circumstances under which member units of family networks will provide a more than custodial environment for its aged members. What are the optimal conditions and situations for providing an attractive environment and relationship for all members across two or more generations? Some of these conditions and situations are location of the household (rural/urban), stage in the family cycle of the household (beginning, middle-age family), socioeconomic and ethnic status of family, and the provision of financial and social incentives such as cash allotments, tax rebates, health care, homemaking, and similar types of services.

Space does not allow for summarizing past research or the theoretical premises of this particular investigation. What can be done is to present some findings from our group of 101 elderly persons and sample of 356 households. First, some findings from 101 older respondents.

Respondents were volunteers present at meetings of organizations who agreed to allow us to come to their meeting to present our study and to interview their members; hence this is not a random sample but a group. Eighty-five percent of the respondents are women; 73 percent are white. Respondents range in age from 55 to 89. The mean age is 74. Respondents' income ranges from under $1,000 per year to $15,000. Twenty-six percent are presently married and living with their spouse. Sixty-four percent live alone, seven percent live with one of their children, and three percent live with either another relative or a friend. Thirty-two percent say that they would have problems that would make it hard for them to continue to live in their home if there was no one to help them.

The study inquired how this group of older people felt about the government offering incentives to families who would take in their aged relatives. Eighty-seven percent had positive reactions to the program. Thirty-six percent of these people thought it was good because it would help the older person. Of those giving negative opinions about the incentive program, the most frequent reasons given for this view was that older people and their families should not live together because of the problems in getting along with relatives and because of their belief that older people should remain independent.

Forty-two percent thought that the monthly check was the best incentive in our proposed program because it was the most flexible, it helped older people stay independent, and it would help with both the older person's and the family's expenses. Twenty-six percent of the respondents liked the medical care incentive best because they perceived it as the most useful one for older people because of the high risk of getting sick and needing costly medical attention.

If the incentive program could offer families two incentives, one financial and one service, the majority of older people in this sample would want families to receive both the monthly check (71 percent) and the medical care (54 percent). In the interview, we described two older persons, one healthy and one not, who wanted to move in with their nieces. We asked respondents in our sample if they thought that the niece should invite the older person to come to live with the niece's family. Forty-three percent thought the niece should take in the able older person. Sixty-two percent of those who were opposed to the move said that the older person should not move in because it would interfere with the family's privacy and life style and would thus cause friction in the family. Fifty percent of the sample thought that the niece should take in the older woman recovering from a stroke. Nineteen percent of the sample was against the move because they felt the older person needed more care than the family could give. Most of the respondents (78 percent) said that the program would be an incentive to the families to take in both of the older people we described in our scenarios. In both cases, there was strongest agreement that the monthly check would be the most appropriate incentive because it would help with the expenses of the family and the older person.

The majority (76 percent) of the sample said that they preferred to live in their own home. It seems that only when older individuals cannot fend for themselves is there an expressed willingness by the elderly person to live with a family.

There does seem to be some relationship between an older person, in our sample, identifying with an ethnic group and their willingness to live with relatives if asked. Those who identify with an ethnic group were more likely to be willing to live with their kin than were those who have no such identification.

Two other variables were found to be related to the older people's willingness to live with relatives. These are the number of people the older person has a lot of contact with, and the number of people the older person can count on to help him or her in times of trouble. Older people, in our sample, who have more relatives that they can count on and/or who have more relatives that they have a lot of contact with are also more inclined to be willing to live with kin, if asked, than are those who have less or no relatives whom they have contact with and/or can count on.

Turning to the larger sample of 356 households selected at random and stratified by race and socioeconomic status, we present only a summary of our major findings. It will be recalled that one major focus was whether incentives provided to member units of extended family networks would facilitate the process of reintroducing elderly persons into the household.

The incentives the respondents were asked to evaluate included both financial and service programs. The financial programs consisted of a monthly check ($200-$400) to reimburse the family for expenses in caring for an older person, a tax deduction, a low cost loan for home improvement, food stamps, and a rental allowance or property deduction. The service programs included medical care for the elderly person, a visiting service which could provide companionship for the older person and someone to stay with him/her when necessary, a social center for older people, an information center which could provide information on services available to the family, a meals on wheels program for the noon meal, and a home aide service to help with household tasks or in the personal care of the older relative.

The respondents ranked each group of incentive programs from most to least desirable. Data show a clearcut first preference for the monthly check among the financial incentives and a preference for the program of medical care among the service incentives. Over six times as many respondents preferred the monthly check program to the next highest ranking financial incentives (tax deduction and food stamps), and over seven times as many respondents preferred medical care to any of the other service incentives.

When the respondents were asked to consider all incentive programs and pick the one they felt was most desirable, the same pattern was apparent. Also of interest is the fact that the incentives liked least were the low cost loan and the meals on wheels. In general, the respondents as a group feel that incentive programs can be useful. They are perceived as being helpful to older people and their families. Only 5.8 percent gave generally negative responses when asked about the overall usefulness of the programs.

General Willingness to Provide a Home for Older People

The majority of respondents do not believe that institutionalization is a desirable alternative for older individuals who do not want to live alone. Slightly over 58 percent indicated that older persons should not have to go to a home for the aged.

A direct question concerned with the willingness of an individual to accept an older person who wants to live in his/her home revealed about the same distribution of responses as noted above. Approximately 60 percent said yes and about 33 percent said no, with the remainder being unsure. Respondents who answered no were then asked if they would *ever* accept an older person in their household. Slightly less than 30 percent of those who originally answered no said that under certain circumstances they would accept an older person in their household.

In summary, the data suggest that most families (assuming the respondent acts as a spokesman for the family) will accept older people in the household in some circumstances. There is, however, a hard core of approximately 19 percent (of the total 356 cases) who have indicated that they would not take in older persons under any conditions.

Responsibility for the Elderly

Individuals who initially said they were not willing (hard core and others) to accept an older person in the household were also asked who should take the responsibility for old people when they can no longer live alone. Over half of the respondents indicated that family or relatives were responsible. Of particular interest, however, is the fact that almost 40 percent said that the government was responsible. Although these individuals are a fairly small proportion of the total sample, they do indicate a willingness of at least some part of the public to place the responsibility for care of the elderly in the domain of the government.

Incentives and Willingness to Care for the Elderly

In order to determine the respondents' willingness to care for the elderly in different situations, and the perceived value of the incentive programs under these conditions, six scenarios were presented (see Table 1). The respondents were asked, for each situation, whether or not they would be willing to have the older person(s) live with them, if any of the above programs would be an incentive to them (or the hypothetical niece or nephew in the scenarios) to accept the older person, and if so, which program.

With respect to the respondents' willingness to accept an older person, the data reveal a particularly interesting result. The one scenario in which the older person is a solitary man is the only one to show less than 50 percent of the respondents willing to accept him in the household. The same is true with respect to the incentive programs. Again, this is the only scenario in which less than 50 percent indicated that any of the incentive programs would act as an impetus to accept him in the household.

This finding may simply reflect an awareness that the reason for wanting to live with his relatives is more trivial than in any of the other

---

Table 1.   Scenarios

1. Mrs. M's husband died recently and since then she has been feeling rather useless. Now at age 68 she has decided that she would like to live with her niece's family in order to help care for the children and help out in other ways.

2. Mrs. W. is a 74-year-old active member of the neighborhood senior citizen group. She also makes beautiful quilts which she then sells for extra income. Recently she has been thinking of moving in with her niece who lives in the same neighborhood. Mrs. W. has had some problems with the plumbing in her house and thinks it is time to sell the house.

3. Miss D. has never been married. Three weeks ago she had a stroke. The hospital now wants to release her. She is not able to return to her second floor apartment because, at least for a while, she is confined to a wheel chair and needs help with getting a bath and with meals. She is thinking about asking her niece if she could stay with them for a while.

4. Mrs. B. is a very lonely 69-year-old woman. Almost daily she calls up her niece to talk with her. Her greatest desire would be to live with her niece's family.

5. Mr. Z., who is 66, is very active and independent. His wife suddenly passed away a few months ago. Mr. Z. has tried but can't cook. He has been unsuccessful in having someone come in and cook his meals, but he has been able to take care of all the household tasks, such as laundry and cleaning, as well as to continue working at this part-time job. He is thinking of asking his nephew if he could stay with them a while.

6. Mr. and Mrs. H have lived in the same small house for nearly sixty years. Last month they received a letter from the state informing them that their property is part of the land being purchased by the state for a new freeway. The couple cannot afford to buy another home. Because of long waiting lists, they have been unable to find housing in any of the subsidized apartments for the elderly. They are thinking about asking their niece and nephew if they can live with them a while.

---

scenarios, or it may reflect a bias on the part of the respondents (mostly women) against solitary older males. The latter possibility bears further investigation.

The choice of incentive programs for each scenario at least partially reflects the particular problems faced by each elderly person. For the most part, the monthly check is seen as the most desirable incentive. However, in the scenario where the older person is a stroke victim, the home aide service and medical care are seen as the most important incentives by a large percentage of the respondents. In the scenario where loneliness is the problem, the social center is seen as the most desirable incentive by a relatively large percentage of the respondents.

In general, the data support earlier results and suggest that at least a small majority of respondents would be willing to take in an older relative in most situations. The data also suggest that at least a small majority feel the different programs would act as an incentive to accept an older relative in the home in most situations. However, these data are somewhat misleading in that (1) the majority of the respondents are willing to accept older relatives with no incentives, and (2) the question concerning the value of incentives was also generalized to the hypothetical niece or nephew.

Respondents who answered no when asked if they would accept an older relative who wanted to live with them were also asked, in a more general context, if any of the incentive programs would influence them. Only 13 percent responded positively. Over 95 percent, however, felt the incentives would influence other people to accept elderly persons. Thus, it may be that the incentive programs will be most valuable in providing support to the majority of families already willing to accept older relatives, and have little effect in encouraging families who currently are opposed to accepting elderly persons in their household.

Summary of Research Results

An analysis of the respondents' ranking of the financial and service incentives revealed that a monthly check was the highest ranked financial incentive by approximately two-thirds of the respondents. Similarly, medical care was rated the most desirable service incentive by about two-thirds of the respondents. Consideration of all incentive programs simultaneously reinforced the perceived importance of these incentives. Slightly less than half the respondents selected a monthly check as the most desirable incentive, and about 22 percent considered medical care the most desirable incentive. The incentives liked least were the low cost loan and the meals on wheels program. With only a few exceptions, this same pattern for incentives liked best and least is found among the various race, class, and marital status-duration of marriage subgroupings.

The results also indicated that the majority of respondents felt some responsibility for older relatives and would be willing to accept an older person in their home, at least under certain circumstances. Only about 19 percent of the respondents definitely indicated that they would not be willing to accept an older person under any circumstances. Also significant is the fact that approximately 70 percent of the respondents not willing to accept an older person (including those who would accept under some circumstances) feel it is the government's responsibility to care for older people.

A more specific examination of the willingness to accept an older person in the household in different situations suggested that in most cases (the respondents were presented with six scenarios) at least a small majority would be willing to take in an older relative. An interesting exception is when the older person is a solitary male. In addition, at least a small majority feel that the financial and service programs would act as an incentive to accept an older person in the home in most situations. It is important to note, however, that when individuals who initially indicated they were not willing to take in an older person were asked in a more general context if any of the incentive programs would influence them, only 13 percent answered yes.

Further analysis of the willingness to accept an older person in the household suggested an interesting pattern of interaction by race, class, and marital status. Among single respondents, blacks are somewhat more willing to accept an older person than are whites, regardless of income. On the other hand, among married respondents this pattern is found only for lower-income families. Upper-income whites are somewhat more willing to accept an older person than are upper-income blacks.

The Cleveland data indicate that the majority of respondent families will take in a near or distant elderly relative and that incentives play a passive, or at best, an enhancing role. Incentives facilitate the process and make it easier for the already committed and do little to change the minds of the refusers. The issue is whether "people do what they say." After our replication study, we recommend demonstrations or model projects which will relate the most appropriate family network, stage of life cycle, and life style with specific incentives, physical and mental status of elderly, attitudes and perceptions of elderly and relatives, physical and social capabilities of relatives and household.

These will determine the actual social and economic cost/benefits for varied types of family network/home care arrangements. Those of least cost that provide maximum supports for the elderly person can be advocated in the formulation of new policies and programs.

The finding—if found to be salient as a consequence of a proposed replication study to begin in January, 1977—that member units of family networks are open to or welcoming of their less well and impaired elderly members, will require public reeducation along these lines and closer attention to what the elderly think and feel about this prospect. Data collected in Cleveland on elderly perceptions and feelings provides guidelines for estimating the conditions and circumstances under which a satisfactory "contract" of family and elderly members can be achieved. Demonstrations or model projects are now required to test the routinized reply of most elderly persons, "I do not want to be a burden to my children."

Nevertheless, from the perspective of family members, as our data indicate, serious attention should be given to the development of the family network as a living environment for the elderly. This may require a reevaluation of current policies and programs of institutionalized care of the elderly, especially in the direction of human service systems providing supportive activities to help the family in maintaining the elderly member in the home. Currently there is increasing interest and the beginning of a social movement to develop more responsive client-centered programs of service. This may require regrouping of institutionalized care systems around individuals (bringing services into the home) rather than requiring clients to enter large-scale bureaucratized care and custodial systems. Discovering an interstitial system of using a combination of family and professional labor power should augur well for existing human service systems. It provides a rationale for a new policy and changed functions for their continued existence in the future.

Reference

Wake, S. and Sporakowski, M.   An Intergenerational Comparison of Attitudes toward Supporting Aged Parents. *Journal of Marriage and the Family*, 34, 42-48, 1972.

5.4

Legal Aspects of Aging

Paul Nathanson

Introduction

A vast array of complex statutory, regulatory, and decisional law is superimposed on the lives of the elderly. Their shelter may be provided or secured under federal and state public and subsidized housing laws, relocation laws, environmental protection laws, and zoning laws. Their health is often dependent upon Medicaid, Medicare, laws regulating nursing homes, and regulations relating to the advertisement of prescription drugs. Their nutrition is often secured by the Food Stamp Program and nutrition programs established by federal law. The source of their income may be Social Security, Supplemental Security Income under Title XVI of the Social Security Act, or private pensions. The dignity of personal freedom and control of property is subject to the vagaries of the law of guardianship, conservatorship, and involuntary commitment.

These various rights, benefits, and protections conferred by the law only exist if the intended elderly beneficiaries have actual knowledge of the rights and protections and have a truly effective means of enforcing them. Thus, issues relating to information about and access to the legal system are also appropriately addressed in a discussion of "law and the elderly." In a more radical sense, the question of alternative methods of resolving disputes between individuals and governmental agencies (*without* using the present legal system) evolves as an important topic for discussion.

An abbreviated version of this paper appeared in *The Humanist*, September/October 1977.

We must recognize that the law that affects the elderly is a composite of judicial (court orders and decisions), legislative (statutes), and administrative (rules and regulations) promulgations. Since these activities involve the three branches of our state and federal governments within the broader context of our state and federal constitutions, it becomes extremely important to understand and orchestrate the interrelationship of legislative, judicial, and administrative processes, as well as the dissemination of information about these processes. This broad view of the law can be better understood when we recognize that the law is at one time an instrument of change and at the same time the codification of existing inequities and imbalances from which change is sought.

The interrelationship of these different spheres of activity might be better brought into focus by a few examples. On Labor Day, September 3, 1973, the following headline appeared on the front page of the *Los Angeles Times:* "Laborers' 'Rich' Pension Plan Challenged as Unfair in Lawsuit." The lawsuit itself was to drag on for several years—but the information regarding the actual *filing* of the lawsuit was a community-organizing event. The National Senior Citizens Law Center (which brought the lawsuit) was flooded with calls from present and past construction plan participants. Those who had participated in the plan and felt that they had been treated unfairly, but had not done anything because they felt they could not "fight city hall" alone, were spurred on to pursue their own claims because they finally felt someone with some access to the power system *cared* and might provide needed assistance. Those who were presently participating in the plan and who had been assuming all would be fine with respect to their own retirement pensions were alerted to the fact that, unless they became immediately concerned with their pension plan, problems might arise in the future. When the Center was subsequently called by a state legislator wanting to hold hearings prior to drafting and introducing state pension legislation, the Center's staff was, due to the contacts arising out of the newspaper article, able to provide the legislative staff with appropriate and effective case histories and witnesses for the hearings.

I was recently in attendance at a U.S. Senate hearing on Women and Social Security. At the hearing, I had the opportunity to meet Mr. Weisenfeld, the plaintiff in a recent U.S. Supreme Court case, *Weinberger* v. *Weisenfeld*, 420 U.S. 636 (1975), which held unconstitutional the provision of Social Security benefits to widows of covered workers with children in the home while denying such benefits to similarly situated widowers. Although his court victory was already several months old, his name was "not yet in the computer." This crystallized a very common problem: the successful resolution of a court case does not necessarily spell real relief for the victor; and administrative machinery must still be activated and made to conform with the courts' edicts. Further, for thousands of similarly situated (and potentially entitled) individuals who have not even heard of the successful Supreme Court case, the newly articulated and clarified right does not exist.

At the same Senate hearing, several other clearly sexually discriminatory provisions of the Social Security Act were challenged and the legislators were asked for relief. Several witnesses and legislators indicated that perhaps this was an area (given the numerous other problems of women and Social Security which required attention) that could be left to the courts since they had already indicated (in *Weisenfeld*) how favorably they would deal with similar issues. Actually, the U.S. Supreme Court had, subsequent to its decision in *Weisenfeld*, decided the case of *Weinberger* v. *Salfi*, 422 U.S. 749 (1975), which created procedural difficulties to bringing a constitutional challenge to such discriminatory provisions. Thus, the lack of knowledge of judicial holdings could have had a detrimental impact on the creation of positive legislation.

Substantive Legal Issues of Concern to the Elderly

The National Senior Citizens Law Center (NSCLC) is a national resource center and focus point for those concerned with addressing the legal needs of the elderly. NSCLC has (through a process which utilizes a Board of Directors familiar with the field of aging and the law and the network of some 3,000 Legal Services Corporation attorneys around the country who deal with poverty clients) determined to focus its attention on: nursing homes, Medicare, Medicaid, consumer issues, housing issues, private pensions, public pensions, Supplemental Security Income, Social Security, involuntary commitment and guardianship, age discrimination and mandatory retirement, veterans, and older women. With respect to each of these areas, NSCLC and other attorneys around the country are involved in court cases, administrative, and legislative advocacy. Merely listing these topics, however, does not really provide much of a framework for understanding specific problem areas and I would like to isolate several issues and highlight them as examples of legal problems affecting the elderly.

Age Discrimination in Employment

It would appear axiomatic in a society which places a premium on individuality, that the right to work as long as one is able would be a basic tenet of life. Unfortunately, one of the most widespread and harmful types of discrimination that affects the elderly is age discrimination in employment. If one is denied the basic right to earn a living, the reliance on various governmental benefits is often the result. And the loss of individuality and dignity may well follow. The forms of employment-related age discrimination vary from failure to hire an individual because of age, to mandatory retirement because of age.

Individuals between the ages of 40 and 65 do receive some measure of protection from the Federal Age Discrimination in Employment Act of 1967 (hereinafter the "Act") (29 U.S.C. §§621, *et seq.*). In general, the Act applies to employers who have 20 or more employees, to employment agencies, to labor organizations, to states and their political subdivisions and agencies, and to the federal government.[1] All sorts of conceivable discrimination is prohibited by the Act, including hiring, discharge, compensation, terms and conditions of employment, classification or referral for employment, and advertisements indicating or implying a preference based on age. If a violation is found, the Act allows for judicially ordered employment, reinstatement, promotion, and the award of back pay. It is also possible that, if discrimination can be proven to have resulted in the loss of pension benefits, a court might order the actual provision of these lost benefits.

What looks good at first is, however, replete with problems going to the very core of the Act's effectiveness. The Act is inapplicable to persons over 65. Although there have been attempts in both the House of Representatives and the U.S. Senate to pass legislation removing the upper age limit of the Act, they have failed. Discrimination on the basis of age is allowed if it can be proven that age is a bona fide occupational qualification for the particular job (the part of a teenager in a TV commercial, for example). Of extreme significance is the provision that exempts retirement and pension plans from the coverage of the Act. As will be discussed below, it is unclear whether this exception condones mandatory retirement *prior* to age 65. To further complicate the situation, numerous states have enacted legislation that protects workers against discrimination on the basis of age. In some states, the coverage of such legislation extends beyond the age of 65; and, several states have no upper age limit at all.

As noted earlier, the lack of effective enforcement of any judicial decision, legislative enactment, or administrative promulgation may emasculate what would otherwise be a favorable law. The courts have thrown numerous procedural obstacles in the way of claimants trying to utilize the Act and tended to narrowly construe the availability of the judiciary for purposes of enforcement of the Act.[2] In addition, the Labor Department, which is charged with enforcing the Act (except with respect to federal employees, in which case the Civil Service Commission is involved), has not been overly zealous in its efforts. More significantly, congressional appropriations for this particular

Labor Department activity have been ridiculously low.[3] The problems with securing adequate enforcement through the Labor Department have recently come to the attention of Congress by the introduction of H.R. 3504 by Representatives Donald Edwards and Robert Drinan. Their legislation, entitled "Civil Rights Amendments Act of 1977," proposes to repeal the Age Discrimination in Employment Act and add age discrimination to the jurisdiction of the Civil Rights Act of 1968. Thus, the Equal Employment Opportunity Commission, rather than the Department of Labor, would be charged with enforcement of the Act.

The situation with respect to workers over the age of 65 is unfortunately even dimmer. Absent coverage by a specific state statute or a specific collective bargaining agreement, employees have been forced to rely on U.S. or state constitutional arguments based upon the due process or equal protection clauses. These arguments have been met at varying judicial levels with a primarily negative response, and in any case, would appear to be of little assistance to individuals working for private employers where no "state action" (i.e., involvement of federal, state, or municipal government) can be shown. It should be noted, however, that on March 4, 1977, the 7th Circuit Court of Appeals in *Christie* v. *Marston*, 45 Law Week 2446, construed the Act to apply to federal employees between the ages of 65 and 70. The court relied to a large extent on the overall mandatory retirement provision for federal workers, which states the general retirement age as 70.

Specifically with respect to mandatory retirement, one of the most blatant examples of age discrimination in employment, the outlook has been particularly bleak. In *Brennan* v. *Taft Broadcasting Company*, 500 F.2d 212 (5th Cir. 1974), the worker had participated in a retirement plan containing a 60-year-old mandatory early retirement provision. The 5th Circuit Court of Appeals upheld the forced retirement at age 60 because of the bona fide retirement pension plan exemption to coverage of the Act. Thus, the court allowed age discrimination on the basis of age even within the age limits set by the Act. However, on February 12, 1977, the U.S. Supreme Court agreed to review the case of *McMann* v. *United Airlines, Inc.*, Civ. No. 75-2206 (4th Cir. 1976), *Cert. granted*, 45 U.S.L.W. 3570 (U.S. Feb. 22, 1977) (No. 76-906), which held that forced early retirement at an age prior to 65 was *not* allowed by the pension plan exception. Instead, the court examined the legislative history of that provision and pointed out that it was intended to further the primary purpose of the Act, i.e., the hiring of older workers, by allowing employment without necessarily including such workers in benefit plans. Thus, the Supreme Court has decided to rule on this split of authority between the federal circuit courts. A decision with respect to mandatory retirement prior to age 65 should be rendered shortly. With respect to areas not covered by the Act, arguments against mandatory retirement have been unsuccessful. Thus arguments based on either equal protection or due process clauses of the U.S. Constitution have failed to bear fruit—

even with respect to public employees. See *Massachusetts Board of Retirement* v. *Murgia*, 96 S. Ct. 2562 (1976).

Intervention: Protection from Protective Services

Intervention in the lives of older people may take many forms: guardianship proceedings; life in an institution for long-term care; the decision to refuse treatment even if death results; and governmental beneficent encroachment. The freedoms at stake may well be the most fundamental in the society, and concern the rights to manage, buy or sell property, control one's own body, enter into contracts, be a party in litigation, dispose of one's assets by gift, and even exercise one's personal liberty, including the freedom to travel, and to associate with whom one pleases. In questions of intervention, the efforts of advocates for the elderly have focused upon preserving individual control over one's own affairs to as great an extent as possible. The hope is that freedom, if it must be limited, be only limited in the most appropriate and least restrictive way, and pursuant to a procedure that affords the utmost protection and benefit of the doubt to the individual before any form of intervention is condoned.

Older people deemed not able to manage their personal or economic affairs are often subject to the imposition of protective services in the form of guardianships. Significant litigative and legislative activity centers around requiring due process *prior* to the declaration of such protective services and limiting, as much as possible, the type of intervention that is ultimately provided. Thus, advocates are seeking to provide means by which the proposed ward will receive the clearest and most informative actual notice of the fact that a guardianship hearing (with specifically enumerated consequences) is about to take place. With respect to the actual hearing itself, efforts center around securing the physical presence of the proposed ward, if at all possible, and the representation of the proposed ward by independent counsel. Consideration is being given to drafting guardianship statutes that insure that guardianship can only be triggered by definitions of functional as opposed to medical disability and that require proof beyond a reasonable doubt (the more severe burden required in criminal cases where individual liberty is also at stake) as opposed to only a mere preponderance of the evidence. Even when intervention may to some extent be justified, the form this intervention takes should be limited. Thus, the proposition of the "least restrictive alternative" as a protection from protective services is currently being discussed. For example, in the case of *Lake* v. *Cameron*, 364 F.2d 657 (D.C. Circuit 1966), the court held that a person who was not a danger to others ought not to be indeterminately committed to an institution without prior exploration of various *other* alternatives available for her assistance within the community in which she lived.

The law even concerns itself with the question of whether or not an individual can have control over his or her own body and ultimate death. Much current discussion centers around the "right to die" and the right to "death with dignity" but it is not at all clear that such rights generally exist. An exciting new legislative approach is contained in the California Natural Death Act (California Health and Safety Code, §§7185 *et seq.*). The Act provides a way for an individual to refuse—in advance—medical treatment that would artificially prolong life. It should be noted that "living wills" which have attempted to achieve the same type of result as the Natural Death Act have had dubious legal affect and validity.

Many individuals who have voluntarily entered nursing homes have probably never undergone any sort of legal declaration of incompetency. They may nevertheless give up many of their basic freedoms, (often without any sort of due process), simply by entering the home. Thus, the freedom to associate with visitors and others of one's choosing, to travel, to receive mail, to eat and drink what one likes, and to refuse "beneficial" medication or activities, may be severely limited within the context of the nursing home. Some sort of protection for these basic rights within the nursing home context has been attempted through the "Patients' Bill of Rights." Unfortunately, such enactments generally depend upon the good will of physicians, staff, and nursing home administrators who all too often may act to limit individual freedoms for staff or community convenience. Among the numerous issues presently being addressed by litigative and/or legislative efforts are: the strengthening of enforcement mechanisms for the Patients' Bill of Rights; the right to the least restrictive alternative and most appropriate treatment; the right to some sort of protection from, or prior to, transfer to a new home because of reclassification (for Medicare or Medicaid purposes) of a patient to a new level of care, or because the patient is on Medicaid; and freedom of access to the home and its resident by advocates (whether they be lawyers or other community representatives).

Once older people are forced to rely on the government for housing, health, income, or other benefits, their dignity and individuality may well suffer also. Thus, in *Wilkie* v. *O'Connor*, 25 N.Y. 2d 617 (App. Div. 1941), where the plaintiff's benefit payments were cut off because the local welfare office did not approve of his personal habits the court stated:

Appellant . . . argues that he has a right to live as he pleases while being supported by public charity. One would admire his independence if he were not so dependent, but he has no right to defy the standards and conventions of civilized society while being supported at public expense. This is true even though some of those conventions may be somewhat artificial.

Even the fairly limited procedural protections of guardianship law are unavailable to recipients of governmental benefits under the Social Security and Supplemental Security Income programs. Thus, payment of the beneficiary's check may be made to a "representative payee" (relative or some other person) if it appears to the Social Security Administration that the interests of the beneficiary would be best served thereby, *regardless of the legal competency or incompetency of the beneficiary*. Further, under the Supplemental Security Income program, representative payees are *automatically* appointed for all drug addicts and alcoholics.

Older Women

Numerous questions of concern to older women are currently being addressed by legislators and courts. In addition to issues that specifically affect older women, there are those that affect the poor or elderly in general, but which may have a special impact upon older women. To the extent such issues can be characterized as "older women's issues," the advocate is able to draw on support from new and separate constituencies. Thus, for example, the fact that a vast majority of single black women over age 65 are poor makes aging welfare issues relevant and important to not only aging advocates, but also to women's groups and black groups.[4]

In addition to general efforts to expand and improve Social Security coverage, the efforts of some advocates revolve around trying to change obvious and overt sex discrimination in the Social Security Act (i.e., the provision of certain types of benefits to the beneficiaries of working men and, at the same time, not to similarly situated beneficiaries of working women). Such discrimination would be eliminated by several legislative proposals being considered in Congress. Some sort of pension coverage (whether it be through Social Security or other mechanisms) for work in the home is also very much under discussion, and Representative Fraser has introduced H.R. 3247, which attempts to provide coverage for homemaking under the Social Security laws. Legislative attempts are also underway to try to reduce the number of years of marriage (presently twenty) required before qualifying for a divorced wife's benefit. In addition, a lawsuit has been filed to try to provide divorced husband's benefits similar to those provided for divorced wives.

In the private pension field, numerous lawsuits are underway challenging unreasonable break-in-service and vesting provisions, and attempts are being made to improve the coverage of the Employee Retirement Income Security Act. Obviously, these efforts are important for both men and women. However, the clarification and expansion of survivor rights under pension plans (so that, for example, the nonworking spouse is at least afforded an opportunity of notice about the worker spouse's election not to have survivor coverage) are especially important for older women. Present litigation concerned with challenging, under various Civil Rights enactments, the use of sex-based actuarial tables to provide lower pensions to women or require higher payments from, or on behalf of, women in order to receive pensions equal to men, may have far-reaching impact.

Interesting legislative efforts (both on the federal and state levels) are attempting to address the problem of "displaced homemakers"— women who are usually in their 50s, have no specific job training that is very marketable, have worked in the home most of their lives, and suddenly find themselves widowed or divorced with no real job prospects or special welfare or relief programs directly available. California and Maryland have passed legislation setting up centers for these women where they can receive assistance as to job opportunities, job training, various available benefit programs, and other kinds of counseling to assist them in their new roles and situations. Similar legislation has been introduced on the federal level by Senator Birch Bayh and Congresswoman Yvonne Burke.

Access to the System

As has been discussed earlier, benefits created by legislation, judicial decisions, or administrative rulemaking are only *real* if the intended beneficiaries know about these benefits, and in addition, have a means of enforcing or protecting them. Thus, "access" to the judicial, administrative, and legislative processes is of extreme importance to the population at large, and specifically to the elderly.[5]

A crucial threshhold part of the access problem is whether or not individuals can find qualified and able representation at a price that they can afford.[6] Significant advances have been made in the last several years with respect to publicly funded free legal services for the elderly. In addition to the legal services programs for the poor supported by the Legal Services Corporation, special elderly law projects have been created primarily under the Older Americans Act. Senator

Kennedy has just introduced S. 1282 which would provide in excess of $20 million through the mechanism of the Older Americans Act for legal services for the nation's elderly. An advantage of funding legal services through the Older Americans Act is that eligibility for the services provided is not subject to a means test; and therefore, those individuals who are not absolutely indigent may receive legal assistance (as is not the case with respect to clients of Legal Services Corporation grantees).[7]

The vast need for legal services cannot really be met by publicly funded free legal services. The resources of the private bar must be brought into play. Thus, consumer questions relating to legal services are currently being widely discussed. For example, several groups of senior citizens (e.g., the Gray Panthers, the Mountain Plains Congress of Senior Organizations, the National Association of State Units on Aging, and the California State Office on Aging) have recently filed an *amicus* brief in the case of *Bates and O'Steen* v. *State Bar of Arizona*, No. 76-316 (as of this writing the Supreme Court has already heard oral argument but has not yet issued a written opinion) that seeks to allow certain limited advertising of attorneys' fees and services based on the First Amendment of the United States Constitution and on antitrust statutes. It is hoped that if advertising is permitted, lower fees (i.e., hopefully, reasonable fees) and a better-educated legal services consumer will result.

Those interested in providing low-cost legal services are presently also concerned with questions surrounding the use of paralegals to provide various types of individual assistance and representation. Federal statutes specifically allow representation by nonattorneys at the administrative hearing level for certain government benefit programs, such as Social Security and the Supplemental Security Income program. However, in several instances, state bar associations have attempted to limit the activities of paralegals even in these areas. These and similar efforts by some bar associations to limit the activities of paralegals—to the extent that these are unjustified attempts at restricting access to reasonable services and, thereby, access to the system—must be carefully watched and, if appropriate, resisted.

Other limitations that can affect access and that have specific implications for the elderly relate to: limits on the jurisdiction of federal courts to hear certain types of controversies which affect the poor;[8] various procedural restrictions that tend to cause access to the system (especially against governmental agencies) to be made more difficult (such as rules concerning sovereign immunity and the Eleventh Amendment to the United States Constitution); requirements on exhaustion of all state remedies before being able to go into federal court; and various recent limitations on class actions imposed by the U.S. Supreme Court.

With respect to access to and review of the administrative agency activity, significant discussions have centered around two issues: first, the access to information about these agencies, and their operations (Freedom of Information Act, 5 U.S.C. §§552; the Privacy Act, 5 U.S.C. §§552a; and, the Government in the Sunshine Act, P.L. 94-409 [Sept. 13, 1976]); and second, trying to devise ways to provide fees for attorney and other representation in administrative proceedings.[9]

Of course, the resolution of disputes between individuals and agencies need not necessarily be done by attorneys or paralegals; and, the search for alternative methods for resolving disputes (whether it be through various kinds of community-based dispute resolution centers or special ethnic courts such as rabbinical courts) is of extreme importance. Simplifying or redirecting the law so that neither the legal system nor lawyers are required is perhaps most significant for the elderly. They oftentimes do not have the several years required to pursue a matter through the court system; or, because they have grown up in a different era, they may distrust that strange and alien system and would much prefer to have their disputes resolved in a more informal way. The movement toward consumer advocacy and ombudsmen programs may be viewed as an integral part of this approach.

Notes

1. For a lengthy discussion of the Act, see Fried and Dowell, *The Age Discrimination in Employment Act of 1967*, Volume 6, CLEARING-HOUSE REVIEW 196 (1972); and Gillan, *The Federal Age Discrimination Act Revisited*, Volume 9, CLEARINGHOUSE REVIEW, 761 (March 1976).

2. Ibid.

3. Two million dollars for all nationwide enforcement efforts.

4. See, generally, Hearings of the Special Committee on Aging of the United States Senate, 94th Congress, Women and Social Security, Oct. 22, 1975. The printed proceedings reprint in its entirety a broader paper prepared by the National Senior Citizens Law Center entitled "Legal Problems Affecting Older Women in America."

5. An excellent recent article that discusses access to the courts and administrative agencies in detail is, Trister, *Legislative Proposals to Improve Access to Federal Courts and Administrative Agencies*, Volume 10, CLEARINGHOUSE REVIEW, page 1023, April 1977.

6. Specifically with respect to *legal services for the nation's elderly*, see Nathanson, *Legal Services for the Nation's Elderly*, Volume 17, Number 2, ARIZONA LAW REVIEW, 1975; and Testimony by Paul

Nathanson, *Improving Legal Representation for Older Americans*, before the U.S. Senate, Special Committee on Aging, September 29, 1976.

7. For discussion of legislation providing financial support for public interest litigation in general, see Trister, cited *supra*, at 1030 *et seq.*

8. A recent Justice Department proposal to expand the role of federal magistrates in hearing Social Security and black lung cases is also to be noted here. Thus, federal district courts would be allowed authority to delegate a percentage of their case loads to magistrates. An appeal to the District Court would be allowed, but the review of factual and legal issues would be fairly limited. Federal Circuit courts of appeal would have discretionary review of district court decisions, but only as to questions of law decided by the district courts. Numerous questions arise in this regard, not the least of which is in a very general sense why the questions of the law affecting primarily the elderly and the poor should be delegated to lesser judicial authorities and have less right to review by the actual federal courts involved.

9. See the Trister article for discussion of these provisions, especially, S. 2715 which was introduced in the last Congress by Senator Kennedy.

CHAPTER VI

POLICY DEBATES AND THE FUTURE OF AGING

The possibility of anticipating future societal conditions with reasonable accuracy is very tenuous indeed. Yet projections in the public policy arena are a necessary, even if a risky, enterprise: forecasting events early enough may enable more effective intervention, in order to lessen impending problems and to facilitate better social conditions.

This chapter takes up three future related issues: retirement, the demographic composition of the aging cohorts, and the organization of social services.

The future of mandatory retirement and the future viability of the social security program have been a major source of concern lately, not only for policy analysts, but also for the public at large. There is hardly an American worker, both young and old, who has not pondered lately whether the social security program will go broke or whether there will be enough for him or her to collect at the time of retirement.

When Congress recently voted to raise the minimum age for mandatory retirement from sixty-five to seventy, it implicitly sanctioned a trend lifting mandatory retirement altogether. The debate that preceded the Congressional action thus remains open. Those who oppose mandatory retirement argue their case primarily in human rights terms. They insist that requiring an elderly worker to retire at sixty-five, just because of age and regardless of merits and fitness, is wasteful, discriminatory, and morally wrong. Those who wish to retain the mandatory retirement claim instead that a worse injustice would be perpetuated against younger workers, whose promotional opportunities may fade away. Furthermore, a uniform retirement age, they add, will spare obsolete and competent workers the embarrassment of dismissal at a later age in life. Behind this last argument lies the myth that all older people are senile or disabled.

Doing away with or modifying mandatory retirement provisions may respond, however, to demographic and economic imperatives not sufficiently highlighted during the 1977 Congressional inquiries, even if they probably were on most policy-makers' minds. Juanita M. Kreps, currently Secretary of Commerce, delivered a lecture entitled "Social Security in the Coming Decades: Questions for a Mature System" in which she summarized the forty year history of the social security program and discussed population shifts in today's society. This lecture was the second in the Robert M. Ball Lecture Series, established in 1973 as a tribute to the former Commissioner of Social Security, and was delivered when Professor Kreps was Vice President of Duke University and James B. Duke Professor of Economics.

The author deals with the questions of income transfer between generations, the declining proportions of workers to retirees, the impact of the rising labor force activity of women, and the possible benefits of delaying the retirement age. Her analysis was a welcome prelude to the above mentioned debate on mandatory retirement, but it also analyzes the issues that may influence the social security program in the years to come.

Gerontologists at the University of Chicago put forth a few years ago a series of predictions concerning aging in the year 2,000. Their analysis primarily relied upon demographic, social, familial, health, and social service changes that are anticipated to occur in the next two decades. Two of these studies are presented in this final chapter. The first by Bernice L. Neugarten inventories a series of population projections and expands on the distinction between the "young-old" and the "old-old" that the author formulated in preceding publications. Although Neugarten is more concerned with life styles than with chronological age limits, she anticipates an early rather than late retirement orientation among the first of these groups, the 55-74 cohort. This will be a cohort engaged in improving the quality of their life and searching opportunities for self-enhancement. The "young-old" may constitute the first age group to reach the society of the future and probably build what Neugarten defines as an "age irrelevant" society, that is, a social environment free of age related constraints, in which all individuals will have choices consonant with their aspirations and abilities, regardless whether they are young or old.

The second study is our concluding paper. It is written by Sheldon S. Tobin and deals with "Social and Health Services for the Future Aged." These services may take new forms, including networks of community service that provide changing but continuing supportive care; new, smaller local institutions, operating as prosthetic environments, and finally, terminal care centers or hospices where terminal patients are helped through the dying process. The service system anticipated by Tobin will be better coordinated at the local level, and it will assume the yeoman task of preventing the risks of unnecessary or premature institutionalization.

True, it is difficult to anticipate what the future holds for the elderly, but we may assume that the quality of their life and well-being in the year 2000 largely depends on adequate preparations today.

Sound policy decisions and program designs are in turn contingent upon a better public awareness and more reliable knowledge of the issues and problems of aging. More substantive information and a more compassionate understanding of what aging is all about are required as a prelude to the "Age of Aging."

6.1

Social Security in the Coming Decade: Questions for a Mature System

Juanita M. Kreps

There is really no way to support retired Americans comfortably and cheaply (Shapiro, 1975).

For a 40-year old, social security retains a remarkable capacity to catch the public eye. Perhaps no other legislative mandate has held our interest so consistently; certainly, none has touched our lives as intimately. Almost no one in the course of his or her lifetime will be beyond the reach of this law, passed four decades ago in an era of depression-inspired social reform. Indeed, the social security system stands as a striking tribute to innovation in an era when lesser minds might well have succumbed to the numbing pain of economic contraction.

For all its breadth of vision, however, the grand design of social security is as little understood today as in 1935. Note, for example, current public concern over the solvency of the system—the fear that "the social security fund will go broke" as the ratio of wage earners to retirees declines. Or alternatively, one hears that the taxes necessary to support retirees will grow ever more burdensome on the smaller

Reprinted from the *Social Security Bulletin*, U.S. Department of Health, Education and Welfare, Social Security Administration, March 1976.

Table 1.

Age Group	Population (percent)			
	1974	1980	1990	2000
School age, 0-19............	36	32	31	30
Working age...............	54	57	58	58
20-44	34	37	39	36
45-64	20	20	19	22
Retirement age, 65 and over .	10	11	12	12

number of workers, reducing their capacity to support themselves and their children. In their more exaggerated expressions these worries pose a threat to further improvements in living standards for older people whose income levels, despite recent increases, remain substantially lower than those of the working-age population.

The concern over future tax receipts is not an idle one, of course. The total population of the United States has grown rapidly since the passage of the Social Security Act and the numbers of persons of working age have continued to provide a growing base for tax collections with which to support retirees. In addition to increasing numbers of wage earners, economic growth helped to lift hourly rates of pay and made it possible for both the benefit levels and the range of persons receiving benefits to improve through time. It was this growth that led economist Paul Samuelson to speak of a "social security paradox" in which everybody got back more than he put into the retirement insurance system.

Social insurance proponents have always recognized the possibility of a slower rate of population growth that ultimately would result in fewer people entering the work force. In the case of the United States the population growth rate was 1.7 percent during the two decades following the Second World War; it dropped to 1.0 percent in 1965-72 and is now 0.7 percent. This decline means that the school-age population has stopped growing; it is not expected to be any higher in 1990 than it is now. The number of working-age persons, however, will continue to increase rapidly—from 115 million to 141 million in the next 15 years. Those persons born in the period of the baby boom are now swelling the labor force and not until the last decade of the century will there be a leveling-off in the size of the working-age group. Persons aged 65 and over will continue to be in the fastest growing segment of the population during the next two decades. If the fertility rate were to reach 2.11, the average needed to maintain a stable population, the proportion of the population in various age groups would be as shown in the following tabulation for selected years.

Such public concern with maintaining the integrity of the social security trust fund implies a failure to understand the nature of the system—essentially a pay-as-you-go tax and benefit scheme. Since no actuarially determined fund is called for, total benefits are limited only by the amount of payroll (or other) taxes Congress wishes to impose. But today's worries about the viability of the system bear out one essential aspect of the problem it now faces—namely, adequate financing. This problem is a special concern not only because the social security program is reaching maturity—when the number of beneficiaries is large enough to call for greater tax revenues than ever before—but also because the worker-beneficiary ratio seems likely to be less favorable after the turn of the century.

In its maturity, the program will face other questions of similar magnitude—questions that were not of such pressing importance in its youth. Can the social security system assume the obligation of having benefits keep pace with growth as well as the cost of living? How high a replacement ratio should be maintained? Should the benefit vary with the age at which one retires, either beyond or before age 65? Will it be necessary to establish a later age of eligibility for benefits to offset the increasing number of elderly persons relative to middle-aged and younger workers? Most troublesome of all, perhaps, is the question of whether imposition of the additional payroll taxes needed to pay for benefits will be acceptable to workers or whether some significant portion of the funds will be collected via other taxes. In the ensuing review, several of these issues are looked at in the context of the probable demographic and labor-force patterns of the coming decades.

Intergenerational Transfers: How Much Smoothing of the Humps and Valleys?

Some time ago Ida Merriam noted that "Earnings . . . have a very poor fit over time to the individual's changing consumption needs" (Merriam, 1967). The problem of smoothing out the "humps and valleys," handled through individual savings and family care in simpler societies, now falls to social institutions that are able to develop procedures for universal coverage. Having such institutions in place, however, the society also has to decide the level of income to be maintained in old age, compared with the level of earnings or, in brief, the extent to which income is to be made even between generations.

Transfers of income between generations may be viewed differently by different age groups, as James Morgan points out. We have, he says, a social contract,

> where each generation helps to pay for increased benefits of the previous generation on an implicit promise that the next generation will do the same for them. From this point of view, the system looks like a bargain in retrospect to each older generation and like a rip-off in prospect to each young cohort if they ignore the probable future increase in benefits (Morgan, 1975).

In a similar vein, Kenneth Boulding earlier spoke of the fact that

> One of the things we know for certain about any age group is that it has no future. The young become middle-aged and the middle-aged become old and the old die. Consequently, the support which the middle-aged give to the young can be regarded as the first part of a deferred exchange, which will be consummated when those who are now young become middle-aged and support those who are now middle-aged who will then be old. Similarly, the support which the middle-aged give to the old can be regarded as the consummation of a bargain entered into a generation ago (Boulding, 1961).

The need for such a support pattern between generations has grown during social security's lifetime; financial arrangements previously made within the family are now met largely through fiscal measures. What appears in the social accounts as a huge increase in the income allocated to old people obscures the fact that in the absence of the payroll or other taxes, workers would need to support their aged parents directly. Or alternatively, persons at work would have to save enough to support themselves in their own retirement. The difficulties of the latter method are emphasized in a recent paper by A. J. Jaffe, who shows that a worker would need to save about one-third of his earnings throughout worklife in order to pay for his retirement (Jaffe, 1975).

Although few people would challenge the need for income transfers from workers to nonworkers, including retirees along with the unemployed, the disabled, dependent children, and handicapped adults, the question of the size of the transfer is constantly under debate. As retirement benefit levels have improved, payroll taxes have increased and the amount of income shifted from young and middle-aged workers to retirees has grown.

Professor Robert Clark, making certain assumptions, estimates that the intergenerational transfer in the social security program grew from about 2.1 percent of a young worker's income in 1950 to approximately 9.0 percent in 1970. Although the replacement ratio—that is, the benefit paid to a retiree as a proportion of his preretirement earnings—has not increased significantly, the increase in tax receipts made it possible to extend coverage, raise minimum benefits, and lower the retirement age (Clark, 1975).

Clark then asks whether this 9.0 percent is likely to increase under conditions of zero population growth. On the assumption that the fertility rate moves to the replacement level of 2.11 immediately and remains there (and assuming a constant rate of income growth and a constant replacement ratio), he shows that the ensuing changes in age structure will necessitate an increase in the tax rate. Specifically, the 1970 tax rate would have to be increased by 50 percent by the year 2050, when stable population is reached, assuming that retirement age and age of entry into the labor force remain constant. Noting that retirement age has been falling steadily during recent decades, however, he speculates on the effect of a continuation of this trend. If the age of exit from work has fallen to 60 by 2050, for example, more than a two fold increse in taxes will be required; if it has fallen to 55, more than a threefold increase would ensue.To the extent that age of entry into the working force is rising, the tax rate would need to be even higher.

The fairly low proportion of earnings maintained under the social security system, compared with the replacement ratios in certain other nations, raises the question of whether the level of pensions should not be improved in the future. To do so, Clark points out, the cost would have to be offset by an equal increase in tax receipts. Hence, in order to raise the present pension level from a replacement ratio of 40 percent to a ratio of 60 percent it would be necessary to raise taxes by 50 percent.

Showing the percentage tax increases needed to support higher replacement ratios in various years before reaching a stable population, he notes further that even maintenance of the present ratio means that the tax rate will need to be 17.55 (an estimated intergenerational transfer of 14 percent) by 2050, if retirement age remains at age 65. These rates are compatible with the Social Security Administration's long-range projections of a 17-18 percent tax after the year 2025.

In evaluating future tax levels it is instructive to compare the tax rates now being paid in other countries. Various attempts have been made to estimate the worker's total tax liability or, conversely, the proportion of his earnings an employee is allowed to retain for current use or savings.

A recent study by the Organization for Economic Cooperation and

Development shows that on the basis of disposable income as a percentage of gross earnings, the typical production worker in the United States ranks above a few nations (Denmark, Sweden, the Netherlands, Germany, Norway, and Finland), about equally with several others (Switzerland, the United Kingdom, Australia, and Canada), and below a third group (including Japan, New Zealand, Belgium, Austria, Italy, Spain, and France). In terms of total payments in social security contributions plus income taxes, as a percentage of the gross national product (GNP), the United States worker fell somewhat below the median paid in the nations under review. Employees in the United States paid less than those in Denmark, Sweden, the Netherlands, Germany, Norway, Finland, the United Kingdom, Canada, New Zealand, Luxembourg, and Austria. They paid more than employees in Switzerland, Australia, Ireland, Japan, Greece, Portugal, Italy, Spain, and France (Organization for Economic, 1975).

These findings are confirmed by a recent Social Security Administration report indicating that, of the several countries studied, the Netherlands and Sweden spent the highest proportions of GNP on all social security programs. The United States devoted a relatively low level of its resources to these purposes; only Japan ranked lower. In expenditures for old-age, survivors, and disability insurance as a percentage of GNP, the nations ranged from Germany's high of 7.59 percent to the United States figure of 3.42 and Japan's 0.31 percent. Sweden and the Netherlands were close behind Germany, followed by Belgium (whose figure excluded disability coverage), France, the United Kingdom, and Canada (Horlick, 1974).

Our relative position would not seem to give cause for alarm, even with the probable growth in tax liability as the social security system matures. Concern over the change in demographic profile may also appear premature, since a reduction in the number of workers relative to retirees will not occur until after the turn of the century. But if retirement age is lowered without an offsetting rise in the labor-force participation of others in the working-age population, tax rates could rise quite sharply.

Ratio of Workers to Retirees

Ultimately, serious problems could emerge as a result of a decline in the proportion of the population of working age and the consequent necessity for transferring a larger percentage of a worker's income to retirees. To the extent that levels of living in old age are raised, these problems will be intensified.

The central question of the relationship between a population's age composition and the economic security of the nation's elderly was reexamined recently by Joseph J. Spengler (Spengler, 1975). He points out that the ratio of working age to total population is at or near maximum when population growth is zero. Whether this maximum is achieved depends on whether the labor-force participation rates in the years before age 65 remains high or, as in recent years in the United States, the work-force rates are declining. He notes that "Continuous increases in the relative number of older persons, together with decline in work-life expectancy, could contribute to financial problems in a country in which payments to retired persons from such programs as social security rest essentially on a pay-as-you-go basis." Early retirement, he concludes, is particularly unfavorable in a stationary population. Removing those aged 55-66 from jobs would reduce the ratio of workers to retirees by 20 percent and increase the number of older dependents by 46 percent.

Earlier or later retirement?

The notion of retiring workers as early as age 55 appears farfetched. Indeed, there is discussion, for the first time, of arrangements for later retirement (and incentives to encourage a postponement of withdrawal from work beyond age 65) that would encourage longer work-life in order to offset the aging of the population.

The condition that led first to fixing the age of eligibility for social security benefits at age 65 and subsequently to encouraging even younger work-force withdrawals was one of a seeming excess of workers. Unemployment was massive when the Act was passed and quite severe when the decision was made to allow men to retire at age 62 with a reduced benefit. Not only Government policy but industry-union bargains as well now make it possible for workers to leave the work force at least 3 years earlier than was initially envisioned. In response to the availability of early pensions and in the face of job shortages, many men have come to view early retirement as a desirable option, provided benefits and other retirement income sources are thought to be adequate (Barfield & Morgan, 1969).

The level of unemployment declined somewhat after the initial arrangements allowing for early retirement, but it is now higher than at any time since the depression of the nineteen-thirties. Labor-market conditions would therefore indicate a possible further lowering of retirement age, on the assumption that a reduced labor-force size would help to assure jobs to those still actively seeking work. In the absence of greater flexibility in wage rates or working schedules, the allocation of jobs among jobseekers may well be achieved by a reduction in labor-force participation rates for men at both the beginning and the end of worklife—a process that has been underway since the early nineteen-hundreds, and particularly since the end of the Second World War.

Pressure for early retirements appears to be likely if unemployment continues. But offsetting this pressure is the overall need to lengthen worklife in order to maintain a favorable ratio of workers to nonworkers. As the social security system matures and the numbers of beneficiaries grow relative to the size of the labor force, appropriate policy for the system would seem to be one that encourages persons to work through their late sixties, perhaps by offering some increment to beneficiaries who retire after age 65. Were this movement to occur, a number of gains could accrue to the individual worker: Increased income, both before and after retirement; reduced dissatisfaction, perhaps, with mandatory retirement; and greater flexibility in varying work-leisure arrangements to match individual preferences.

Retirement age and rising labor-force activity of women

Women's labor-force activity rates were of course much lower at the time of the social security legislation, and there is no evidence that the framers of the Act expected the sharp rise in these rates that began only a few years later. Much of the current concern with unequal treatment of men and women under the law emerges from provisions designed to meet income needs in an era when most married women were not engaged in market work but relied instead on their husbands' earnings during worklife and their retirement income thereafter.

But what was not foreseen or planned for has nevertheless come to be one of this century's major social developments. Married women have supplied most of the increase in the work force during recent decades; the worklives of single women, which have traditionally resembled those of men, have continued in much the same pattern. In more than half of all husband-wife families of the age group 25-64, both members are now at work.

The sharp rise in women's labor-force rates during World War II has had a lasting effect on their propensities to work outside the home: First, on the work rates of older women, then on those with children in school, and, most recently, on mothers of preschool children. During the period 1965-73 the labor-force activity for women aged 20-24 rose from 50 percent to 60 percent; among the college graduates of this age group the rate moved from 70 percent to 86 percent. Among those aged 25-34, the proportion with market jobs increased from 37 percent to 50 percent, while for those with no children it reached 75 percent. Clearly, the worklife pattern for married women has changed dramatically, with younger cohorts, particularly those with college degrees, staying in the labor force through most of the childrearing period (Women and Social Security, 1975).

But women have not always observed the same work patterns as men. Women have felt, for example, that they needed shorter market hours in order to meet their traditional nonmarket obligations. Even when the woman worker was typically single and young she exerted a downward pressure on working hours, according to Clarence Long, since she "needed to be able to type till five o'clock and still have time to search for a cheap roast or a rich husband" (Long, 1958). Women may find such a remark chauvinist. It is certainly true that those with husbands have felt a similar need for shortened workdays. But an equally important effect of women's entrance into market jobs has been the addition of female workers in sufficient numbers to offset the male workers' withdrawal, leaving the percentage of adults engaged in market work relatively stable during the past half a century.

For purposes of anticipating the future ratio of workers to retirees it is necessary to make explicit one's assumption regarding the labor-force activity of women in the decades ahead. Will the decline in work rates for men, occasioned by their longer period of schooling and retirement, continue to be offset by women's higher levels of market activity, or will one change faster than the other?

Projections are difficult to make because of the number of factors affecting both the supply and the demand sides of labor. Women have been drawn into the labor market by the availability of jobs and rising wage scales. In the past, they have sometimes dropped out of the work force for childbearing and childrearing and also when they were discouraged by poor job prospects. But there is increasing evidence that young women now in the labor force have much stronger attachments to the labor force than was true of earlier cohorts and that they are less likely to return to fulltime home work either to meet family responsibilities or because the job market is unfavorable.

If the expectations of these women are borne out, their participation in the labor force will have greater continuity through worklife and their numbers will surely swell the proportion of the adult population seeking work. Whether men will experience further reductions in the length of their worklives, thereby continuing the secular decline in the labor-force activity of men, depends in large measure on the rate of economic growth and the availability of jobs. What both sexes might reasonably demand is shorter workweeks—or work interspersed with longer vacations, sabbaticals, education, and training. This pattern would be especially helpful if men and women come to share more evenly the home work, as they are now sharing the market work.

The net effect could be to produce a favorable ratio of workers to retirees and possibly to retard the downward drift of retirement age for men. By contrast, slower economic growth and heavy unemployment in the last quarter of this century could lead to some discouragement of workers and probably to a continued pressure for postponed entry to and early retirement from the work force. The impact of a reduction in worklife on the considerations before the Social Security Administration is critical, whether such reduction is a result of the population's age structure or an outgrowth of shrinking job opportunities. Consequently, it will be necessary to return to these questions in the subsequent discussion of financing.

Financing: New Questions and Old

In a recent statement, Wilbur J. Cohen, noting that the number of aged persons would grow from the present 22 million to 30 million in the year 2000 and to 50 million by 2030, made some recommendations for changes in financing. Instead of the scheduled rise in taxable base from the current $14,100 to $17,000 in 1977, he suggests that the base be raised to $24,000. This increase would "restore the financial integrity" of the program and would allow for other needed reforms: Benefits to persons aged 55 and over totally disabled for their customary work; actuarially reduced benefits for persons aged 60-62; changes that would eliminate discrimination against women under the Act and would extend its coverage to unpaid household workers. With regard to financing health insurance, he recommends that general tax revenues, employers, and employees each contribute a third of the needed funds (*N.Y. Times*, 1975).

Demographic and deficits

An extensive review of the financing of the old-age, survivors, and disability insurance (OASDI) program prepared by the Quadrennial Advisory Council on Social Security pointed to the demographic changes that began with the low birth rates of the 1930's and noted two important statistics: (1) there are now 30 beneficiaries per 100 workers and (2) in 2030 there will be 45 beneficiaries per 100 workers. Unless these ratios are improved by immigration, increased market work by women, or a later retirement age, the Council report concludes, a long-run OASDI deficit of 2.98 percent of payroll will ensue, three-fourths of it due to the demographic change (Advisory Council, 1975). Even higher deficits were projected by the Trustees of the Federal OASDI trust funds. Specifically, the Trustees estimated that on the average the deficit would be: 1.26 percent of taxable earnings for the

25 years, 1975-1999; 4.10 percent of taxable earnings for the second 25 years, 2000-2024; and 10.19 percent of taxable earnings for the third 25 years, 2025-2050.

The average cost over the entire period is expected to be 5.32 percent of taxable payroll. The assets of the trust funds, given the early deficit rates, would be exhausted soon after 1979 (1975 Annual Report).

In view of these possible deficits, it is not surprising to hear criticisms and advice from every hand. The Advisory Council focused its primary attention on the instability of replacement rates caused by the automatic cost-of-living formula written into legislation in 1972 and recommended a "decoupling" system instead. The new formula " . . . will cause benefits to rise solely in keeping with wages during an individual's working years, and after retirement his benefits will increase solely on the basis of increases in the Consumer Price Index" (Advisory Council, 1974).

It is important to distinguish between the impact of the automatic benefit mechanism, which compounds the cost-of-living adjustment by raising the worker's potential benefit through higher wages *and* by increasing the schedule of benefits, and the problems associated with a changing demographic pattern. Policy can easily be changed, if the public wills it, in such a way as to stabilize replacement ratios; the "decoupling" proposal appears to answer this problem. But the second question—the number of workers in relation to the number of non-workers, old or young—is a more complex issue composed of changing fertility rates, retirement age, the labor-force activity of young and older men and, even more significantly, of women. The proportions of young to old or men to women cannot be changed quickly; they result from earlier events.

To change the ratio of workers to nonworkers is not impossible, however. Indeed, such a change can be accomplished fairly easily in a period of economic expansion. It would be feasible, for example, to extend working age from 65 to 68 and thereby keep a more favorable ratio, when jobs are available for both the middle-aged and the older worker. Moreover, the proportion of women in the job market would be greatly increased if a strong demand for their services pushed up their wages. In view of women's greater life expectancy, an extension of worklife could be particularly beneficial to them. The Social Security Advisory Council suggests that retirement age might be extended by 2 months a year, beginning in the year 2005 and ending in 2023. The result would be to lower payroll taxes as shown below (Advisory Council, 1975).

A later retirement age is appealing for individual as well as societal reasons: Personal preferences can be accommodated; earnings can be extended later into the lifespan; the worker's sense of self-worth is enhanced. But the probability that social policy will move toward a

Table 2.

| Calendar Year | Tax Rate | |
	Scheduled	With 68 as Retirement Age by 2023
2005-2014	12.3	12.1
2015-2024	14.2	13.5
2025-2050	16.1	14.6

lengthened worklife is low in an era characterized by job shortages and high unemployment, as we noted earlier. The reverse movement toward earlier retirement has been occuring, with departure from the work force before age 65 becoming the norm. Hence, an extension of working years in later life would seem unlikely unless the rate of growth is accelerated.

Funds and funding

Economists have frequently raised questions regarding the possible impact of OASDI on saving and capital formation, hypothesizing that the incentive to save privately is reduced by the assurance of public benefits. Interest in this interrelationship has increased with the work of Martin Feldstein (1974), Alicia Munnell (1974), and others. Feldstein concludes that social security halves personal saving, thereby leading to substantial reductions in the stock of capital and the level of national income. Specifically, the GNP would have been 11-15 percent higher in 1972 had private capital not declined in response to social security taxes and transfers. Thus "a pay-as-you-go social security system reduces aggregate saving and lowers the level of real income" (1974). Edgar Browning argues further that the cost of social insurance is concentrated on the young, the benefits on those who are older. As a result, older voters will favor a larger commitment of funds for social security than younger voters, but both groups will underestimate the effects of social insurance on capital accumulation (Browning, 1975).

Other economists, notably John Brittain, have raised objections to using the payroll tax to collect funds to pay benefits, primarily on the basis of the regressivity of the tax. Writing in 1972, he concluded that "As the tax rate on the working poor nears 13 percent (11 percent for OASDHI and 2 percent for UI), it would seem especially patronizing for their more affluent fellows to assert that it is good for the poor to be forced to save for their old age" (Brittain, 1972). As to its impact on saving, Brittain reasons that the payroll tax cuts into saving less sharply than a progressive income tax and is therefore less of a constraint on growth (1972). Moving toward income taxation and away from payroll taxes is recommended.

None of these objections to the pattern of financing social security are new. They take on added force, however, because tax rates are higher than in the earlier days of the program and because of current publicity over the declining size of the trust fund. It is clear that the pressure to consider alternative funding procedures will continue, with recommendations ranging from relatively mild suggestions for raising the taxable base for the payroll tax to a reform that would involve the building up of a social security fund to offset any decline in private saving and yield a return on the accumulation (Feldstein, 1975).

Summary

Current public preoccupation with the future of social security is perhaps a good sign. It may signify an interest in one's own retirement, admittedly, rather than a concern for the general welfare. Still, recognition of the need to provide income for the future forces a wage earner to confront the costs of retirement benefits and the problems inherent in offsetting any demographic shifts along the way. A typical editorial recently declared:

> Retirement age may have to be pushed back to 68 or even 70 simply to keep the social security system solvent.
>
> For unless birth rates rise dramatically, the ratio of workers to retired persons will drop from 3 to 1 to 2 to 1 in the not-too-distant future, putting a heavy financial burden on people who pay social security taxes.
>
> . . . There are good reasons for mandatory retirement. One is the need to maintain an efficient, alert work force. Another is to make room for young leadership.
>
> But it's beginning to look as though retiring workers at 65—or even younger—is a luxury our children and grandchildren may not be able to afford (*The Cleveland Press*, 1975).

Although such statements tend to exaggerate the impact of current trends, it is nevertheless important to call attention to a possible reversal of the downward drift of retirement age and to the basic explanation for the existence of a younger or later age. General acceptance of extended worklife or higher taxes for the support of retirement benefits is essential to the further growth of the system, and such growth is more difficult to achieve in the wake of frequent warnings that the fund is depleted.

The problems facing a mature system need to be addressed, with perhaps more attention to public sentiment than has been necessary in the past. The costs of substantial increases in the level of benefits, the growing proportion of the population to be supported, new questions on the manner of funding, and the possible impact of social insurance on private saving—these are the issues that lie ahead. The more clearly these issues are stated, the greater the chances of developing a consensus that the gains of the system far outweigh its costs.

It is an error to play down the costs of adequate retirement benefits, as Harvey Shapiro argues:

> At the heart of social security's burgeoning costs are some important demographic shifts in American society. When social security was created in 1935, much of the population was going to work at the age of 16 and retiring at 65 with a life expectancy of another 5 or 6 years. More recently a number of middle-class young people have been entering the labor force at age 25 or so, and when they retire at 65, many can expect to live another 10 or more years. Thus individuals have fewer years to save up for longer retirements (Shapiro, 1975).

Coupled with increased longevity and lower birth rates, he concludes, retirement benefits are bound to be expensive. The question before the public is not whether the clock can be turned back four decades to a time when a tax of 2 percent of the first $3,000 of earnings covered a small number of retirees, and those only meagerly. The debate turns, instead, on the proportion of earnings we wish now and in the future to maintain in retirement, and how we wish to finance that benefit. There can be no doubt that the costs will be high, even if we merely hold to the present replacement ratio. For when the retirement stage of life extends to one-third the length of worklife, the transfer of earnings is necessarily large, even when the humps and valleys are only partially smoothed.

References

Advisory Council on Social Security, *Report of the Quadrennial Advisory Council on Social Security*, Committee on Ways and

Means, U.S. House of Representatives (94th Congress, 1st Session), 1975, chapter 7.

Barfield, R. & Morgan, J. *Early Retirement: The Decision and the Experience*, Institute for Social Research, University of Michigan, 1969.

Boulding, K. Reflections on Poverty. *The Social Welfare Forum*. Columbia University Press, 1961, p. 45.

Brittain, J. A. *The Payroll Tax for Social Security*, The Brookings Institution, 1972, p. 20

Browning, E. K. Why the Social Insurance Budget Is Too Large in a Democracy. *Economic Inquiry*, September 1975, pp. 373-388.

Clark, R. N. *Age Structure Changes and Intergenerational Transfers of Income*, Duke University, 1975.

Feldstein, M. Social Security, Induced Retirement, and Aggregate Capital Accumulation. *Journal of Political Economy*, Sept.-Oct. 1974, pp. 905-26.

————.Toward a Reform of Social Security. *The Public Interest*, Summer 1975, pp. 75-95.

Horlick, M. *National Expenditures on Social Security in Selected Countries, 1968 and 1971*, (Research and Statistics Note #29), Social Security Administration, Office of Research and Statistics, 1974.

Jaffe, A. J. *Pension Systems—How Much Myth? How Much Reality?* Paper presented at the 10th International Congress of Gerontology, Jerusalem, June 1975.

Long, Clarence. *The Labor Force Under Changing Income and Employment*, Princeton University Press, 1958.

Merriam, I. C. Implications of Technological Change for Income, in Kreps, J. *Technology, Manpower, and Retirement Policy*, World Publishing, 1966, p. 167.

Morgan, J. N. *Economic Problems of the Aging and their Policy Implications*. Paper presented for a Conference on Public Policy Assessment of the Conditions and Status of the Elderly, February 1975, p. 3.

Munnel, A. H. The Impact of Social Security on Personal Savings. *National Tax Journal*, December 1974, pp. 553-68.

1975 Annual Report of the Board of Trustees of the Federal Old-Age and Survivors Insurance and Disability Trust Funds, Committee on Ways and Means, U.S. House of Representatives (94th Congress, 1st Session), 1975, p. 2.

Organization for Economic Cooperation and Development. The Effect of Tax and Welfare Programs on Workers' Incomes. *OECD Observer*, March-April 1975, pp. 37-39.

Shapiro, H. *New York Times Book Review*, November 15, 1975, p. 8.

Spengler, J. J. *Stationary Population and Changes in Age Structure: Implications for the Economic Security of the Aged,* Duke University, 1975.

The Cleveland Press, November 10, 1975, p. A6.

The *New York Times,* August 18, 1975, p. C-25.

Thompson, L. *An Analysis of the Factors Currently Determining Benefit Level Adjustments on the Social Security Retirement Program* (Technical Analysis Paper No. 1), Department of Health, Education, and Welfare, 1974.

Women and Social Security: Adapting to a New Era, Special Committee on Aging, U.S. Senate (94th Congress, 1st Session), 1975, p. 9.

6.2

The Future and the Young-Old

Bernice L. Neugarten

A wide range of predictions regarding the future of our society and the future of the world have been put before the American public in the past few years. In the flood of statements that are now appearing there are—to oversimplify it—perspectives that are grandly optimistic, others that are grossly pessimistic. The economy will continue to expand, and the good life will soon be here for us all, or the economy is on the verge of collapse. With continued growth of science and technology, man will solve the problems of overpopulation, food shortages, energy crises, inflation, environmental pollution, and the threat of nuclear war; or because of the very growth of science and technology, such problems are now so unprecedented in scale that man's efforts are doomed to fail.

Within one or the other perspective, the future status of the aged is also differently described. In the optimistic world-view, where at least the developed countries are moving from a production orientation to a quality-of-life orientation, it is said that more equitable social systems are arising. Older persons will get their fair share of the new abundance. In the pessimistic view, where among other things there will be increasing alienation, conflict over employment opportunities and competition between age groups, the old will become newly disadvantaged.

Copyright 1975 by The Gerontological Society. Reprinted by permission. *The Gerontologist*, Vol. 15, No. 1 (Supplement), February 1975, pp. 4-9.

We ourselves have taken a mid-way position, one we regard as conservatively optimistic, and one that might be called a view of the relatively "normal, expectable future." This we regard as the most expeditious view in furthering our own more circumscribed approach to future research.

In very brief terms, we are assuming that for the American society there will be slowed economic growth together with slowed population growth, with Zero Population Growth occurring in about 50 years; increasing urbanization and growth of metropolitan agglomerations; continuing technological advances and an increasingly rapid rate of their application. Levels of education will continue to rise, although at a less dramatic rate than in the past few decades, producing less difference between age groups.

We are assuming a value orientation which—to borrow a phrase from Denis Johnston (1972) and others—is neither the "blue" world of the work ethic nor the "green" world of the leisure ethic, but a "turquoise" world in which new concepts of work and new flexible life styles will appear, so that in both the work setting and the leisure setting there will be greater concern for personal growth and fulfillment. We are presuming also a society in which there will be more, rather than less planning, and in which the role of government in the affairs of everyday life will increase rather than decrease. We are assuming that persons of all ages will expect "more" from life, although "more" may mean a changing value system in which the pursuit of affluence may become less significant than the pursuit of meaningful ways of self-enhancement and community enhancement.

How Many Older Persons Will There Be?

Whatever the uncertainties in other areas, population projections for the middle-aged and old are relatively safe for the next 25 years because they depend on mortality rates, not fertility rates. Everybody who will be old by the year 2000 is already alive. But will he live a great deal longer than his predecessors?

Two general strategies for lengthening life are being pursued by biomedical and biological researchers: the first is the continuing effort to conquer major diseases; the other, to alter the intrinsic biological processes which are presumed to underlie aging and which may proceed independently from disease processes—that is, to discover the genetic and biochemical secrets of aging, then to slow the biological clock that is presumably programmed into the human species. This second approach is directed at rate control, rather than disease control.

Thus far all the increases in life expectancy have been due to in-

Table 1.   Numbers of Older Persons in U.S.A. in 1975 and in 2000 (in millions)

	1975[a]		2000 (A)[a]		2000 (B)[b]	
	M	F	M	F	M	F
Total 55+	18.0	23.2	19.7	27.5	24.8	32.4
65+	8.9	12.8	10.2	16.3	14.4	20.8
75+	3.1	5.2	4.0	7.7	6.9	11.2
55-75	14.9	18.0	15.7	19.8	17.9	21.2

[a]If age-specific death rates continue as of 1968.
[b]If age-specific death rates are reduced after 1970 by 2 percent per year for persons aged 20+.
Projections carried out by David D. McFarland and Grace Chiu.

creased controls over disease but not, so far as is known, to any decrease in the rate of aging. The question then becomes, are there likely to be dramatic discoveries with regard to rate control that will lead to a mushrooming in numbers of older persons by the year 2000?

In attempting to answer this question, we have made inquiries of leading biological researchers, asking for their assessments. With the striking exception of a few who are saying that if research efforts were generously enough supported, the life-span could be extended some 20 to 25 years within the next two decades, for example, Comfort (1959) and Strehler (1970), the responses we have thus far received are consistently negative. The overwhelming majority have responded that they see no such possibility. We have therefore proceeded on the conservative view that there will be no dramatic changes in the length of the human life span within the next few decades, but that, instead, there will be relatively regular improvements with regard to medical knowledge and health care that will produce steady but slow reduction in mortality rates.

Table 1 shows the estimated numbers of older persons in the United States in 1975 and two different projections for the year 2000. The columns marked 2000 (A) are based—as is true also for the 1975 entries—on the age-specific mortality rates of 1968, the latest year for which good data are available. The columns marked 2000 (B) are based on age-specific mortality rates reduced by 2% per year after 1970 for all persons aged 20+.

This latter projection may be overly optimistic, for it will depend upon improved health practices such as reduced cigarette smoking and reduced consumption of foods that increase the likelihood of heart

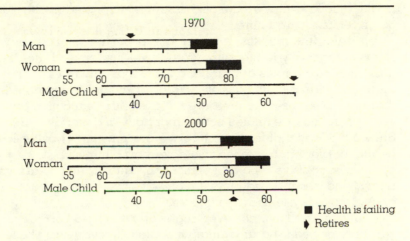

Figure 1. The Timing of Life Events: 1970 and 2000

disease, as well as upon reduction in atmospheric pollution and improved health services. This projection has seemed to us not unreasonable, however, in light of the most recent data on heart disease in United States, as well as other health data for this and other countries. In any case, the figures shown for 2000 (B) serve to show the cumulative effect of a relatively conservative improvement in mortality rates if that improvement continues from year to year. For example, the 65+ population in the year 2000 is expected to be about 26.5 million under present mortality rates, but about 35.5 million under the reduced rates. For the 75+ population the difference is even greater, for the number would be under 12 million in the one instance, but over 18 million in the other instance.

This 2% per year reduction in mortality rates would add about 5 years to average life expectancy for persons aged 65. This prediction is shown graphically in Figure 1, where it is suggested that men who reached 65 in 1970 could expect, on the average, to live to 78; but men who reach age 65 in 2000 can expect to live to 83 (the parallel figures for women are 81.5 and 86).

What Will Be the Health Status of Older People?

Given our assumption that average life expectancy will increase over the next 25 years, and the assumption that this increase will come, not from a slowing of the rate of aging, but from continuingly improved health, it follows that we are also assuming improved health status for older persons in the future.

In truth, the realities are more complex. The relations of various forms of morbidity to mortality are not well understood, nor the relations of mortality rates at younger ages to mortality rates at later ages; there are various definitions of "health" or "vigor" and various indices that have been used for measurement; levels of education and socio-economic status are related both to morbidity and mortality, and so on. Suffice it to say that for the future we are presuming better levels of health for older persons because poverty is diminishing over the life-cycles of successive cohorts of persons, because educational levels are rising, and because we predict more effective forms of public health and improved systems of health care.

All this says little, however, regarding the period of disability that can be expected to occur for many people in the very last phase of life; and for the moment, we have little basis for predicting that this period will become shorter. We have merely suggested in Figure 1, therefore, that a period of disability or failing health will continue to occur toward the end of life.

What Will Be the Role of the Family?

Keeping in mind that "family" is not synonymous with "household," and looking first at family structure, it is clear from census data that there has been a significant shift in marital status of older persons in the past 20 years, with an increase in the proportions of both men and women who are married and living with spouse present, and with offsetting decreases in the proportions never married, widowed, or divorced. Whether these trends will continue into the next 25 years will depend upon a whole host of factors, social as well as economic, not least upon changing attitudes toward marriage, divorce, and remarriage. Some observers believe that nontraditional forms of family life and various manifestations of women's liberation are spreading rapidly into the present middle-aged group; and if so, these will carry forward into old age by the decade 1990-2000, but in fact such evidence as is presently available indicates that the "nonmarried" family, the commune, and other such family forms constitute a very tiny proportion even of the present-day young.

With regard to intergenerational family structure, we can be fairly sure that the four- and five-generation family will be the norm because of increasing longevity and because the length of generations has been shortening.

It is often overlooked that for persons who will be old in 2000, there

Table 2.   Numbers of Children Surviving to Women of Various Ages, USA, 1975 to 2000[a]

Calendar Year	Age of Women			
	55	65	75	85
1970-1974	2.40	2.12	—	—
1980-1984	2.84	2.35	2.02	—
1990-1994	3.06	2.78	2.24	1.80
2000-2004	2.68[b]	2.99	2.65	2.00
2010-2014	—	2.62	2.85	2.37

[a]Projections calculated by David D. McFarland (Assumptions: mortality rates constant at levels shown in 1969 U.S. life table; children ever born at observed levels for cohorts which have already completed their fertility; women at younger ages have completed the same fraction of total fertility that older women had completed at the same age; children are 25 years younger than their mothers.
[b]This smaller number reflects the drop in fertility that began in the 1960s.

will be more, rather than fewer children and other relatives. Table 2 shows, for instance, the projected numbers of children who will be surviving to women at various ages in successive decades. Given the assumptions stated in the footnote of that Table, it appears that the woman who will reach 55 in the year 2000 will have more surviving children than the women who reached 55 in 1975; and that for women who will reach 75, the increases will be even more striking. These projections are based on stable mortality rates throughout the next 25 years, but the differences reflect, of course, the fluctuating birth rates of past decades. (If, as was suggested earlier, mortality rates are reduced in the future, the rates of surviving children will be further affected.)

Numbers of surviving children do not, of course, tell us about interactions or patterns of assistance between parent and child. Projections of the latter type are difficult. We do not, for example, have national data for the 1970s similar to those for the 1960s reported by Shanas, Townsend, Wedderburn, Friis, Milhoj, and Stehouwer (1968) by which to assess present patterns of family interaction, to say nothing of future patterns. Yet a whole range of smaller studies leads to the conclusion that the family has thus far remained a strong and supportive institution for older people. Our review of this literature adds up to the following: most old people want to be independent of their families as much as possible, but when they can no longer manage for themselves, they expect their children to come to their aid. Not only do such expectations exist, but they are usually met. A complex pattern of exchange of services exists across generations, and both ties of affection and ties of obligation remain strong. Perhaps expectations will change in these regards by the year 2000, but if so, the changes are likely to be slow.

When it comes to living in the same household, there has been a dramatic trend toward separate households for older persons. While there are more families having older relatives, fewer are living with them. Yet even as late as 1970, the latest year for which national data are available, it was clear that the older the individual, and the sicker, the more likely he would be found living with a child. For all persons aged 75+, one of five women, and one of ten men were living with a child (a few percent were living with another relative). It is a neglected fact that, in 1970, a total of 2¼ million persons aged 65+ were living in the same household with a child or other relative.

Here again it is not easily predicted whether or not the trend toward separate households will continue. The trends will be affected by economic factors and by housing policies. One significant factor is the increasing numbers of families in which persons of advanced old age have children who are themselves old, a trend that will become even more marked in the next few decades. What its effects will be is difficult to foresee. If a more effective network of supportive social and home health services arises, more intergenerational households may appear in which both generations are old.

One thing is likely: that families will want more options in the settings and types of care available for an aged family member whose health is failing. Such institutions as nursing homes may be necessary for a part of the population, but many families may seek ways of maintaining an older person at home, either in his own household or in the child's household.

The Young-Old

Because the papers to follow deal with economic status, residential location, mental health, and social and health services, we shall not pursue these as separate questions here. Instead, to return to Figure 1, we have suggested there that the age of retirement—or, perhaps more accurately, the age of "first retirement"—will come about age 55 in the year 2000 rather than, as now, at about age 65. With the anticipated increase in life expectancy the post-retirement period of the life-span for men will be about 25 to 28 years instead of the present 13 years. The implications of this change, together with various other sets of data regarding the characteristics of older persons, suggests a meaningful division between the "young-old" and the "old-old."

Although it is life styles rather than chronological ages that concern us, nevertheless most of the young-old can be expected to come from the group who are 55 to 75, and most of the old-old from those who are 75+.

Age 55 is beginning to be a meaningful age marker in the lifecycle because of the lowering age of retirement. The large majority of persons now retiring are doing so earlier than "required" by mandatory rules, with many retiring just as soon as they can live comfortably on their retirement incomes. One example is the auto workers who exercise the option to retire at 55. In an increasing number of occupational groups, eligibility for pensions is determined not by age, but by numbers of years of service, with the result that some men are retiring in their early 50s or even earlier. In other industries, where over-all employment is declining, the downward trend in age of retirement is dramatic. The 1970 census already shows only 81% of all 55- to 64-year-old men in the labor force, compared to 92% in the next younger age group.

The trend toward earlier retirement will depend upon rates of economic and technological growth, international as well as national, the numbers of young workers, the number of women workers, the extent to which the work setting becomes more attractive, the adequacy of retirement income, the value of leisure time, and so on. But most observers predict that the downward trend in age of retirement will continue over the next two or three decades. By and large, the young-old will become increasingly a group of retirees.

As suggested by our earlier comments on health status, the young-old are already a relatively healthy group. The data have not been aggregated in age categories most appropriate to our purposes, but at present, about 15% of the group aged 45 to 64 need to limit their major activities because of health, while for all those 65+, it is about 40%. We estimate that, if our young-old group were differentiated in these data, the proportion with health limitations would probably be between 20 and 25%.

In distinguishing further between the young-old and the old-old, we should look again at the population data and the family data. As shown in Table 1, women outnumber men by a sizable proportion, but less so in the 55+ and 65+ than in the 75+. Furthermore, because most men marry women somewhat younger than themselves, the young-old as a total group are more like younger than like older age-groups. About 80% of the young-old men, and well over half the women were married in 1970 and living with their spouses. By far the common pattern is the husband and wife living in their own household, with some 80% owning their own homes.

The economic status of the young-old is less easily assessed. For most persons income drops precipitously upon retirement, and if present trends continue, the adjustment to lower incomes may be timed closer to age 55 than to age 65. The anticipation of a longer period of life at a reduced income may affect monetary savings plans in young adulthood just as it affects pension plans, but such consequences are presently unpredictable. However, current income is only part of total economic resources. (For instance, government in-kind transfers such as Medicare, value of rent to homeowners, net worth holdings, tax adjustments, intrafamily transfers, and other components need to be included in assessing economic well-being.) It is an open question whether, in the next few decades, economic well-being will be increasingly equalized across age groups, but the trend has clearly been thus far toward improved economic status for older people.

It is likely that economic hazards for both the young-old and the old-old will be further reduced in the near future. Threats of inflation notwithstanding, the rises in Social Security together with their cost-of-living increases, and the new federalization of the welfare system (the Supplemental Security Income system that makes the incomes of the poorest older people somewhat more adequate than before) together constitute one major step forward. It is almost certain also that a form of national health insurance will soon be instituted which will meet an increasing proportion of health costs for persons of all ages. In addition, private and public pensions and profit-sharing plans have spread, and greater numbers of workers will collect benefits, given the newest federal legislation that monitors the operation of private pension plans. To the extent these and other changes occur, the major threats to economic well-being of older persons will be effectively diminished, with the outcome that the future young-old should be more financially secure than their predecessors.

The young-old are already much better educated than the old-old, and in the near future they will be in a less disadvantaged position in comparison to the young. The gains in educational level in successive cohorts of the population have been so substantial that by 1990 the young-old group will be, on the average, high school graduates. Furthermore, with the anticipated growth in higher education for adults, whether degree-oriented or not, and the even greater growth in what the Carnegie Commission (1973) calls "further education" (that education, both part-time and full-time, which occurs in settings other than college campuses and which is not aimed at academic degrees) it can be anticipated that the educational differences that presently exist between young, middle-aged, and young-old will be further reduced.

With regard to political participation, the young-old group is a highly active group compared to other age groups. Verba and Nie (1972) show that, when their national data are corrected for income and education, over-all political participation is highest for the age group 51-65 (i.e., voting, persuading others how to vote, actively working for party or candidate, working with others on local problems); and it falls off only a little for persons over 65. Thus, in the electorate as a whole the young-old are disproportionately influential.

What Will the Young-Old Want?

These, then, are some of the characteristics of that 15% of the total population who are the young-old. As a group, they are already markedly different from the out-moded stereotypes of old age. They are relatively free from traditional social responsibilities of work and family, they are relatively healthy, relatively well-off, and they are politically active. We predict that these characteristics will become increasingly salient by the year 2000.

A vigorous and educated young-old group can be expected to develop new needs with regard to the meaningful use of time. They will want a wide range of options and opportunities both for self-enhancement and for community participation.

With regard to work, some will opt for early retirement; some will want to continue to work beyond 65; some will want to undertake new work careers at one or more times after age 40. The young-old are likely to encourage economic policies that hasten the separation between income and work, with the goal of providing retirees with sufficient income to approximate their pre-retirement living standards.

We are already seeing a trend which will probably accelerate: a wider range of life patterns with regard to work, education, and leisure. More middle-aged and older people are seeking education, some because of obsolescence of work skills, others for recreation or self-fulfillment. Plans are now in progress in various parts of the country to create intergenerational campuses, and in this and other ways to help bring into reality the so-called "learning society."

The needs of the young-old in housing, location, and transportation will be increasingly affected by the decisions they make with regard to the use of leisure time. The desire to find interesting things to do will lead them to seek environments which will maximize options for meaningful pursuits. If opportunities are provided for meaningful community participation in their present communities, fewer rather than more are likely to move to age-segregated retirement communities.

The young-old are likely to want greater options for what generally might be called an "age-irrelevant" society, one in which arbitrary constraints based on chronological age are removed, and in which all individuals have opportunities consonant with their needs, desires, and abilities, whether they be young or old.

Over-all, as the young-old articulate their needs and desires, the emphasis is likely to be upon improving the quality of life and upon increasing the choices of life styles.

The Old-Old

The visibility of the young-old is not to denigrate the old-old, nor to neglect their needs.

An increasing minority of the old-old will remain active and productive and, because this is true, will want increased options in all areas of life. The majority will probably live independently, but many will need supportive social services, or home health services, or special features in the physical environment to enable them to function as fully as possible. Without taking an overly optimistic view, it is likely that such services will grow, and that they will become more effective not only in slowing physical and mental deterioration, but in preventing unnecessary decline in feelings of self-worth and dignity.

There is no denying the fact that at the very end of life there will be a shorter or longer period of dependency, nor that there will be increased numbers of the old-old who will need special care, either in their own homes or in institutional settings. New and difficult ethical questions will arise regarding what share of the health and services budget of the nation should go to the old-old. For persons who are terminally ill or incapacitated, the problems for the society will continue to be how to provide the maximum care and comfort, the assurance of dignified death, but also how to provide a greater element of choice for the individual himself or for members of his family regarding how and when his life shall end. The future will probably see the spread of educational programs aimed at the public at large as well as at various professional groups for achieving a "best death" for each individual.

The Future Roles of the Young-Old

To turn now to the broader question of the relation between age groups and how they may change in the future, older persons will probably continue to move away from the roles of economic producer and increasingly become the users of leisure time. In those new roles, the young-old may be the first age group to reach the society of the future. How will they experiment with what some observers would call the truly human condition—the condition of freedom from work and freedom from want?

With their relative good health, education, purchasing power, free time, and political involvement, they are not likely to become neglected members of the society. Will they, instead, become social contributors? Will they create new service roles with or without financial remuneration?

Will they become major agents of social change in building an age-irrelevant society? If they create an attractive image of aging and thus allay the fears of the young about growing old, they will play a significant role in shaping the society of the future.

References

Carnegie Commission on Higher Education, *Toward a learning society*. McGraw-Hill, New York, 1973.

Comfort, A. Longer life by 1990? *New Scientist*, Dec., 1959, 549-551.

Johnston, D. F. The future of work: Three possible alternatives. *Monthly Labor Review*, U.S. Dept. of Labor, Washington, May, 1972.

Neugarten, B. L. Age groups in American society and the rise of the young-old. *Annals of the American Academy of Political & Social Science*, Sept., 1974, 187-198.

Shanas, E., Townsend, P., Wedderburn, D., Friis, H., Milhoj, P., & Stehouwer, J. *Old people in three industrial societies*, Atherton Press, New York, 1968.

Strehler, B. Ten myths about aging. *Center Magazine*, July, 1970, 41-48.

6.3

Social and Health Services
for the Future Aged

Sheldon S. Tobin

It is anticipated that future cohorts of older persons will not only live
about 5 years longer than the present cohorts but they will also stay
healthier to a more advanced age. There is no evidence to suggest,
however, that they will be less incapacitated in the final phase preceding their death, nor that the length of a pre-terminal phase will be
shorter. Thus, it can be anticipated that about 1 of every 5 Americans
aged 65 and over will need a combination of intensive and extensive
social and health services.

This amount of need is reflected in current survey data: about 5%
of older Americans currently reside in institutions, and for every older
person in an institution there are at least 2 others who are homebound,
1 of 4 of whom are bedridden (Shanas, Townsend, Wedderburn, Friis,
Milhoj, & Stehouwer, 1968). Corroboration for this amount of need for
social and health services comes from the planners of protective service programs for the elderly, who have estimated that about 1 of 6
older Americans who are not institutionalized are so impaired as to
necessitate one or more types of direct social and health services (see,
for example, Hall, Mathiasen, & Ross, 1973). When this 15% to 16% of
community-dwelling elderly who need services are added to the 5%
who reside in institutions, the total again is about 20%—or about 1 of 5

Copyright © 1975 by The Gerontological Society. Reprinted by permission. *The Gerontologist*, Vol. 15, No. 1 (Supplement), February 1975, pp. 32-37.

older Americans. Most of these 20% are among the old-old, those aged 75+, who, in successive decades, will be increasingly older when they need social and health services.

It is impossible to forecast how well the needs will be met of these very old impaired individuals. The *effectiveness* of future social and health services are obviously more speculative questions than the characteristics of the future aged population—characteristics such as their number, sex distribution, family structure, and residential location. It is possible, however, to make some educated inferences on the *form* of future social and health services. To be explicit, three current trends will, in all likelihood, be translated into structural forms in the next decade or two. First is the community-based, local or neighborhood organization that is now being developed to deliver and to integrate a wide range of social, health and other services in order to prevent premature institutionalization. Second is the smaller long-term care institution for those aged persons who must have custodial care; institutions that will be an inextricable part of community based service organizations. Third is the terminal care center or the hospice, for persons who are in the terminal phase of life, centers that will be visible and important components of hospitals. These three forms of social and health services will, on the surface, remarkably change the topography of organizations and institutions devoted to long-term care for elderly individuals, but their effectiveness may not be any greater than that of the current *nonsystem* of social and health care.

Actually, within the current *nonsystem*, the components for a system are already in evidence. These components, as listed in Table 1, however, are not effectively linked one to another and they are not so organized that they are readily available either simultaneously or sequentially. The integration that is now lacking will be achieved only if sufficient funds are allocated for that purpose.

Community-Based Organizations

The possibility for realizing the first form of social-health services—the community-based organization that under one auspice attempts to integrate a range of services—is reflected in legislation that was proposed by Kennedy and Mills (in HR 13870, 93rd Congress, 2nd Session, 1974). This legislation included a modification of Medicare that would cover the costs of providing those social and health services that would help older persons avoid institutionalization for as long as possible, and that would also cover institutional care when such care becomes necessary. The proposed legislation incorporated the Morris (1971) proposal for local Personal Care Organizations to be developed and

Table 1.   Some Current Services for the Elderly

A continuum of services: From services for the comparatively well elderly through services that provide alternatives for preventing premature institutionalization to services for those who need institutional care.

Home-Delivered (Service delivered to the home)	Congregate-Delivered	
	Congregate Organized (Person travels to the Service)	Congregate Residence
Outreach	Adult education	Senior housing (includes retirement hotels)
Information and referral	Recreational senior center	Senior housing with recreation
Telephone reassurance		Senior housing with recreation and social services
Friendly visiting	Nutrition sites (wheels to meals)	
Work at home		
Senior wheels to shopping doctor dentist social functions		
Escort service	Multipurpose senior center (all of the above plus outreach, health and social follow-up)	Sheltered care
Homemaker service (housekeeping, handyman, etc.)		Half-way houses
Meals-on-Wheels		Mental hospital
Home health care (visiting nurse, rehabilitation, speech therapy, dentist and doctor)	Day care (day and night hospital)	Institutional care (nursing homes and homes for the aged)
Foster home care (complete social and health care for bedridden person at home)		Intermediate nursing care
		Skilled nursing care
		Short-term crisis care
		Vacation plan
		Terminal care

funded through nonprofit corporations that would purchase care for all beneficiaries within a substate area. The intent of the Morris proposal was to create for each beneficiary a package of social and health services that would be tailor-made to meet his particular needs.

This particular proposed legislation reflects the political pressures of various types that led prestigious legislators such as Kennedy and Mills to endorse what, if passed by the Congress, would surely eventuate in far-reaching changes in social and health services, ones that would be costly as well. Foremost is the pervasive discontent with the quality of institutional care, care that ultimately is being paid for by the taxpayer. Recent cutbacks in federal and state allocations for institutional care have only raised further public concerns that institutional care is not available for those persons who need it, nor are alternatives available for those persons who might otherwise be institutionalized prematurely (see, for example, Church, 1971). The development of viable alternatives to institutionalization has also been urged by voluntary service agencies and by not-for-profit provider groups, primarily by administrators of not-for-profit institutions—especially administrators of sectarian homes for the aged. Although these groups have not been as effective in arguing their cause with Congress as have the lobbyists for the proprietary nursing home industry, their voices have nevertheless begun to be heard. Their cause is strengthened by the increasing pressures from families of older people and from older people themselves—from families who would prefer not to institutionalize their aged member and older people who are increasingly trying to avoid entering what they perceive to be a "death house."

Although the present cohort of the elderly may have strong feelings against entering an institution, they are more likely to passively accept their adverse circumstances than will future cohorts. Aged persons in the future will be more inclined to see their personal problems as being remediable either by informal or by professional help from others; and to a greater extent, they will have already used professional help in meeting earlier personal problems. These changed attitudes are likely to occur regardless of educational level. At the same time, the use of professionals is more frequent among persons with higher educational levels, and the fact that future cohorts of the aged will be more highly educated—the average educational level for those 65 years of age and over will rise in the next 20 years from an 8th-grade to a 12th-grade level—is likely to lead to the increased use of professional care-givers.

In addition to the heightened expectations of future cohorts, the results of current social experiments in the delivery of social health care to the impaired elderly may also influence the shape of future legislation. Local personal care organizations are now being developed which may prove to be financially feasible. A singular effort, for example, is that represented in the Greater Hartford Process (1972), where public and private monies have been pooled in Hartford for setting up a city-wide Community Life Association. In this experiment, the locus of service integration is within the Neighborhood Life Center. Beyond offering services to persons of all ages, these Centers provide special programs for maternal and infant care, for adolescents, and for personal care services for the impaired elderly. If data on benefits become available—especially, if favorable cost/benefit ratios can be demonstrated—the data may supply decision-makers with a clear rationale for developing local, and specifically neighborhood, systems of integrated social-health services.

Data such as those presented by Golant (1975) will also be important, data that suggest the persistence of neighborhoods with high concentrations of elderly people, where such local service systems will be welcomed, if not demanded.

It is only, however, if such local systems make a prior commitment to the very old—and specifically to the prevention of premature institutionalization—that they will be effective. This problem is well recognized by all those who developed and are now implementing Title III of the 1973 amendments to the Older Americans Act. This legislation mandates the development of linkage networks by mobilizing and coordinating services so that there can be maximum "independence and dignity in a home environment for older persons capable of self-care with appropriate supportive services" (Section 301). Unless there are adequate resources—not only for the linkage function but also for the actual services that are to be coordinated—a viable service system for the very old cannot be developed by the Area Agencies on Aging (see, for example, the discussion by Hudson, 1974, of the problems inherent in implementing the intent of this legislation).

The Local Institution

The second future form of social and health care, the small local institution, is not now a reality. Although small institutions are potentially less dehumanizing for their residents than are large institutions, they are not perceived as economically feasible. Professionals have not yet been able to mobilize sentiment for constructing more humane but possibly more costly institutional facilities. If, however, local care *systems* are developed, the developers and managers might play an important role in developing local institutions that provide more desirable environments for those elderly people who need them. If a continuum of care is created that includes both community and institutional components, older people who reside in a local institution might be regarded as being the continued responsibility of the local provider organization. Once having delivered services to an older person with the intent of maintaining him in the community, the local system might well assume a larger responsibility for assuring him optimal institutional care if and when he needs it.

What type of institution is likely to become available? Will there be no choice but to send the older person to a "warehouse for the deteriorated and infirm?" Many argue (see, for example, Anderson, 1974) that our society will not allocate sufficient funds for therapeutic institutional care for the very old, saying, among other things, that it is very costly to hire personnel for the unpleasant task of caring for the chronically-ill aged. Yet it may become feasible to limit costs, if small institutions can make use of new technologies and can then use paraprofessionals in implementing modern theories of human service organizations.

If, for example, the local primary care system is effectively linked to secondary general hospitals and to the specialized services in tertiary medical care centers, it would be more possible to design feasible local, prosthetic environments for the impaired older person. Such prosthetic environments could make use of computerized systems in helping the person with the tasks of everyday living. Architectural design could facilitate independence. New technologies and new attitudes on the part of older persons toward using technological devices may make these innovations more feasible. The future aged, who will have experienced the increased benefits of science and technology, are likely to become increasingly more comfortable with sophisticated medical technology and advanced electronic gadgetry.

Many devices and systems are now being developed that will be helpful for the impaired elderly person within an institutional setting, as well as in his own home. For example, in a recent issue of *Aging*, Culclasure (1974) discusses several ways in which NASA space research led to technology that can be adopted for the elderly. One picture showing a patient in a hospital bed has the caption: "Above, an immobilized patient, by merely moving her eyes, can dial a telephone, turn pages of a book or magazine, or change TV channels." Using computers, as in this case, for supporting and enhancing life functions, seems to offer unlimited possibilities (see, for example, Gordon, 1969).

Another type of technological advance that will be useful for the future impaired elderly is that of telemetric monitoring. The impaired person can be monitored for changes in various physiological parameters if he wears a simple unobtrusive device (see, for example, Milsum, 1970). Through this monitoring device, the person in an institutional setting, or in his own home, could be assured that a marked change in physiological function would be responded to at once by human service personnel. The efficient use of monitoring obviously necessitates various combinations of paramedical personnel, biomedical instrumentation, transportation, and communication technology. One example of this technology is that now used in Nebraska in emergency care for highway accident victims (Stratbucker & Chambers, 1971). Vital function telemetry permits monitoring of the accident victim as he is being transported to the hospital, at the same time that the physician in the hospital transmits instructions to prepare for receiving the patient in the emergency room. Telemetry and computers, in turn, can be incorporated into architectural designs that enhance security and mobility. Housekeeping could be made easier by employing devices now in use in modern hotels such as suction-cleaning systems that are built into the floor. Various writers (see, for example, Fozard & Thomas, 1973) have suggested other ways of redesigning the environment to optimize the functioning of an older person.

Given, then, new attitudes in elderly persons and rapid advances in technology, the local small institution becomes more possible for the future aged. This type of institution, a free-standing congregate housing facility for even as few as 20 to 50 impaired elderly persons—architecturally designed to assure maximum mobility and social interaction, telemetrically equipped so that the individual could control food preparation, room cleaning, and other tasks of daily living—need not lack the all-important human component. Social service personnel could be available, but the personnel would also include architects and engineers as well as physicians, nurses and therapists. A critical factor in controlling costs would be to maximize the use of paraprofessionals.

The "decentralized" institutional facility could be articulated with other components of the long-term care system. In addition to linkages with other medical facilities, a major linkage would be with the social-provision system.

This type of institution appears unrealistic in terms of our present orientation and our present economic realities. Current thinking is that about 180 beds is the efficient size for a long-term care institution, given the costs of operating a combination hotel, hospital, and social community. Once the basic costs are established, the effort then turns to humanizing the environment. Less, however, may be more: an optimal size, from the perspective of the resident, is much smaller than 180. Small institutions could be efficient if professional expertise of a wide variety of types was used to develop and coordinate the delivery of diverse, high-quality services. The "decentralized" long-term care facility would also appear more realistic if the Kennedy-Mills proposal or similar legislation were passed. Indeed if the small institution were embedded in a community social-provision organization that was directed at preventing premature institutionalization, then there could be a more cogent argument for adequate reimbursement to the institution.

Given current social and health practices it is more economical to deliver social and health services in the community than in long-term care institutions. But this may not be so if these community services were to become more widely available and if they were coordinated. They would then be very different from the "hit and miss" programs that are now operating. More costly still would be the delivery of services to the homebound and to the bedridden who now all too often suffer in silence and who receive no services. Thus, gearing-up to offer extensive services to all who could benefit from them would be costly, indeed; but in the long run, such services might cost less because they would prevent or delay the individual's deterioration. At present, because of the absence of preventive care, more older persons are being placed in total institutions than is warranted. If, therefore, the social and health system were efficient, institutional care could be prevented for many and, for others, could be used more selectively. Examples of *selective* use of institutions include post-hospital stays where realistic efforts are made at once to return the person to a less institutional environment; and brief stays during crises, or when family members who care for the older person wish to have a vacation.

In sum, the local institution could become a flexible resource for the community provision system. In the long run, if effectively linked to the secondary and tertiary components of the health system, it could be less costly than other forms of care, possibly less costly than our present reliance on the proprietary nursing home industry which articulates with neither other community providers nor hospitals.

Terminal Care

The third form of social-health service that may emerge in the near future is the terminal care center, the hospice modeled after Saunder's (1972) center in England where terminal patients are helped through the dying process by the careful management of pain and the maintenance of maximal social supports. Because Saunder's hospice is embedded in a hospital complex it becomes a legitimate and specialized service, much like a surgical service. The hospice helps both the dying person and the family at the "bedside." The staff of the hospice, much in the English tradition, could also go into the community to help the dying patient and his family at home.

Hospices are beginning to be developed in this country, some in hospitals where a fixed number of beds is designated for terminal care. The development of these centers is possibly a reaction to the increasing preoccupation in our society with euthanasia, as well as to the growing awareness that current hospital practices do not ease the crisis for the patient nor for the patient's family. At present it is in these very hospital and other institutional settings that over 60% of all deaths occur. Furthermore, deaths are increasingly concentrated in old age rather than being spread more evenly across the life-span. Three of four deaths in 1967 (77%) occurred in the 55+ age group (Vital Statistics of the United States, 1969). Given the present situation, as more people live longer, they are also more likely to die in settings that are least conducive to easing the dying process for themselves and their families.

The development of terminal-care centers may be hastened by the evidence that is being amassed that the process of dying can indeed be eased for the person himself as well as for close family members. Students of thanatology believe that sensitive and trained personnel can be helpful to both the dying patient and the family. The work of Kubler-Ross (1969) and others emphasizes the importance to the dying person of completing a series of psychological stages in preparation for death. These stages, if worked through, eventuate in a final resolution in which there is an evaluation of one's own life as meaningful and in which death becomes more acceptable. However we may conceptualize the "best death," or even the "successful death," the aged of the future will, in all likelihood, manifest a different set of attitudes and expectations regarding societal responsibilities for easing the dying process. The demand will grow for a wider range of options for the family in maintaining some degree of control over the management of death. Indeed these issues are already under discussion in various voluntary organizations that are now developing hospices.

The trend toward establishing hospices is also related to the current misuse of institutional settings. Some mental hospitals, for example, have been admitting increasing numbers of terminal patients who are simply identified as mentally ill (Markson & Hard, 1970). If the patients so misclassified were treated as "dying," it might be possible to improve their terminal experience. In other institutional settings patients are labeled terminal, and then ignored. Efforts to reach these patients have at times proved successful. Kastenbaum (1972), for example, used a "reach out" procedure for mental hospital patients who were treated by staff as if they were already dead, and he identified half such patients as capable of sentient experiences and responses. Efforts such as these have illuminated the possibilities for more humane practices in the care of the dying patient.

The creation of specialized terminal care institutions within the hospital system would make it possible not only to provide better care for patients in the center itself, but also throughout the hospital system.

Professionals and paraprofessionals from the center could be mobilized to provide terminal care and counseling in the same way that other therapies are now ordered for patients in the hospital. With these personnel being used throughout the hospital, practices in caring for the medical and psychological needs of the elderly patient would be modified. At present, efforts to change practices for the terminal patient in hospitals—usually limited to offering seminars to change the attitudes of service personnel—have not been very successful. The presence of a terminal care *service* may, however, have much better outcomes.

In addition to being articulated with the total hospital system, the hospice could also make a needed contribution to the efforts of other community agencies if personnel could also go into people's homes to facilitate the dying process. Thus, the terminal care center draws attention again to the need for coordinated *systems* of social and health services.

Overview

The forms of social and health services discussed here are likely to become more visible in future years. Currently there is a broad array of services for the elderly, but they lack articulation. Fortunately these issues are now being seriously confronted by service providers and legislators alike. The problems inherent in developing services that can be delivered both simultaneously and sequentially—currently referred to as the issue of "continuity of care," "service integration," "unnecessary duplication of services," and "appropriate level of institutional care"—are becoming better understood. As older people age their needs shift—from general life-enhancing services, to services that maintain the individual as a viable member of the community, to survival needs that often necessitate institutional care. As self-care capacity deteriorates among the heterogeneous cohort of the old-old, a *wide variety* of services are helpful, including home delivered services, congregate organized services, and congregate residential services. It is recognized that only through efficient linkages will there be a fit between changing needs and services.

The local provision system that has as one task the prevention of premature institutionalization, the community institution that has the task of humanizing custodial care for those severely debilitated elderly who need institutional care, and the terminal care center that has the task of helping the dying person—these may indeed be the emerging service forms of the future. The question remains whether they will accomplish the lofty tasks for which they will have been developed.

References

Anderson, O. W. The sick aged and society: Some dismal implications for public policy. Paper presented at the Annual Meeting of American Public Health Assn., New Orleans, 1974.

Church, F. *Alternatives to nursing home care: A proposal.* USGPO, Washington, 1971.

Culclasure, D. T. NASA space research aids civilians, including the elderly. *Aging,* No. 239-240, Sept.-Oct., 1974, 14-17.

Fozard, J. L., & Thomas, J. C. Why aging psychologists ought to get interested in aging. Paper presented to the Symposium on Human Aging and Engineering Psychology, American Psychological Assn., Montreal, Aug., 1973.

Golant, S. M. Residential concentrations of the future elderly. *Gerontologist,* 1975, *15,* 1:2, 16-23.

Gordon, T. J. The feedback between technology and values. In K. Baier & N. Escher (Eds.), *Values and the future.* Free Press, New York, 1969.

Greater Hartford Process, Inc. A new system of social services for 1980. Hartford, CT, March, 1972. (mimeo)

Hall, G. H., Mathiasen, G., and Ross, H. A. *Guide to development of protective services for older people.* National Council on the Aging. Charles C Thomas, Springfield, IL, 1973.

Hudson, R. B. Rational planning and organizational imperatives: Prospects for area planning in aging. *Annals of the American Academy of Political and Social Science,* 1974, *415,* 41-54.

Kastenbaum, R. While the old man dies: Our conflicting attitudes toward the elderly. In B. Schoenberg (Ed.), *Psychosocial aspects of terminal care,* Columbia Univ. Press, New York, 1972.

Kübler-Ross, E. *On death and dying.* Mcmillan, New York, 1969.

Markson, E. W. & Hard, J. Referral for death: Low status of the aged and referral for psychiatric hospitalization. *Aging & Human Development,* 1970, *1,* 261-272.

Milsum, J. H. Biological engineering. In A. B. Bronwell (Ed.), *Science and technology in the world of the future.* Wiley Inter-Science, New York, 1970.

Morris, R. *Alternatives to nursing home care: A proposal.* Printed for use of the Special Committee on Aging. USGPO, Washington, Oct., 1971.

Saunders, C. A therapeutic community: St. Christopher's Hospice. In B. Schoenberg (Ed.), *Psychosocial aspects of terminal care.* Columbia Univ. Press, New York, 1972.

Shanas, E., Townsend, P., Wedderburn, D., Friis, H., Milhoj, P., & Stehouwer, J. *Old people in three industrial societies.* Atherton, New York, 1968.

Stratbucker, R. A., & Chambers, W. A. Vital function telemetry as part of a mobile emerging medical care system. Paper presented to the Biomedical Science Instrumentation Symposium, Milwaukee, Aug.-Sept., 1971.

Vital Statistics of the United States, 1967, Vol. II, *Mortality*, Part B. National Center for Health Statistics, Washington, 1969.

TEAR OUT CONVENIENT ORDER FORM:

PAPERBACKS AVAILABLE FROM PROMETHEUS BOOKS

CRITIQUES OF THE PARANORMAL

____ESP & PARAPSYCHOLOGY: A CRITICAL RE-EVALUATION *C.E.M. Hansel* $7.95

____EXTRA-TERRESTRIAL INTELLIGENCE *James L. Christian, editor*   5.95

____OBJECTIONS TO ASTROLOGY *L. Jerome & B. Bok*   3.95

____THE PSYCHOLOGY OF THE PSYCHIC *David Marks & Richard Kammann*   7.95

____PHILOSOPHY & PARAPSYCHOLOGY *J. Ludwig, editor*   8.95

HUMANISM

____ETHICS WITHOUT GOD *K. Nielsen*   4.95

____HUMANIST ALTERNATIVE *Paul Kurtz, editor*   4.95

____HUMANIST ETHICS *Morris Storer, editor*   6.95

____HUMANIST FUNERAL SERVICE *Corliss Lamont*   1.95

____HUMANIST MANIFESTOS I & II   1.95

____HUMANIST WEDDING SERVICE *Corliss Lamont*   1.50

____HUMANISTIC PSYCHOLOGY *I. David Welch, George Tate, Fred Richards, editors*   8.95

____MORAL PROBLEMS IN CONTEMPORARY SOCIETY *Paul Kurtz, editor*   4.95

____VOICE IN THE WILDERNESS *Corliss Lamont*   4.95

PHILOSOPHY & ETHICS

____ART OF DECEPTION *Nicholas Capaldi*   4.95

____BENEFICENT EUTHANASIA *M. Kohl, editor*   7.95

____ESTHETICS CONTEMPORARY *Richard Kostelanetz, editor*   9.95

____EXUBERANCE: A PHILOSOPHY OF HAPPINESS *Paul Kurtz*   3.00

____FREEDOM OF CHOICE AFFIRMED *Corliss Lamont*   4.95

____HUMANHOOD: ESSAYS IN BIOMEDICAL ETHICS *Joseph Fletcher*   6.95

____JOURNEYS THROUGH PHILOSOPHY *N. Capaldi & L. Navia, editors*   9.95

____MORAL EDUCATION IN THEORY & PRACTICE *Robert Hall & John Davis*   7.95

____TEACH YOURSELF PHILOSOPHY *Antony Flew*   5.95

____THINKING STRAIGHT *Antony Flew*   4.95

____WORLDS OF PLATO & ARISTOTLE *J.B. Wilbur & H.J. Allen, editors*   5.95

____WORLDS OF THE EARLY GREEK PHILOSOPHERS *J.B. Wilbur & H.J. Allen, editors*   5.95

SEXOLOGY

_____THE FRONTIERS OF SEX RESEARCH *Vern Bullough, editor*   6.95

_____NEW BILL OF SEXUAL RIGHTS & RESPONSIBILITIES *Lester Kirkendall*   1.95

_____NEW SEXUAL REVOLUTION *Lester Kirkendall, editor*   4.95

_____PHILOSOPHY & SEX *Robert Baker & Fred Elliston, editors*   6.95

_____SEX WITHOUT LOVE: A PHILOSOPHICAL EXPLORATION *Russell Vannoy*   6.95

SKEPTICS BOOKSHELF

_____ANTHOLOGY OF ATHEISM & RATIONALISM *Gordon Stein, editor*   8.95

_____ATHEISM: THE CASE AGAINST GOD *George H. Smith*   6.95

_____CLASSICS OF FREE THOUGHT *Paul Blanshard, editor*   5.95

_____CRITIQUES OF GOD *Peter Angeles, editor*   6.95

_____WHAT ABOUT GODS? (for children) *Chris Brockman*   3.95

SOCIAL ISSUES

_____AGE OF AGING: A READER IN SOCIAL GERONTOLOGY

     Abraham Monk, editor   8.95

_____REVERSE DISCRIMINATION *Barry Gross, editor*   7.95

The books listed above can be obtained from your book dealer
or directly from Prometheus Books.
Please check off the appropriate books.
Remittance must accompany all orders from individuals.
Please include 85¢ postage and handling for each book.
(N.Y. State residents add 7% sales tax)

Send to _____
                    (Please type or print clearly)
Address _____

City _____ State_____ Zip_____

                              Amount Enclosed_____

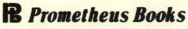 **Prometheus Books**
1203 Kensington Avenue
Buffalo, New York 14215